THE INTERNATIONAL DIMENSIONS OF HUMAN RIGHTS

THE INTERNATIONAL DIMENSIONS OF HUMAN RIGHTS

Karel Vasak
General Editor

Revised and edited for the English edition
by Philip Alston

Volume 2

GREENWOOD PRESS
WESTPORT, CONNECTICUT

unesco

UNESCO, PARIS, FRANCE

Library of Congress Cataloging in Publication Data

Dimensions internationales des droits de l'homme.
English.
The International dimensions of human rights.

Translation of: Les dimensions internationales des
droits de l'homme.
Bibliography: v. 2, p.
Includes indexes.
1. Civil rights (International law)—Addresses, essays,
lectures. 2. Civil rights—Addresses, essays, lectures.
I. Vasak, Karel. II. Alston, Philip. III. Unesco.
IV. Title.
K3240.6.D5513   341.48'1   81-22566
ISBN: 0-313-23394-2 (set)   AACR2
ISBN: 0-313-23395-0 (vol. 1)
ISBN: 0-313-23396-9 (vol. 2)

Library of Congress Catalog Card Number: 81-22566
Greenwood Press ISBN: 0-313-23394-2 (set)

Unesco ISBN: 92-3-101477-3

First published 1982 by the United Nations Educational, Scientific and Cultural
Organization, 7, Place de Fontenoy, 75700, Paris, France, and Greenwood Press,
a division of Congressional Information Service, Inc.
88 Post Road West, Westport, Connecticut 06881

Printed in the United States of America

10 9 8 7 6 5 4 3 2 1

Contents

Tables

THE INTERNATIONAL DIMENSIONS OF HUMAN RIGHTS

13 Unesco and Human Rights

Hanna Saba

According to the Constitution of Unesco, the purpose of the Organization is "to contribute to peace and security by promoting collaboration among the nations through education, science and culture in order to further universal respect for justice, for the rule of law, and for the human rights and fundamental freedoms which are affirmed for the peoples of the world, without distinction of race, sex, language or religion.[1]"

Since its inception, all the programmes of the Organization have been consequently established with due regard for these supreme goals. All the sectors of Unesco—education, natural sciences, social sciences, culture and communication—treat the defence of human rights which is indissolubly linked to the safeguarding of peace, as the ultimate goal of their efforts. All that is not explicitly aimed at developing respect for those rights in general, and at implementing specific rights, consists essentially, however, in creating the indispensable material, intellectual, moral and cultural conditions whereby human rights may pass from being principles to becoming tangible realities in the lives of all human beings. From the standpoint of Unesco, economic and social development must itself be defined as an indispensable precondition for the full exercise of those rights.

The advance of science and its utilization in the service of development are bound to transform the material conditions of men's lives. By means of science it should be possible to make it considerably easier to meet men's needs, and, by increasing the resources of governments, to overcome the difficulties encountered, particularly with regard to the achievement of economic, social and cultural rights.

Furthermore, at a time when science and technology are changing the face of the planet and the living conditions of its inhabitants, a minimum of scientific knowledge is becoming one of the fundamental rights of human beings. Scientific knowledge is in fact indispensable if we are to understand the world in which we live, our place in it, our possibilities and limits.

The dissemination of cultures, access by all peoples to the masterpieces of the spirit or of art that each of them has produced, lead us to understand each other better and to appreciate more fully that which runs through the diversity of cultures, and constitutes a common universal heritage. In such circumstances, cultural exchanges greatly contribute to the promotion of international understanding and friendship among peoples.

The new techniques of information and communication provide particularly effective means of making human rights known and of disseminating the principles that the United Nations has established in this field.

The struggle against discrimination and racial or religious prejudice often calls for studies to be carried out in the social sciences.[2] In addition, such studies make it easier to analyze the different conceptions that men may form of their rights; they make it possible to cope better with the difficulties encountered in the implementation of certain rights, in which, it should be noted, account must be taken of the diversity of traditions and differences in economic and social conditions.

The task of philosophical thinking in this context is to examine the universality of human rights from the perspective of the diversity of religions, absolutes and traditions. Sacrificing neither the concrete diversity of mankind for some abstract universality, nor the fundamental unity of the human race for the sake of the multiplicity of absolutes which have generated war in the course of history, philosophy seeks an understanding more rooted in concrete situations which, over and above confrontations of logic or dogma, makes it possible to give universal expression to human rights by actually going to the core of diversity.[3]

Thus, by virtue of both its nature—and the fields in which it is pursued—and its purpose, Unesco's action helps to ensure respect for all human rights.

The execution of a programme, laid down by the General Conference of Unesco in which all its members are represented, and which provides for the utilization of highly diverse methods and techniques adapted to the complex problems arising from the development of education, science and culture, is the principal means whereby Unesco endeavours to attain its objectives.

In order for it to pursue its goals, the Organization, besides taking direct responsibility for the implementation of its activities, formulates standards and principles intended to direct the action of governments. Unesco's policy in regard to the numerous problems arising from this promotion and observance of human rights is consequently defined not only in its direct activities, but also in the various legal instruments, declarations, conventions and recommendations that it has adopted since it was founded in 1946.

1. UNESCO'S NORMATIVE ACTIVITIES IN THE FIELD OF HUMAN RIGHTS

One of the functions of Unesco according to its Constitution is to recommend such international agreements and conventions as may be necessary to promote the purposes of the Organization.[4] The Constitution further distinguishes between conventions and recommendations[5] to which practice has added the category of declarations. Of the twenty-seven conventions, protocols and other agreements, adopted either by the General Conference or special intergovernmental conferences convened by Unesco, the twenty-nine recommendations and five declarations, many concern human rights and particularly the rights to education, culture and information set out in Articles 26, 27 and 19 of the Universal Declaration.[6]

With regard to the implementation of the Conventions and Recommendations adopted by the General Conference, the Constitution of Unesco is modelled upon certain methods and practices of the International Labour Organisation.

According to Article IV, paragraph 4, each Member State undertakes to submit recommendations or conventions to its competent authorities within a period of one year from the close of the session of the General Conference at which they were adopted with a view to their adoption and application. Moreover, each Member State shall submit "at such times and in such manner as shall be determined by the General Conference reports. . . on the action taken upon the recommendations and conventions referred to in Article IV, paragraph 4."

In contrast with the Constitution of the ILO, however, the Constitution of Unesco does not establish a procedure for appeals and complaints concerning the non-observance of the provisions of a ratified convention. As will be seen, it was by means of a special protocol that a Conciliation and Good Offices Commission was established within the Organization, and was instructed to seek to settle differences arising between States party to one of the most important Conventions of Unesco, that against discrimination in education.

The conventions and recommendations drawn up by *special* Conferences convened by Unesco are not subject to the forementioned provisions of the Constitution: these relate only to the implementation of instruments adopted solely by the *General* Conference of the Organization. Most of those conventions and recommendations nevertheless provide for special measures of implementation and such, in particular, is true of the Convention for the Protection of Cultural Property in the Event of Armed Conflict adopted by a special diplomatic conference which was held at The Hague from 21 April to 14 May 1954, and which was convened by Unesco.

2. IMPLEMENTATION OF THE CONVENTION FOR THE PROTECTION OF CULTURAL PROPERTY IN THE EVENT OF ARMED CONFLICT[7]

This Convention, adopted at The Hague on 14 May 1954, is founded on the principle that damage to cultural property belonging to any people whatsoever means damage to the cultural heritage of all mankind. The purpose of the Convention is to provide international protection for this heritage which, in order for it to be effective, must be organized in time of peace. To that end, the Contracting Parties undertake, on the one hand, to safeguard cultural property against the foreseeable effects of an armed conflict, by taking such measures as they consider appropriate (building of shelters against bombardments, prevention of fires and the collapse of buildings, etc.). They undertake, on the other hand, to respect cultural property situated within their own territory as well as within the territory of other Contracting Parties by refraining from any use of the property and its immediate surroundings or of the appliances in use for its protection for purposes which are likely to expose it to destruction or damage in the event of armed conflict and by refraining from any act of hostility directed against such property.

Furthermore, the contracting States undertake to prohibit, prevent and, if necessary, put a stop to any form of theft, pillage or misappropriation of, and any acts of vandalism directed against, cultural property. They also undertake to refrain from requisitioning moveable cultural property situated in the territory of another Contracting Party.

The Convention also contains special provisions concerning occupied territories and the obligations of the Occupying Powers in respect of cultural property situated in those territories.

(a). Control of the execution of the Convention

This control is the subject of extensive provisions in the 1954 Convention and the Regulations for its execution. However, practice, and in particular Unesco's action in the Middle East conflict, have considerably increased the impact of those provisions and improved the operation of the machinery for international supervision established by them.

There is scarcely any need to stress the importance of the organization and operation of machinery for international control in ensuring that the rules to be observed in cases of armed conflict are respected. The mere fact that such machinery exists is likely to influence the responsible agents of the parties to the conflict to give attention and consideration to rules since their violation could be brought to the attention of, and denounced before, the entire world.

Although the provisions relating to the organization of supervision come under the heading of control, the machinery established by the 1954 Convention goes beyond the strict framework of the mere control of the application of the Convention. The powers and responsibilities conferred upon the different agents whose appointment is provided for immediately upon the outbreak of an armed conflict enable them to have, besides a supervisory role, a positive function in ensuring the implementation of important provisions of the Convention and the Regulations, particularly in regard to the organization of the transport of cultural property threatened by an extension of the conflict, the granting of special protection for improvised refuges, and so on.

(b). Organization of control

The organization of the machinery for control and implementation takes account of international practice whereby, when two countries enter into war or simply break off diplomatic relations, they entrust a neutral State—"a Protecting Power"—with the task of defending their interests in the country with which they are in conflict. The Regulations stipulate (Art. 3) that the protecting Power shall appoint from among the members of its diplomatic staff delegates with special responsibility, together with the Commissioner-General whose role is described below, for controlling the execution of the Convention.

The Commissioner-General for Cultural Property is a neutral person chosen from an international list compiled by the Director-General of Unesco and containing the names of the candidates presented by the different countries party to the Convention (Art. 1 of the Regulations). As soon as an armed conflict breaks out a Commissioner-General for Cultural Property is appointed to each State in conflict by joint agreement between, on the one hand, the Government of the country to which he will be accredited and, on the other, the Protecting Power acting on behalf of the opposing party. In addition, each belligerent appoints a representative for cultural property situated in its territory. If it is in occupation of another territory, it is required to appoint a special representative for cultural property situated in that territory.

Commissioners-General, Representatives for cultural property and Delegates of the Protecting Powers are the agents principally responsible for control. Their mission is of a general character. In addition, provision has been made for inspectors and experts to be appointed and charged with specific missions. We shall now see how this machinery operates and what are the powers and functions of the different agents.

The Commissioners-General for Cultural Property are principally responsible for ensuring that the rules of the Convention are observed by the belligerents. Whereas the Representative for cultural property and the Delegates of the Protecting Powers represent the parties engaged in conflict and are appointed for the purpose of defending their respective interests, the Commissioner-General, appointed to each country at war, has an essentially impartial and international mission the purpose of which is to safeguard property forming part of a cultural heritage which, as is emphasized in the Preamble to the Convention, belongs to all mankind.

The Commissioner-General's role is similar at the cultural level to that exercised by the International Committee of the Red Cross at the humanitarian level but, in addition, it is enshrined in legal texts and his functions are recognized and accepted by Governments. He deals with all matters referred to him in conjunction with the representative of the party to which he is accredited and with the delegates of the opposing Protecting Power (Art. 6, para. 1, of the Regulations). It falls to the latter to draw attention to any

violations of the Convention constituting grounds for complaint by the belligerent whom they are duty bound to protect; when such violations occur, to
investigate, with the approval of the party to which they are accredited, the
circumstances in which they have occurred and to make representations
locally to secure their cessation. If necessary, they notify the Commissioner-
General whom they must keep informed of their activities (Art. 5 of the
Regulations).

The Commissioner-General makes any representations to the parties to
the conflict or to their Protecting Powers which he deems useful for the
application of the Convention. He can, with the agreement of the State to
which he is accredited, order an investigation or conduct it himself. He can
appoint inspectors or experts and charge them with specific missions.

Lastly, and this is particularly important, he draws up such reports as may
be necessary on the application of the Convention and communicates them to
the parties concerned and to their Protecting Powers (Art. 8 of the Regulations). The Commissioner-General may thus be led to note violations of the
Convention in his report, to describe the representations made by himself as
well as by the delegates of the Protecting Powers and to put on record the
positive or negative outcome of his representations.

The fact that the report is drawn up by an eminent figure whose impartial
character and official responsibilities derive from the Convention cannot fail
to have an effect on international public opinion; this often acts as an effective
means of pressure and undoubtedly encourages the State concerned to give
very serious consideration to the observations of the Commissioner-General.

*(c). Application of the provisions of the Convention and the Regulations to
the Israel-Arab conflict*

Following the events of June 1967 and the resumption of fighting between
Israel and Egypt, Jordan, Syria and Lebanon, the Director-General of Unesco
took the initiative of inviting the parties to the conflict to give effect to the
provisions of the Convention and Regulations of 1954 concerning control.

One of the principle difficulties to be surmounted consisted in the fact that,
as Israel had never been recognized by the Arab countries and diplomatic
relations had never been established between it and its neighbours, no Protecting Power had been appointed to protect the interests of each of the
belligerents in the territory of the opposing party. Thus, as has been seen, it
falls to the Protecting Powers to play a decisive role not only in appointing
Commissioners-General but also at all stages of control, of which they are
important agents.

However, such a situation had been expressly provided for by the Regulations which had adopted a proposal made by the delegate of Israel to the
Hague Conference in 1954 to the effect that a neutral State, chosen by joint
agreement by the parties to the conflict, be entrusted with those functions of
a Protecting Power which concern the appointment of Commissioners-General

(Art. 9 of the Regulations), and that the Commissioners-General be invested with the powers and functions of the Protecting Powers in discharging the mission of control (Art. 6, para. 6, of the Regulations).

The belligerents by joint agreement had chosen Switzerland as the neutral State required to appoint Commissioners-General, who then made the appointments at the end of September 1967. Mr. Reinnick (Netherlands) was accredited to Israel and Mr. Brunner (Switzerland) was accredited to the four Arab countries, the latter having decided to choose the same person.

However, it became clear both to the Director-General of Unesco and to the States engaged in the conflict that the provisions of the Regulations concerning the discharge of the mission of control were inadequate, particularly in that specific instance where there did not exist a Protecting Power possessing the facilities, privileges and immunities of an embassy required for it to discharge the mission in the country to which it was accredited.

It was also indispensable that the Commissioner-General be entrusted, in addition to his own responsibilities, with those of the Protecting Power, acquire an adequate status and that he be able, in particular, to communicate freely with the belligerent whose interests he was required to defend. It was consequently necessary for the Commissioner-General to be granted the privileges and immunities, which would ensure him complete independence in respect of the government to which he would be accredited, and to receive the benefit of minimum material facilities, particularly in respect of premises, staff and communication.

The 1954 Regulations contained a serious omission in this respect. In Article 10 it merely stipulated that: "The remuneration and expenses of the Commissioner-General for Cultural Property, inspectors and experts shall be met by the Party to which they are accredited. Remuneration and expenses of delegates of the Protecting Powers shall be subject to agreement between those Powers and the States whose interests they are safeguarding". Such a text makes the Commissioner-General dependent upon the State to which he is accredited.

The situation consequently had to be remedied and a revision of the Convention was contemplated by some. In view of the time required for any new texts to enter into force, this solution proved to be impracticable and the view was taken that the best way to proceed would be to give a new interpretation to the established provisions on the basis of joint agreement between the various parties concerned.

On the initiative of the Director-General of Unesco, Ambassador Rappart, delegate of the neutral State, Switzerland, and myself, representing Unesco in my capacity as Assistant Director-General and Legal Adviser of the Organization, engaged for ten days in discussions for that purpose with the representatives of Israel and with those of the four Arab countries. Following these discussions during which the belligerents expressed the same views with regard to the status of the Commissioners-General, the Executive Board of

Unesco took a number of important measures. It decided to set up a special
fund on the basis of contributions from the parties to the conflict enabling the
international organization itself to remunerate the Commissioners-General
and to meet their expenses. Thus, one of the shortcomings of the Regulations
was remedied in that, as has already been pointed out, it was stipulated that
such remuneration and expenses be paid by the State to which the Commissioner-
General is accredited: thus, the independence and international character of
the Commissioner-General are henceforth more clearly marked.

Moreover, the Executive Board of Unesco instructed the Director-General
of the Organization to take the necessary steps for the Commissioners-General
to be able, on taking up office, to:

a) enjoy the recognized immunities granted to high officials of the United
   Nations system;
b) benefit from the services and assistance of the offices of the United
   Nations and Unesco in the countries party to the conflict, particularly in
   regard to communication facilities.

Lastly, the Executive Board expressed a desire to be informed of any
subsequent developments in the implementation of the Convention and, in
particular, of the legal and practical conditions under which the Commissioners-
General had discharged their mission.

This decision is particularly important. It undoubtedly indicates, more
clearly than the 1954 Regulations, the international character of the mission
of the Commissioners-General who, thanks to Unesco and the United Nations, are granted the facilities necessary for them to carry out their task. It
normalized and strengthened relations between the Commissioners-General
and Unesco and from that time onwards assigned to the Organization, and in
particular to its Executive Board which was henceforth to receive regular
reports from the Commissioners-General, a role and a responsibility which
had not been expressly provided for in the Convention, but which undeniably
improve the effectiveness of the machinery for controlling its application.

*(d). Consideration by the Executive Board of Unesco of reports from the
Commissioners-General on the application of the Convention*

The Executive Board of Unesco received the first reports of the two
Commissioners-General in May 1968. They indicated in those reports that
they had been able to fulfil their functions thanks to the facilities placed at
their disposal by the representatives of Unesco and the United Nations (particularly in regard to communications) in the countries to which they had been
assigned and thanks to the immunities and status granted to them by the
Governments of those countries.

The method of work adopted by them consisted for each Commissioner in
receiving the complaints of the Government to which he was accredited concerning violations alleged to have been committed by the opposing party and
in transmitting them to his colleague accredited to that party. The latter then

made an investigation and, where appropriate, made the necessary representations in order to ensure that the Convention be respected.

Apart from two complaints concerning the bombing, prior to the cease-fire,
of a convent in Jerusalem and of a museum and church in Suez, the reported
violations related essentially to the occupied territories.

The complaints formulated by the Arab countries concerned in particular:
-the removal of the famous Dead Sea manuscripts which had been on
  exhibition in the Rockefeller Museum, situated in the Arab part of Jerusalem, and their transfer to Israeli territory;
-the destruction of certain buildings in Jerusalem (Jordan);
-the removal of certain movable objects and a staircase from the Mosque of
  Abraham in Hebron (Jordan);
-the carrying out of systematic excavations in occupied territory, particularly in Jerusalem (Jordan) and in the region of Banias (Syria).

Subsequent reports from the Commissioners-General noted complaints from
the Arab countries concerning both the lack of maintenance of Moslem monuments in Jerusalem and certain alterations being carried out in the Arme-
nian district of that city, opposite the Wailing Wall, in the ancient Jewish
district and in the Magrebeen Moslem district, the purpose of which seemed
to be radically to transform the very character of Jerusalem, in particular
through the destruction of buildings and monuments in the Arab or Moslem
style.

Israel on the other hand had invited the Commissioner-General accredited
to it to investigate the state of certain Jewish monuments (synagogues and
cemeteries situated in various Arab countries).

This request was rejected by the Arab countries who contended that it
was not based on any of the provisions of the Convention in that it contained no reference to any act of hostility carried out by virtue of the armed
conflict.

The reports of the Commissioners-General were considered in turn by the
Executive Board and then by the General Conference of Unesco which adopted,
in December 1968, two resolutions in this connection.

The first (Resol. 3.342—15th session) recommended "Member States to
take, with the help of the two Commissioners-General, all necessary measures to conform to the articles of the Convention and to the provisions of the
recommendation concerning the international principles applicable in the case
of archaeological excavations adopted by the General Conference of Unesco
at its ninth session (1956)".

The second (Resol. 3.343—15th session), after referring in its preamble to
the exceptional importance of the cultural property in the old city of Jerusalem to all humanity, and to a United Nations General Assembly resolution
concerning Jerusalem (Resolution 2253 adopted on 4 July 1967), addressed
"an urgent international appeal in accordance with the said United Nations
resolution, calling upon Israel:

(a) to preserve scrupulously all the sites, buildings and other cultural prop-
     erties, especially in the old city of Jerusalem;
(b) to desist from any archaeological excavations, transfer of such proper-
     ties and changing of their features or their cultural and historical
     character."

3. THE IMPLEMENTATION OF THE CONVENTION AGAINST DIS-CRIMINATION IN EDUCATION

The methods and procedures for implementing and supervising the application of the Convention against Discrimination in Education differ from those
just described and more closely resemble the procedures of the International
Labour Organisation.

The Convention and Recommendation against Discrimination in Education
was adopted by the General Conference at its eleventh session, on 14 December 1960.[8] The Convention entered into force on 22 May 1962.

The purpose of these two instruments is not only to eliminate and prevent
all discrimination, but also to promote equal opportunity and treatment in
education. They thus contribute to the attainment of two separate but complementary objectives, included in the Constitution of the Organization. The
injustices to be fought and eliminated include not only discrimination which,
resulting from legislative provisions or administrative practices, involves
deliberate denial of the right to education of certain members of the community, but also inequalities which often derive not so much from deliberate
intention as from a set of social, geographical, economic and historical circumstances, often referred to as a form of "static discrimination" in order to
better distinguish it from active and deliberate discrimination.

The nature of the undertakings entered into by the States party to the
Convention varies according to whether what is involved is the elimination of
discrimination or the assurance of equal opportunity. According to Article 3,
those states agree to undertake forthwith a series of measures; in particular,
they are to abrogate or modify any statutory provisions and to discontinue
any administrative practices which involve discrimination, and also not to
allow any different treatment or preference based solely on the ground that
people belong to a particular group. On the other hand, the measures to be
taken to ensure equal opportunities necessitate, in many countries, a far-
ranging effort which is not limited to education, as well as substantial budg-
etary expenditures which have to be spread out over time.

The Convention thus stipulates that the States shall formulate, develop
and apply a national policy which, by methods appropriate to the circumstances and to national usage, will tend to promote equality of opportunity
and of treatment in the matter of education.

The adoption by the General Conference of a Recommendation at the same
time as a Convention corresponds to a desire to take account of the difficul-

ties that some Member States might encounter, for various reasons and, in particular, on account of their federal structure, in ratifying the Convention. Except for differences in formulation and in legal bearing inherent in the nature of these two categories of instruments, the content of the Recommendation is identical to that of the Convention.

The procedures for supervising the execution of the Convention hinge essentially on the reports submitted by States. According to Article VIII of the Constitution of Unesco, each Member State shall submit to the Organization reports on the action taken upon the recommendations and conventions adopted by the General Conference. In addition, the States who are Parties undertake, by virtue of Article 7 of the Convention, to give to the Organization information on the legislative and administrative provisions which they have adopted for the application of the said Convention. A similar provision is included in the Recommendation.

As was recalled by the General Conference at its fourteenth session (1966), "the taking cognizance by an international organization of the extent to which its Member States apply the conventions adopted by it and give effect to its recommendations constitutes an essential function". It is able to discharge this task by examining periodically the reports that Member States are obliged to submit to it for that purpose.

The object of this method is to enable the Organization to be apprised of and to evaluate both the progress achieved by the various countries in implementing an international instrument and the difficulties encountered by them. The Organization is then in a position to determine its future action more effectively.

This is particularly important when, as in the case of the 1960 Convention and Recommendation, the instrument in question does not merely define rules for immediate application but also constitutes the starting point for progressive measures that States are invited to take in the future, with a view to achieving to the fullest extent the objectives and goals pursued and which the Organization is duty bound to guide.

It is to be pointed out that Article 6 of the Convention and a similar provision of the Recommendation stipulate that the General Conference of Unesco may adopt subsequent recommendations defining the measures to be taken against the different forms of discrimination in education and for the purpose of ensuring equality of opportunity and treatment.

The procedure for submitting and considering reports from Member States on the application of the 1960 instruments was laid down in a decision taken by the General Conference in 1964.[9] Pursuant to this decision three consultations of Member States have been held: the first in 1965-66, the second in 1971-72, and the third in 1975-80.[10] Detailed questionnaires were drawn up by the Secretariat for each of these consultations. These questionnaires covered all the provisions of the 1960 Convention and Recommendation. By the importance given to certain questions, they also reflect the particular concerns of the Organization. Moreover, considerable latitude is given to the Secretariat in determining the subjects to be dealt with in the reports and the form and periodicity of these reports.

The reports received were analyzed by the Secretariat and examined by a special committee of the Executive Board of Unesco, composed of twelve members.

The question arose however as to whether the organ called on to make a first examination of the States' reports should not, in conformity with the practice of the ILO, be completely non-governmental in character. Moreover, the committee, which considers the reports of States on the Recommendation concerning the Status of Teachers adopted in 1966 by a special Conference convened by Unesco and drawn up with the full collaboration of the ILO, is composed of independent persons appointed in their personal capacity.

The Executive Board of Unesco considered that, pending reconsideration of the matter in the light of the experience of the Committee on the Application of the Recommendation concerning the Status of Teachers, the system in force should be maintained.

After considering the reports of States, the special committee of the Board itself establishes a report, in which it formulates its conclusions and recommendations and which is submitted in turn to the Executive Board and then to the General Conference.

The special Committee generally gives in its report an overall evaluation of the situation and formulates a number of suggestions concerning the future action of the Organization. In some cases, the special Committee gives its interpretation of certain provisions of the Convention whose application has given rise to difficulties. Such in particular was the case in regard to the definition of national minorities and the significance to be given to article 5 (c) of the Convention which refers to "the right of national minorities to carry on their own educational activities, including the maintenance of schools, and, depending on the education policy of each State, the use or the teaching of their own language". In its report, Finland drew attention to the particular situation existing in the County of Aland.[11] The fact of the matter was that by virtue of special legislation deriving from specific historical and political circumstances and whose purpose was to safeguard the Swedish language and culture in the Aland Islands, it was prohibited, except with the special consent of the commune concerned, to dispense education in a language other than Swedish.

In its report, the Special Committee, after furnishing explanations concerning the significance to be attached to the term "national minorities", stated its views as follows: "In the case of multilingual countries which have a federal system or a special system for certain provinces or administrative units, another problem of interpretation arises. In such countries, responsibility for education generally lies with the local authorities. However, population groups which are in the majority in the country as a whole may be in the minority in certain regions (provinces, States or cantons) which are more or less autonomous in the matter of education. In the opinion of the Special Committee, such groups should be regarded as national minorities within the meaning of Article 5 (c) of the Convention or Section V (c) of the Recommendation mentioned above, and consequently benefit from their provisions".

It should be noted that Finland has since deposited its instruments of ratification of the Convention.

The 1960 Convention also contains a reference to disputes between States concerning the interpretation or application of its provisions. Article 8 provides that such disputes may be referred to the International Court of Justice. However, the jurisdiction of the Court is optional and for each dispute may be referred to the International Court of Justice. However, the jurisdiction of the Court is optional and for each dispute the agreement of the States concerned is necessary.

The proposal that the Court's jurisdiction be recognized as compulsory, originally laid before the General Conference, came to nought on account of the opposition of the socialist States of East Europe, whose traditional position in this regard is well-known. They were joined by the Arab States and many Latin American States.

The General Conference, however, by way of compromise, adopted in 1962 a Protocol instituting a Conciliation and Good Offices Commission to be Responsible for Seeking the Settlement of Disputes Which May Arise between States Parties to the Convention. This Protocol obliges the States party to it to recognize the jurisdiction of the Commission. Now ratified by 22 States, the Protocol entered into force in October 1968.

In drafting it, Unesco was guided by various precedents, in particular those of the European Commission of Human Rights, established by the European Convention for the Protection of Human Rights and Fundamental Freedoms, the Fact-Finding and Conciliation Commission on Freedom of Association and the Human Rights Committee, set up by the International Covenant on Civil and Political Rights.

The Commission established by the Unesco Protocol is permanent. It is composed of eleven members elected by the General Conference upon submission of their candidatures by the States Parties, but the members elected sit in their personal capacity.

The draft Protocol established by the Director-General contained a proposal that two of the eleven seats should be assigned to candidates presented by non-governmental organizations in consultative relationship with Unesco and recognized by its Executive Board as representing, on the one hand, the teaching profession, and, on the other, the interests of pupils and students at the various levels of education. This proposal was not adopted.

The members of the Commission must be nationals of the States Parties to the Protocol, but the Commission cannot include more than one national of the same State. The General Conference must seek to include in it persons qualified in the field of education and persons with legal experience, either as lawyers, jurists or members of tribunals, while taking into account the needs for equitable geographical distribution and the representation of the various forms of civilization and of the principal legal systems.

In addition to the eleven members of the Commission, *ad hoc* members may be appointed when the Commission does not include a member whose nationality is that of one of the States party to the dispute. The Secretariat is ensured by the Director-General of Unesco.

Originally, recourse to the Commission was open only to States party to the Protocol. If one of those States considers that another of them is not applying the provisions of the Convention, it can, by written communication, draw the attention of that State to the matter. The State receiving the communication has three months to make its answer known. If, within six months after the receipt of the initial communication, nothing has been settled to the satisfaction of the two States, both have the right to refer the matter to the Commission.

However, the Protocol stipulated that six months after its entry into force, in other words, since October 1974 in fact, the Commission may be instructed to seek to settle any dispute between States which, without being party to the Protocol, are party to the Convention, if the said States so agree. Despite this possible extension of the competence of the Commission, it is to be noted that it remains limited to disputes between States and that no recourse is directly accessible to private persons.

The Commission can, for any case brought before it, request the States concerned to provide it with all relevant information. It must, however, hear and determine a case only after exhausting domestic remedies in the sense given to that expression by international law.

The role of the Commission, when it has obtained the information that it considers necessary, consists essentially in establishing the facts and placing its good offices at the disposal of the States concerned in order to reach a friendly settlement of the matter "on the basis of respect for the Convention." In such cases, the report will be confined to a brief statement of the facts and of the settlement reached. If, on the contrary, no settlement of the dispute has been reached, the report contains, in addition to a statement of the facts, an indication of the recommendations which have been formulated. Individual opinions are allowed.

The Commission may also recommend that the Executive Board or the General Conference of Unesco, depending on the case, request the International Court of Justice to give an advisory opinion concerning any legal question relating to a case brought before it. Moreover, it is expressly stipulated that the setting up of the Commission does not impair the right of States to have recourse to other procedures for settling their disputes and, *inter alia,* to submit by joint agreement their disputes to the Permanent Court of Arbitration of The Hague.

Although the Commission has been established since 1971 and has met on several occasions, in particular to establish and adopt its Rules of Procedure, recourse has not been had to it so far.

Declaration on Race and Racial Prejudice and Resolution for its Implementation*

In addition to the studies already mentioned, Unesco's contribution to the struggle against racism, racial discrimination and *apartheid* has involved normative action.

The most noteworthy early activities of Unesco concerning racism were the drafting of scientific statements. The first of these was issued in 1950 as the "Statement on Race".[12] It was followed in 1951 by the "Statement on the Nature of Race and Race Differences".[13] Both these statements, drafted by specialists, stress the biological and anthropological aspects of race based on the latest findings of scientific research at the time and unequivocally reject theories of racial superiority. The biological aspects were again predominant in the "Proposal on the biological aspects of race", drafted by 22 specialists convened by Unesco in 1964.[14]

At an expert meeting convened by Unesco in September, 1967, a much broader range of social scientists was represented among the 18 specialists, who drafted the fourth document on the subject, "Statement on Race and Racial Prejudice".[15] That statement dwells on the political, economic, social and cultural dimensions of the problem.

While these four documents carried the authority of the eminent specialists who drafted them, they could in no way be said to be binding on the Member States of Unesco. In order to reinforce the validity of the propositions especially those in the 1967 statement, the General Conference of Unesco invited the Director-General at its seventeenth session (1972) to prepare, on the basis of the 1967 statement, a draft Declaration on Race and Racial Prejudice,[16] which was adopted at the twentieth session of the General Conference in 1978.

The Declaration contains a number of original features which deserve special mention.

For the first time in an international instrument, Unesco's Declaration on Race and Racial Prejudice proclaims the *right to be different*, which is immediately qualified to exclude the misuse of this right to justify discriminatory practices.[17]

After defining "racism" and its consequences, the Declaration stipulates that "it is contrary to the fundamental principles of international law and,

*The information in this section was revised with the collaboration of S. Marks on the basis of a chapter by him to appear in another publication.

consequently, seriously disturbs international peace and security".[18] The Declaration also asserts that "any form of racial discrimination practised by a State constitutes a violation of international law" for which the State is accountable to other States in accordance with the rules of international responsibility.[19]

The Declaration not only condemns *apartheid* as "one of the most serious violations" of the principle of equality in dignity and rights but also qualifies *apartheid* as a "crime against humanity [which] gravely disturbs international peace and security".[20] *Apartheid* thus has the same criminal status as genocide according to this Declaration, a status it had already been given by the International Convention on the Suppression and Punishment of the Crime of *Apartheid*.

The Declaration has the additional feature of having its own resolution for implementation.[21] According to this resolution, Member States are urged "to communicate to the Director-General all necessary information concerning the steps they have taken to give effect to the principles set forth in the Declaration".[22] The Director-General is invited by the Resolution "to prepare a comprehensive report on the world situation in the fields covered by the Declaration, on the basis of the information supplied by Member States and of any other information supported by trustworthy evidence which he may have gathered by such methods as he may think fit, and to enlist for this purpose, if he deems it advisable, the help of one or more independent experts of recognized competence in these fields".[23] The very existence of such provisions as well as the potential they hold for pressuring States to comply with the Declaration contribute to making the Declaration and Resolution novel contributions to the international protection of human rights.

4. PROCEDURES ESTABLISHED BY THE EXECUTIVE BOARD OR THE GENERAL CONFERENCE

Alongside the procedures laid down on conventions which have just been summarized, certain procedures have been established by the Executive Board or the General Conference to provide for the study of specific cases or questions concerning the exercise of human rights in Unesco's fields of competence. The main such procedures are those used by the joint ILO/Unesco Committee of Experts on the Application of the Recommendations concerning the Status of Teachers and those of the Committee on Conventions and Recommendations concerning communications alleging violations of human rights.

(a). Joint ILO/Unesco Committee of Experts on the Application of the Recommendation Concerning the Status of Teachers[24]

The decision to set up this Committee was taken at the fourteenth session of the General Conference of Unesco (Paris, October-November 1966) and the

167th session of the ILO Governing Body (Geneva, November 1966). The Committee's terms of reference are to examine the reports received from governments on action taken by them on the Recommendation concerning the Status of Teachers (adopted at Paris on 5 October 1966 by a special intergovernmental conference) and to report thereon to the two bodies which set it up. In accordance with a decision taken by the ILO Governing Body (170th session) and the Executive Board of Unesco (77th session), the Joint Committee consists of 12 members sitting in their personal capacities and chosen on the basis of their competence in the principal domains covered by the Recommendation, each organization designating six members for the domains falling mainly within its province.

Four sessions of the Committee have been held: (Geneva, 1968; Paris, 1970; Geneva, 1976; and Paris, 1979). In determining its methods of work, the Committee decided that it could take into consideration information on implementation of the Recommendation which might be received from national organizations representing teachers or their employers, and from international teachers' organizations having consultative status with Unesco, without excluding information from other authoritative sources.[25] Information concerning a particular country is communicated to it for any observations it may wish to make. The Committee also drew up a questionnaire with a view to obtaining information on the application of the main provisions of the Recommendation by the Member States of both organizations. Apart from these sources, the Committee makes use only of official information contained in United Nations, ILO and Unesco documents. The Committee's Secretariat (provided by Unesco and the International Labour Office) undertakes a preliminary analysis of all information received, and this analysis is then examined by a working group of the Committee. After studying the information provided, the Committee, in its report, adopts conclusions and recommendations concerning any studies it may consider necessary on situations where it feels that the application of the Recommendation is unsatisfactory. The Committee's report is then submitted to the governing bodies of the two Organizations. In the case of Unesco, the report is first studied by the Committee on Conventions and Recommendations after which it is transmitted, together with the latter Committee's recommendations, to the Executive Board, which in turn, transmits it to the General Conference with the Board's recommendations.

Several of the Recommendation's provisions are directly concerned with the exercise of human rights, particularly those relating to non-discrimination in the training and employment of teachers, the right of association of teachers, etc. Particular mention may be made of Article 80, which stipulates that "Teachers should be free to exercise all civic rights generally enjoyed by citizens". From this point of view, the Joint Committee's report constitutes a valuable source of information which can influence the evolution of law and practice in these matters. The Joint Committee has observed, however, that the number of Member States replying to the questionnaire is diminishing and that the replies are often not sufficiently detailed.[26] The report has nevertheless enabled the Executive Board[27] and the General Conference[28] to make fairly detailed recommendations on the improvements needed in regard to application of the Recommendation.

*(b). The handling of communications addressed to Unesco in connection with cases and questions involving the exercise of human rights in the Organization's spheres of competence.**

The procedure for handling communications alleging violation of human rights is determined by the text of the Executive Board Decision 104 EX/3.3, adopted in 1978, and by the practice of the Committee on Conventions and Recommendations.[29] Five phases may be distinguished in the handling of communications according to this procedure.

1. *Preparation of the file by the Secretariat*

Upon receipt by the Unesco Secretariat of a communication which appears to concern alleged violations of human rights, the communication is transmitted to a specialized unit for handling communications, which acknowledges receipt, informing the author of the procedure laid down in Decision 104 EX/3.3, drawing his attention to the conditions of admissibility listed in para. 14(a) of that decision and inviting him to fill in a form.[30] At the end of the form is a declaration by which the author expresses his agreement to the application of the procedure. As soon as possible after receipt of the signed form, a copy is sent to the government concerned informing it that any reply it may wish to make will be brought to the notice of the Committee and that a representative of the government concerned may attend the meeting of the Committee at which the communication will be examined in order to provide additional information or answer questions asked by members of the Committee.

A file is then prepared by the Secretariat containing a summary of the communications, the form, any reply from the government and other such information or documents from the government or the author which may be necessary for the proper examination of the communication.

2. *Examination of the admissibility of the communication*

Whether or not the government concerned has replied, the file is transmitted to the Committee, whose first task is to determine if all of the ten conditions of admissibility set out in para. 14(a) Decision 104 EX/3.3 have been met. These conditions are the following:

Conditions

(a) Communications shall be deemed admissible if they meet the following conditions:

*This section has been revised in collaboration with S. Marks on the basis of a chapter by him to appear in another publication.

(i)   the communication must not be anonymous;

(ii)   the communication must originate from a person or a group of persons who, it can be reasonably presumed, are victims of an alleged violation of any of the human rights referred to in paragraph (iii) below. It may also originate from any person, group of persons or non-governmental organization having reliable knowledge of those violations;

(iii)   the communication must concern violations of human rights falling within Unesco's competence in the fields of education, science, culture and information and must not be motivated exclusively by other considerations;

(iv)   the communication must be compatible with the principles of the Organization, the Charter of the United Nations, the Universal Declaration of Human Rights, the international covenants on human rights and other international instruments in the field of human rights;

(v)   the communication must not be manifestly ill-founded and must appear to contain relevant evidence;

(vi)   the communication must be neither offensive nor an abuse of the right to submit communications. However, such a communication may be considered if it meets all other criteria or admissibility, after the exclusion of the offensive or abusive parts;

(vii) the communication must not be based exclusively on information disseminated through the mass media;

(viii) the communication must be submitted within a reasonable time-limit following the facts which constitute its subject-matter or within a reasonable time-limit after the facts have become known;

(ix)   the communication must indicate whether an attempt has been made to exhaust available domestic remedies with regard to the facts which constitute the subject-matter of the communication and the result of such an attempt, if any;

(x)   communications relating to matters already settled by the States concerned in accordance with the human rights principles set forth in the Universal Declaration of Human Rights and the international covenants on human rights shall not be considered;

3. *Examination of the merits of the communication*

Once a communication is declared admissible, the Committee examines its merits in order to determine whether it warrants further action. If it does not, it is dismissed and the author and government are notified.[31] If it does warrant further action, the Committee's task is to help "to bring about a friendly solution designed to advance the promotion of human rights falling within Unesco's fields of competence".[32]

The general terms of this mandate guarantee the Committee the necessary flexibility to utilize the confidentiality of the meetings, the presence of the representative of the government concerned and the additional information which the Director-General may place at the disposal of the Committee to encourage the government to resolve the issue. The effectiveness of this phase of the procedure, of course, depends on the nature of the claim and the attitude of the government concerned. It should be borne in mind that, at any stage of the procedure, even before the Committee has begun considering admissibility, the Director-General can intercede on behalf of the victim. This role is defined as "initiating consultations, in conditions of mutual respect, confidence and confidentiality, to help reach solutions to particular problems concerning human rights".[33] During the Committee's consideration of either the admissibility or merits, it can avail itself of the information at the disposal of the Director-General,[34] keep a communication on its agenda while seeking additional information[35] or even, in exceptional circumstances and with the prior approval of the Executive Board, hear the author of the communication or other qualified persons.[36]

The language of the preamble of Decision 104 EX/3.3 is particularly relevant to the examination of the merits and the search for a friendly solution. After recalling the provision of Unesco's Constitution on non-intervention,[37] the preamble states that, "in matters concerning human rights within its fields of competence, Unesco...should act in a spirit of international co-operation, conciliation and mutual understanding", and recalls "that Unesco should not play the role of an international judicial body".[38] This provision accurately reflects the approach taken by the Committee in dealing with governments concerned with communications declared admissible, an approach based essentially on a search for a dialogue.

4. Report to the Executive Board

According to paragraph 15 of Decision 104 EX/3.3, "the Committee shall submit confidential reports to the Executive Board at each session on the carrying out of its mandate under the present decision". The paragraph stipulates further that these reports "shall contain appropriate information arising from its examination of the communications which the Committee considers useful to bring to the notice of the Executive Board" as well as "recommendations which the Committee may wish to make either generally or regarding the disposition of a communication under consideration".

The Committee has established the practice of reporting on every communication examined at the session, whether it has been declared admissible or not. The report usually sets out for each one a brief summary of the facts, the views of the Committee's members and of the representative of the government concerned, and the decision reached by the Committee. The decision on admissibility is either that the communication is admissible, inadmissible, suspended (for further information) or postponed. As regards admissible communications, the Committee either reports its decision to apply the special procedure concerning disappeared persons or to request further information from the government concerned, the author of the communication, or both, or the Committee recommends appropriate action. It can, for example, request the Executive Board to invite the Director-General to address to the government concerned an appeal for clemency or for the rapid release of a detained person. The Board examines the report of the Committee in closed meetings.[39]

Communications alleging violations of human rights fall into either one or both of two categories defined in the Decision. The first category encompasses communications which concern "individual and specific" cases of human rights violations.[40] The second category encompasses communications which concern "questions of massive, systematic or flagrant violations" resulting "either from a policy contrary to human rights" applied by a State or "from an accumulation of individual cases forming a consistent pattern".[41]

Although there are as yet no precedents for the examination by the Board of questions concerning large-scale violations of human rights, Decision 104 EX/3.3 provides that communications transmitted to the Board by the Committee which "testify to the existence" of such a question "should be considered by the Executive Board and the General Conference in public meetings".[42]

The fact that the procedure deals with both individual and large-scale violations is no doubt one of its more original features and one of the reasons for the success of the negotiation process which led its adoption. Indeed, as the debates which preceded the adoption of Decision 104 EX/3.3 demonstrated,[43] certain Board members felt that only large-scale violations of human rights should be considered, whereas others felt that the Organization should be authorized to deal with individual cases.

The procedure does not specify at what stage a communication is to be qualified as concerning only a specific case, rather than a pattern of human rights violations.

It will be recalled that the public examination of communications involving "questions" concerns both the Executive Board and the General Conference.

5. *The procedure before the General Conference*

There is no indication in Decision 104 EX/3.3 as to what procedure the General Conference is to follow with regard to communications concerning allegations of human rights violations. Should a communication concerning a question of large-scale violations be brought before the General Conference, it would most likely be under an item included in the agenda by the Board.[44] There are no precedents to date.

The Committee started examining communications at its session of September 1978. It has been meeting since then in April and August or September. Some 400 communications have been handled according to the newly established procedure.[45]

The legislative measures taken by Unesco to define human rights and the resulting obligations for governments and perhaps even more its activities for the purpose of supervising the application of the standards adopted, have only recently been systematized and become a regular feature of its practice. However, it is now quite apparent that the Organization has become fully aware of the responsibilities incumbent upon it in this field. This awareness is all the more timely in that the extraordinary development of science and technology currently raises problems which need to be resolved at the level of the entire world community. International law must protect the individual against attacks upon his privacy and his intellectual and moral independence resulting from the abusive use of new techniques or certain forms of advertising and publicity; it must also protect him against the growing and serious dangers of the total pollution of his environment, following wholesale industrialization.

It has become necessary more than ever before to draw up a code for science and technology defining their moral purpose and formulating principles governing their utilization in the exclusive service of man with a view to the harmonious development of mankind at the spiritual and material levels.

The coming years open up vast and bright prospects for Unesco's standard-setting activities, as it does for those of other major organizations of the United Nations system.

ANNEX

LIST OF NORMATIVE INSTRUMENTS ADOPTED EITHER
BY THE GENERAL CONFERENCE OR BY
INTERGOVERNMENTAL CONFERENCES CONVENED
SOLELY BY UNESCO OR JOINTLY WITH OTHER
INTERNATIONAL ORGANIZATIONS OF RELEVANCE
TO HUMAN RIGHTS

A. CONVENTIONS AND AGREEMENTS

Universal Copyright Convention, with Appendix Declaration relating to Article XVII and resolution concerning Article XI. 6 September 1952.

Protocol 1 annexed to the Universal Copyright Convention, concerning the application of that Convention to the works of stateless persons and refugees. 6 September 1952.

Protocol 2 annexed to the Universal Copyright Convention, concerning the application of that Convention to the works of certain international organizations. 6 September 1952.

Protocol 3 annexed to the Universal Copyright Convention, concerning the effective date of instruments of ratification or acceptance of, or accession to, that Convention. 6 September 1952.

Convention for the Protection of Cultural Property in the Event of Armed Conflict, with Regulations for the Execution of the Convention. 14 May 1954.

Protocol for the Protection of Cultural Property in the Event of Armed Conflict. 14 May 1954.

Convention against Discrimination in Education. 14 December 1960.

Protocol instituting a Conciliation and Good Offices Commission to be Responsible for Seeking the Settlement of any Disputes which may Arise between States Parties to the Convention against Discrimination in Education. 10 December 1962.

Convention on the Means of Prohibiting and Preventing the Illicit Import, Export and Transfer of Ownership of Cultural Property. 14 November 1970.

Universal Copyright Convention as revised at Paris on 24 July 1971 with Appendix Declaration relating to Article XVII and resolution concerning Article XI. 24 July 1971.

Protocol 1 annexed to the Universal Copyright Convention as revised at Paris on 24 July 1971 concerning the application of that Convention to works of stateless persons and refugees. 24 July 1971.

Protocol 2 annexed to the Universal Copyright Convention as revised at Paris on 24 July 1971 concerning the application of that Convention to the works of certain international organizations. 24 July 1971.

Convention concerning the Protection of the World Cultural and Natural Heritage. 16 November 1972.

B. RECOMMENDATIONS

Recommendation concerning the Most Effective Means of Rendering Museums Accessible to Everyone. 14 December 1960.

Recommendation against Discrimination in Education. 14 December 1960.

Recommendation concerning Technical and Vocational Education. 11 December 1962.

Recommendation on the Means of Prohibiting and Preventing the Illicit Export, Import and Transfer of Ownership of Cultural Property. 19 November 1964.

Recommendation concerning the Status of Teachers. 5 October 1966.

Recommendation concerning the Preservation of Cultural Property Endangered by Public or Private Works. 19 November 1968.

Recommendation concerning the Protection, at National Level, of the Cultural and Natural Heritage. 16 November 1972.

Recommendation concerning Education for International Understanding, Cooperation and Peace and Education relating to Human Rights and Fundamental Freedoms. 19 November 1974.

Revised Recommendation concerning Technical and Vocational Education. 19 November 1974.

Recommendation on the Status of Scientific Researchers. 20 November 1974.

Recommendation on the Development of Adult Education. 26 November 1976.

Recommendation on Participation by the People at Large in Cultural Life and their Contribution to it. 26 November 1976.

Recommendation concerning the Safeguarding and Contemporary Role of Historic Areas. 26 November 1976.

Recommendation concerning the International Exchange of Cultural Property. 26 November 1976.

Recommendation for the Protection of Movable Cultural Property. 28 November 1978.

Recommendation concerning the Status of the Artist. 27 October 1980.

C. DECLARATIONS

Declaration of the Principles of International Cultural Co-operation. 4 November 1966.

Declaration of Guiding Principles on the Use of Satellite Broadcasting for the Free Flow of Information, the Spread of Education and Greater Cultural Exchange. 15 November 1972.

Declaration on Race and Racial Prejudice. 27 November 1978.

Declaration on Fundamental Principles concerning the Contribution of the Mass Media to Strengthening Peace and International Understanding, to the Promotion of Human Rights and to Countering Racialism, Apartheid and Incitement to War. 28 November 1978.

NOTES

1. Article I, para. 1, of the Convention creating the United Nations Educational, Scientific and Cultural Organization.

2. The following may be cited as examples: *The Race Question in Modern Science*, Unesco, Paris, 1956; *Race as News*, Unesco, Paris, 1974; *Racism and Apartheid in Southern Africa (South Africa and Namibia)*, Unesco, Paris, 1974, etc.

3. See *The Birthright of Man*, Unesco, Paris, 1968.

4. See Article 1, paragraph 2 of the Constitution.

5. See Article 4, paragraph 4, of the Constitution.

6. A complete collection of the normative instruments of Unesco will be published soon. The list of those instruments which are particularly relevant to human rights appears as an annex to this chapter.

7. See also Jean De Breucker, "Pour les vingt ans de la Convention de la Haye du 14 mai 1954 pour la protection des biens culturels", in *Revue belge de droit international*, Vol. XI (1975), pp. 525-547; and *Information on the Implementation of the Convention for the Protection of Cultural Property in the Event of Armed Conflict*, Unesco document CL/MD/41 (1979).

8. See H. Saba, "La Convention et la Recommandation concernant la lutte contre la discrimination dans le domaine de l'enseignement", in *Annuaire français de Droit International*, 1960, pp. 646-652.

9. See P. Merens, "L'application de la Convention et de la Recommandation de l'UNESCO concernant la lutte contre la discrimination dans le domaine de l'enseignement: un bilan provisoire", in *RDH/HRJ*, 1968, Vol. I, pp. 91-108.

10. The most recent reports of the Committee on the Convention and Recommendation on the third consultation were submitted to the General Conference at its twentieth session (1978) in document 20 C/40 and to the twenty-first session (1980) in document 21 C/27.

11. See in this connection T. Modeen, "La protection internationale des minorities: les Iles d'Aland", in *RDH/HRJ*, Vol. VI, 1973, pp. 287-302.

12. The text of this Statement along with the four others to be mentioned are reprinted in *Unesco, Declaration on Race and Racial Prejudice*, 23 (1979) [Hereafter cited as *Declaration*].

13. *Ibid.*, p. 29

14. *Ibid.*, p. 35

15. *Ibid.*, p. 41

16. Resolution 17 C/10.1, para. 14

17. Article 1, para 2. See also the "Explanatory report on the draft Declaration on Race and Racial Prejudice," document 20 C/18 Annex, page 1. [Hereafter "Explanatory Re-

port"]. Drawing on the allusion made to "right to development as a human right" by the UN Commission on Human Rights in its resolution 4 (XXXIII), the drafters also consecrated the new concept of "right to full development". See Article 3; Explanatory Report, p. 3.

18. Article 2, para 2. See also Explanatory report, page 3. The implications of the terms used in the light of the UN Charter were clearly in the minds of the drafters of the text.

19. Art. 9, para. 1. *See also* Explanatory Report, p. 8.

20. Art. 4, para. 2. *See also* Explanatory Report, p. 4.

21. *Declaration*, p. 18

22. *Ibid.*, para. 1. (c)

23. *Ibid.*, para. 2. (a)

24. Information given in this sub-section is mainly drawn from documents 100 EX/CR.2 and 102 EX/19 prepared by Unesco's Secretariat.

25. Since no definition was given of "other authoritative sources," the Secretariat of the Joint Committee has not considered itself entitled to pass on to the Committee reports from organizations, particularly research organizations, that did not fall into the other categories mentioned, nor communications from individuals. In principle, the latter are handled in accordance with the procedure laid down by 77 EX/Decision 8.3, which will be examined below.

26. 19 C/23 and CEART/III/1976/10, paragraph 171.

27. 100 EX/Decision 5.2.1, based on documents 100 EX/13 and 19 C/23, containing the Joint Committee's report, and document 100 EX/14, containing the report of the Committee on Conventions and Recommendations in Education.

28. 19 C/Resolution 1.171.

29. For a summary of the history, to 1976, of the communications received and of the recommendations for in procedure, see Unesco Doc. CR.2 (1976). For a detailed analysis of the question see Unesco Doc. 102 EX/19 (1977)

30. The text of the standard letter to the authors of communications and the form are reproduced in Unesco, The Executive Board of Unesco p. 53 (1979).

31. Decision 104 EX/3.3, para. 14 (j).

32. *Ibid.*, para. 14 (k).

33. *Ibid.*, para. 8(b), *See* also 103 EX/19 para. 47.

34. 104 EX/Decision 3.3, para. 14(f).

35. *Ibid.*, para. 14(h)

36. *Ibid.*, para. 14(g), referring to Rule 29 of the Board Rules of Procedure, which provide for this possibility.

37. *Ibid.*, para. 6.

38. *Ibid.*, para. 7.

39. *See e.g.*, the announcement concerning the private meeting held on 17 October 1979. Unesco Doc. 108 EX/Decisions, at 43 (1979).

40. Decision 104 EX/3.3, para. 10.

41. *Ibid.*

42. *Ibid.*, paras. 17&18.

43. Unesco Doc. 102 EX/SR. 5,6,7,8,9,10&17 (1977); Unesco Doc. 103 EX/WP/HR/INF 1 & Adds, 1 & 2, Unesco Doc. 103 EX/18 & Unesco Doc. 103 Ex/19 (1977).

44. Art. 11 of the Rules of procedure of the General Conference allows the Director General, the Executive Board or Member States to request the inclusion or to include supplementary items to the agenda established according to arts. 9&10. Standing items or supplementary items could include such questions.

45. For further information on the functioning of this new procedure see Document 21 C/13, paragraphs 59-67.

14 The Implementation of Humanitarian Law

Christian Dominicé

1. THE SYSTEM OF SUPERVISION INSTITUTED BY THE GENEVA CONVENTIONS

The law of armed conflicts[1] is largely inspired by humanitarian considerations. Its main object is to endeavour to contain military necessities—namely, the search for effectiveness in operations undertaken against the opposing party— within the narrowest possible limits, in order to protect to a certain extent the lives, health and dignity of human beings.[2] It can therefore be stated that humanitarian rules include not only those governing the conduct of operations— methods and means of combat—but also those concerning the victims of conflicts (the wounded, the sick, prisoners and the civilian population). Thus, the *Hague law*, as it is traditionally known, should, to a large extent, be included in the notion of international humanitarian law, like the *Geneva law*, even though, sometimes, the latter alone has been placed in the category of humanitarian law. Moreover, it will be noted that while the Hague and Geneva laws have for a long time presented obvious points of contact (the question of prisoners of war is one example, among others), the recent tendency is towards a more thorough integration of these two groups of complementary norms, as is borne out more particularly in the two Additional Protocols to the Geneva Conventions—Protocol I relating to the protection of victims of international armed conflicts and Protocol II relating to the protection of victims of non-international armed conflicts—adopted in 1977 by the Diplomatic Conference on the Reaffirmation and Development of International Humanitarian Law Applicable in Armed Conflicts, which held four sessions in Geneva between 1974 and 1977. The Protocols entered into force on December 7, 1978. The first contains provisions relating to methods of combat and means likely to be used by the belligerents, which is a field that comes traditionally under Hague law.[3]

While the definition of international humanitarian law should not be limited solely to the rules of the humanitarian Conventions, it is to be noted that the

Geneva Conventions of 1949,[4] as contrasted with the Conventions concerning the conduct of hostilities, establish international machinery for the purpose of ensuring their implementation. While this machinery, established by the general provisions of the four Conventions of 1949, is at the centre of the present study, consideration is not given to the question of the institution of criminal proceedings against persons committing infractions of the Conventions.[5]

Common article 1 of the four Conventions of 1949 stipulates: "The High Contracting Parties undertake to respect and to ensure respect for the present Convention in all circumstances." This is an important reminder which leaves no doubt as to the role and function of the machinery instituted by the Conventions, which appears essentially as a procedure for supervision rather than a system of application.

The texts which call for particular attention are articles 8, 9 and 10 of the first three Conventions and 9, 10 and 11 of the fourth. They establish what may be described as a system possessing several tiers.

First of all, it is stipulated that the Conventions shall be applied "with the co-operation and under the scrutiny of the Protecting Powers whose duty it is to safeguard the interests of the Parties to the conflict" (art. 8/8/8/9).

Second, it is stated that the High Contracting Parties "may at any time agree to entrust to an organization which offers all guarantees of impartiality and efficacy the duties incumbent on the Protecting Powers by virtue of the present Convention" (art. 10/10/10/11, first paragraph). What is being referred to here is the "organization acting in place of a Protecting Power" envisaged in various proposals made on several occasions, but of which no concrete example has so far been afforded by practice.

Lastly, the Conventions provide for the establishment of a "substitute" for cases where the persons protected by the Conventions do not benefit or cease to benefit from the activities of a Protecting Power or of an organization such as that referred to above: the Detaining Power must then request a neutral State, or such an organization, to undertake the functions incumbent on the Protecting Powers by virtue of the Conventions (art. 10/10/10/11, second paragraph). If protection cannot be arranged accordingly, the Detaining Power shall request or shall accept the offer of the services of a humanitarian organization, such as the International Committee of the Red Cross,[6] to assume the humanitarian functions performed by Protecting Powers under the Conventions (art. 10/10/10/11, para. 3).

In addition, it is important to emphasize that article 9/9/9/10 states that the provisions of the Conventions constitute no obstacle to the humanitarian activities which the ICRC (or any other impartial humanitarian organization) may undertake for the protection and relief of the beneficiaries of the Conventions. In other words, it should not be overlooked that while the ICRC, as the final substitute, appears at the bottom of the list in the system just described, it also holds a special or parallel position, by virtue of its specific mission, expressly identified by the texts.[7]

It is therefore worthwhile examining in turn, from the point of view of the implementation of the humanitarian Conventions, the role of the Protecting Powers, including the organization acting in their place and the substitute, and then the functions and terms of intervention of the ICRC.

2. THE PROTECTING POWERS AND THEIR SUBSTITUTE

(a) The institution of the Protecting Power

The institution of the Protecting Power is not a creation of the humanitarian Conventions. In referring to the "Protecting Powers whose duty it is to safeguard the interests of the Parties to the conflict", the Conventions of 1949, following the precedent created by Article 86 of the Geneva Convention of 1929 (Code of prisoners of war), take as their foundation an institution long enshrined in the law of nations. Thus a practice had arisen whereby a State (the State of origin), in the event of its breaking off diplomatic relations and, more particularly, engaging in war, with another State (the State of residence), would entrust to a third State responsibility for protecting its interests and those of its nationals in the State of residence.

This practice, established by custom, to which the belligerents of the last two world wars had great recourse, was enshrined in treaty form in article 45 of the Vienna Convention of 1961 on diplomatic relations.[8]

It is worthwhile briefly recalling the main features of the institution of the Protecting Power:

Appointment of a Protecting Power presupposes a three-sided agreement. In other words, the State of origin must ensure that the Protecting Power agrees to accept the mandate and that the State of residence agrees to recognize the Protecting Power in that capacity.

The Protecting Power is the mandatory of the State of origin. It acts as a delegate of the latter and consequently cannot assert any more rights than are enjoyed by its mandator vis-à-vis the State of residence.

In discharging its mandate, the Protecting Power benefits, however, from a certain measure of discretion, notably as regards the manner in which it proposes to act upon the instructions it receives from the State of origin. It is not a mere organ of transmission.

Lastly, there is nothing to prevent the same State being assigned the functions of Protecting Power by two States in their mutual relations (system of the double mandate). At the time of the Indo-Pakistani conflict in 1971, the Helvetic Confederation (Switzerland) exercised such a double mandate. In addition, those functions that may be described as regular functions (in contrast with those resulting from the Geneva Conventions) exercised by the Protecting Power may vary to a large extent. The Protecting Power may not only discharge various administrative functions (supervision of buildings, establishment of acts, etc.) but also may carry out more specifically political activities, such as requests for explanations, protests, etc., or representations on behalf of the nationals of the State of origin.

While it is not appropriate to dwell at length here on the regular functions of the Protecting Powers—those customarily referred to under the heading of the "Vienna mandate"—it is nevertheless worth stressing that this mandate may be fairly heavy for the State that assumes it, especially when it is a small State. It may, in addition, be sometimes awkward to carry out, especially since, be it not forgotten, the Protecting Power is also concerned with the protection of its own interests and those of its nationals.

(b) The Protecting Powers in the framework of the Geneva Conventions

It is understandable that, in order to facilitate the effective application of the Geneva Conventions, the High Contracting Parties in 1949, taking account of the positive experience resulting from Article 86 of the 1929 Convention, decided to have recourse to the Protecting Powers, an institution already firmly established by international practice, while at the same time not excluding the development of other institutions.

(i) THE ORIGIN AND LEGAL NATURE OF THE MANDATE OF THE PROTECTING POWER

Since they do not create a new institution but refer to a customary practice between parties to an armed conflict, it is to be expected that the Conventions should pass over in silence the designation of Protecting Powers. The principles emerging from international practice consequently remain valid here, and particularly the necessity of the three-sided agreement. When a belligerent has entrusted to a third State (a neutral State), with its agreement, the defence of its interests with the adversary State, and the latter has accepted the Protecting Power in that capacity, the arrangement provided for by the Geneva Conventions is in place. In this connection, the following remarks need to be made.

(1) It seems clear from the text of article 8/8/8/9 that, once a Protecting Power has been designated and accepted, it is automatically entrusted, in addition to its regular tasks, with the functions assigned to it by the Conventions. This does not necessarily mean to say that the "Vienna mandate" and the "Geneva mandate" cannot be dissociated. Indeed it can be envisaged, even if such an eventuality remains fairly theoretical, that a party to the conflict may wish to make one Power responsible for safeguarding its political and diplomatic interests and another for ensuring that the Geneva Conventions are respected. This would be possible, provided that the adversary party was in agreement. In addition, it is important not to forget the terms of the first paragraph of article 10/10/10/11, which specifically provides that the duties incumbent on the Protecting Powers may, with the agreement of the parties, be entrusted to a particular organization. In other words, it is perfectly possible for the Geneva mandate to be covered by a special agreement aimed at entrusting it to a State or to an organization distinct from the neutral State responsible for safeguarding the interests of the originating Power. However, if such an agreement is not reached, and if there exists a Protecting Power accepted as such by the State of residence, it is automatically assigned, *ipso jure*, the duties resulting from the Geneva Conventions. Such is undoubtedly the sole interpretation authorized by the texts and which

corresponds to the desire of the Contracting Parties when they resolve to have recourse to an institution enshrined in general international law.

(2) Should it be deduced from the imperative character of the text that there exists an obligation, for the belligerent States, to designate a Protecting Power? It would seem, rather, that the basic premise was that the parties to the conflict would be naturally led to do so in their own interests, and this was an additional reason for the Geneva mandate being added to the regular diplomatic mandate. It should be pointed out, however, that the designation of a mandatory Power (Vienna mandate) is optional, with the result that uncertainty remains as to the obligation to designate a Protecting Power for the purpose of implementing the humanitarian Conventions.

(3) As has already been emphasized, the powers of the Protecting Power are delegated to it by the State of origin, the latter being the mandator of the former. Is this exactly the case in respect of the application of the Conventions of 1949? The commentators insist on the fact that the Protecting Power is a sort of general mandatory.[9] In other words, while its power to act as a Protecting Power is indubitably founded upon the particular mandate entrusted to it by a specific State, its responsibilities under the Geneva Conventions are assigned to it by all of the Contracting Parties. This is certainly important in respect of the general conception of the supervision and authority which the Protecting Powers may claim to be entitled to exercise.

(ii) THE MEANS AVAILABLE TO THE PROTECTING POWER

The Protecting Power acts through the intermediary of its representatives or delegates. These of course are primarily its diplomatic and consular staff, appointed in accordance with established rules and practice. However, the case may arise where the Protecting Power does not have a sufficient number of staff at its disposal. The Geneva Conventions have consequently provided for the possibility of the Protecting Power having recourse to the services of delegates appointed from amongst its own nationals or the nationals of other neutral Powers. It is stated, however, that such persons shall be subject to the approval of the Power with which they are to carry out their duties (art. 8/8/8/9, first paragraph).

(iii) THE MISSION ENTRUSTED TO THE PROTECTING POWER

Common article 8 (article 9 of the 4th Convention), as has been seen, stipulates: "The present Convention shall be applied with the co-operation and under the scrutiny of the Protecting Powers...". How is this mission to be considered? It is to be noted, first of all, that, in addition to this general provision, each of the Conventions of 1949 contains specific provisions defining the circumstances and modalities of the intervention by the Protecting Powers. The number of these specific provisions, however, varies a great deal from one Convention to another. Thus, apart from the reference to them in the general provisions common to the four Conventions, the Protecting

Powers are mentioned only in two articles in the first Convention and one in the second, while numerous specific tasks are assigned to them in the third and fourth.[10] No doubt this is on account of the different purposes of these texts. Clearly, specific and detailed tasks and responsibilities can more easily be assigned to the Protecting Powers in the case of the protection of prisoners of war, or of the civilian population, than in that of the protection of wounded, sick and shipwrecked persons in the combat zone.

The fact remains that the question immediately arose as to whether the role of the Protecting Powers is strictly circumscribed by the specific provisions relating to them or whether, by virtue of article 8/8/8/9, it should be understood as being appreciably more far-ranging. Persuasive arguments, based both on principle and on the texts, support the latter interpretation.[11] Thus, it must be acknowledged that the tasks of the Protecting Powers cover all that concerns the implementation and observance of the prescriptions and obligations resulting from the four Conventions, subject to the two restrictions defined in the texts themselves.

The first, which at least in its first part, is not so much a true restriction as a simple reminder of the rules of general international law, is common to the four Conventions. It results from the third paragraph of article 8/8/8/9, according to which: "The representatives or delegates of the Protecting Powers shall not in any case exceed their mission under the present Convention. They shall, in particular, take account of the imperative necessities of security of the State wherein they carry out their duties". It is obvious that the agents of the Protecting Powers cannot either exceed their mission or exercise an activity harmful or dangerous to the State of residence. Moreover, that State can demand that any representatives or delegates not exercising their functions with the sole objective of ensuring the application of the Conventions be recalled. However, this provision should not provide grounds for unduly restricting the activities of the Protecting Powers.

The second restriction is contained only in the first two Conventions. It is worded as follows: "Their activities shall only be restricted as an exceptional and temporary measure when this is rendered necessary by imperative military necessities". It is to be noted however that provisions of the same kind are contained in the other two Conventions, concerning visits to camps and places of internment, which fortunately gives them a more limited bearing. The danger presented by such a provision should indeed be emphasized, since it may easily serve as an excuse for unduly impeding the activities of the Protecting Powers, even though it is clearly worded in such a way as to guard against its being invoked lightly.

It now remains necessary to define more specifically the mission of the Protecting Power. The decisive text, as we have seen, is that which lays down that each of the Conventions "shall be applied with the co-operation and under the scrutiny of the Protecting Powers". What exactly does this mean?

It should not be forgotten that the primary responsibility for implementation of the Conventions falls to the parties to the conflict. Most of the obligations resulting from the Conventions are stated to be their responsibility, with the result that the scale and importance of activities of "co-operation" are less than those relating to "scrutiny". The Protecting Power co-operates each time that it assists a party to the conflict in discharging its obligations, or carries out acts expressly assigned to it.[12] Under this heading can also be included relief activities—the forwarding of foodstuffs and medicines, etc. —on behalf of protected persons, such activities being intended to help ensure that certain obligations relating to the treatment of persons are respected.

As for activities under the heading of "scrutiny", which was a subject of considerable discussion at the Diplomatic Conference of 1949, these should be understood as corresponding to the right—and the obligation—of the Protecting Power to verify that the parties to the conflict respect the obligations imposed on them by the Conventions. A large number of specific provisions in the third and fourth Conventions provide illustrations of such supervisory activities,[13] but, as has already been stressed, they do not constitute an exhaustive list of all the possible forms of supervision. In the case of the first two Conventions, the problems are more complex since it becomes necessary for the Protecting Power to be present on the battlefield, with the units engaged in combat, or on board ships. This is both an onerous and difficult task. What is certain is that the State of residence is obliged to recognize the right of the Protecting Power to carry out checks, not only in the camps and places of internment, but also wherever there are persons protected by the Conventions, be it on the battlefield or in occupied territories.

What might be the results of these supervisory activities? It is probable that they constitute an incentive, for the parties to the conflict, to respect the Conventions. The Protecting Power may set down the results of its investigations in reports addressed to the State of origin, and notify the State of residence of the protests of the former. However, by virtue of the margin of discretion allowed it, which is further reinforced by its status as a general mandatory, it may prefer not to transmit all its reports to the State of origin if the interests of the persons protected seem to it to be better served by discreet action rather than by measures likely to increase tension.

Can it, on its own authority, intercede with the Government of the State of residence in order to deplore violations of the Conventions and to request that they be halted? This can unhesitatingly be stated to be the case, since responsibility for scrutiny, within the meaning of article 8/8/8/9, is both entrusted to and imposed upon the Protecting Power by all of the Parties to the Conventions. Any supervisory activity not involving the right and the duty to draw the attention of a party to the conflict to its violations would be meaningless. It is important to stress, however, that in carrying out its supervisory activities the Protecting Power should not be so much a censor—that is not its role—as a means of effective support for protected persons.

(c) The system of Protecting Powers and the reality of armed conflicts

Article 8/8/8/9 of 1949, despite certain shortcomings of a formal rather than substantive nature, was generally hailed as an important advance. There was reason to rejoice because genuine machinery of scrutiny was thereby established in a particularly sensitive area. And such rejoicing was all the more justified in that the experience of the Second World War had shown that the condition of prisoners who had benefited from the system of the 1929 Convention had been incomparably better than that of prisoners to which that system had not been applied.

However, the fact must be faced that the system of Protecting Powers has not lived up to expectations. Until recently, although Protecting Powers had been present in the Suez conflict (1956) and in the Goa conflict (1961), the system of implementation sought by the Geneva Conventions had been scarcely used. Attempts were made on various sides to explain why this was so,[14] among which mention may be made of the following reasons:

—many conflicts were non-international armed conflicts and hence did not entail the application of the system of Protecting Powers;

—owing to the fact that the institution of the Protecting Power serves to fill the gap left once diplomatic relations have been broken off, no Protecting Power was appointed in certain conflicts in which the belligerents had not broken off their diplomatic relations, or in other conflicts involving States one of which was not recognized by the others;

—mention was also made of other reasons of a practical kind, such as for instance the brief duration of certain conflicts or the unwieldiness of the system of Protecting Powers.

These observations led to various proposals being made, the purpose of which was to make improvements in the system of the 1949 Conventions. These will be dealt with subsequently.

It should be pointed out, however, that use was made of the system of the Protecting Power in the Indo-Pakistani conflict of December 1971, linked to the events which led to the secession of eastern Pakistan to form the independent State of Bangladesh.[15] During the agitated period from the proclamation of independence of Bangladesh (26 March 1971) to the outbreak of hostilities between India and Pakistan, the Swiss Confederation had occasion to exercise its good offices. Its co-operation proved to be useful in successfully bringing about the repatriation of the members of two diplomatic missions which had been closed in Dacca and Calcutta, an operation which was all the more complicated in that a number of Pakistani officials in Calcutta had declared their allegiance to Bangladesh. Immediately after the breaking off of diplomatic relations Switzerland was instructed to safeguard Pakistani interests in India and Indian interests in Pakistan. It thus assumed a double mandate, a situation with precedent during the Second World War. Switzerland thus performed useful services of a diplomatic character, such as the exchange of diplomats, the establishment of numerous documents, and a good offices mission which promoted the resumption of direct contacts between the two opposing parties.

There remained the problem of the application of the Geneva Conventions which was further complicated by the emergence of a legal controversy. Switzerland contended that, in being chosen as the mandatory State, it was simultaneously assigned the duties and prerogatives of the Protecting Power within the meaning of the 1949 Conventions. It considered in particular that its agents should be able to visit prisoners' camps. In the view of the Swiss Government, based on article 8/8/8/9, the "Vienna mandate" entailed *ipso jure* the "Geneva mandate", unless the parties to the conflict had agreed to entrust the Geneva mandate to a substitute organization or to another neutral State, which had not occurred in this case.

While Pakistan did not raise any objections—it held only a small number of prisoners—the Indian Government was opposed to this view. It held that the Vienna and Geneva mandates were distinct from each other, and that it had authorized Switzerland to exercise only the former. It added that the Pakistani prisoners of war captured on the eastern front had surrendered to the joint command of the Indo-Bengali troops, that they were therefore held jointly by the two countries and that the mandate entrusted by Pakistan to Switzerland did not cover Bangladesh.

In fact, the Pakistani prisoners taken on the western front were able to be visited by representatives of Switzerland.[16] This being so, the view may be taken that this controversy concerning the Geneva mandate should not be dissociated from its particular political context in which the question of the recognition of Bangladesh by the other States, and Pakistan in particular, played a cardinal role for India.

The fact remains that, while maintaining its legal stand, and without ceasing to enjoy good relations with the Indian Government, the principal role played by Switzerland consisted of the use of its good offices. This enabled it to do useful humanitarian work. In a subsequent agreement between India and Pakistan, in 1973, concerning the repatriation of various categories of persons, Switzerland was requested by the three States concerned to assist in its implementation. It accepted that responsibility and contributed, in collaboration with the ICRC and the Office of the United Nations High Commissioner for Refugees, to the gradual repatriation of the various persons referred to in the agreement.

What lessons can be drawn from this experience?

The controversy concerning the "Geneva mandate", which seems on the basis of the Geneva Conventions of 1949 and in the absence of any agreement concerning a substitute organization, automatically to complement the "Vienna mandate", is disturbing. At the very least, it reveals the obstacles still standing in the way of a system of supervision which requires intervention by another State, and particularly when it is the mandatory of the opposing party. This is a handicap from which the ICRC does not suffer, although its responsibilities are, in any event, more limited. All the same, in the case of the Indo-Pakistani conflict of 1971, it may be noted that the controversy concerning the Geneva mandate would not perhaps have been quite so acute had it not been for the problem relating to the recognition of Bangladesh. The mandate of the Protecting Power was able to be exercised in regard to prisoners from the western front, from which it might be adduced that the underlying principle was not necessarily being questioned. However, care must be taken not to jump to hasty conclusions in this matter.

Experience in the Bangladesh case seems to confirm that, as was shown earlier, the institution of the Protecting Power is severely handicapped and that it is based on the system of traditional diplomatic relations. Each time that, in one form or another, a question of recognition is being disputed between the parties to a conflict, the resulting political problems hinder the appointment of a Protecting Power or the full exercise of its mandate. In the Bangladesh case Switzerland found itself at a particular moment in an awkward situation, since it was being urged by India to recognize Bangladesh and by Pakistan not to do so. Its freedom of decision in this matter, as a sovereign State, was to a certain extent limited by its obligation to jeopardize as little as possible the exercise of its mandate. In addition, of course, the problem of recognition was all the more difficult since Pakistan did not intend to appoint the mandatory State in its relations with the secessionist entity.

While certain shortcomings of the system of Protecting Powers came to light, it is however important to stress that the 1971 conflict also revealed its benefits. The speed with which the Protecting Power was appointed and was able to get to work reveals the fundamental quality of the system: it is based upon an existing diplomatic infrastructure. The representatives of the Protecting Power are on the spot, they are familiar with the country, they have their contacts with the administration, and they benefit from a status which facilitates their task. No other body can offer these advantages to the same extent. No doubt humanitarian organizations sometimes have possibilities of action which are denied the Protecting Power, owing to its being a State, and a mandatory State. This brings out the complementary character of the two institutions, it being noted in addition that the diplomatic efforts of the Protecting Power, through the medium of its good offices, appear on certain occasions to be such as to facilitate the task of humanitarian organizations "in the field".

(d) Organizations acting in place of and as substitutes for Protecting Powers

(i) ORGANIZATIONS ACTING IN PLACE OF PROTECTING POWERS

In stipulating, in the first paragraph of article 10/10/10/11, that the contracting States may at any time agree to entrust to an organization which offers all guarantees of impartiality and efficacy the duties incumbent on the Protecting Powers, the Conventions of 1949 offer to the parties to a conflict the possibility of having recourse to a special organization, rather than to a neutral State.

The text is set out in terms sufficiently broad to allow of various solutions. Thus, the parties to the conflict may, as soon as it breaks out, and even if they appoint other mandatory Powers to safeguard their interests, agree to entrust the Geneva mandate to a special body which may be an existing organization (international organization, private institution), and, especially if there is no Protecting Power at a given time (the mandatory State ceases to be neutral or renounces its mandate), transfer the mandate to such an organization.

It is also conceivable that, in time of peace, all or some of the contracting States might agree to appoint or to set up such an organization, to which the Geneva mandate would be automatically entrusted upon the outbreak of hostilities. Mention should perhaps be made, in this context, of the proposal made in 1949 by the French delegation to establish an International High Committee capable of replacing the Protecting Powers. This proposal was not adopted in the text of the Conventions, but it is to be noted that one of the resolutions of the Diplomatic Conference of 1949 requests that the desirability of setting up an international body be studied.[17]

However, the fact remains that on no occasion have the parties to a conflict agreed to entrust the Geneva mandate to a special body, despite the apparent soundness of such an approach.

A governmental organization would perhaps be subject to even greater political handicaps than a neutral State, while it would be difficult for a private body to command resources comparable to those of a Protecting Power.

(ii) SUBSTITUTES FOR PROTECTING POWERS

The entire system of the Geneva Conventions, deriving very largely from experience during the Second World War, is founded on the idea that it is in the interest of States engaged in a conflict to appoint mandatory Powers to safeguard their interests with their adversaries. The mandate resulting from the Conventions is in addition to the regular diplomatic mandate.

Experience had also shown, however, that situations may arise in which there is no Protecting Power. Nevertheless it is necessary to find a means of ensuring the protection of victims, and it is here that the notion of the substitute comes into play.

We may immediately discount the case where the mandatory Power, having ceased to exist as such for reasons specific to it, the State of origin entrusts the defence of its interests to another neutral State. Such is the situation which arises when the mandatory Power itself becomes a party to the conflict, as was the case for the United States of America in December

1941. The new mandatory Power is not a substitute, its status is that of the original Protecting Power.

Substitutes are provided for in cases where there is no Protecting Power, either because the parties to the conflict have not appointed one or because during the conflict events arise which put an end to the mandate. Particular mention may be made of the annexation or occupation of the State of residence, or the disappearance of the State of origin.[18]

If it turns out that the persons protected by each of the Conventions do not benefit, or cease to benefit, by the activities of a Protecting Power, it is stipulated (article 10/10/10/11, second paragraph) that the Detaining Power shall request a neutral State, or an organization acting in place of a Protecting Power (in the sense seen above, on the assumption that there exists one) to undertake the functions performed by the Protecting Power. It may seem strange at first sight that responsibility for taking such a step falls to the Detaining Power, but the fact should not be overlooked that humanitarian considerations are of priority importance here. This being so, whatever the reasons for the default of the Protecting Power, it is preferable for protected persons to benefit by the activities of a neutral State, even if it is appointed by the Detaining Power itself, rather than be deprived of all support.

With respect to this provision, it may be noted that several contracting States have made reservations by virtue of which the request made by the Detaining Power to a neutral State shall not be deemed valid unless the Power, of which the protected persons are nationals, consents to it.[19]

As this substitute system has not yet been tested there is little point in further expounding upon it or in raising the question as to whether a distinction should have been made based on whether the Power of origin has continued to exist or has disappeared (following annexation).

Lastly, this being the final tier of the system, the Conventions also provide for cases where protected persons do not benefit by the activities of a neutral State (or an organization acting in its place) acting in the capacity of a Protecting Power or of a substitute. The third paragraph of article 10/10/10/11 stipulates that in such cases the Detaining Power shall request or accept the services of a humanitarian organization, such as the ICRC, to assume the humanitarian functions performed by Protecting Powers under the Conventions. The Detaining Power is obliged to accept such an organization's offer of services, provided that it furnishes sufficient assurances of impartiality and efficacy.

The assumption by the ICRC or any other impartial humanitarian organization of the humanitarian functions performed by Protecting Powers in no way restricts other general humanitarian activities which may be undertaken, subject to the consent of the Parties concerned (article 9/9/9/10).

As the question of the ICRC's intervention is discussed below, I shall limit myself here to two remarks. It should be noted first of all that, while the Detaining Power is obliged to request the assistance of a humanitarian organization at this ultimate stage when no other protection is forthcoming, it is not obliged to accept such an organization's offer of services unless two conditions have been met: it must not have already obtained the assistance of an institution, and the organization which proposes its services must furnish the assurances defined in paragraph 4 of the same article.[20]

Secondly, it will be noted that the text defines the nature of the responsibilities of the humanitarian organization: it falls to it to assume the humanitarian functions performed by Protecting Powers. While thus clearly stressing that the humanitarian organization intervenes in a different capacity from that of the Protecting Power or its substitute (it is not a mandatory but an auxiliary), this provision seems to indicate that the functions of the Protecting Powers, in the framework of the Conventions of 1949 are not all of a humanitarian nature. In other words, some of them are more specifically diplomatic or political. This is a question to which we shall return in connection with the role of the ICRC. It may be noted here, however, that virtually all of the functions performed by the Protecting Powers under the "Geneva mandate" seem to be of a humanitarian character.

3. THE DELEGATIONS OF THE INTERNATIONAL COMMITTEE OF THE RED CROSS

(a) The ICRC and the Geneva Conventions

It is neither necessary nor possible to describe here all the highly varied activities of the ICRC and its specific role in the whole of the Red Cross movement. It is sufficient to recall that, while it is closely linked to the Geneva Conventions, the ICRC also undertakes its activities in circumstances other than those which make the Conventions applicable.

It should be emphasized that the activities of the ICRC are not confined to armed conflicts—either international or non-international—which define the scope of the humanitarian Conventions. Thus, for example, they also cover situations of internal disturbances or tensions. The best illustration of this is that afforded by its activities on behalf of political prisoners. What characterizes all the various types of activity carried out by the ICRC, whether or not they are based on the Conventions, is their exclusive concern to ensure the protection of human beings whose lives are threatened and also, from this perspective, their constant concern for impartiality, on which their effectiveness essentially depends. The fact remains that action on behalf of victims of armed conflicts, which was the purpose for which the ICRC was set up, constitutes its principal function and one which is amply enshrined in the Geneva Conventions.

In what capacity is it required to contribute to the implementation of these Conventions? As has been seen in connection with the Protecting Powers, implementation of the Conventions comprises various elements. It devolves primarily upon the parties to the conflict. It is they that must apply the Conventions and not other States or organizations, but the latter perform a function which can be broken down into three major types of activities:

(i) Relief activities proper, which provide victims of conflicts with material, medical or moral assistance. These activities are not aimed at the implementation of the Conventions in the strict sense,[21] but it seems obvious that, by contributing to the amelioration of the condition of victims of conflicts, they help, albeit indirectly, to ensure that the obligations laid down by the Conventions are respected.

(ii) Acts and activities—generally of an administrative and technical character—specifically entrusted by the Geneva Conventions to the Protecting Power or its substitute, either because the Detaining Power is not in a position to perform them itself, or because it is preferable that someone else take responsibility for them. Into this category can be placed all activities designed to help the parties to the conflict to discharge their obligations.

(iii) Supervisory activities, which may have somewhat different characteristics according to the way in which they are conceived. If what is principally involved is, by means of visits and checks, to call the Detaining Power's attention to its obligations to help it to discharge them and to intercede on behalf of protected persons, then it can be said that supervision serves an essentially humanitarian purpose. It would be quite different if such supervision were performed with a view principally to exposing violations of law to obloquy, distributing blame and, generally acting as a censor.

While these three types of activities are not entirely separate from each other, it is useful to distinguish between them and to keep them in mind in attempting to appraise the question of the ICRC's role in the application of the Geneva Conventions. In this connection, the principal provisions constituting the legal basis for its activities should be recalled.

We have already considered the general provision of article 9/9/9/10, which grants the ICRC the possibility, subject to the consent of the parties to the conflict, of undertaking its humanitarian activities for the protection of those protected by the Conventions, and for their relief. We have also seen that in cases where no protection is afforded (there being neither a Protecting Power nor a substitute), the Detaining Power must request or accept the offer of the services of a humanitarian organization, such as the ICRC, to perform the humanitarian functions performed by Protecting Powers under the Conventions (article 10/10/10/11). To this should be added the important express mention of the ICRC in common article 3. This provision concerns cases of "armed conflict not of an international character," and constitutes what has been described as a sort of "miniature Convention" for this particular type of conflict. But, more particularly, it states that "an impartial humanitarian organization, such as the International Committee of the Red Cross may offer its services to the parties to the conflict".

Confining myself to the essential points, it seems to me that three main remarks need to be made concerning these provisions of the Conventions:

(i) The ICRC, unless another body of the same type is able to take its place, benefits from a genuine right of intervention, but one which is limited to certain circumstances. For this to be so there must be an armed conflict of an international character (within the meaning of common article 2) and, in addition, no protection must be provided for the beneficiaries of the Conventions. In such a case, what is the ICRC entitled to do? In stating that it falls to it to assume the humanitarian functions performed by the Protecting Power under the Conventions, the text seems to indicate that certain functions performed by those Powers, owing to their not having a humanitarian character, fall outside the competence of the ICRC. However, if one discounts the regular diplomatic activities of the Protecting Powers (Vienna mandate), which fall completely outside the field of application of article 10/10/10/11, it is difficult to discover, among the activities entrusted to the Protecting Powers by the Conventions (Geneva mandate), any which do not have a humanitarian character or purpose. One might perhaps be tempted thus to identify supervisory activities. However, as has been pointed out, unless it gives rise to public protest or criticism, supervision remains essentially a humanitarian activity. Moreover, the right to carry out certain acts for the benefit of prisoners or internees, for instance, which makes it necessary to enter into contact with them, would seem necessarily to involve the right to draw the Detaining Power's attention to its obligations. It consequently seems to me that the ICRC, in this case, is to all intents and purposes assigned all the functions performed by Protecting Powers under the Conventions, for they are all of a humanitarian character, including functions performed by way of good offices under article 11/11/11/12, except for the fact that the ICRC is the mandatory of none of the parties to the conflict.

(ii) It is not so much a right as a faculty, subject to the consent of the parties to the conflict, which is granted to the ICRC in the case of international conflict in which the system of the Protecting Power is applied. In addition to relief activities, can it perform other functions? It is to be noted that the tasks performed by the Protecting Power under the Conventions may prove to be fairly onerous, especially if there are numerous prisoners of war and civilian internees. There is consequently room for collaboration by the Protecting Power with the ICRC, which will be able to exercise a parallel activity, both at the administrative level and in the matter of supervision, which is provided for by the texts themselves in certain circumstances.[22]

(iii) The irreplaceable role of the ICRC assumes a particular dimension in armed conflicts not of an international character, which fall outside the field of application of the system of Protecting Powers and cause difficult problems to arise in respect of the protection of victims. The activities which it will endeavour to carry out, with the agreement of the parties to the conflict, include relief activities, co-operation in the implementation of the provisions of common article 3, starting with the calling of attention to the obligations resulting therefrom, and measures aimed at inducing the parties to the conflict to bring into force all or part of the provisions of the Conventions.[23]

(b) The means of action available to the International Committee of the Red Cross

In the framework of this chapter, it is possible to make only a few brief remarks in this connection.

One observation seems to me to deserve mention over all others. The ICRC's essential tool, on which the implementation and effectiveness of all its means of action depend, is its reputation for impartiality. Its moral authority derives from its exclusive dedication to the cause of victims of conflicts, regardless of who they are. This is true both of the governing bodies of the ICRC and its delegations.

Secondly, and particularly in regard to the implementation of the Geneva Conventions, it is clearly the delegations that are of leading importance.[24] Set up and directed by the Geneva headquarters, they are required to play a decisive role since it is they who, locally, keep in contact with the parties to the conflict, intercede on behalf of protected persons, visit them, ensure that relief is properly provided and, if need be, discharge all the functions performed under the Conventions by the Protecting Powers.

In view of the necessity of impartiality and efficacy, these delegations have to be carefully selected. It is to be noted, however, that while, by virtue of its statutes the Committee itself is composed solely of Swiss citizens, there is no such rule as regards the members of delegations, although, for reasons which are easy to understand, the ICRC is obliged to be careful if it wants to guard against any suspicion of partiality as regards those acting on its behalf.[25]

As for the status of the delegates, it is to be noted that article 8/8/8/9 provides that the parties to the conflict shall facilitate, to the greatest extent possible, the task of the representatives or delegates of the Protecting Powers. This provision holds good for the ICRC each time that it is assigned the functions of auxiliary substitute in the sense of article 10/10/10/11, paragraph 3. It also, in my view, holds good by analogy when the ICRC's action has the consent of the parties to the conflict, be it in the framework of article 9/9/9/10 (international armed conflicts) or of the common article 3 (armed conflicts not of an international character). This means, on the one hand, similar immunities to those of diplomatic staff[26] for their *ex officio* activities, and, on the other, freedom of movement and adequate facilities for entering into contact with protected persons.

Furthermore, and this must be the conclusion, the delegations of the ICRC possess the outstanding characteristic of being the mandatories of the human spirit. It is by striving scrupulously to preserve that characteristic, secure from all prejudice or political influence, that they are in a position to play a decisive role in the implementation of the Geneva Conventions and to be granted the facilities required by them for that purpose.

4. RECENT DEVELOPMENTS AND APPRAISAL

It is apparent that the Geneva Conventions of 1949, in instituting the system of Protecting Powers and in confirming the specific role of the ICRC (or any other impartial humanitarian organization accepted by the Parties to a conflict), created an elaborate mechanism aimed at ensuring the correct application of the Conventions.

It is nonetheless true that the results have been considered disappointing, since the system of Protecting Powers has been used only occasionally and the ICRC has been able to administer its services in only about half the conflicts which have occurred since 1949. It is understandable then that a great deal of discussion has been devoted to the problem of reinforcing the use of humanitarian law,[27] and that the Diplomatic Conference examined this question carefully.[28] Before a brief analysis of the dispositions the Conference adopted in this domain, two observations are called for.

First of all, the essence of the problem concerns the will of the Parties to the conflict. If they are resolved to ignore the humanitarian rules, it is not the mechanism of application, to which they accord little value, which will be able to do much about it. On the other hand, if the will to respect the conventions is present, it is important that the system of implementation should not be burdened with defects which complicate its application.

In the second place, if one intends to ensure optimal aid to protected persons, which is the principal goal of the scrutiny system, supervision confided to a third party must clearly aim to incite the Parties to the conflict to assume their obligations. Indeed it must help them to do so. Inquiries on violations, public criticism, and condemnations of all kinds belong to another outlook, which is beyond the scope of this discussion. It is submitted that during hostilities, this type of control frequently risks being more prejudicial than useful in the application of humanitarian law. That is why, concerning the reinforcement of this application, we leave aside propositions dealing with the creation of bodies with the essential vocation of establishing the facts about and condemning infractions, whatever their merits may be from an overall point of view.[29]

The preparatory work and debates of the Conference clearly demonstrate that the principle of the system of Protecting Powers is not contested.[30] While pointing out difficulties which have arisen, the majority of commentators have recognized its merits and asserted that it was necessary to improve the system, not to abolish it.

In adopting article 5 of Protocol I additional to the Geneva Conventions, the Diplomatic Conference clearly declared itself in favor of reinforcing the Protecting Powers system, with the goal of applying the Conventions of 1949. The first two paragraphs of this document state:

1. It is the duty of the Parties to a conflict from the beginning of that conflict to secure the supervision and implementation of the Conventions and of this Protocol by the application of the system of Protecting Powers, including *inter alia* the designation and acceptance of those Powers, in accordance with the following paragraphs. Protecting Powers shall have the duty of safeguarding the interests of the Parties to the conflict.
2. From the beginning of a situation referred to in Article 1, each Party to the conflict shall without delay designate a Protecting Power for the purpose of applying the Convention and this Protocol and shall, likewise without delay and for the same purpose, permit the activities of a Protecting Power which has been accepted by it as such after designation by the adverse Party.[31]

Difficulties arose from the fact that by virtue of the Conventions of 1949 the mandate of Protecting Power is added to the ordinary diplomatic mandate. It can be noted that Protocol I, without expressing an opinion on whether the "Vienna Mandate" entails *ipso jure* the "Geneva Mandate," in any case imposes on the Parties to the conflict the duty to act so that the system of Protecting Powers is set up for the purpose of applying the Conventions and the Protocol. It is true that this system continues to be based on a three-sided agreement. However, in making the attribution of the "Geneva Mandate" an autonomous obligation, article 5 represents an advance capable of offering a solution in situations where the designation of a Mandatory Power in the sense of the Vienna Convention must not be counted on (see Protocol I, art. 5, paras. 5 and 6). To this obligation to designate and accept a Protecting Power, article 5 adds a mechanism designed to facilitate attribution of this mandate in case the Parties to the conflict should delay doing so. It also reserves in this respect a special role to the ICRC (see Protocol I, art. 5, para. 3).

Parallel to the improvement and reinforcing of the Protecting Powers system, the position of the ICRC as substitute is strengthened. Without causing damage to its own particular tasks (especially relief activities), it can offer to act as substitute, and this offer must be accepted. The same provision is equally valid for any other impartial body (see Protocol I, art. 5, para. 4).

There remains the serious problem of the application of humanitarian law in armed conflicts not presenting an international character. It could be wished that Parties to conflicts were obliged to resort to the services of the ICRC. Taking into account the opinion of the majority of experts that it had consulted, the ICRC did not go so far in the draft of Protocol II that it submitted to the Diplomatic Conference. It suggested a provision which, under the title, "Aid to Observation of the Present Protocol," limited itself to instituting the option for the Parties to the conflict to resort to the services of the ICRC or any other impartial body. This proposition thus went hardly further than the common article 3 of the Conventions. Even in this scarcely restrictive form, it did not find favour in the eyes of the Diplomatic Conference, with the result that there is no provision in Protocol II which adds to what already exists concerning our subject.

Finally, then, it can be said, concerning armed conflicts of an international character, that the system designed to deal with them, while not perfect, is of a sort to favor correct application of humanitarian law in all cases where the Parties to conflict intend to fulfill their obligations in good faith. The assistance of a Protecting Power ought to be assured, even if conditions are such that no State has been invested with an ordinary diplomatic mandate.

Protocol I undoubtedly created a new difficulty, because it considers situations, such as "wars of liberation" against Colonial Powers or insurrections against racist regimes, as international armed conflict (see Protocol I, art. 1, paras. 3 and 4).

In situations of this kind, attribution of the Geneva Mandate to a Protecting Power frequently runs up against considerable political difficulties. Nevertheless, the obligation remains to accept the ICRC as a substitute.

Concerning armed conflicts of a non-international character, the situation remains uncertain. It has proved to be impossible to develop or strengthen the system of assistance and control beyond the terms of the common article 3. To tell the truth, the problem in question is one that would be suitable to examine in the general context of international humanitarian law. For the moment, this is a law between States. The Conventions and Protocols are open only to States. Reflection ought to be given to the manner in which it could prove desirable and possible to broaden this structure, which would perhaps permit improvement in its implementation.

NOTES

1. The rules of the law of armed conflicts and the links which exist between those rules and international norms for the protection of human rights are examined *supra*, in Chapters 3 and 8.

2. See G. Schwarzenberger, *The Law of Armed Conflicts*, London, Stevens, 1968, Vol. 2, p. 9.

3. See the *Diplomatic Conference on the Reaffirmation and Development of International Humanitarian Law Applicable in Armed Conflicts, Final Act, Geneva, 1977*.

4. These, it may be recalled, are Convention I for the amelioration of the condition of the wounded and sick in armed forces in the field, Convention II for the amelioration of the condition of wounded, sick and shipwrecked members of armed forces at sea, Convention III relative to the treatment of prisoners of war and Convention IV relative to the protection of civilian persons in time of war. When mention is made of the same article in the four Conventions, the following system is employed: 8/8/8/9.

5. In this regard the Conventions provide for an inquiry procedure. See art. 52/53/132/149.

6. Referred to hereinafter as the ICRC.

7. Concerning the system of application of the Geneva Conventions, see in particular the *Commentary* of the 1949 Conventions, published under the general editorship of J. Pictet, 4 Vols., Geneva, ICRC, 1952-1966; F. Siordet, *The Geneva Conventions of 1949: The Question of Scrutiny*, Geneva, 1953; P. de La Pradelle, "Le contrôle de l'application des conventions humanitaires en cas de conflit armé," *Annuaire français de droit international*, 1956, p. 343 *et seq.*

8. Concerning the Protecting Power within the meaning of general international law, see e.g. K. Doehring, "Schutzmacht," in Strupp-Schlochauer, *Wörterbuch des Völkerrechts*, Band III, Berlin, 1962, pp. 218-222; P. Guggenheim, *Traité de droit international public*,

Vol. II, Geneva, 1954, p. 332 *et seq.*; M. Whiteman, *Digest of International Law*, Vol. 7, Washington, 1970, pp. 448-464. See also R. Bertschy, *Die Schutzmacht im Völkerrecht*, Fribourg thesis, 1952 and A. Janner, *La Puissance protectrice en droit international d'après les expériences faites par la Suisse pendant la seconde guerre mondiale*, trad. Monney, 2nd ed., Basel, 1972.

9. Cf. F. Siordet, *op. cit.*, pp. 36-37.

10. A complete table of all the references to the Protecting Powers in the four Conventions is given in F. Siordet, *op. cit.*, pp. 73-78.

11. Cf. *Commentary, op. cit.*, Conv. I, p. 106.

12. Numerous activities provided for by Conventions III and IV which are of an administrative character, in the broad sense, or of a medical character, come under the heading of such "co-operation". See the list given of them in the table mentioned *supra*, note 10.

13. The most typical examples are visits to prisoners' camps and places of internment, Convention III, art. 126, and Convention IV, art. 143.

14. Cf. documents submitted by the ICRC to the Conference of Government Experts of 1971, Vol. II, Geneva, January 1971; and UN Docs. A/7720 (1969) and A/8052 (1970).

15. See Rousseau, "Chronique des faits internationaux," *Revue générale de droit international public*, 1972, p. 538, and 1973, p. 857.

16. It is important to point out that the ICRC, for its part, was able to perform its traditional humanitarian role in regard to all prisoners.

17. See *Commentary, op. cit.*, Conv. I, p. 127, and P. de La Pradelle, *loc. cit.*, p. 344. The resolution of the Conference of 1949 is reproduced in the *International Red Cross Handbook*, 11th ed., Geneva, 1971, p. 225.

18. For an analysis of the various cases where there is no Protecting Power revealed by the Second World War, cf. F. Siordet, *op. cit.*, p. 50.

19. Cf. *Commentary, op. cit.*, Conv. I, p. 128.

20. Art. 10/10/10/11, para. 4.

21. The parties to the conflict do however assume some obligations in respect of relief activities, cf. in particular Conv. IV, art. 23.

22. Convention III, art. 126, and Convention IV, art. 143.

23. Art. 3, para. 3.

24. See H.G. Knitel, *Les délégations du Comité international de la Croix-Rouge*, Geneva, 1967 (Etudes et travaux de l'Institut universitaire de Hautes Etudes internationales, No. 5).

25. Note that, in regard to the performance of certain specific functions, the appointment of delegates is submitted to the approval of the Detaining Power. Cf. art. 126 of Convention III, art. 143 of Convention IV.

26. See H.G. Knitel, *op. cit.*, p. 107.

27. See references cited in note 14, *supra* and Council of Europe Consultative Assembly doc. 3336 (1973).

28. This Section was written after the conclusion of the Diplomatic Conference, with the collaboration of Mr. Antoine Martin, former deputy head of the Legal Division of the ICRC, whom the author would like to thank.

29. In the Geneva Conventions, inquiries on violations are referred to in a separate article (art. 52/53/132/149), which shows clearly that they fall under a different heading than supervision of the Conventions' application. Also see art. 90 of Protocol I (International Fact-finding Commission).

30. See "Questionnaire concerning measures intended to reinforce the implementation of the Geneva Conventions of August 12, 1949: replies sent by Governments", ICRC, Geneva, 1973; J. Patrnogic, "Contrôle de l'application des conventions humanitaires et problème des sanctions", *Annales de droit international médical*, No. 24, September 1973, p. 75; Diplomatic Conference, Report of Commission I.

31. Protocol I gives the following definition of Protecting Power in its article 2, paragraph c: " 'Protective Power' means a neutral or other State not a Party to the conflict which has been designated by a Party to the conflict and accepted by the adverse Party and has agreed to carry out the functions assigned to a Protecting Power under the Conventions and this Protocol".

Sub-Part II
Regional Institutions for the Promotion and Protection of Human Rights

15 Introduction

Karel Vasak

1. THE UNITED NATIONS AND REGIONAL HUMAN RIGHTS INSTITUTIONS

The Charter of the United Nations, Chapter VII of which is devoted to "Regional Arrangements", contains nothing which precludes the existence of such arrangements and indeed provides encouragement for them, especially insofar as they are likely to contribute to the pacific settlement of "local" disputes. What is revealed here once again is a *negative rather than a positive conception of peace*, which is that of the authors of the San Francisco Charter: *peace understood as a period without conflicts* and, in particular, without violent conflicts. Moreover, the Charter specifically assigns only one obligation to regional agencies: to contribute to the settlement of local disputes.

Despite the emphasis laid on the settlement of conflicts, the Charter does not preclude action by regional agencies in other fields: paragraph 1 of article 52 of the Charter, in referring to the purposes and principles of the United Nations (article 1), which include the promotion of respect for human rights, opens the way for regional action in the field of human rights, without however making it obligatory.

For a long time, regionalism in the matter of human rights was not popular at the United Nations: there was often a tendency to regard it as the expression of a breakaway movement, calling the universality of human rights into question. However, the continual postponements of work on the International Human Rights Covenants led the UN to rehabilitate, and to be less suspicious (less jealous, some would say) towards, regionalism in human rights, especially after the adoption of the Covenants in 1966.

By Resolution 2200 C (XXI) of 19 December 1966, the General Assembly requested the United Nations Commission on Human Rights to study, *inter alia*, the question of the setting up of appropriate regional institutions for the purpose of discharging certain functions relating to observance of the Covenants. Consequently, the Commission on Human Rights (resolution 6 (XXIII) of 1967) set up an *ad hoc* group to study the possibility of establishing regional human rights commissions within the framework of the United Nations. The 1968 report of the Group, which contained neither conclusions nor recommendations, simply stressed that the initiative in this matter must emanate from the States of the region concerned[1]. Nevertheless, the United Nations has subsequently organized three regional seminars in Africa which have dealt with the subject of regional commissions.

The first of these was organized in Cairo in September 1969[2]. On the basis of the report of that seminar and of the report of the ad hoc study group the Commission adopted another inconclusive resolution in which it requested the Secretary-General "to arrange for appropriate consultation and exchange of information between the Commission and the Organization of African Unity as regards the possible establishment of the suggested regional commission" (resolution 6 (XXVI) of 1970). In 1973 a seminar held in Dar-es-Salaam on "new ways and means for promoting human rights with special attention to the problems and needs of Africa" concluded that an African Convention on human rights should be prepared under OAU auspices and accepted in principle the need for an African Commission.[3]

In a series of resolutions between 1977 and 1979 the General Assembly appealed "to States in areas where regional arrangements in the field of human rights do not yet exist, to consider agreements with a view to the establishment within their respective regions of suitable regional machinery for the promotion and protection of human rights"[4]. In July 1979 the 16th ordinary session of the OAU Assembly of Heads of State and Government called on the OAU Secretary-General to organize a "meeting of highly qualified experts to prepare a preliminary draft of an 'African Charter on Human and Peoples' Rights' providing inter alia for the establishment of bodies to promote and protect human and peoples' rights".[5]

A subsequent United Nations regional seminar on "the establishment of regional commissions on human rights with special reference to Africa" was held in Monrovia in September 1979. It adopted the "Monrovia Proposal for the Setting Up of an African Commission on Human Rights" which contains a possible model for such a commission[6]. Finally, the African Charter of Human and Peoples' Rights was adopted in Nairobi in June 1981.

In relation to other regions, it may be noted that the August 1979 Conference of the Law Association of Asia and the Western Pacific (LAWASIA) recommended that the Council of Lawasia establish a Permanent Standing Committee on Human Rights with a view to establishing a Centre or Centres for Human Rights in the region and the working towards the creation of an Asian Commission and/or Court of Human Rights.

Finally although not strictly a regional initiative, mention may be made of the fact that in 1979 the Heads of Government of Commonwealth nations invited the Commonwealth Secretary-General to appoint a Working Group to examine a proposal, put forward by The Gambia, to establish a Commonwealth Human Rights Commission. In October 1981, the Commonwealth

Heads of Government agreed in principle to establish a special unit within the Commonwealth Secretariat for the promotion of human rights.

2. REGIONAL HUMAN RIGHTS INSTITUTIONS—THE PRESENT POSITION

Signs of the regionalization of human rights are now to be seen in every continent, although only in a very embryonic form in Asia.

This movement was first launched, chronologically, on the European continent. Today the international promotion and protection of human rights has acquired three institutional dimensions in Europe, but there are great disparities, both in the extent to which this particular branch of European law has been developed, and in the machinery established for its implementation.

These three dimensions are as follows:

(i) The *Community dimension*. Within the European Communities, respect for basic rights "forms an integral part of the general principles of law whose observation is ensured by the Court of Justice" and "the protection of these rights, consonant with the constitutional traditions common to Member States, must be assured within the context and aims of the Community" (Case 11-70, Internationale Handelsgesellschaft, Collected Texts XVI, p. 1135). Thus, community law in respect of human rights, which is still in embryonic form, is essentially jurisprudential in nature except when it is based upon an express provision of constitutional treaties as is, for instance, article 7 of the EEC Treaty, affirming the principle of non-discrimination. It is also to be noted that, during 1979-1980, a number of steps have been taken in the direction of securing formal adherence by the European Communities to the European Convention.[7]

(ii) The *pan-European, or greater European dimension* found institutional expression in the Conference on Security and Co-operation in Europe (CSCE) and its follow-up activities and review conferences in Belgrade in 1978 and in Madrid in 1980-1982. Apart from the fact that, in the Final Act, human rights are considered to be one of the "principles governing the mutual relations of the participating States"[8], specific aims are set forth in the field of human rights —a field, moreover, described preferably as the "humanitarian field" in that document—and, more particularly, in respect of freedom of movement of men, ideas and information.

(iii) The *"Roman" dimension*, the most developed of all, whose institutional framework is the Council of Europe and whose legal basis is the Rome Convention for the Protection of Human Rights and Fundamental ·Freedoms and the Turin European Social Charter is of particular interest in the context of this treatise.

Outside Europe, the regional protection of human rights is not marked by the same degree of development nor by the same level of institutionalization.

On the *American continent*, the problem has been theoretically received along the same lines as in Europe since the Organization of American States, after setting up in 1959 an Inter-American Commission on Human Rights, succeeded in providing it with a supporting framework in the form of the American Convention on Human Rights adopted in 1969, and which entered into force on July 18, 1978.

On the *African continent*, after proclaiming their adherence to the Universal Declaration of Human Rights, the authors of the Charter of Addis Ababa creating the Organization of African Unity did not reserve a leading place for human rights since no African organ with special responsibility for human rights has so far been created. However, we have noted above the recent initiatives which have been taken within Africa with a view to the establishment of a regional commission.

In the *Arab world*, the League of Arab States did, it is true, set up in 1968 a permanent Arab Commission on Human Rights, but this body is insufficiently well-known, even in the Arab countries, and so far its activities have passed unnoticed, with the exception of its work to draw up a Declaration of the Rights of Arab Citizens. One cannot fail to note the links being forged between the African world and the Arab world: the Arab-African dialogue has already given rise to close co-operation in the economic and social fields; it is to be hoped that the field of human rights will soon follow.

3. HUMAN RIGHTS AND REGIONAL INTEGRATION

Intended to pave the way towards a united Europe of which it would constitute the "axis", the European Convention on Human Rights—which is manifestly the most developed system for the regional protection of human rights—both sustains and is sustained by a policy of European integration. It is a fact that the supra-national elements which it contains (right of individual petition before a court, powers of decision of the Court, in particular) would not resist for long in a purely intergovernmental organic body or in one not of a nature to transcend itself through a process of legal and even constitutional integration. Expressed in terms of the geopolitical character of existing European organizations, what this means is that in order to continue to exist and to develop, the Rome Convention requires not only the institutional support of the Council of Europe, but also the political implications of the European Communities, just as the Council of Europe and the European Communities would not be able without peril to remain cut off from the Convention. Logically, it was seen that the outcome of the Greek case—that is to say, of the applications brought by several European governments against the Greek government of the Colonels before the European Commission of Human Rights—affected both the frontiers of the Council of Europe—Greece withdrew from the Organization—and those of the European Communities, since the operation of the Agreement setting up an Association between the EEC and Greece had to be suspended.

The experience of the European Convention of Human Rights thus tends to show that the regional protection of human rights can achieve full success only if it constitutes an element in a policy of integration on the part of the States of a given region. Only at this price is it possible to permit the blow struck by regionalism in the "matter of human rights against that necessary universalism which springs from the intrinsically identical nature of all human beings. The recent entry into force of the United Nations Covenants on Civil and Political Rights and on Economic, Social and Cultural Rights, which should be preserved as a legal expression of the universal character of the human being, should even lead us to be more exacting in the future in respect of regionalism than we were in the past when no universal system for the effective protection of human rights seemed feasible. In the last analysis, regional protection must come within the framework of regional organization in accordance with the Charter of the United Nations and become one aspect of the policy of integration. If, however, regional protection were but *a form of intergovernmental co-operation*, the parochial and perhaps even selfish attitudes of which it would also be the expression, would by no means justify the danger of such a serious blow to universalism[9].

NOTES

1. Doc. E/CN.4/966 and Add. 1.

2. See the basic document for this seminar by K. Vasak, published in *Mélanges Cassin*, Pédone, Paris, 1968. Vol. 1, p. 467, under the title "Vers la création de commissions regionales des droits de l'homme". The report of the Cairo seminar was published in doc. ST/TAO/HR/38.

3. UN doc. ST/TAO/HR/48, paras. 127-28.

4. See General Assembly resolutions 32/127 (1977), 33/167 (1978) and 34/171 (1979).

5. AHG/Dec. 115 (XVI) reproduced in United Nations document A/34/552 (1979) Annex II. A draft of the Charter is reprinted in the Bulletin of Peace Proposals, Oslo, Vol. II, No. 4, 1980.

6. United Nations document ST/HR/SER.A/4, para. 83 and Annex 1.

7. See EEC doc. COM (79) 210 final, 2 May 1979; H.G. Schermers, "The Communities under the European Convention on Human Rights", *Legal Issues of European Integration*, 1978/1, p. 1; and the articles in Vol. 5, No. 4, 1972 of RDH/HRJ.

8. This is Principle VII entitled "Respect for human rights and fundamental freedoms, including the freedom of thought, conscience, religion or belief".

9. A similar idea is to be found in the General Agreement on Tariffs and Trade: it is permissible to limit the application of the most-favoured-nation clause to certain countries only if the goal pursued is the establishment of a free-trade area or a customs union.

16 The Council of Europe

Karel Vasak

According to article 1, paragraph (a), of the Statute of 5 May 1949, the aim of the Council of Europe is to achieve a "greater unity" between its members, of which there are now twenty one (Austria, Belgium, Cyprus, Denmark, Federal Republic of Germany, France, Greece, Iceland, Ireland, Italy, Liechtenstein, Luxembourg, Malta, Netherlands, Norway, Portugal, Spain, Sweden, Switzerland, United Kingdom and Turkey). It should in fact be possible, in realizing this aim, to attain two objectives: To safeguard and promote the ideals and principles which are the common heritage of its Member States; and to facilitate their economic and social progress. According to the Statute, this common heritage which is to be safeguarded and promoted includes "the spiritual and moral values which are. . . the true source of individual freedom, political liberty and the rule of law, principles which form the basis of all genuine democracy".

The desire to defend and promote freedom—and consequently democracy—therefore permeates the entire Statute of the Council of Europe: It is reflected in particular in articles 3, 4, 5 and 8 which govern the various aspects of the membership of the Council. Only democratic States can become members of the Council of Europe which, as a result, constitutes no less than a "club" of European democracies, the rules of admission to which seem particularly strict. Some authors go so far in this view as to contend that the European Convention on Human Rights has, for the Council of Europe, a constitutional value in the sense that all Member States should ratify it and that a State applying for admission must undertake to do so. This view, however, is contradicted by the provisions of article 65, paragraph 1, of the Convention which authorize a Contracting State to denounce the Convention while remaining a member of the Council of Europe.

It nevertheless remains true that this thesis has a political value in that it reflects the pre-eminence of human rights among the concerns of the Council of Europe. Today, the organization is increasingly identified with human rights, striving to become the home of freedom, the haven of democracy, the ultimate recourse of the persecuted. This being so, it is easy to understand the spirited reactions within the Council of Europe to the *coup d'état* of the Greek colonels in 1967, followed two years later by the withdrawal of Greece from the Council.

It is easy to understand why the European Convention on Human Rights was the first multilateral treaty concluded in the framework of the Council of Europe, of which it provides an extension of the statutory basis, and why the Strasbourg organization sought to complement this first treaty on human rights by a second agreement for the protection of the economic and social rights of man: this was to be the role of the European Social Charter.

1. THE EUROPEAN CONVENTION ON HUMAN RIGHTS

The Convention for the Protection of Human Rights and Fundamental Freedoms was signed in Rome on 4 November 1950 and entered into force on 3 September 1953 after the tenth instrument of ratification had been deposited. The Convention is supplemented by five additional Protocols which fall into two different categories:

The (first) additional Protocol, signed in Paris on 20 March 1953 and which came into force on 19 May 1954, and Protocol No. 4, signed in Strasbourg on 16 September 1963 and which came into force on 2 May 1968, recognize certain rights and freedoms other than those already included in the Convention; the provisions concerning them are considered to be additional articles to the Convention which consequently applies to them.

Protocols Nos. 2, 3 and 5 concern the operation of the two principal organs of the Convention, the European Commission and Court of Human Rights. Protocol No. 2, signed at Strasbourg on 6 May 1963, confers upon the Court competence to give advisory opinions. Protocol No. 3, also signed at Strasbourg on 6 May 1963, amends articles 29, 30 and 34 of the Convention concerning the procedure of the Commission. These came into force on 21 September 1970. Protocol No. 5, signed at Strasbourg on 20 January 1966, entered into force on 20 December 1971. It amends articles 22 and 40 of the Convention governing the election of members of the Commission and of the Court; it was ratified by nineteen Member States of the Council of Europe. Mention should also be made here of the European Agreement Relating to Persons Participating in Proceedings of the European Commission and Court of Human Rights, which was signed in London on 6 May 1969. The purpose of this Agreement is to grant certain strictly enumerated immunities and facilities to persons who, as applicants, witnesses or in other capacities, take part in the proceedings of the Commission and Court. The Agreement came into force on 17 April 1971.

As of January 1982, the Convention was binding upon twenty members of the Council of Europe, namely: Austria, Belgium, Cyprus, Denmark, Federal Republic of Germany, France, Greece, Iceland, Ireland, Italy, Luxembourg, Malta, Netherlands, Norway, Portugal, Spain, Sweden, Switzerland,

United Kingdom and Turkey. The First Additional Protocol has been ratified by the same States, with the exception of Switzerland. Protocol No. 4 has been ratified by the following States: Austria, Belgium, Denmark, Federal Republic of Germany, France, Iceland, Ireland, Luxembourg, Norway, Portugal and Sweden.

The human rights (civil and political)[1] protected by the Convention are enumerated in it and in Protocols Nos. 1 and 4. These human rights cover protection of physical well-being (right to life, prohibition of torture, inhuman or degrading treatment or punishment, prohibition of slavery, servitude, forced or compulsory labour); protection of freedom (freedom of movement, right to freedom and security); protection of the right to justice (right to be granted effective remedy, right to a fair hearing, rights of the accused); protection of privacy (right to marry, right to respect for private and family life, right to respect for one's home and correspondence); protection of intellectual activity (freedom of thought, conscience and religion, freedom of expression, right to education and right of parents over the education and teaching of their children); protection of political activity (freedom of assembly and association, free elections); protection of economic activity (right to enjoy one's possessions). At the same time, discrimination, on whatever grounds, in the exercise of the rights protected is prohibited.

But the originality of the Convention does not lie in the list of rights which it protects. It indisputably lies in the institutional part of the Convention, and more precisely in the machinery for the international supervision of the observance of its provisions. The authors of the Convention devised a lasting institutional framework, and one which is relatively complex and unwieldy, comprising an organ of inquiry and conciliation, the European Commission of Human Rights, a political decision-making organ, the Committee of Ministers of the Council of Europe, a judicial decision-making organ, the European Court of Human Rights, and an auxiliary organ of the Convention, the Secretary-General of the Council of Europe.

(a). An organ of inquiry and conciliation: the European Commission of Human Rights

Under article 19 of the Convention, the European Commission of Human Rights is one of the two organs whose purpose is to "ensure the observance of the engagements undertaken by the High Contracting Parties". While the constitution of the European Court of Human Rights, the other organ instituted by the Convention, presupposed prior acceptance of its compulsory jurisdiction by eight States, the Commission could come into being once the Convention came into force on 3 September 1953. The first election of the members of the Commission took place on 18 May 1954.

The general rules concerning the organization, operation, competence and procedure of the Commission are contained in Section III of the Convention.

They are more clearly defined in the Rules of Procedure established by the Commission in pursuance of article 36 of the Convention, the revised version of which came into force on 15 May 1980.

As a compromise solution between the conflicting requirements of the individual to whom the promoters of the Convention wished to open the doors of the international court, and those of the State, which had to be protected against improper individual appeals, the creation of the Commission no doubt expresses in succinct form the originality of the Convention. Serving as a substitute for the Court for the individual and yet as a tribute to the sovereignty of States, the Commission has many and varied functions. The sole link between these tasks is often merely the identity of the parties in the case laid before it. Like certain characters in Greek mythology, it changes face when it changes function. A Chamber of Petitions at the beginning, when it decides whether an application is admissible, it goes down a notch in the judicial hierarchy to become a mere examining magistrate when it establishes the facts of the case. As a conciliating magistrate when it seeks a friendly settlement, it must also possess the qualities of a diplomat since the interests of a State are at stake. Then, required to give its "opinion" as to whether there has been a breach of the Convention, the Commission becomes an auxiliary of justice in the guise of the professional expert on human rights. Finally, in order to perform the entire spectrum of judiciary functions, the role of an attorney-general falls to the Commission before the Court.

Only the affirmation of its jurisdictional character could enable the Commission to carry out these functions without too many clashes. Originally envisaged as a simple administrative organ entrusted with conciliation and with the sorting out of applications, the Commission found in fact that these tasks were too numerous for a body that did not sit in a permanent capacity. To circumvent this it organized and imposed itself on States and individual applicants as an international judicial organ. The rules governing both its organization and operation as well as its practice—which has become a genuine case-law—provide a striking confirmation of this unanimous desire on the part of its members.

(i). ORGANIZATION AND OPERATION

Membership

The Commission consists of a number of members equal to that of the High Contracting Parties. No two members may be nationals of the same State (Conv., art. 20). The Commission consequently consists at the present time of twenty members. The members of the Commission are elected by the Committee of Ministers of the Council of Europe by an absolute majority of votes, from a list of names drawn up by the Bureau of the Consultative Assembly of the Council of Europe. Each group of the Representatives of the High Contracting Parties in the Consultative Assembly puts forward three candidates, of whom at least two are its nationals (Conv., art. 21).

The Convention does not lay down the qualifications required to be a candidate. However, the national groups in the Assembly have always taken care to put forward candidates possessing high qualities and in fact complying with the conditions laid down by article 39, paragraph 3, of the Convention, for candidates for membership of the European Court of Human Rights, namely: to be of high moral character and either possess the qualifications required for appointment to high judicial office or be jurisconsults of recognized competence.

The members of the Commission, except for those elected at the time of the first election which was held on 18 May 1954, are elected for a period of six years, half of whom are replaced every three years. However, once new members had to be elected because of new ratifications of the Convention, the purpose of article 22 of the Convention could not be achieved since their six-year period of office began at a date often very different from that of the other members of the Commission. Consequently, Protocol No. 5 of the Convention, of 20 January 1966, provides that, in order to ensure that as far as possible one half of the membership of the Commission shall be renewed every three years, the Committee of Ministers may decide, before proceeding to any subsequent election, that the term or terms of office of one or more members to be elected shall be for a period other than six years but not more than nine and not less than three years.

The members of the Commission may be re-elected. Resignation of a member constitutes vacation of office. A member of the Commission elected to replace a member whose term of office has not expired holds office for the remainder of his predecessor's term. However, the members of the Commission hold office until replaced.[2] After having been replaced, they continue to deal with such cases as they already have under consideration (Conv., art. 22).

The Convention passes over in silence the question whether the holding of the office of member of the Commission is incompatible with certain professions or functions. It would have been difficult for it to have been otherwise owing to the fact that the members of the Commission are not required to sit in a permanent capacity within an organ which is, however, a permanent one. It is self-evident, however, that it is not possible to be simultaneously a member of the Commission and a member of the Court. The Rules of Procedure merely provide that a member of the Commission may not take part in the consideration of any case in which he has a personal interest, or has had to be apprised of the facts of the case as the advisor of one of the parties or as a member of a tribunal or commission of inquiry, or in any other capacity (art. 21, para. 1). Moreover, the Rules of Procedure reserve each member of the Commission the right to withdraw from consideration of a particular case for some special reason (art. 22). Likewise, if a member or the President of the Commission considers that one of the members should not take part in the consideration of a particular case, because a circumstance is involved which may affect the impartiality of that member, the question is submitted to the Commission for decision (art. 21, para. 2).

The Commission elects its President and its first and second Vice-Presidents for a period of three years (or, more exactly, for the period separating two partial renewals of members of the Commission, that period being, in pursuance of Protocol No. 5, inferior or superior to three years). The President directs the work and presides at the meetings of the Commission. The first Vice-President replaces the President if the latter is unable to carry out his duties or if the office of the President is vacant (Rules of Procedure 6 and 7); the second Vice-President replaces the first under the same conditions. If the President is a national of, or was put forward as a candidate by, a High Contracting Party which is party to a case brought before the Commission, he must relinquish the office of President in respect of that case (Rule 9).

No provision of the Convention deals with the question of the remuneration of the members of the Commission. This silence is accounted for by the fact that when the Convention was being drafted, it was not known what would be the volume of work of the Commission and whether the continual presence of its members would be necessary. It was thus not possible to decide whether a fixed remuneration should be opted for or compensation for each day of duty. At the present time, the members of the Commission receive a compensation, the sum of which is determined by the Committee of Ministers of the Council of Europe.

Place, sessions and organization of work

The seat of the Commission is the seat of the Council of Europe in Strasbourg. The Commission may decide at any stage during the consideration of an application that it is necessary for itself or one or more of its members to carry out an enquiry or perform any other of its functions elsewhere. Thus, increasingly frequently, local enquiries or visits to the scene of the alleged violation by several delegates of the Commission have been organized.

A quorum of the Commission is ten members out of the twenty who currently constitute the Commission. However, seven members may constitute a quorum, in particular in the case of an individual application not communicated to the State against which it is brought (Rule 16, para. 2).

The sessions of the Commission and its organs are held *in camera* (Conv., art. 33, Rules of Procedure, 17). It follows that, in the course of proceedings, the parties involved are not authorized to give information concerning the procedure. The Commission alone may publish a press release from time to time.

This rule which often creates difficulties has been much criticized particularly in cases with political implications in which it is important, if not essential, for the hearing to be made public. *A priori*, it ill befits the nature of the role assigned by the Convention to the Commission: to be the custodian of human rights. As the Committee of Ministers also meets *in camera*, a case which has not been brought before the Court—whose hearings are in principle public— will have been examined from the time that it was introduced right up to the final decision in the course of sessions held *in camera*. In fact, the *in camera* rule is justified, or at least accounted for, in the case of the Commission, by the conciliation mission which the Convention entrusts to it at a particular stage of the procedure. In addition, it is motivated by the desire of the authors of the Convention to provide States with further protection against ill-willed or ill-intentioned applications.

The rules concerning administration proper reveal that close links exist between the Commission and the Council of Europe. Thus, the Secretariat of the Commission is provided by the Secretary-General of the Council of Europe, who also appoints the Secretary of the Commission (Conv. art. 37, Rules of Procedure, 11 to 13). The Secretary of the Commission performs functions similar to those of the registrar of an international court (cf. Rules of Procedure, 12 and 13).

(ii) COMPETENCE OF THE COMMISSION

"Ratione loci"

The Commission is competent, *ratione loci*, to take cognizance of facts which occur on territories where the Convention is being applied. These are, first of all, the national territories of the contracting States. It is to be noted that the Federal Republic of Germany has made a declaration to the effect that the territory to which the Convention applies also includes the *Land* of Berlin.

In order for the Convention to apply to the non-metropolitan territories for whose international relations the contracting States are responsible, an express notification of extension is necessary (art. 63). Three States have had recourse to this faculty: Denmark with respect to Greenland (the notification has become inapplicable since Greenland has become an integral part of the national territory); the Netherlands with respect to Surinam which has since become independent and the Dutch West Indies; the United Kingdom with respect to forty-two territories: most of these territories have also become independent (in which case the Convention ceases to apply to them since, according to article 66, it is open for signature solely by Members of the Council of Europe).

The competence *ratione loci* of the Commission is not limited, however, solely to the national territory or to the non-metropolitan territories to which the Convention has been extended pursuant to article 63. For it emerges from article 1 of the Convention that the contracting States are obliged to secure the rights and freedoms defined in the Convention to everyone "within their jurisdiction". That is to say, according to the interpretation given by the Commission, in particular in its decision concerning the admissibility of the application *Cyprus v. Turkey*, to everyone effectively under their authority or responsibility, whether such authority is exercised in their territory or abroad.

It is to be noted that the Committee of Ministers has decided to preserve the Convention's character as a closed treaty. In February 1963, it agreed not to take action upon a recommendation of the Assembly requesting that States which are not members of the Council of Europe and which possess the required qualifications be granted the opportunity to accede to the Convention.

"*Ratione personae*"

The Commission may receive petitions from:

—any High Contracting Party (Conv., art. 24);

—any person, non-governmental organization or group of individuals provided that the High Contracting Party against which the complaint has been lodged has declared that it recognizes the competence of the Commission to receive such petitions (Conv., art. 25).

At first sight, the right of a Contracting Party to address a petition to the Commission is but a reaffirmation of the right of a State to stand up for its nationals. However, the fact is that there is no requirement concerning nationality in the system of the Convention. Thus, in almost all the "State" applications brought so far, the alleged victims whose defence was taken by the applicant State were not its nationals (although certain links may have existed between the applicant State and the victims).

This solution clearly conforms to the logic of the system of the "collective guarantee" established by the Convention. Thus, each contracting State is in fact responsible for the observance of the guaranteed rights on all the territory where the Convention applies. In such circumstances, one is tempted to say that the possibility for a State to bring an application is not so much a right as a duty and that, in the last analysis, the State merely sets public action in movement in the interest of the entire European Community of human rights. The power of the Commission and of the Court to prevent the parties from withdrawing their applications confirms this interpretation.

The Commission has only been empowered to receive individual applications since 5 July 1955, the date on which the condition for the entry into force of the right of individual application (art. 25, para. 4) was fulfilled, six States having made the declaration of acceptance. As of January 1982, sixteen of the twenty States which had ratified the convention had made such a declaration: Austria, Belgium, Denmark, Federal Republic of Germany, France, Iceland, Ireland, Italy, Luxembourg, Netherlands, Norway, Portugal, Spain, Sweden, Switzerland and the United Kingdom. It is worth pointing out that two of these States extended the application of the right of individual application to several territories for whose international relations they are responsible and which do not all belong to the European continent. The Netherlands so acted with respect to the Dutch West Indies; the United Kingdom with respect to the following territories: Bermuda, Cayman Islands, Falkland Islands, Gibraltar, and Turks and Caicos Islands.

It is undeniable that the right of individual application constitutes the greatest innovation introduced by the Convention since what is involved is not a mere right of gracious petition, but a genuine right to institute proceedings before an international judiciary organ.

For a person, a non-governmental organization or a group of individuals to be able validly to bring an application before the Commission, that person, non-governmental organization or group of individuals must claim to be the victim of a violation of the protected rights. The notion of victim may be understood, *a priori*, in more or less broad terms, with the result that the ground for action which must be demonstrated by the applicant may be more or less direct. In actual fact, the question is whether the right of action provided for by article 25 is a subjective right or, as in the case of applications brought by States, not so much a right as a duty on the part of the individual to set European legal procedure in movement. The latter interpretation is intellectually attractive in that it provides a legal expression of the *de facto* interdependence which exists between the observance of human rights from one individual to another and from one country to another.

The first decisions of the Commission seemed to give a fairly broad interpretation to the notion of "victim." Thus, "article 25 of the Convention relates not only to the victim or victims of the alleged violation, but also to any indirect victim to whom the alleged violation is prejudicial or who has a genuine personal interest in the termination of the violation" (Application No. 282, *ECHR Yearbook* I, p. 164). Other decisions such as in the Klass and the Preikhzas cases seem to limit the meaning of the concept of victim (Applications Nos. 5029/71 and 6504/74).

It is not enough for the applicant to claim to be the victim of a violation; the alleged violation must have been committed by a High Contracting Party which has recognized the right of individual application. Applications lodged against the following are consequently declared to be inadmissible:

—against States which are not Members of the Council of Europe;
—against private individuals;
—against Member States of the Council of Europe which have signed but not ratified the Convention;
—against States which have ratified the Convention but which have not recognized the right of individual application;
—against institutions which are not within the jurisdiction of the Contracting States (cf., for instance, Application No. 235/56, *ECHR Yearbook* II, p. 257, alleging the responsibility of the Federal Republic of Germany for the acts of the Supreme Restitution Court operating on its territory and set up under an agreement concluded between the German Govern-

ment and the three Occupying Powers, the United States, the United Kingdom and France; see also C.F.D.T. case, Application No. 8030/77).

"Ratione materiae"

Any Contracting Party may refer to the Commission "any alleged branch of the provisions of the Convention by another High Contracting Party" (art. 24). Thus, a Contracting Party may refer to the Commission any case of violation of the right protected under Section I which comes to its knowledge. But it could also refer to the Commission any "breach" of other provisions of the Convention, such as articles 25, 28, 31, 32, 57, 59, 60, 61, 62 and 65. In practice, no case of the latter has ever arisen.

On the request of an individual, the Commission can consider any alleged violation of the rights set forth in the Convention by one of the Contracting Parties. These rights are those listed in Section I of the Convention and in Protocols Nos. 1 and 4 to the Convention.

Are there any other provisions of the Convention or its Protocols which set forth rights for the individual? The answer is in the affirmative as regards article 25 which, provided that the State has made a declaration of acceptance of the right of individual application, ensures that the individual will not be hindered in the effective exercise of his right to refer applications to the Commission. However, this right for an individual not to be hindered in the effective exercise of his right of application to the Commission is not comparable with other human rights protected by the Commission. It is a right *sui generis* to which, consequently, the ordinary rules of admissibility do not apply.

Moreover, the Commission acknowledged in its decision of 30 June 1959 (Application No. 434/58, *ECHR Yearbook* II, p. 355) that a State which has signed and ratified the European Convention of Human Rights and Fundamental Freedoms "must be understood as agreeing to restrict the free exercise of its rights under general international law...to the extent and within the limits of the obligations which it has accepted under that Convention". Thus, a right which is not set forth in the Convention may nonetheless be protected indirectly through recourse to a right explicitly mentioned in the Convention.

"Ratione temporis"

The competence *ratione temporis* of the Commission extends to all facts which took place prior to the entry into force of the Convention in respect of the Contracting Party against which a complaint has been lodged.

In a particular decision, the Commission took the view that "facts occurring before the date when the Convention came into force in respect of a Contracting Party shall be within the competence of the Commission if, and to the extent that, they may lead to a continuous violation of the Convention extending beyond that date" (Application No. 214/56 *De Becker v. Belgium, ECHR Yearbook* II, p. 215).

In the latter case, what was involved was a judicial decision given before the Convention came into force with respect to Belgium, which initiated the automatic application of a legal provision giving rise to a permanent situation which the applicant considered to be contrary to the Convention.

The competence *ratione temporis* of the Commission is of an objective character and is therefore not the consequence of undertakings entered into by Contracting States towards each other. In the *Austria v. Italy* case, the incompetence *ratione temporis* of the Commission was argued by the Italian government after expressing a line of reasoning based on the idea of the reciprocity of the engagements undertaken.

The Italian argument was in substance as follows: in ratifying the Convention on 26 October 1955, Italy entered into an undertaking solely with respect to States which at that time were High Contracting Parties. As, however, the events to which the application related had taken place in 1956 and as the main part of the proceedings had taken place before Austria became a Contracting Party to the Convention (3 September 1958), consideration of the application fell outside the competence *ratione temporis* of the Commission.

The Commission did not agree with the Italian argument. After noting that no clause of the Convention limited a State's right to bring an application to complaints in regard to facts occurring before that State had ratified the Convention, the Commission went on to express the following view: "The purpose of the High Contracting Parties in concluding the Convention was not to concede to each other reciprocal rights and obligations in pursuance of their aims and the ideals of the Council of Europe...".

The Commission deduced from this that "it follows that the obligations undertaken by the High Contracting Parties in the Convention are essentially of an objective character, being designed rather to protect the fundamental rights for the High Contracting Parties themselves". The conclusion follows from the premises: "The fact that in the Assize Court and the Court of Appeal, Italy had no obligations towards Austria under the Convention does not debar Austria from now alleging a breach of the Convention with respect to those proceedings".

(iii) PROCEEDINGS BEFORE THE COMMISSION

Institution of proceedings before the Commission, representation of the Parties and legal aid

Any claim submitted under article 24 (by a Contracting Party) or article 25 (by a person, a non-governmental organization or a group of individuals) must be submitted in the form of an application in writing signed by the applicant or his representative (Rules of Procedure, 37).

The application is addressed to the Secretary-General of the Council of Europe who transmits it, along with any relevant documents, to the President of the Commission. It is then registered at the Secretariat of the Commission and assigned a number which is communicated to the applicant. The proceedings are thus instituted.

The Contracting Parties are represented before the Commission by their agents who may obtain the assistance of counsel.

Persons, non-governmental organizations and groups of individuals may present their case in person before the Commission; it is consequently not compulsory for them to have recourse to a member of the bar. They may, however, if they so desire, be assisted or represented by a lawyer or by any other person residing in the territory of a State Party to the Convention, barring a decision to the contrary, which the Commission may take at any time (Rules of Procedure, 26, para. 2).

The Convention passes over in silence the question of legal aid for individual applicants. Although the proceedings before the Commission are free of charge and the formalities reduced to the strict minimum, an individual applicant will nevertheless have to meet costs which are frequently considerable, principally from the time that his application has been declared to be admissible. At the proposal of the Commission, the Committee of Ministers established, by its Resolution (63) 18 of 25 October 1963, for a period of two years, a system of legal aid. Since then, it has been regularly renewed. Its operation is governed by the provisions contained in the Addendum to the Rules of Procedure (arts. 1 to 7 of the Addendum).

Consideration of the admissibility of the application by the Commission

The proceedings instituted by the lodging of the application entail first of all an examination of its admissibility. The procedure followed is different, at the beginning at least, according to whether the application is brought by a State (Conv., art. 24) or by an individual (art. 25).

If a State application is referred to the Commission, the President, through the intermediary of the Secretary-General of the Council of Europe, gives notice of such application to the Contracting Party against which the claim is made and invites it to submit to the Commission its observations in writing on the admissibility of such application.

If, on the other hand, an individual application is submitted to the Commission, it is not immediately communicated to the government against which the claim is made. The President submits it first of all to a member of the Commission who, as a rapporteur, carries out a prior examination of its admissibility. The result of this examination, during which the rapporteur may request relevant information on matters connected with the application, from the applicant or the State concerned, is the subject of a report to the Commission. The latter may then either declare at once that the application is inadmissible or strike it off its list, or request relevant information from the applicant or the State concerned and/or invite the said State to present observations on the admissibility of the application.

Whether the application is by a State or an individual, the Commission may, before deciding on its admissibility, invite the parties to submit further observations in writing. It may also invite them, if it considers it useful, to submit explanations at an oral hearing, which will then be held *in camera*.

The substance of a State or individual application which comes within the competence of the Commission will be considered only if it surmounts the formidable hurdle of admissibility. The great majority of applications are declared inadmissible because they do not fulfill the conditions governing admissibility. These are laid down by articles 26 and 27 of the Convention which deserve to be quoted in their entirety:

"Art. 26. The Commission may only deal with the matter after all domestic remedies have been exhausted, according to the generally recognized rules of international law, and within a period of six months from the date on which the final decision was taken.

Art. 27.1. The Commission shall not deal with any petition submitted under Article 25 which:

(a) is anonymous, or

(b) is substantially the same as a matter which has already been examined by the Commission or has already been submitted to another procedure of international investigation or settlement and if it contains no relevant new information.

2. The Commission shall consider inadmissible any petition submitted under Article 25 which it considers incompatible with the provisions of the present Convention, manifestly ill-founded, or an abuse of the right of petition.

3. The Commission shall reject any petition referred to it which it considers inadmissible under Article 26."

The foregoing conditions governing admissibility can be placed in two categories:

a) Conditions governing both State applications and individual applications:
- prior exhaustion of all domestic remedies;
- the period of six months from the date on which the final decision was taken, within which the application must be brought.

b) Specific conditions governing individual applications:
- they must not be anonymous;
- they must not be the same as a matter already examined by the Commission;
- they must not have already been submitted to another procedure of international investigation or settlement;
- they must not be incompatible with the provisions of the Convention;
- they must not be manifestly ill-founded;
- they must not constitute an abuse of the right of petition.

The admissibility of any application, brought either by a State or by an individual, is subject to *the prior exhaustion of all domestic remedies* "according to the generally recognized rules of international law". In an important decision, the Commission made it clear that this rule is "founded upon the principle that the Respondent State must first have an opportunity to redress by its own means within the framework of its own domestic legal system the wrong alleged to have been done to the individual" (Application No. 343, *ECHR Yearbook* II, p. 413). In other words, the competence of the Commission is essentially of a subsidiary character, since the State is the first organ responsible under the Convention for ensuring the observance of the guaranteed rights. It follows that the lodging of an application does not create any *Litis pendens* which can be invoked in the national courts dealing with the case, the rule of the prior exhaustion of domestic remedies can be interpreted as imposing a *Litis pendens* on the Commission (Applications Nos.1420/62, 1477/62, 1478/62, 16 December 1964, *ECHR Yearbook* VI, p. 591).

Any application must be brought within a *period of six months* from the date on which the final decision was taken. There is an obvious link between this rule and that of the prior exhaustion of all domestic remedies which is contained in the same article 26. Moreover, the Commission has had occasion to make this clear in interpreting the concept of final decision: "The term 'final decision'...in Article 26 refers exclusively to the final decision concerned in the exhaustion of all domestic remedies according to the generally recognized rules of international law, so that the six months period is operative only in this context" (Application No. 214, *ECHR Yearbook* II, p. 215). The Commission establishes such a close link between the two rules that no "prescription" of the alleged violation of the Convention seems possible once the applicant has been relieved of the obligation to exhaust all domestic remedies (31 May 1968, "Greek Case": *Collection of Decisions*, No. 26, p. 80).

The first condition governing admissibility, specific to individual application, concerns the *identity of the applicant*. The Commission does not accept any anonymous application. An application is not considered to be anonymous if the case-file relating to it contains any elements enabling the applicant to be identified (cf. Application No. 361/58).

To be admissible, the application must not be "*substantially the same as a matter which has already been examined by the Commission*". Does this rule mean that the decisions of the Commission are invested with the authority of *res judicata* and that consequently the Commission does indeed exercise jurisdictional power when it decides on the admissibility of applications? The answer seems bound to be in the affirmative. True, the Commission has affirmed in several decisions that "considering the scope of its functions and powers, the Commission believes that, in the matter of the protection of human rights, it ought not to follow strict rules which would lead to its decisions being invested with the authority of *res judicata*, as is the case of ordinary courts of law when there are *eadem personae, eadem res, eadem causa petendi*" (cf. Application No. 202, *ECHR Yearbook* I, p. 190). In fact, it will reconsider an application declared inadmissible only if there is "relevant new information," a notion to which, moreover, it gives a fairly strict interpretation, seeking always to determine whether the new application contains material likely to affect the substance of the first application (cf. Application No. 2606/65: *Collections of Decisions*, No. 26, p. 22).

The application must not have *already been submitted to another procedure of international investigation or settlement*. This condition governing admissibility, which has remained fairly theoretical up to now, is likely to find an application when other international human rights organs may participate in the investigation or settlement of the same case: such may indeed prove to be so following the entry into force of the Optional Protocol to the United Nations, Covenant on Civil and Political Rights which also provides for a procedure for individual applications. The question of the co-existence of the two procedures was examined at the Council of Europe by the Committee of Government Experts on Human Rights, which recommended that the States parties to both the Convention and the Optional Protocol to the Covenant formulate, when ratifying the Protocol, a reservation to the effect that they would give preference and priority to the procedure of investigation and settlement provided for by the Convention.

The application must not be *incompatible with the provisions of the Convention*. It follows from the case-law of the Commission that applications which do not fall within the framework of the competence of the Commission *ratione materiae, ratione personae* and *ratione loci* are considered to be incompatible with the provisions of the Convention. As regards applications for which the Commission is not competent *ratione temporis*, it simply declares them inadmissible *ratione temporis*.

The application must not be manifestly ill-founded. It is somewhat surprising at first sight to encounter a condition relating to the substance of a case when the application has reached only that stage at which its admissibility is being examined. The Commission has explained itself as follows: "the preparatory work for the Convention shows that this special terminology and unusual extension of the notion of admissibility is explained by the concern of the Contracting Parties to prevent applications unworthy of the Commission's attention; whereas, however, the Commission is not thereby entitled to reject, at the stage of its decision as to admissibility, an application which is not obviously ill-founded" (Application No. 214, *ECHR Yearbook* II, p. 215). Thus, the applicant must supply proof that his application discloses the appearance of a violation of a right protected by the Convention.

The application must not constitute an *abuse of the right of petition*. This ground of inadmissibility seldom appears in the rulings of the Commission. Generally speaking, it constitutes a sanction for an abuse of the individual's right to apply to the Commission. However, the fact that an application was inspired by motives of publicity or propaganda does not necessarily have the consequence of making it abusive (Application No. 332, *ECHR Yearbook* II, p. 309). The Commission has also availed itself of this ground of inadmissibility to sanction the defamatory and insulting statements made by the applicant in regard to the Respondent Government in the course of the proceedings (24 May 1966, Application No. 2424/65: *Collection of Decisions*, No. 20, p. 54).

The decision taken by the Commission on the admissibility of an application must be accompanied by reasons. The Secretary of the Commission communicates it to the applicant party. He also communicates it to the respondent party, except when the application has been rejected *de plano*, that is to say, without having been communicated to the State concerned.

A decision declaring an application inadmissible terminates the proceedings. If, however, the Commission accepts the application, the second phase of the proceedings begins, which now takes place before the Commission meeting in plenary, whereas up until the entry into force of Protocol No. 3 to the Convention, such proceedings took place essentially before a Sub-Commission of seven members.

Examination of admissible applications

During the second phase of the proceedings the Commission has three tasks:
- to establish the facts;
- to endeavour to achieve a friendly settlement of the case and, in the event of failure,
- to draw up a report on the case.

It is to be observed that under new article 29 of the Convention, introduced by article 1 of Protocol No. 3 to the Convention, the Commission may henceforth, after declaring an individual application admissible, unanimously decide to reject the application if, in the course of the examination as to substance, it notes the existence of one of the grounds of inadmissibility. However, such cases of rejection have been few.

Establishment of the facts. The Commission, like an examining magistrate, is provided with very broad powers for the purpose of ascertaining the facts. Article 28 of the Convention states that the Commission "shall undertake together with the representatives of the parties an examination of the petition and, if need be, an investigation, for the effective conduct of which the States concerned shall furnish all necessary facilities, after an exchange of views with the Commission." In other words, the Commission is free to organize the investigation of the application as it sees fit.

In practice, the investigation almost always consists of a written phase and an oral phase. During the first phase, the parties exchange statements setting forth their motives, conclusions and offers of proof.

The oral phase consists of one or more hearings with the parties, during which the parties develop their motives and conclusions. The Commission may, at the request of a party or *proprio motu*, decide to hear as a witness or expert or in any other capacity any person whose evidence or statements seem likely to assist it in the carrying out of its task.

The Commission may also carry out a visit of inquiry or instruct one or more of its members to do so. Thus, as part of its investigation of the Greek Application No. 176/56, several members of the Commission visited Cyprus in order to collect information. Similarly, in the *Matznetter Case* (Application No. 2178/64), several members of the Commission went to Austria to hear witnesses. Similar visits of enquiry have taken place in other cases before the Commission.

For some years the Commission, when it considered it advisable or more practical for the efficient carrying out of its tasks, has not hesitated to visit the countries concerned or to hold hearings in other countries. Thus, in the *Greek Case* (Application Nos. 3321, 3322, 3323 and 3344/67), the Commission, after having heard some twenty witnesses—often in dramatic circumstances— in Strasbourg, went to Greece at the beginning of 1969 to continue its investigation of the case. Similarly, in the *Ireland v. United Kingdom* case, numerous witnesses were heard both in Strasbourg and, for reasons of security, in Norway; lastly, in the *Cyprus v. Turkey* case, a delegation from the Commission went to the island to hear witnesses.

Attempt to secure a friendly settlement. Once the investigation has been completed, when the Commission is sufficiently familiar with the views of the parties and is able to form a first overall idea of the merits of the application, it places itself at the disposal of the parties with a view to securing a friendly settlement of the matter.

It is certain that the authors of the Convention attached great importance to the attempt at conciliation. Several provisions of the Convention reveal that they wanted at any cost to guard against the chances of a friendly settlement being jeopardized from the outset. In particular, the rule according to which the Commission must meet *in camera* is calculated to prevent the case from being discussed by all and sundry and in the heat of passion.

Have the hopes placed in the conciliatory function of the Commission been disappointed? It might seem so at first sight, since a formal friendly settlement has been reached so far in only a relatively small number of cases (a total of 22 as of 1 January 1982).

Reality, however, is more complex than one might be led to think by the texts. For, if one consults the list of applications for which a settlement has been reached, it is seen, on the contrary, that a solution has been found for several of them which, while not constituting formally a decision as to whether there has or has not been a violation of the Convention, have been settled to the satisfaction of the alleged victims. Thus, a solution was found for the De Becker Application (No. 214/56), the nineteen applications concerning criminal proceedings in Austria, the Gericke Application (No. 2294/54), the Televizier Application against the Netherlands (No. 2690/65), more recently Giama Application (No. 7612/76) and many others which, while not constituting a "friendly settlement" within the meaning of article 28, nevertheless greatly resemble such a settlement in the sense that each of the parties benefited from it, without its being prejudicial to observance of the Convention. What is reflected here is a development which is also to be seen in other fields, namely, the constant introduction of greater flexibility into international legal provisions, to the benefit of less formal methods of settlement not provided for by the texts.

If the Commission secures a friendly settlement of the application "on the basis of respect for human rights as defined in this Convention", it draws up a report which is transmitted to the interested States, to the Committee of Ministers and to the Secretary-General of the Council of Europe. This report consists of a brief statement of the facts and the terms of the solution reached. It is published.

Drawing up of the report. If the Commission does not secure a friendly settlement of the case, it is required to "draw up a report on the facts and state its opinion as to whether the facts found disclose a breach by the State concerned of its obligations under the Convention".

While, legally, the report is not a verdict since it contains only an "opinion" which is not binding upon the parties, it does, however, have the appearances of one. As in a verdict, the main part of the report is devoted to establishing whether the facts ascertained comply or do not comply with the provisions of the Convention.

The report is transmitted by the Secretary of the Commission to the Committee of Ministers of the Council of Europe; the Commission may, in transmitting the report, make "such proposals as it thinks fit" (Conv., art. 31, para. 3), which proposals will be aimed at facilitating settlement of the case. The report is also transmitted to the States concerned, which are not at liberty to publish it (Conv., art. 31). Is the report also communicated to an individual applicant in the case of an application brought before the Commission under article 25? The Convention is silent on this point. In Rule 61 of its Rules of Procedure, the Commission has provided that, if a case brought before it under article 25 is then referred to the European Court of Human Rights, the report will, barring a decision to the contrary by the Commission, be communicated to the applicant so that he may present his observations in writing on the said report.

(iv). TERMINATION OF THE PROCEEDINGS

The proceedings instituted before the Commission under article 24 (State applications) or under article 25 (individual applications) may lead to any one of the following:

- a decision by the Commission declaring the application inadmissible;
- a report drawn up by the Commission recording the friendly settlement of the case;

- a report drawn up by the Commission containing its "opinion" as to whether the facts found disclose a violation of the Convention.

Mention must be made of a fourth possibility which is not provided for by the Conventions: the application may be withdrawn and struck off the Commission's list.

As regards State applications, the Commission, in considering the joint request of the Greek Government and the British Government to withdraw Application No. 299/57 without deciding on the merits, has declared that "when an application alleging a violation of the Convention has been referred to it, the question of the withdrawal of the application concerns it as well as the parties and (that) it must be sure that the withdrawal of the case is likely to help and not hinder the realization of the objectives of the Convention". This attitude on the part of the Commission is to be compared with the right of the European Court of Human Rights to refuse to recognize the withdrawal of the applicant party, even if such withdrawal is accepted by the other parties.

Concerning individual applications, the decision by which the Commission decides to strike them off its list constitutes a termination of the proceedings which, while not expressly provided for by the Convention, is nevertheless inherent in the exercise of any judicial body's functions. In the first years after it came into operation, the Commission confined itself to mentioning the decision to withdraw an application in the minutes drawn up after each application had been examined. Increasingly, however, the Commission strikes an application off its list by virtue of a genuine "decision as to admissibility".

While there has been a change in form, the Commission's position as to substance has never varied: acting along the lines indicated by article 28 (b) with respect to a friendly settlement, the Commission has always asserted that it is free to take or not to take action upon a request formulated by an applicant that an application be struck off its list (cf. Dec. of 2 Oct. 1964, Applications Nos. 2169, 2204, 2326/64: *Collection of Decisions*, No. 14, p. 76). Henceforth the Commission may, under Rule 43 of its Rules of Procedure, strike an application off its list "unless it considers that any reason of a general character affecting the observance of the Convention justified further examination of an application".

The report containing the Commission's opinion as to whether the facts of the case disclose or do not disclose a breach of the Convention, far from bringing the case to an end, is on the contrary the starting point for a new procedure which culminates in the *decision as to the merits*. At the end of a period of three months from the date of the transmission of the report to the Committee of Ministers of the Council of Europe, two courses of action are open:

- before the expiry of the three months period the case has been referred to the Court by the Commission or by the Contracting Party concerned;

Table 16.1
Applications Declared Admissible

A. *Inter-State Applications*

Serial number	Registration number	Parties Applicant Resp. State	Date of decision on admissibility	References for the decision	Alleged violation(s) accepted	State of proceedings as of 1 Oct 1980
1	176/56	Greece v/ U.K.	2 June 1956	Yearb. 2, pp. 182-187	Art.3 Conv.	Res. (59) 12 of 20 April 1959
2	299/57	Greece v/ U.K.	12 Oct. 1957	Yearb. 2, pp. 187-197	Art.3 Conv.	Res. (59) 32 of 14 Dec. 1959
3	788/60	Austria v/ Italy	11 Jan. 1961	Yearb. 4, pp. 112-183	Art.6§1;6§2; 6§3d; 14 Conv.	Res. (63)DH 3 of 23 Oct. 1963
4 to 7	3321/67 3322/67 3323/67 3344/67	Denmark Norway Sweden Netherlands v/Greece	24 Jan. 1968	Yearb. 2, pp. 689-729	Art. 5,6,8,9, 10,11,13,14, 15 Conv.	Res. DH(70)1 of 15 April 1970
8	4448/70	Denmark Norway Sweden v/Greece	16 July 1978	Yearb. 13, pp. 123-137	Art.3,6 Conv.	Struck off list
9	5310/71	Ireland v/ U.K.	1 Oct. 1972	Yearb. 15, pp. 81-257	Art.3,5,6 in association with art.15 Conv; 14 Conv.	Judgement of 18 Jan. 1978

10	6730/74	Cyprus v/ Turkey	26 May 1975	Yearb. 18, pp. 83-124	Art.1,2,3,4, 5,6,8,13,14, Conv.; Art.1 Add. Protocol.	Res.DH (79) of 19 Jan. 1979
11	6950/75					
12	8007/77	Cyprus v/ Turkey	10 July 1978	Yearb. 21, p. 100	Art.1,2,3,4, 5,6,8,13,14,	Pending before the Commission

B. Individual Applications

1	214/56	De Becker v/Belgium	9 June 1958	Yearb. 2, pp. 215-255	Art.10 Conv.	Judgement of 27 March 1962
2	332/57	Lawless v/Ireland	30 Aug. 1958	Yearb. 2, pp. 309-341	Art.5,6,7, Conv.	Judgement of 1 July 1961
3	343/57	Nielsen v/Denmark	2 Sept. 1959	Yearb. 2, pp. 413-473	Art.6§1 Conv.	Res.(61)28 of 25 Oct. 1961
4	524/59	Ofner v/Austria	19 Dec. 1960	Yearb. 3, pp. 323-355	Art.6§1-3c Conv.	Res.(63)DH 2 of 5 April 1963
5	17/59	Hopfinger v/Austria	19 Dec. 1960	Yearb. 3, pp. 371-393	Art.6§1-3c Conv.	Res.(63)DH 1 of 5 April 1963
6	596/59	Pataki v/Austria	19 Dec. 1960	Yearb. 3, pp. 357-371	Art.6§1-and 3c Conv.	Res.(63)DH 2 of 16 Sept. 1963
7	789/60	Dunshirn v/Austria	15 March 1961	Yearb. 4, pp. 187-197	Art.6§1 and 3c Conv.	
8	834/60	Glaser v/Austria	28 March 1963	Yearb. 6, pp. 140-151	Art.6§1-3b and c Conv.	Res.(64)DH 1 of 5 June 1964
9	964/60	Steinko v/Austria	"	"	Art.6 Conv.	"

Table 16.1 (Continued).

Serial number	Registration number	Parties Applicant Resp. State	Date of decision on admissibility	References for the decision	Alleged violation(s) accepted	State of proceedings as of 1 Oct 1980
B. *Individual Applications*						
10	1180/61	Steinhauser v/Austria	"	"	Art. 6 Conv.	Res.(64)DH 1 of 5 June 1964
11	1207/61	Maurer v/Austria	"	"	Art. 6 Conv.	"
12	1308/61	Pietsch v/Austria	"	"	Art.6§1-3c Conv.	"
13	1526/62	Eichberger v/Austria	"	"	Art. 6 Conv.	"
14	1543/62	Nemec v/Austria	"	"	Art.6§1-3c Conv.	"
15	1567/62	Lettl v/Austria	"	"	Art.6§1-3b and c Conv.	"
16	1632/62	Cerny v/Austria	"	"	Art.6,§1a Conv.	"
17	1634/62	Schleritzko v/Austria	"	"	Art.6§1-3b and c Conv.	"
18	1735/62	Albrecht v/Austria	28 March 1963	Yearb. 6, pp. 140-151	Art. 6 Conv.	Res.(64) DH 1 of 5 June 1964
19	1631/62	Vesezky v/Austria	20 June 1963	Yearb. 7, pp. 419-435	Art. 6 Conv.	
20	1640/62	Schostal v/Austria	20 June 1963	Yearb.7, pp. 419-435	Art. 6 Conv.	

478

21	1549/62	Mölzer v/Austria	2 Sept. 1963	Yearb. 7, pp. 253-263	Art.681-3c Conv.	
22	1446/62	Plischke v/Austria	19 June 1963	Yearb.6, pp. 253-263	Art.681-3c Conv.	Res.(65) DH 1 of 9 April 1965
23	1474/62	23 inhabitants of Alsemberg v/Austria	26 July 1963	Coll. Dec. 11, pp. 50-58	Art.8-14 Conv.; art.2 Add. Prot.	Judgement of 23 July 1968
24	1677/62	5 inhabitants of Kraainem v/Belgium	26 July 1963	Yearb. 7, pp. 141-163	Art.8,14 Conv.; art.2 Add.Prot.	"
25	1691/62	64 inhabitants of Antwerp v/Belgium	26 July 1963	Yearb. 7, pp. 141-163	Art.8,14 Conv.; art.2 Add.Prot.	"
26	1769/63	Charlent and consorts inhabitants of Ghent v/ Belgium	26 July 1963	Yearb. 6, pp. 445-459	Art.8,14 Conv.; art.2 Add. Prot.	"
27	1994/63	57 inhabitants of Louvain v/Belgium	5 March 1964	Yearb. 7 pp. 253-261	Art.8,14 Conv.; art.2 Add.Prot.	"
28	2126/64	Inhabitants of Vilvorde v/Belgium	29 June 1964	Yearb. 7, pp. 281-299	Art.8,14 Conv.; art.2 Add.Prot.	"

Table 16.1 (Continued).

Serial number	Registration number	Parties Applicant Resp. State	Date of decision on admissibility	References for the decision	Alleged violation(s) accepted	State of proceedings as of 1 Oct 1980
B. Individual Applications						
29	1727/62	Boeckmans v/Belgium	29 Oct. 1963	Yearb. 6, pp. 371-423	Art.6§1,2, 3c Conv.	Friendly settlement
30	2013/63	Inhabitants of Mol v/Belgium	5 March 1964	Published		Struck off list
31	2122/64	Wemhoff v/FRG[1]	2 July 1964	Yearb. 7, pp. 281-299	Art.5§3; 6§1 Conv.	Judgement of 27 June 1968
32	1936/63	Neumeister v/Austria	6 July 1964	Yearb. 7, pp. 225-251	Art.5§3; 6§1 Conv.	Judgement of 27 June 1968
33	1602/62	Stögmüller v/Austria	1 Oct. 1964	Yearb. 7, pp. 169-193	Art.5§3 Conv.	Judgement of 10 Nov. 1969
34	2178/64	Matznetter v/Austria	16 Dec. 1964	Yearb. 7, pp. 331-349	Art.5§3; 6§1; and 6§1 in association with 5§4 Conv.	Judgement of 10 Nov. 1969
35	2209/64	Inhabitants of Fourons v/Belgium	15 Dec. 1964	Inhabitants of Fourons case, EC, pp. 85-94	Art.8,14 Conv.; art.2 Add. Prot.	Res.DH(74)1 of 30 Apr. 1974
36	2294/64	Gericke v/FRG	16 Dec. 1964	Yearb. 7, pp. 349-557	Art.5§3 Conv.	Struck off list

Source: RDH/HRJ VIII, 2-3, pp. 475-490. Table prepared by D. Giuliva.
[1]FRG—Federal Republic of Germany

37	2299/64	Grandrath v/FRG	23 April 1965	Yearb. 8, pp. 325-337	Art.14,4, 9 Conv.	Res.(67)DH 1 of 29 June 1967
38	2120/64	Poerschke v/FRG	14 Feb. 1966	Yearb. 9, pp. 329-391	Art.5§3, 6§1 Conv.	Friendly settlement
39	2208/64	Binet v/Belgium	14 Feb. 1966	Yearb. 9, pp. 392-407	Art.5,6, 13 Conv.	Struck off list
40	1850/63	Köplinger v/Austria	29 March 1966	Yearb. 9, pp. 241-267	Art.5§4; 6§1 and 3c Conv.	Res.(69)DH 1 of 1 May 1969
41	2686/65	Zeidler-Kornmann v/FRG	13 Dec. 1966	Yearb. 9, pp. 495-511	Art.3 Conv.	Res.(68)DH 1 of 26 June 1966
42	2690/65	Televizier v/Netherlands	15 Dec. 1966	Yearb. 9, pp. 513-551	Art.10, 14 Conv.	Struck off list
43	2689/65	Delcourt v/Belgium	6 April 1967	Yearb. 10, pp. 283-321	Art.6§1 Conv.	Judgement of 17 Jan. 1970
44	2832/66	De Wilde v/Belgium	7 April 1967	Yearb. 10, pp. 420-459	Art.5§1,3,4; art.4,6,3,13 Conv.	Judgement of 18 June 1971
45	2835/66	Ooms v/Belgium				
46	2899/66	Versyp v/Belgium				
47	2991/66	Alam and Khan v/ U.K.	15 July 1967	Yearb. 10, pp. 479-507	Art.8, 6§1 Conv.	Friendly settlement
48	2604/65	Jentzsch v/FRG	19 Dec. 1967	Yearb. 10, pp. 219-239	Art.5§3 Conv.	Res.DH(71)2 of 5 May 1971

Table 16.1 (*Continued*).

Serial number	Registration number	Parties Applicant Resp. State	Date of decision on admissibility	References for the decision	Alleged violation(s) accepted	State of proceedings as of 1 Oct 1980
B. Individual Applications						
49	2396/65	X v/FRG	20 Dec. 1967	Not published	Admissible *in toto*	Struck off list
50	2257/64	Soltikow v/FRG	5 April 1968	Yearb. 11, pp. 181-229	Art.6§1 Conv.	Res.DH(71)1 of 19 Feb. 1971
51	2614/65	Ringeisen v/Austria	18 July 1968	Yearb. 11, pp. 269-321	Art.5§3,6§1 Conv.	Judgement of 16 July 1971
52	2645/65	Scheichelbauer v/Austria	3 Oct. 1969	Yearb.12, pp. 157-173	Art.6§1 Conv.	Res.DH(71)3 of 12 Nov. 1971
53	3897/68	Sepp v/FRG	17 July 1970	Coll. Dec. 35, pp. 83-96	Art.6§1 Conv.	Friendly settlement
54 to 78	4404/70 and others	25 appl. by East African Asians v/U.K.	10 Oct. 1970	Yearb.13, pp. 929-1007	Art.3,5,14; and art. 8 combined with art.14 Conv.	Res.DH(77)2 of 21 Oct. 1977
79	4115/69	Knechtl v/U.K.	17 Dec. 1970	Yearb. 13, pp. 731-763	Art.6§1 Conv.	Friendly settlement
80 to 85	4501/70 and 4526/70 to 4530/70	6 appl. by East African Asians v/U.K.	18 Dec. 1970	Yearb. 13, pp.1015-1027	Art.3,5,14; and art.14 combined with art.8 Conv.	Res.DH(77)2 of 21 Oct. 1977

No.	Appl.	Name	Date	Reference	Article	Outcome
86	4340/69	Simon-Herold v/Austria	2 Feb. 1971	Yearb. 14, pp. 353-399	Art.2,3 Conv.	Friendly settlement
87	4451/70	Golder v/U.K.	30 March 1971	Yearb. 14, pp. 417-445	Art.6§1; 5§3 Conv.	Judgement of 25 Feb. 1975
88	4465/70	Vampel v/Austria	31 March 1971	Yearb. 14, pp. 477-497	Art. 5§3 Conv.	Struck off list
89	4475/70	Svenska Lotsförbundet v/Sweden	24 May 1971	Yearb. 14, pp. 497-523	Art.11 Conv.	Rejected under art. 29 Conv.
90	4517/70	Huber v/Austria	14 July 1971	Yearb. 14, pp. 573-616	Art.6§1 Conv.	Res.DH(75)2 of 15 April 1975
91	4733/71	Karnell and Hardt v/Sweden	13 Dec. 1971	Yearb. 14, pp. 677-693	Art.2 Add. Prot. combined with art.14 Conv.	Struck off list
92	5207/71	Raupp v/FRG	13 Dec. 1971	Yearb. 14, pp. 699-711	Art.2,3 Conv.	Rejected under art. 29 Conv.
93	2551/65	La Haye De Wilde				
94	3155/67					
95	3174/67	Nys Swalens v/Belgium	17 Dec. 1971	Yearb. 14, pp. 138-161	Art.5§4 Conv.	Res.DH(72)1 of 16 Oct. 1972
96	3499/68					
97	4464/70	National Union of Belgium Police v/Belgium	8 Feb. 1972	Yearb. 15, pp. 309-329	Art.11 Conv.	Judgement of 27 Oct. 1975

Table 16.1 (*Continued*).

Serial number	Registration number	Parties Applicant Resp. State	Date of decision on admissibility	References for the decision	Alleged violation(s) accepted	State of proceedings as of 1 Oct 1980
B. Individual Applications						
98	4897/71	Gussenbauer v/Austria	22 March 1972	Yearb. 15, pp. 449-467		
99	5219/71		14 July 1972	Yearb. 15, pp. 559-563	Art. 4,14 Conv.; art. 1 Add. Prot.	Friendly settlement
100 to 104	5100/71 5101/71 5102/71 5354/72 5370/72	Five Dutch soldiers v/Netherlands	17 July 1972	Yearb. 15, pp. 508-559	Art.5,6,14 Conv.; and for last 2 applications, art. 10, 11, 17, 18 Conv.	Judgement of 8 June 1976
105	5614/72	Svenska Lokmanna-förbundet v/Sweden	20 July 1972	Yearb. 15, pp. 594-603	Art.11,13,14 Conv.	Judgement of 6 Feb. 1976
106	4771/71	Kamma v/Netherlands	21 July 1972	Yearb. 15, pp. 414-443	Art.18 combined with art.5 Conv.	Res.DH(75)1 of 13 March 1975
107	5095/71	Kjeldsen v/Denmark	16 Dec. 1972	Yearb. 15, pp. 482-509	Art.2 Add. Prot.	Judgement of 7 Dec. 1976
108	5920/72	Busk-Madsen v/Denmark	19 July 1973	Coll Dec. 44, pp. 96-100	Art.2 Add. Prot.	Judgement of 7 Dec. 1976

484

No.	Application	Case	Date	Reference	Article	Result
109	5926/72	Pedersen v/Denmark	19 July 1973	Coll. Dec. 44, pp. 96-100	Art.2 Add. Prot.	Judgement of 7 Dec. 1976
110	5589/72	Schmidt and Dahlström v/Sweden	18 Dec. 1972	Yearb. 15, pp. 577-593	Art.11,14 Conv.	Judgement of 6 Feb. 1976
111 112 113 114 115 116 117	5577/72 5578/72 5579/72 5580/72 5581/72 5582/72 5583/72	Donnelly and others v/U.K.	5 April 1973	Coll. Dec, 43, pp. 122-149	Art.3 Conv.	Rejected under art. 29 Conv.
118	5765/72	Mellin v/FRG	16 July 1973	Coll. Dec. 44, pp. 81-92	Art.6§1 Conv.	Friendly settlement
119	5961/72	Amekrane v/U.K.	11 Oct. 1973	Coll. Dec. 44, pp. 101-114	Art.3,5&4, 8 Conv.; art.5§1,2,3 Conv.	Friendly settlement
120	5178/72	De Geillu-streerde Pers v/Netherlands	12 Oct. 1973	Coll. Dec. 44, pp. 13-24	Art.10,14 Conv.	Res.DH(77) 1 of 17 Feb. 1977
121	6066/73	Levy v/FRG	17 Dec. 1973	Coll. Dec. 45, pp. 99-108	Art.5§3 Conv.	Res.DH(76)1 of 10 March 1976

Table 16.1 (Continued).

B. Individual Applications

Serial number	Registration number	Parties Applicant Resp. State	Date of decision on admissibility	References for the decision	Alleged violation(s) accepted	State of proceedings as of 1 Oct 1980
122	5943/72	Handyside v/U.K.	4 April 1974	Coll. Dec. 45, pp. 23-53	Art.10 Conv.; art.1 Add. Prot. combined with art.10 Conv.	Judgement of 7 Dec. 1976
123	6242/73	Brückmann v/FRG	27 May 1974	Coll. Dec. 46, pp. 202-210	Art.6§1,7,8 9,10,11 Conv.; art. 3, 5§1c and f Conv.	Struck off list
124	5856/72	Tyrer v/U.K.	19 July 1974	Coll. Dec. 46, pp. 128-133	Art.3 Conv. combined with art.14 Conv.	Judgement of 25 April 1978
125	6181/73	Hätti v/FRG	5 Oct. 1974	Coll. Dec. 46, pp. 188-201	Art. 6§1 Conv.	Res.DH(76)3 of 19 Nov. 1976
126	5849/72	Müller v/Austria	16 Dec. 1974	Dec. and Rep. 1, pp. 46-50	Art.1 Add. Prot. combined with art.14 Conv.	Res.DH(76)2 of 7 April 1976
127	5029/71	Klass and others v/FRG	18 Dec. 1974	Dec. and Rep. 1, pp. 20-40	Art.6§1, 8§1, 13 Conv.	Judgement of 6 Sept. 1978

No.	Appl. No.	Name	Date	Yearbook	Article	Judgement/Decision
128	6538/74	Times, Newspapers, Sunday Times, Evans v/U.K.	21 March 1975	Yearb. 18, pp. 203-236	Art.6, 10 Conv.	Judgement of 26 April 1979
129	6232/73	König v/FRG	27 May 1975	Yearb. 18, pp. 179-191	Art.6§1 Conv.	Judgement of 28 June 1978
130	6301/73	Winterwerp v/Netherlands	30 Sept. 1975	Yearb. 18, pp. 192-201	Art. 5§1 Conv.	Judgement of 24 Oct. 1979
131	6833/74	Marckx v/Belgium	29 Sept. 1975	Yearb. 18, pp. 248-275	Art.3,8 and 14 Conv.	Judgement of 13 June 1979
132	5613/72	Hilton v/U.K.	5 March 1976	Yearb. 19, p. 257	Art.3,6 Conv. and 8 Conv.	Res.DH(79)3 of 21 April 1979
133	6281/73	Neubecker v/FRG	5 March 1976	Yearb. 19, p. 305	Art.6§1 and 2 Conv.	Friendly settlement, Dec. and Rep. VIII, p. 30
134	6210/73	Luedicke v/FRG	11 March 1976	Yearb. 19, p. 291	Art.6§3e; art.14 Conv.	Judgement of 28 Nov. 1978
135	6959/75	Brüggemann v/FRG	19 May 1976	Dec. and Rep. V p. 103	Art.8,9,11, 12 and 14 Conv.	Res.DH(78) 1 of 17 May 1978

Table 16.1 (Continued).

B. Individual Applications

Serial number	Registration number	Parties Applicant Resp. State	Date of decision on admissibility	References for the decision	Alleged violation(s) accepted	State of proceedings as of 1 Oct 1980
136	6650/74	Liebig v/ FRG	15 July 1976	Yearb. 19, p. 331	Art.6§2 Conv.	Friendly settlement
137	6877/75	Belkacem v/ FRG	27 Sept. 1976	Dec. and Rep. VI p. 76	Art. 6§3e, art. 14 Conv.	Judgement of 28 Nov. 1978
138	7132/75	Koc v/FRG	27 Sept. 1976	Dec. and Rep. VI, p. 135	Art. 6§3e, art. 14 Conv.	Judgement of 28 Nov. 1978
139	6878/75	Lecompte v/ Belgium	6 Oct. 1976	Dec. and Rep. VI, p. 79	Art.6 and 11 Conv.	Pending before the Court
140	7412/76	Haase v/ FRG	11 Dec. 1976	Dec. and Rep. VII, p. 127	Art.5§3 and 6§1 Conv.	Res.DH(78)2 of 18 April 1978
141	7341/76	Eggs v/ Switzerland	11 Dec. 1976	Dec. and Rep. VI, p. 170	Art.5§1a, 4 and 6 Conv.	Res.DH(79)7 of 19 Oct. 1979
142	6224/73	Kiss v/ U.K.	16 Dec. 1976	Dec. and Rep. VII, p. 55	Art.6§1 Conv.	Res.DH(78)3 of 19 April 1978
143	6694/74	Artico v/ Italy	1 March 1977	Dec. and Rep. VIII, p. 73	Art.6§3c Conv.	Judgement of 13 May 1980

No.	Application No.	Case	Date	Dec. and Rep.	Articles	Status
144	7367/76	Guzzardi v/Italy	1 March 1977	Dec. and Rep. VIII, p. 185	Art.3,5,6,8 and 9 Conv.	Pending before the Court
145	6903/75	Deweer v/Belgium	10 March 1977	Dec. and Rep.VIII, p. 90	Art.6§1,2 and 3 Conv.	Judgement of 27 Feb. 1980
146	7238/75	Van Leuven-Demeyere v/Belgium	10 March 1977	Dec. and Rep. VIII, p. 140	Art.6 and 11 Conv.	Pending before the Court
147	6840/74	X v/U.K.	12 May 1977	Dec. and Rep.X, p.5	Art.3 and 5 Conv.	Pending before the Commission
148	6998/75	Hinchliff v/U.K.	14 May 1977	Dec. and Rep. VII, p. 106	Art.3 and 5 Conv.	Pending before the Committee of Ministers
149	6870/75	X v/U.K.	14 May 1977	Dec. and Rep.X, p.37	Art.3 and 5 Conv.	Pending before the Commission
150	7050/75	Arrowsmith v/U.K.	16 May 1977	Dec. and Rep. VIII, p. 123	Art.9 and 10 Conv.	Res.DH(79)4 of 12 June 1979
151	7360/76	Zand v/Austria	17 May 1977	Dec. and Rep. VIII, p. 167	Art.6§1 Conv.	Res.DH(79)6 of 12 June 1979
152	6323/73	Bochieri v/Italy	19 May 1977	Dec. and Rep. VIII, p. 59	Art.6§1 Conv.	Struck off list

489

Table 16.1 (*Continued*).

Serial number	Registration number	Parties Applicant Resp. State	Date of decision on admissibility	References for the decision	Alleged violation(s) accepted	State of proceedings as of 1 Oct 1980
B. Individual Applications						
153	6289/73	Airey v/ Ireland	7 July 1977	Dec. and Rep. VIII, p. 42	Art.6§1,8,13 and 14 Conv.	Judgement of 9 Oct. 1979
154	7215/75	X v/U.K.	7 July 1977	Dec. and Rep. XI, p. 36	Art.8 and 14 Conv.	Res.DH (79)5 of 12 June 1979
155	7601/76	Young and James v/ U.K.	11 July 1977	Dec. and Rep. IX, p. 126	Art.9,10,11 and 13 Conv.	Pending before the Court
156	7710/76	Schiesser v/ Switzerland	12 July 1977	Dec. and Rep. X, p. 238	Art.5§3 Conv.	Judgement of 4 Dec. 1979
157	7629/76	Krzyeki v/ FRG	14 July 1977	Dec. and Rep. IX, p. 175	Art.5 Conv.	Res.DH(78)4 of 13 Oct. 1978
158	5947/72	X				
159	6205/73	Y				
160	7052/75	Colne				
161	7061/75	Tuttle	4 Oct. 1977	Dec. and Rep. X p. 154	Art.8,10 and 13 Conv.	Pending before the Commission
162	7107/75	Z				
163	7113/75	McMahon				
164	7136/75	Carne v/U.K.				

165	7114/75	Hamer v/ U.K.	13 Oct. 1977	Dec. and Rep. X, p. 174	Art.12 Conv.	Pending before the Committee of Ministers
166	7614/76	Nagel v/ FRG	6 Dec. 1977	Dec. and Rep. XII, p. 97	Art.6§1 Conv.	Friendly settlement
167	7648/76	Christinet v/ Switzer-land	6 Dec. 1977	Dec. and Rep. XI, p. 175	Art.5 Conv.	Res.DH(79)9 of 25 April 1979
168	6504/74	Preikhzas v/ FRG	7 Dec. 1977	Dec. and Rep. XII, p. 5	Art.6§1 Conv.	Res.DH(79)8 of 19 Oct. 1979
169	7759/77	Buchholz v/ FRG	7 Dec. 1977	Dec. and Rep. XII, p. 163	Art.6§1 Conv.	Pending before the Committee of Ministers
170	7397/76	Peyer v/ Switzerland	13 Dec. 1977	Dec. and Rep. XI, P. 58	Art.5 Conv.	Friendly settlement
171	6699/74	X v/FRG	15 Dec. 1977	Dec. and Rep. XI, p. 16	Art.3 and 8 Conv.	Friendly settlement
172	7511/76	Campbell v/ U.K.	15 Dec. 1977	Dec. and Rep. XII, p. 49	Art.3 Conv. and Art.2, Prot. 1	Pending before the Committee of Ministers
173	7743/76	Cosans v/ U.K.	15 Dec. 1977	Dec. and Rep. XII, p. 140	Art.3 Conv. and Art.2, Prot. 1	Pending before the Committee of Ministers
174	7612/75	Giama v/ Belgium	15 Dec. 1977		Art.3 Conv.	Friendly settlement

Table 16.1 (*Continued*).

Serial number	Registration number	Parties Applicant Resp. State	Date of decision on admissibility	References for the decision	Alleged violation(s) accepted	State of proceedings as of 1 Oct 1980
B. Individual Applications						
175	6871/75	Caprino v/ U.K.	3 March 1978	Dec. and Rep. XII, p. 14	Art.5(4) Conv.	Pending before the Committee of Ministers
176	7806/77	Webster v/ U.K.	3 March 1978	Dec. and Rep. XII, p. 168	Art.9,10,11, and 13 Conv.	Pending before the Court
177	7525/76	Dudgeon v/ U.K.	3 March 1978	Dec. and Rep. XI, p. 117	Art.8 and 14 Conv.	Pending before the Court
178	7640/76	Geerk v/ Switzerland	7 March 1978	Dec. and Rep. XII, p. 103	Art.6 and 10 Conv.	Friendly settlement
179	7438/76	Ventura v/ Italy	9 March 1978	Dec. and Rep. XII, p. 38	Art.5 and 6 Conv.	Pending before the Commission
180	7819/77	Campbell v/ U.K.	6 May 1978	Dec. and Rep. XIV, p. 186		
181	7654/76	Van Ooster-wijck v/ Belgium	9 May 1978	Dec. and Rep. XIV, p. 133		Pending before the Commission

No.	App. No.	Case	Date	Dec. and Rep.	Article	Status
182 to 185	7604/76 7719/76 7781/76 7913/77	Foti Lentini Cenerini Gully v/ Italy	11 May 1978	Dec. and Rep. XIV, p. 133	Art.6§1	
186	7907/77	X v/ U.K.	12 July 1978	Dec. and Rep. XIV, p. 205	Art.27 Conv. Art.2 Add. Prot.	
187	7464	Karrer and others v/ Austria	5 Dec. 1978	Dec. and Rep. XIV, p. 51	Art.1.a.2 Add.Prot.	
188	8224/78	Bonnechaux v/Switzerland	6 Dec. 1978	Dec. and Rep. XV, p. 211	Art.5§3 Conv.	Pending before the Committee of Ministers
189	7975/77	Bonazzi v/Italy	13 Dec. 1978	Dec. and Rep. XV, p. 169	Art.5§1, §4 Conv.	Pending before the Commission
190	7598/76	Kaplan v/U.K.	14 Dec. 1978	Dec. and Rep. XV, p. 120	Art.6§1 Conv.	"
191	7151/75	Sporrong v/Sweden	5 March 1979	Dec. and Rep. XV, p. 15	Art.6 Conv.	"
192	7152/75	Lonnroth v/Sweden	5 March 1979	Dec. and Rep. XV, p. 15	Art.6 Conv.	"
193	8186/78	X v/U.K.	1 May 1979		Art.12 Conv.	"
194	8244/78	Singh and Uppal v/ U.K.	2 May 1979		Art.8, 14 Conv.	"

Table 16.1 (*Continued*).

B. Individual Applications

Serial number	Registration number	Parties Applicant Resp. State	Date of decision on admissibility	References for the decision	Alleged violation(s) accepted	State of proceedings as of 1 Oct 1980
195	8130/78	Eckle v/ FRG	9 May 1979	Dec. and Rep. XVI, p. 120	Art.6§1 Conv.	"
196	8209/78	Sutter v/ Switzerland	11 July 1979	Dec. and Rep. XVI, p. 179	Art.6§1 Conv.	"
197	7906/77	Van Droogenbroeck v/Belgium	5 July 1979		Art.5§4 and 5§1 Conv.	Pending before the Committee of Ministers
198	8269/78	Adolf v/ Austria	6 July 1979		Art.6§1,2, 3 Conv.	Pending before the Commission
199	7984/77	Pretto v/ Italy	11 July 1979		Art.6§1 Conv.	Pending before the Commission
200	8273/78	Axen v/ FRG	11 July 1979		Art.6§1 Conv.	"
201	8339/79	Schertenleib v/Switzerland	12 July 1979		Art.5§3 Conv.	"
202	8304/78	Corigliano v/Italy	2 Oct. 1979		Art.6§1 Conv.	"

No.	Application No.	Case	Date	Articles	Pending before the Commission
203 to 208	7161/75 7291/75 7939/77 8111/77 8246/78 8253/78	6 prisoners' correspondence cases v/U.K.	11 Oct. 1979	Art.8 Conv.	
209	7299/75	Albert v/Belgium	4 Dec. 1979	Art.6, 11 Conv.	"
210	7496/76	Le Compte v/Belgium	4 Dec. 1979	Art.6, 11 Conv.	"
211	7630/76	Reed v/U.K.	6 Dec. 1979	Art.3,6, 8,Conv.	"
212 to 214	8022/77 8025/77 8027/77	A B v/U.K. C	8 Dec. 1979	Art.5,8 Conv.	"
215	7987/77	X Industries v/Austria	13 Dec. 1979	Art.6§1 Conv.	"
216	8289/78	Peschke v/Austria	5 March 1980	Art.6§1 and 6§3c Conv.	"
217	8427/78	Hendricks v/Netherlands	13 March 1980	Art.8,6§1 Conv.	"
218	7365/76	Gleaves v/U.K.	13 March 1980	Art.8§1,2 Art.10§2 Conv.	"
219	8077/77	Baker v/U.K.	13 March 1980	Art.8§2 Conv.	"

495

Table 16.1 (*Continued*).

Serial number	Registration number	Parties Applicant Resp. State	Date of decision on admissibility	References for the decision	Alleged violation(s) accepted	State of proceedings as of 1 Oct 1980
B. Individual Applications						
220 to 227	7468/76 7938/77 8106/77 8018/77 8325/78 8778/79 8797/79	7 Swiss men under military service	8 July 1980		Art.5§1,§4 Art.5§1,§4 Art.5§1 Art.5§1 Art.5§1,§4 Art.5 Art.5§1 Conv.	Pending before the Commission
228	7889/77	Arrondelle v/U.K.	15 July 1980		Art.6,8,13 Conv.,Art.1 Prot.1,Art.14 combined with art.8,art.1 Prot.1	"
229	8692/79	Piersack v/ Belgium	15 July 1980		Art.6§1 Conv.	"

- the case not having been referred to the Court within the three months period, the Committee of Ministers is required to take the decision (cf. Conv., art. 32).

There thus exists two organs with powers of decision in the system of the Convention: a judicial organ, the European Court of Human Rights, and a political organ, the Committee of Ministers of the Council of Europe.

(b). A political decision-making organ: the Committee of Ministers of the Council of Europe

(i). GENERAL REMARKS

The Committee of Ministers, as the "organ which acts on behalf of the Council of Europe" (Statute, art. 13), already plays a part in the workings of the Convention on account of the links which attach the Convention to the Council of Europe.

The Committee of Ministers is thus required to elect the members of the Commission. While it does not elect the judges of the Court, it nevertheless plays a part in their election since, after grouping together the lists of candidates submitted by the Member States of the Council, it submits a single list to be voted on by the Assembly.

As the expenses of the Commission are, according to article 58 of the Convention, borne by the Council of Europe, it falls to the Committee of Ministers to meet these expenses within the framework of the budget of the Council. Expenses include: *inter alia*, daily compensation to members of the Commission and judges of the Court, determined by the Committee of Ministers. In accordance with article 38 of the Statute, the expenses of the Council are shared between all the Member States in such proportions as are determined by the Committee of Ministers on the basis of the population of each State. The Committee approves the budget of the Council which is submitted to it each year by the Secretary-General. In practice, a separate section is devoted to the Commission and the Court.

Lastly, the Committee of Ministers plays a role in the execution of the judgments delivered by the Court. Thus, article 54 of the Convention stipulates: "The judgment of the Court shall be transmitted to the Committee of Ministers which shall supervise its execution". It is to be observed straight away that the Committee of Ministers is not responsible for the execution of the judgment but merely for supervising its execution.[3] The nuance is important: it may be assumed from it that the authors of the Convention expected the judgments of the Court to be executed voluntarily and in their entirety. In the event of difficulties, the Committee of Ministers could probably not make do with simply drawing up a report noting a default. It then falls to it to act in the framework of the Statute of the Council of Europe, possibly going so far as to decide that the "guilty" State should be suspended or even expelled from the Council of Europe.

But the Convention does not merely provide for recourse to the Committee of Ministers each time that its links with the Council of Europe make it necessary. By virtue of article 32, the Committee of Ministers in fact becomes the complement to the Court in that it is assigned powers of decision in those cases not referred to the Court.

Article 32 stipulates:

"1. If the question is not referred to the Court in accordance with Article 48 of this Convention within a period of three months from the date of transmission of the Report to the Committee of Ministers, the Committee of Ministers shall decide by a majority of two thirds of the members entitled to sit on the Committee whether there has been a violation of the Convention.

2. In the affirmative case the Committee of Ministers shall prescribe a period during which the High Contracting Party concerned must take the measures required by the decision of the Committee of Ministers.

3. If the High Contracting Party concerned has not taken satisfactory measures within the prescribed period, the Committee of Ministers shall decide by the majority provided for in paragraph 1 above what effect shall be given to its original decision and shall publish the report.

4. The High Contracting Parties undertake to regard as binding on them any decision which the Committee of Ministers may take in application of the preceding paragraphs."

In a Convention wholly based on the idea of legal protection of human rights, the role assigned to a political organ as a decision-making body is bound to be surprising. The result of a compromise, article 32 is at the same time the consequence of resignation accompanied by hope. Resignation on the part of those who championed a Court of Human Rights with compulsory jurisdiction, who, in the face of the insurmountable resistance they encountered in attempting to set it up, had to accept an optional Court. The grounds for hope derive from the two-thirds majority vote by which the Committee has to decide whether there has been a violation each time that a case is not referred to the Court: for the first time indeed, the rule of unanimity was abandoned within the Committee of Ministers in a field of some importance for the Council of Europe.

(ii). ORGANIZATION AND WORKING OF THE COMMITTEE OF MINISTERS

When it is called upon to exercise the functions of a decision-making organ of the Convention, the Committee of Ministers retains the same organization and, in principle, operates according to the same rules as when it acts as an organ of the Council of Europe. Article 32 of the Convention, it is true, contains no provision urging the Committee of Ministers to adopt proper rules of procedure and so far it has not considered it necessary to do so. It has simply drawn up a number of rules concerning particular points, somewhat unmethodically and almost as problems have arisen.[4]

The Committee of Ministers consists of one representative for each Member State of the Council of Europe. This being so, a government which is represented on the Committee of Ministers is fully empowered to participate in the exercise of the functions and powers defined in article 32, even if it has not ratified the European Convention of Human Rights. Similarly, the parties to a dispute retain the right to vote and consequently participate in the discussions and in the decision. This situation has not failed to be criticized since a State becomes at once judge and party. It is to be recognized, however, that this is the consequence of a political organ being assigned judicial functions.

(iii). COMPETENCE OF THE COMMITTEE OF MINISTERS

The Committee of Ministers is competent to exercise the functions assigned to it by article 32 of the Convention only if two conditions are met:

- the case must have been previously investigated by the Commission and a report drawn up by the Commission in which, noting the failure of its attempt to secure a friendly settlement, it gives its opinion concerning the alleged violation of the Convention;
- the three-month period from the date of transmission of the report of the Commission to the Committee of Ministers must have elapsed without the case having been referred to the Court.

In comparison with the Court, the competence of the Committee of Ministers is consequently subsidiary, since the Committee takes a decision only when the Court does not do so. But to say that the Committee of Ministers is but a secondary organ of decision may give rise to misunderstandings and errors of appreciation in regard to the practical importance of the Committee and the Court respectively.

The Committee of Ministers is undeniably a subsidiary decision-making organ if this is taken to mean that, chronologically, it falls first to the Court to deal with a case, since cases can be referred to the Committee only after the three month period has elapsed. However, the Committee could also be described as the principal decision-making organ since, as the jurisdiction of the Court is optional, *all* cases, which have been the subject of a report by the Commission, are referred to it.

When it exercises the functions assigned to it by article 32, the Committee of Ministers has the power to discuss the substance of any case concerning which the Commission has submitted a report, and it can do so while fully exercising its powers of decision by examining, for instance, the written or oral statements of the parties. Thus, the Committee is limited in the exercise of its competence only by the need to act within the framework of article 32 and by the wish, which it has demonstrated on several occasions, not to lose sight of its character as a political organ whenever it acts as an organ of decision of the Convention. This position which it has adopted is not without effect upon the procedure which it has decided to follow in human rights cases.

(iv). PROCEEDINGS BEFORE THE COMMITTEE OF MINISTERS

Article 32 of the Convention contains no provisions regarding proceedings before the Committee of Ministers. The very most it does is determine at what time the proceedings are actually instituted: on the expiration of the period of three months from the date of the transmission of the Commission's report to the Council of Ministers. It is thus seen that, while the possibility of proceedings being instituted before the Committee of Ministers is created when the report is transmitted to it, the proceedings are actually instituted only after three months, during which the case can be referred to the Court. This is the only indication as regards procedure which is given in article 32.

It is certain that the rules of procedure so far adopted by the Committee of Ministers are not sufficient to define the role of the Commission before the Committee and, even less, to make clear the position of the individual applicant in the proceedings. Since the Committee of Ministers and the Court are but two organs of the same mode of settlement, there is a temptation simply to transpose the Rules in force before the Court.

However, the two situations are far from being identical. Despite the fact that its function determines the nature of the organ, it is no less true that the nature of the organ affects the exercise of its function. To be sure, the fundamental reality remains the intervention, as an organ of decision, of the Committee of Ministers which is the political organ *par excellence*, since it is an expression of the sovereign powers of the Member States of the Council of Europe. It is for this reason that purely and simply transposing the rules in force before the Court appears hazardous.

The Commission did not make a mistake here when it abstained from adding to its Rules of Procedure provisions governing its relations with the Committee of Ministers, although a particular section of its Rules defines its relations with the Court. No doubt it considered that its role before a political organ could not be the same, particularly in view of the fact that the Convention contains no provision relating to any participation by the Commission before the Committee of Ministers, whereas articles 44 and 48 of the Convention govern, at least partially, its position before the Court. The Commission would consequently appear to exceed the limits of the functions assigned to it by the Convention, if it were to participate in the proceedings before the Committee of Ministers. Moreover, the Committee of Ministers recognized this when it expressly abstained, and for the same reason, from including in its Rules provisions relating to the participation of the delegates of the Commission in the proceedings before it.

Under these circumstances, the Committee of Ministers has only itself to rely on in reaching the decision required of it by article 32. It is recognized that, although it must possess all the powers necessary to arrive at a decision on the report of the Commission, it is nevertheless possible that it will not wish to take on the task which consists of collecting the grounds of proof, in the event that this proves necessary. The procedure to be followed will be determined by an *ad hoc* decision.

Similarly, the Committee of Ministers has decided not to establish—as the Commission did by Rule 76 of its Rules of Procedure when a case is brought before the Court—a procedure whereby the report of the Commission may be communicated to the individual applicant. It took the view that the report should be so communicated only in exceptional cases in strict confidence and with the consent of the State against which the application brought before the Commission is lodged.

(v). TERMINATION OF THE PROCEEDINGS

Article 32 provides for only one way in which proceedings instituted before the Committee of Ministers can be terminated: the decision taken by a majority of two-thirds of the representatives entitled to sit on the Committee. If this two-thirds majority has not been obtained either for a decision of "guilty" or "not guilty" with respect to the State concerned, it has been recognized, at least in the *Huber v. Austria* case, that no other measures need to be taken, the case thus ending in a deadlock in the absence of a genuine decision as to the substance of the case. It is probable and, at least to be hoped, that the last word has not been said in this connection.

In addition to settlement by decision, mention should no doubt be made of friendly settlement which, while not expressly mentioned in article 32, permeates the entire Convention. Moreover, was not this solution implicitly recognized by the Committee of Ministers when it approved the solution reached in the Cyprus case? By its Resolutions (59) 12 and (59) 32, it in fact decided, taking account in particular of the agreements of Zurich and London concerning the settlement of the Cyprus problem, that "no further action is called for", thus terminating the proceedings instituted by Applications 176/56 and 299/57 by Greece against the United Kingdom. In the same manner, Resolution DH(79) 1 also encourages the Parties to undertake intercommunity negotiations to reach a solution in the case.

The proceedings will normally be terminated by the decision of the Committee as to whether, in the case before it, there has or has not been a violation of the Convention. It will be taken by a "resolution" which, according to article 20 of the Statute of the Council of Europe, is the form assumed by important decisions of the Committee. The Committee of Ministers will thus have to settle a legal dispute. It will have to do so in full possession of its powers of decision, and consequently in no way be bound—nor indeed is the court—by the report of the Commission. A judge is not tied to the person testifying before him, and this principle remains valid, even if the judicial functions are exercised by a political organ.

It must be noted that only the Convention can provide the grounds for a decision by the Committee of Ministers. Moreover, the International Court of Justice very rightly noted in its advisory opinion of 24 May 1948 concerning the conditions of admission of a State to membership in the United Nations (Charter, art. 4) that "the political character of an organ cannot release it from the observance of the treaty provisions established by the Charter when they constitute limitations on its power and criteria for its judgement". The Court stressed that "to ascertain whether an organ has freedom of choice for its decisions, reference must be made to the terms of its constitution". In the case of the Committee of Ministers, reference must be made to the Convention, both to its text and to its spirit.

If the Committee of Ministers decides that there has been no violation of the Convention, the "acquittal" is final and no remedy is available. If the decision concludes that there has been a violation of the Convention, the Committee then determines the time-limits within which the State concerned must take the measures required by its decision. Does it have to define these measures in its decision? Article 32 does not so prescribe and it seems to give the State concerned full liberty to draw itself the necessary consequences from the decision. It has, however, been recognized that the Committee of Ministers is empowered, when it has decided that a violation of the Convention has taken place, to formulate opinions, suggestions or recommendations to the State concerned, provided that they relate directly to the violation. Whether they are or are not founded upon the proposals of the Commission, such opinions, suggestions or recommendations are of course not binding upon the State concerned.

If, following the decision of the Committee of Ministers, the State has not taken "satisfactory measures", article 32 provides that the Committee then decides by a majority of two-thirds of the representatives entitled to sit on the Committee, "what effect shall be given to its original decision". What "effect" can in fact be given? Article 32 gives no indication, thus allowing the Committee of Ministers a large measure of discretion as regards the measures to be taken to sanction the non-compliance of the State which has violated the Convention. No doubt the Committee, like the Court under article 50 of the Convention, could afford to the injured party "just satisfaction", that is to say, financial compensation, if municipal law allows only partial reparation to be made for the consequences of the violation. But it could also initiate the procedure designed to expel the "guilty" State from the Council of Europe, in accordance with article 8 of the Statute of the Council.

Article 32 mentions but one form of sanction: publication of the report of the Commission. It is still necessary for the Commission to have reached the same decision as the Committee of Ministers, that is, for it to have concluded that there has been a violation of the Convention. If such is not the case, there is obviously nothing to be gained by publishing the report and it is probable that the Committee of Ministers would not in fact publish it.

Is it possible for the report to be published when the Committee of Ministers, endorsing the opinion of the Commission, decides that there has not been a violation of the Convention? Article 32 does not prohibit it. It consequently falls to the Committee to decide in the light of the circumstances of each case. Thus, taking into account the wish expressed by the Danish Government, it authorized, in December 1961, the publication of the report of the Commission in the *Nielsen Case*, with the exception, however, of the chapter concerning the attempt to secure a friendly settlement. In subsequent cases, the same *ad hoc* procedure has always been followed.

(c). A judicial decision-making organ: the European Court of Human Rights

(i). GENERAL REMARKS

Like the Commission, the European Court of Human Rights was instituted by the Convention to ensure that the undertakings resulting from that treaty be respected. It thus shares with the Commission responsibility for giving effect to the collective guarantee; however, the power which is the basis and justification of this responsibility—jurisdictional power—is held at the highest level by the Court.

The general rules concerning its organization, its working, its competence and procedure are defined, principally, in Section III of the Convention. However, even more so than in the case of the Commission, rules of procedure were necessary, if not to complete the general rules at least to define their content. Acting under article 55 of the Convention, which gives the Court the power to draw up its own rules and determine its own procedure, the Court adopted its Rules of Court on 18 September 1959 at its third plenary session. Since then, it has amended them several times.

Although the Convention came into force on 3 September 1953 and the Commission consequently went into operation, the Court, for its part, was set up only in 1959. Indeed, under article 56 of the Convention, the first election of the members of the Court, and therefore its establishment, was to take place after eight Contracting Parties had recognized its compulsory jurisdiction. This condition was fulfilled on 3 September 1958, exactly five years after the Convention entered into force.

Whereas for the promoters of the Convention, the Court was to be the basis of the edifice, as the discussions proceeded, it became its summit, to which it was to become increasingly difficult to gain access. Open to everyone in the first draft of the Convention, it does not now provide for the individual as a party. Designed to be the cornerstone of the machinery offering the collective guarantee, it is now but an optional cog in that machinery, the advantages of which, it is true, are not belittled, but whose disadvantages regarding the sovereign powers of States are stressed. If it is true that the human rights controversy relates essentially to the lawfulness of human rights, the European Court of Human Rights takes us back to the heroic ages of administrative law when the State's responsibility could be challenged before a tribunal only with that State's previous agreement, whereas the

Table 16.2

Cases Brought Before the Committee of Ministers

Serial number	Title of the case(s)	Subject of the case	Opinion of the Commission	Decision	Date of decision	Summary of decision	Reference or state of proceedings
A. *Inter-State Cases*							
1	Greece v/ U.K.	legislative measures and administrative practices of British authorities in Cyprus	not published	Res.(59) 12	20 April 1959	no further action called for	Yearb. II, p. 187
2	Greece v/ U.K.	certain cases of torture or maltreatment comparable to torture	not published	Res.(59) 32	14 Dec. 1959	no further action called for	Yearb. II p. 197
3	Austria v/ Italy	court proceedings brought against 6 young people from Upper Adige	no viol. of Conv.	Res.(63) DH 3	23 Oct. 1963	no viol. of Conv.	Yearb. VI, pp. 797-799

No.	Parties	Subject	Commission	Resolution	Date	Committee	Reference
4 to 7	Denmark Norway Sweden and Netherlands v/Greece	legislative measures and administrative practices adopting following coup d'etat	viol. of arts.5,6, 8,9,10,11, 13,14 Conv.	Res.DH (70)1	15 April 1970	viol. art.5, 6,8,9, 10,11, 13,14, Conv.	Yearb. Greek case 1969, 12, pp. 511-514
8 to 9	Cyprus v/Turkey	machinations and practices consecutive to occupation	not published	Res.DH (79)1	20 Jan. 1979	encouragement to undertake negotiations	

B. *Individual Cases*

No.	Parties	Subject	Commission	Resolution	Date	Committee	Reference
1	Nielsen v/Denmark	crim. proc.: right of defence	no viol. of Conv.	Res.(61)28	25 Oct. 1961	no viol. of Conv.	Yearb. IV, pp. 591-593
2 to 3	Ofner and Hopfinger v/Austria	crim. proc.: right of defence	no viol. of Conv.	Res.(63)DH 1	5 April 1963	no viol. of Conv.	Yearb. VI, pp. 709-713
4 to 5	Pataki and Dunshirn v/Austria	crim. proc.: right of defence	art.294§3 of Penal Code not in conformity with Conv.	Res.(64)DH 2	16 Sept. 1963	no action required in present cases (legislative reform)	Yearb. VI, pp. 737-739

Table 16.2 (*Continued*).

Serial number	Title of the case(s)	Subject of the case	Opinion of the Commission	Decision	Date of decision	Summary of decision	Reference or state of proceedings
B. Individual Cases							
6 to 19	Glaser, Steinko, Steinhauser, Maurer, Pietsch, Eichberger, Nemec, Mölzer, Lettl, Vesezcky, Cerny, Schlerizko, Schostal and Albrecht v/Austria	crim. proc.: right of defence	procedures followed in these cases not in conformity with Conv.	Res. (64) DH 1	5 June 1964	no action required in present cases (legislative reform)	Yearb. VII, pp. 435-441
20	Plischke v/Austria	crim. proc.: right of defence	situation remedied during proc. before Comm.	Res. (65) DH 1	9 April 1965	no further action required (legislative reform)	Yearb. VIII, pp. 405-467

21	Grandrath v/FRG	conscientious objection	no viol. of Conv.	Res.(67) DH 1	29 June 1967	no viol. of Conv.	Yearb. X, pp. 695-699
22	Ziedler-Kornmann v/FRG	treatment of prisoner	no viol. of Conv.	Res.(68) DH 1	26 June 1968	no viol. of Conv.	Yearb. XI, pp. 1029-1031
23	Köplinger v/Austria	length of crim. proc.	no viol. of Conv.	Res.(69) DH 1	1 May 1969	no viol. of Conv.	Köplinger case,EC, 1969, pp. 214-215
24	Soltikow v/FRG	length of proc.	no viol. of Conv.	Res.DH (71)1	19 Feb. 1971	no viol. of Conv.	Yearb. XIV, pp. 874-876
25	Jentzch v/FRG	length of prevent. detention	no viol. of Conv.	Res.DH (71)2	5 May 1971	no viol. of Conv.	Yearb. XIV, pp. 899-903
26	Scheichelbauer v/ Austria	conditions of crim. proc.	no viol. of Conv.	Res.DH (71)3	12 Nov. 1971	no viol. of Conv.	Yearb. XIV, pp. 903-907
27 to 30	La Haye, De Wilde, Nys and Swalens v/ Belgium (2nd "vagrancy" case)	measures relating to vagrancy	the system established by the law of 27 Nov. 1891 is not in conformity with Conv.	Res.DH (72)1	16 Oct. 1972	Viol. art.5§4 Conv. but following action taken, no further action required	Yearb. XV, pp. 695-699

Table 16.2 (Continued).

B. *Individual Cases*

Serial number	Title of the case(s)	Subject of the case	Opinion of the Commission	Decision	Date of decision	Summary of decision	Reference or state of proceedings
31	Inhabitants of Fourons v/Belgium	language laws	viol. art.2 Add. Prot. combined with art.14 Conv.	Res.DH (74)1	30 April 1974	no further action required	Inhabitants of Fourons case, EC, 1974, pp. 117-118
32	Kamma v/ Netherlands	diverting of crim. proc.	no viol. of art 18 combined with art.5 Conv.	Res.DH (75)1	13 March 1975	no viol. of Conv.	Kamma case, EC, 1975, p. 61
33	Huber v/Austria	length of crim. proc.	viol. art.6§1 Conv.	Res.DH (75)2	15 April 1975	no further action required	Huber case, EC, 1975, pp. 105-106
34 to 58	25 appl. East African Asians v/U.K.	refusal of right to enter U.K.	viol. art.3	Res.DH (77)2	21 Oct. 1977	no viol. art.3 and 5 nor of art.5 and 14	Yearb. XX, p. 642
59 to 64	6 appl. East African Asians v/U.K.	refusal of right to enter U.K.	not published			no further action required	

No.	Case	Subject	Result	Res.DH	Date	Result	Reference
65	Levy v/FRG	length of provisional detention	no viol. of Conv.	Res.DH (76)1	10 March 1976	no viol. of Conv.	Levy case, EC, pp. 49-50
66	Müller v/Austria	right to pension	no viol. of Conv.	Res.DH (76)2	7 April 1976	no viol. of Conv.	Muller case, EC, p.24
67	Hätti v/FRG	length of crim. proc.	no viol. of Conv.	Res.DH (76)3	19 Nov. 1976	no viol. of Conv.	Yearb. XIX p. 1025; EC, p. 147; Dec. + Rep. VI, p. 56
68	De Geillustreerde Pers N. V. v/Netherlands	legislative measures regarding publications	no viol. of Conv.	Res.DH (77)1	17 Feb. 1977	no viol. of Conv.	De Geillustreerde case, EC, p. 69 Yearb. XX p. 640
69	Brüggemann and Scheuten v/FRG	private life (abortion) freedom of religion	no viol. of Conv.	Res.DH (78)1	17 March 1978	no viol. of Conv.	Yearb. XXI, p. 638
70	Haase v/FRG	provisional detention too long	no viol. of Conv.	Res.DH (78)2	18 April 1978	no viol. of Conv.	Yearb. XXI, p. 640
71	Kiss v/U.K.	access to the court	viol. art.6§1	Res.DH (78)3	19 April 1978	no further action required	Yearb. XXI, p. 642

Table 16.2 (Continued).

B. Individual Cases

Serial number	Title of the case(s)	Subject of the case	Opinion of the Commission	Decision	Date of decision	Summary of decision	Reference or state of proceedings
72	Krzycki v/ FRG	unjustified detention	no viol. of Conv.	Res.DH (78)4	13 Oct. 1978	no viol. of Conv.	Yearb. XXI, p. 646
73	Hilton v/ U.K.	inhuman treatment in prison	viol. art.6§1	Res.DH (79)3	24 April 1979	viol. of Conv.	
74	Arrowsmith v/U.K.	freedom of expression in a military camp	no viol. of Conv.	Res.DH (79)4	12 June 1979	no viol. of Conv.	
75	Wells v/ U.K.	private life (homosexual)	no viol. of Conv.	Res.DH (79)5	12 June 1979	no viol. of Conv.	
76	Zand v/ Austria	proceeding before Labour Court	no viol. of Conv.	Res.DH (79)6	12 June 1979	no viol. of Conv.	
77	Eggs v/ Switzerland	disciplinary punishment during a military service	viol. art. 5§1	Res.DH (79)7	19 Oct. 1979	modification of the Swiss Military Penal Code during the proc.	

No.	Case	Subject	Result	Res.DH	Date	Result	Status
78	Preikhzas v. FRG	length of proceedings before Labour Court	no viol. of Conv.	Res.DH (79)8	19 Oct. 1979	no viol. of Conv.	
79	Christinet v/ Switzerland	re-integration in an internment establishment	no viol. of Conv.	Res.DH (79)9	29 Nov. 1979	no viol. of Conv.	
80	Bonnechaux v/ Switzerland	provisional detention too long	no viol. of Conv.	Res.DH (80)1	27 June 1980	no viol. of Conv.	
81	Droogenbroeck v/ Belgium	lawfulness of detention	viol. art.5§4				Pending before the Committee of Ministers
82	Hinchliff v/U.K.	detention of person of unsound mind					"
83	Hamer v/ U.K.	refusal of right to marry in prison					"
84	Campbell v/U.K.	corporal punishment					"
85	Cosans v/ U.K.	corporal punishment					"

Table 16.2 (*Continued*).

Serial number	Title of the case(s)	Subject of the case	Opinion of the Commission	Decision	Date of decision	Summary of decision	Reference or state of proceedings
B. Individual Cases							
86	Buchholz v/FRG	proceedings before Labour Court					
87	Caprino v/U.K.	lawfulness of detention					,,

first draft of the Convention transposed the most modern rules governing the responsibility of the public authorities to the international level.

While it is easy to criticize that part of the Convention which relates to the Court, it is even easier to justify it: the Convention could not turn a blind eye to that fundamental reality of international life which is represented by States. This being so, it was preferable, in the very interests of the protection of European public order, to give to the Court the usual attributes of an international judicial organ.

(ii). ORGANIZATION AND WORKING OF THE COURT

The Court consists of a number of judges equal to that of the Members of the Council of Europe. No two judges may be nationals of the same State (Convention, article 38). Thus, a difference still exists between the membership of the Commission and that of the Court: whereas the Commission consists of as many members as there are Contracting Parties, the number of judges of the Court corresponds to the number of Member States of the Council of Europe; however, in 1975, and for the first time since the entry into force of the Convention, there was the same number—eighteen—of members belonging to the Commission as to the Court since all the Member States of the Council of Europe were at that time Contracting Parties to the Convention. The adhesion of Portugal in September 1976 made it necessary for a nineteenth judge of the Court to be elected. A twentieth judge was elected in 1978 following Spain's entry into the Council, and finally the twenty-first judge, a Canadian representing Liechtenstein, recently completed the ranks of the Court.

The members of the Court are elected by the Consultative Assembly of the Council of Europe by a majority of votes cast from a list of persons nominated by the Member States. Each State must nominate three candidates, of whom two at least must be its nationals (Convention, art. 39, para. 1). A difficulty arose at the time of the first election because article 39, paragraph 1, does not indicate whether, to be elected, a candidate has to obtain an absolute majority of votes or whether a relative majority is sufficient. Two proposals were placed before the Assembly: the first provided for election by an absolute majority in the first ballot and a relative majority in the second; the second provided for a single ballot with a relative majority. After adopting the first proposal, the Assembly proceeded with the election by secret ballot.

Article 39, paragraph 2, of the Convention stipulates that "As far as applicable, the same procedure shall be followed to complete the Court in the event of the admission of new members of the Council of Europe, and in filling casual vacancies".

Candidates for the office of judge of the Court must be of high moral character and must either possess the qualifications required for appointment to high judicial office or be jurisconsults of recognized competence (article 39, paragraph 3).

The judges are elected for nine years. However, four of the judges elected at the first election held office for three years and the four others for six years. As in the case of the Commission, the purpose of this provision—the renewal of one third of the judges—could not be achieved once the period of office of certain judges began at very different dates. Thus, as for the Commission, the object of Protocol No. 5 to the Convention is also to amend article 40 of the Convention so as to ensure as far as possible the renewal of one third of the members of the Court every three years.

The judges may be re-elected. The resignation of a judge constitutes vacation of office. A judge elected to replace another judge whose term of office has not expired holds office for the remainder of his predecessor's term.

No provision of the Convention stipulates that the judges are independent. No doubt the view was taken that the independence of judges goes hand in hand with the exercise of jurisdictional power.

It is to be noted, finally, that, like the members of the Commission, the judges of the Court enjoy, under article 59 of the Convention, during the discharge of their functions, the privileges and immunities provided for in article 40 of the Statute of the Council of Europe and in the agreements made thereunder. The fourth Additional Protocol to the General Agreement on Privileges and Immunities of the Council of Europe, signed on 16 December 1961 and entered into force on the same date, contains provisions relating to the Court which more clearly define the privileges and immunities provided for in the Statute of the Council of Europe. In general, they are scarcely different from those granted to the Commission by the second Additional Protocol to the same General Agreement, which was signed on 15 December 1956 and which came into force on the same day.

The Convention establishes no incompatibility between the office of judge and certain other functions or professions. In the face of this silence, the Court did not feel entitled to so provide in its Rules. It merely established what constitutes an obstacle to the exercise of the functions of judge. Article 4 of the Rules of Court thus provides that: "A judge may not exercise his functions while he is a member of a Government or while he holds a post or exercises a profession which is likely to affect confidence in his independence".

It is also to be observed that a judge may not take part in the consideration of any case in which he has a personal interest or in which he has previously acted either as the agent, advocate or adviser of a Party or of a person having an interest in the case, or as a member of a tribunal or commission of enquiry or in any other capacity.

The Court elects its President and Vice-President for a period of three years. They may be re-elected (Convention, article 41).

The seat of the European Court of Human Rights is at the seat of the Council of Europe at Strasbourg.

The plenary sessions of the Court are convened by the President and must be so convened at least once a year (Rules of Court, 16).

The quorum of the plenary Court is eleven elected judges.

The Convention is silent on the question of the public character of the work of the Court. In its Rules, the Court adopted the traditional principle concerning the public character of court proceedings: hearings are public, unless the Court in exceptional circumstances decides otherwise (Rule 18). The judgement of the Court is read at a public hearing (Rule 51, para. 2). Lastly, the Registrar is responsible for the publication of judgements, decisions and other documents of the Court (Rule 52) and documents deposited with the Registrar and not published are in principle accessible to the public as well. As the Commission and the Committee of Ministers meet *in camera*, a case consequently loses its secret character only from the time that it is examined before the Court.

No provision of the Convention deals with the question of the registry of the Court: articles 11 and 12 of the Rules of Court stipulate that the Court elects its Registrar and Deputy Registrar after the President has in this respect obtained the opinion of the Secretary-General of the Council of Europe.

(iii). JURISDICTION OF THE COURT AND CONDITIONS UNDER WHICH A CASE CAN BE BROUGHT BEFORE IT

For a case to be brought before the Court, the Court must first of all have been constituted. Article 56 thus provides that no case can be brought before the Court before the first election of its members. Now under the same article 56, this first election could not take place before eight Contracting Parties had recognized the compulsory jurisdiction of the Court. This condition was fulfilled on 3 September 1958: the first election of judges thus took place on 21 January 1959.

No case can be brought directly before the Court. It must first of all have been brought before the Commission in the form of an application, have been declared admissible and investigated by the Commission; then the attempt to reach a friendly settlement must have failed and the Commission must have drawn up its report stating the failure of the attempt to secure such a settlement.

Lastly, the case must have been referred to the Court within a period of three months from the date of transmission of the report of the Commission to the Committee of Ministers.

According to article 45 of the Convention, the jurisdiction of the Court extends to all cases concerning the interpretation and application of the Convention. Thus, within the limits *ratione loci, ratione materiae* and *ratione temporis* of the Convention, the Court appears to exercise a general jurisdiction. In actual fact, it has indirect jurisdiction, derived from that of the Commission in that, to be brought before the Court, a case must, on the one hand, fall within the framework of the competence of the Commission *ratione loci, ratione materiae, ratione personae* and *ratione temporis* and, on the other, meet the various conditions of admissibility pertaining to State and individual applications.

Should it be concluded form this that the Court, in that it does not exercise "direct" jurisdiction, consequently forfeits the general jurisdiction that seems, however, to be reserved for it by article 45 of the Convention? Such is not the case. The Court retains its task of exercising, within the limits of the Convention, a general jurisdiction in the sense that questions of competence *ratione loci, ratione materiae* and *ratione temporis*, as well as questions of admissibility, settled by the Commission in its decision on admissibility, may be brought up again before the Court.

The Court has jurisdiction with respect to any Contracting party that has declared that it recognizes its jurisdiction as compulsory or that has given its consent or agreement to a particular case being brought before the Court.

The declaration may be made unconditionally or on condition of reciprocity, or for an indeterminate period. As of 1 January 1982, eighteen of the twenty-one Contracting States had recognized the compulsory jurisdiction of the Court, namely: Austria, Belgium, Cyprus, Denmark, Federal Republic of Germany, France, Greece, Iceland, Ireland, Italy, Luxembourg, Netherlands, Norway, Portugal, Spain, Sweden, Switzerland and the United Kingdom.[5]

Under article 48 of the Convention, the following may bring a case before the Court: the Commission or the High Contracting Party concerned which is that whose national is alleged to be a victim, that which referred the case to the Commission or that against which the complaint has been lodged.

Article 44 provides, in addition, that "Only the High Contracting Parties and the Commission shall have the right to bring a case before the Court."

While it is natural for States to be granted the right to bring a case before the Court, it seems surprising that the same right is granted to the Commission. Moreover, the situation which presents itself here is one which is fairly rare in international practice (ie., one in which an international judicial organ— the Commission—brings a case before another international judicial organ— the Court). The Commission's right to bring a case before the Court is in fact the result of a compromise between those who were in favour of, and those who were against, a Court which would be accessible to the individual. It clearly results from the aforementioned articles 44 and 48 that the individual cannot, after the failure of efforts for a friendly settlement, refer a case to the Court that he has brought before the Commission using the application procedure. Since, in most cases, the application is brought by an individual against his own Government, no Contracting Party, with indeed the exception of that of which the individual is a national, can, under article 48, bring a case before the Court. The Commission's right to bring a case before the Court makes it possible, to a certain extent at least, to redress the balance. Thus, this right is in fact but the logical consequence of the refusal to grant the individual the right to bring a case before the Court.

(iv). PROCEEDINGS BEFORE THE COURT

Institution of proceedings

A case is brought before the Court either by the Contracting Party concerned by means of an application, or by the Commission by means of a request (Rule 31). Both the application and the request may contain a certain amount of information enabling the Court to ascertain whether the conditions under which a case may be brought before it have been met.

Like an application brought before the Commission, the institution of proceedings before the Court does not have a suspensive effect. Moreover, even though no provision of the Convention accords competence to the Commission or to the Court for ordering interim measures, solutions have been found in the case of the Court such as in matters concerning the Commission especially, either within the framework of its Rules or in practice before the Commission, thanks to the spirit of co-operation of the Contracting States.

The Chamber and the plenary Court

When a case is brought before the Court, the Court is constituted in a Chamber of seven judges. Such is the principle laid down by article 43 of the Convention. Whereas before the International Court of Justice judgement by a Chamber is the exception and under its Statute the Court is not obliged to be constituted in a Chamber, the European Court of Human Rights is in principle required to exercise its functions by means of a Chamber.

The Chamber of the Court required to judge a case must be composed of every judge who has the nationality of the State or States party to the case together with the President of the Court or failing him the Vice-President. If the Court does not include an elected judge having the nationality of a Party, or if the judge called upon to sit in that capacity is unable to sit or withdraws, the President of the Court invites the agent of the Party concerned to inform him within thirty days whether his Government wishes to appoint to sit as judge either another elected judge or an *ad hoc* judge who must possess the qualifications required to be a judge of the Court. The names of the other judges and substitute judges are determined by a drawing of lots affected by the President from among the elected judges not having the nationality of any Party concerned (Rule 21).

Article 43, in providing that "for the consideration of each case brought before it the Court shall consist of a Chamber composed of seven judges", seems at first sight to rule out the plenary Court ever being apprised of a case. If this were so, the European Court of Human Rights, like the Permanent Court of Arbitration, would, to all intents and purposes, be but a list of twenty-one judges from which the Chambers would be constituted. There would be a danger of differences in interpretation between two Chambers of a Court incapable of achieving any unity in its case-law.

Rule 48 of the rules of Court, by providing in certain cases for the relinquishment of jurisdiction by the Chamber in favour of the plenary Court, re-establishes the unity of the Court and consequently of its case-law:

"Where a case pending before a Chamber raises a serious question affecting the interpretation of the Convention, the Chamber may, at any time, relinquish jurisdiction in favour of the plenary Court. The relinquishment of jurisdiction shall be obligatory where the resolution of such a question might yield a result which is inconsistent with a judgment previously delivered by a Chamber or by the plenary Court. Reasons need be given for the decision to relinquish jurisdiction."

"The plenary Court, having been seized of the case, may either retain jurisdiction over the whole case or may, after deciding on the question of interpretation, order that the case be referred back to the Chamber which shall, in regard to the remaining part of the case, recover its original jurisdiction."

A regularly constituted Chamber relinquished jurisdiction for the first time in favour of the plenary Court in the case relating to certain aspects of the laws on the use of languages in education in Belgium. It did so on 3 May 1966 *at the actual request* of the respondent Government, on the ground that the case raised a number of serious questions affecting the interpretation of the Convention. Other instances of such relinquishment occurred subsequently.

Conduct of the proceedings

Whether a case is referred to it by a Contracting Party or by the Commission, the Court "shall take into consideration the report of the latter." The Court is neither bound to accept the conclusions of the report nor bound to accept the facts as they have been established by the Commission. The Court, however, cannot but attach great importance to the report which is the result of a long investigation during which the parties have exchanged several statements of the case and have taken part in several hearings together. In addition, in drawing up its report, the Commission will have been less removed from the facts of the case than the Court, which will come into contact with these several years after they have occurred. In the *Lawless* case, for instance, the facts which led to an application before the Commission in September 1957 occurred in July 1957. The case was brought before the Court, however, only in 1960. In such conditions, the report constitutes the principal item in the case-file of the Court, although the Court does not necessarily accept as established the facts of the case in the report drawn up by the Commission and consequently does not confine itself to finding fault, where appropriate, with their legal interpretation.

The proceedings before the Court are divided into written proceedings and oral proceedings.

A preliminary objection must be filed by a party at the latest before the expiry of the time-limit fixed for the delivery of its first pleading.

When the case is ready for hearing, the President of the Chamber fixes the date of the opening of the oral proceedings. He directs the hearings. He prescribes the order in which the agents, advocates or advisers of the parties and the delegates of the Commission, as well as any other person appointed by them, shall be called upon to speak (Rule 37). The Chamber may, at the request of a party or of delegates of the Commission or *proprio motu*, decide to hear as a witness or as an expert, or in any other capacity, any person whose evidence or statements seem likely to assist it in the carrying out of its task (Rule 38). This provision also enables the Chamber of the plenary Court to hear the applicant as a witness or in any other capacity (provided that he assists the delegates of the Commission before the Court) but not as a party.

Role of the Commission

Whether or not it reaches the conclusion in its report that there has been a breach of the Convention, the Commission may or may not wish to bring the case before the Court. However, it should be noted that in recent years there has been a notable increase in the number of cases that the Commission has presented to the Court. If it decides to refer it to the Court, it is by no means obliged to justify its decision although, in certain cases, it may consider it advisable to state its reasons.

The functions of the Commission do not come to an end when the case has been referred to the Court. In fact, no provision of the Convention expressly states that it cannot take part in the examination of the case before the Court, article 48 merely providing that a case may be brought before the Court by the Commission, *inter alia*. Actually, it is difficult to imagine the Commission refraining from taking part when its report is likely to be at the centre of the discussions. Furthermore, the absence of the Commission would certainly not facilitate the task of the Court; it would even make it practically impossible in cases where only one Contracting Party is entitled to appear before the Court. It is thus already implicit in the ordinary workings of the machinery of the Convention that the Commission take part in the proceedings.

Even if it brings a case before the Court, the Commission still does not become a *party* to the proceedings. The Court recognized this in its Rules, Rule 1 of which stipulates that the term "Parties" means those Contracting Parties which are the Applicant and Respondent Parties.

To understand the role of the Commission, it must not be forgotten that from the moment that a case has been brought before the Court, the proceedings acquire a judicial character. In other words, as long as a case has not been brought before it, the Court has strictly no jurisdiction in a case. But once it has been brought before it, the Court is in possession of its full jurisdictional power. Should it be deduced from this that the Commission, which is not a party, is subject to the supervision of the Court, and that the powers available to it derive from the jurisdictional power of the Court? Such, in substance, was the view upheld by the Irish Government in the discussions relating to the preliminary objections in the *Lawless* case.

In rejecting the conclusions of the Irish Government, the Court considered that it was not "competent to take decisions which would delete a rule from the Commission's Rules of Procedure—a step which would affect all Parties to the Convention". But the judgement defines above all the position of the Commission before the Court. The preambular paragraph relating thereto deserves to be reproduced in its entirety:

"Whereas in Article 19, the Convention sets up both the Commission and the Court 'to ensure the observance of the engagements taken by the High Contracting Parties in the Convention' and assigns to each of these bodies specific functions in the safeguarding of human rights; whereas those of the Commission differ according to the stage reached in the proceedings; whereas, in the initial stage—governed mainly by Section III of the Convention—the Commission's chief function is to carry out an independent inquiry, to seek a friendly settlement and, if need be, to bring the case before the Court: once this has been done, the Commission's main function is to assist the Court, and it is associated with the proceedings; however, even at this stage its action is determined not by a decision of the Court, but directly by the terms of the Convention."

In its Rules of Procedure the Commission has defined its function as an assistant of the Court. Rule 56 confirms that the Commission assists the Court in any case brought before the Court. Although the term employed is different, the idea is the same.

The Commission does not merely make its case-files accessible to the Court. It assists the Court through one or more delegates whom it appoints in plenary session once a case has been brought before the Court. The Rules of the Court indicate in Rule 29 that the delegates "may, if they so desire, have the assistance of any person of their choice". This provision was incorporated, in substance, by the Commission in its Rules of Procedure (Rule 56) which states that that person shall be appointed by the Commission but without giving any other details concerning the qualifications of any persons that might be called on to assist the delegates. The very general terms of this provision make it possible to say, however, that the delegates may be assisted by the applicant himself or by his representative or agent. After creating something of a stir in the vagrancy case against Belgium, this has now become common practice.

The role of the delegates will no doubt be fairly limited in the case of a dispute between two States, either because what is originally involved is an application brought before the Commission by one State against another State, or because a State has set before the Court the complaints formulated in an application by an individual. The delegates will probably do no more than see to it that the report is not misinterpreted by either party and answer any questions put to them by the Court concerning the report. Such an eventuality has never arisen as yet.

Such is not the case when the dispute involves only one party, either because the application has been brought before the Commission by an individual against his own Government, or because a State refrains from setting forth as its own the complaints formulated by its national against the respondent State. As the Court does not wish to become an Attorney General as well and as, above all, it has not instituted a procedure of an inquisitorial type (although in the Belgium linguistic case, it adopted a highly active attitude in its examination of the different complaints), it has a tendency to have recourse to the Commission which, by taking an active part in the proceedings, may redress the balance upset before the Court to the disadvantage of the individual.

The place of the individual

In listing those who may bring a case before the Court, article 48 of the Convention makes no mention of the individual. Article 44 seems to go even further since it stipulates that "Only the High Contracting Parties and the Commission shall have the right to bring a case before the Court." This text, it is true, permits a less strict interpretation than the French text "seules les hautes parties contractantes et la Commission ont qualité pour se présenter devant la Cour", since it simply excludes the individual from those who have the right "to bring the case before the Court" ("de porter l'affaire devant la Cour").

Whatever the case, it is indisputable that before the Court the individual can never be a party, that he can never "appear before the Court", in the words of the judgement in the *Lawless* case of 14 November 1960.

Does this mean that the individual is completely excluded from the proceedings? In its aforementioned judgement, the Court noted that "the whole of the proceedings in the Court, as laid down by the Convention and the Rules of Court, are upon issues which concern the Applicant." It should not be forgotten indeed that the individual actually originates the proceedings since it is he who brings the application before the Commission. He is also the finishing point of the proceedings since, if the Court decides that there has been a violation of the Convention and that the municipal law of the respondent Contracting Party allows only partial reparation to be made for the consequences of the violation, it affords, if necessary, just satisfaction to the injured party, that is to say, to the individual (Convention, art. 50).

Thus, it is impossible to consider the individual to be alien to the proceedings in which he is "directly concerned". The place reserved for him is tied to his being an applicant before the Commission. It is interesting to note in this connection that both in the judgement of 14 November 1960 and in the statements made before the Court by the Delegate of the Commission and by the counsel of the Irish Government, the individual concerned in the proceedings, G.R. Lawless, is always referred to as the "Applicant", and in subsequent cases the same term has been used.

The Rules of Court already contain certain provisions which allow the individual to take part in the proceedings. However, the Court could not go beyond them without disregarding the express provisions of article 44 of the Convention. And yet, it is "in the interests of the proper administration of justice that the Court should have knowledge of and, if need be, take into consideration, the Applicant's point of view". Being empowered neither to appear before the Court nor to formulate conclusions through a representative of his choice, the individual had to turn to the Commission, called upon to be not his representative but that of the public interest before the Court. Moreover, the Commission understood that there was a danger of disequilibrium between the State and the applicant being too great if, in fulfilling its function as an assistant of the Court, it did not give the individual the opportunity to make his voice heard. It therefore provided in Rule 76 of its Rules of Procedure (now Rule 61) that it would communicate its report to the applicant who would be at liberty to submit to it his written observations on the report. But the Commission reserves its decision as to what action, if any, shall be taken with respect to those observations.

In its judgement of 14 November 1960, the Court refused to find fault with this provision of the Rules of Procedure of the Commission. It considered that the Commission is entitled to communicate its report to the applicant, while prohibiting its publication, whenever such communication seems useful to it. Furthermore, the Court made it clear that for the purpose of knowing the individual's point of view, it has at its disposal:

"...in the first place, and in any event, the Commission's report, which of necessity sets out the applicant's allegations with regard to the facts and his legal arguments, even if it does not endorse them; secondly, the written and oral observations of the Delegates and counsel of the Commission which, as the defender of the public interest, is entitled of its own accord, even if it does not share them, to make known the Applicant's views to the Court as a means of throwing light on the points at issue; and thirdly, the Court may also hear the Applicant in accordance with Rule 38 of the Rules of Court, and as part of the enquiry, may invite the Commission, *ex officio*, or authorize the Commission at its request, to submit the Applicant's observations on the Report or on any specific point arising in the course of the debates".

This judgement, as important as it is, did not make it clear in what *form* the applicant's considerations should reach the Court, nor by what *methods* the Commission should collect them. On these two points the judgement of 7 April 1961, also delivered in the Lawless case, provides important clarifications, confirmed by subsequent practice in other cases with which the Court has had to deal.

On the question of *form*, it results implicitly from the aforementioned judgement of 7 April 1961 and above all from the interpretation given to it by the Commission in practice, that the Commission is not and cannot become a purely passive intermediary between the Court and the applicant. The Commission should not constitute a platform for the applicant allowing him to recover, at least in part, the status of a party to the proceedings, and consequently his opinions can be presented to the Court only insofar as they are reflected in the public interest represented by the Commission.

As regards *methods*, the Commission is entirely free to choose them, provided that it does not follow that the applicant "has any *locus standi in judicio*". In fact, the Commission has always sought to keep in contact with the applicant, by communicating to him the report on which he may submit written observations, by "exchanges of views" which the delegates have with the applicant or his lawyer on the occasion of the oral hearings and, lastly, by providing the representative of the applicant, if need be, with the opportunity to speak under the supervision of the delegates at the time of the hearings before the Court.

Thus, thanks to the good will of the Commission, the Court has managed indirectly to provide a place for the individual applicant in the proceedings before it; this will prevent him from considering the subsequent termination of the proceedings to be an *inter alios actum*.

(v). TERMINATION OF THE PROCEEDINGS

Friendly settlement or other arrangement providing a solution of the matter

After bringing a case before the Court, the Commission may, nevertheless, consider it useful to remain in contact with the two parties with a view to continuing its efforts to secure a friendly settlement. If it reaches a friendly settlement "on the basis of respect for human rights", it notifies the competent Chamber of the Court. Although it is not obliged to do so, the Court may strike the case off the list after ascertaining the views of the delegates of the Commission. In the case of an arrangement or of another similar circumstance the same procedure will be followed to provide a solution to the matter (Rule 47, para.2). The Court then strikes the case off its list, no doubt by means of a judgement, as in the *De Becker* case.

Discontinuance

The case may also be terminated by the applicant party deciding not to proceed with it. When that party has notified the registrar of the Court of its intention not to proceed with the case and if the other parties agree to such discontinuance, the Chamber decides, after having obtained the opinion of the Commission, whether or not it is appropriate to approve the discontinuance and accordingly to strike the case off its list. In the affirmative, the Chamber gives a reasoned decision which is communicated to the Committee of Ministers in order to allow them to supervise, in accordance with Article 54 of the Convention, the execution of any undertakings which may have been attached to the discontinuance by order of the Chamber or with its approval.

However, notwithstanding the notice of discontinuance and "having regard to the responsibilities of the Court in pursuance of Article 19 of the Convention", the Chamber may also decide that it should proceed with the consideration of the case (Rule 47, paragraphs 1 and 2).

Judgement

The proceedings will normally terminate with the judgment which will decide whether in the case under consideration there has or has not been a violation of the Convention. The judgement must be accompanied by the reasons on which it is based. It must contain a number of particulars, furnishing unmistakable proof of the fact that it embodies a jurisdictional act.

The judgement of the Court is transmitted to the Committee of Ministers which supervises its execution (Convention, article 54).

Can it be said that the judgement, which is compulsory for the State, is directly enforceable? It does not appear to be. Article 50 of the Convention leaves it to the Contracting party concerned to draw the necessary consequences from the judgement. The judgement does not in fact directly cancel any decision that is taken or any measure that is ordered by a judicial authority or any other authority of a Contracting Party, deemed by the Court to be in conflict with the Convention. It is only when the internal law of the Contracting Party allows only partial reparation to be made for the consequences of the violation of the Convention that the Court can afford the injured party just satisfaction, that is to say, damages. In delivering its judgement on the merits of the case, the Court would be able to grant such damages. But normally it will reserve the rights of the applicant and will give its opinion in another judgement, following proceedings instituted on the initiative of the applicant and in which the Commission will once again have taken part, under the same conditions, through its delegates.

The judgement of the Court is final (Convention, article 52) and, consequently, no remedy can be provided against it. To say that the judgement of the Court is final does not mean that a request for interpretation or revision is not admissible. Indeed, under Rule 53 of the Rules of Court, "A Party or the Commission may request the interpretation of a judgement within a period of three years following the delivery of that judgement. The request shall state precisely the point or points in the operative provisions of the judgement on which interpretation is required". Furthermore, under article 54, "A Party or the Commission may, in the event of the discovery of a fact which might by its nature have a decisive influence and which, when a judgement was delivered, was unknown both to the Court and to that Party or the Commission, request the Court, within a period of six months after that Party or the Commission, as the case may be, acquired knowledge of such fact, to revise that judgement". In both cases, the Court decides by means of a judgement.

Under article 53 of the Convention, the Contracting Parties "undertake to abide by the decision of the Court in any case to which they are parties". Thence it results that the authority of *res judicata* will be relative and not absolute. Execution of the judgements of the Court is consequently founded on the undertaking of the Contracting States, a classic solution in international law. In the event of a refusal to execute the judgement, the Committee of Ministers could probably not, in carrying out its function of supervising such execution, be content with noting the default of a State. It would then be necessary to take action within the framework of the Statute of the Council of Europe against the recalcitrant State by applying the procedure to suspend and to exclude it from the organization.

(d). An auxiliary organ of the Convention: the Secretary-General of the Council of Europe

It would have been abnormal for the Secretary-General of the organization, within the framework of the Convention, not to have been given a part in its functioning. In point of fact, the highest official of the Council is required to take action in a dual capacity: as the representative of the Council of Europe he exercises administrative functions which are the consequence of the links between the Convention and the Council; as an organ of the Convention, he is assigned specific functions by article 57, thus sharing with the other organs of the Convention responsibility for its implementation.

Under the terms of article 57:

"On receipt of a request from the Secretary-General of the Council of Europe any High Contracting Party shall furnish an explanation of the manner in which its internal law ensures the effective implementation of any of the provisions of the Convention".

Article 57 thus grants to the Secretary-General a *right* to which corresponds an *obligation* on the part of the Contracting Parties: the Secretary may ask the Contracting Parties for an explanation of the manner in which their internal law ensures the effective implementation of any of the provisions of the Convention; the Contracting Parties have the obligation to furnish explanations.

This diptych is clear only on the surface and leaves unanswered a whole series of questions concerning, for instance, the subject of the Secretary-General's request, his right to act in all circumstances, on his own initiative and outside the statutory machinery of the Council of Europe, and, perhaps especially at what times it would be appropriate to question the explanations furnished by the Contracting States. Concerning this last point, one thing is certain: as the texts stand at present, the Secretary-General is not empowered

Table 16.3
Cases Referred to the Court

Serial number	Title of the case	State concerned	Initiator of proceedings before Court	Subject of case	Opinion of Commission	Date of judgment	Subject of judgment	Reference or state of proceedings
A. Inter-State Cases								
1	Ireland v/U.K.	U.K.	Ireland	emergency legislative measures in Northern Ireland	viol. art. 1,4; viol. art. 3 Conv.	18 Jan. 78	no viol. art.5 viol. of art.3 (inhuman treatment but not torture)	ECHR series A Vol. 6
B. Individual Cases								
1	Lawless case	Ireland	Commission	detention without judgment in military camp	no viol. of Conv.	14 Nov. 60	prel. obj. role of applicant before Court	ECHR series A vol. 1
						7 April 61		ECHR series A Vol. 2
						1 July 61	MERITS: no viol. of Conv.	ECHR series A Vol. 3

No.	Case	State	Organ	Subject	Result	Date	Decision	Source
2	De Becker case	Belgium	Commission	compatibility art.123 sexies Penal Code with Conv.	viol. art.10 Conv.	27 March 62	Striking off list	ECHR series A Vol.4
3 to 8	case "relating to certain aspects of the laws on the use of languages in education in Belgium"	Belgium	Commission	laws on use of languages	Belgian legislation does not meet the requirements of the Conv.	3 May 66 / 9 Nov. 67 / 23 Aug. 68	prel. obj. MERITS: viol. art.14 combined with art.2 Add. Prot.	ECHR series A Vol. 5 / ECHR series A Vol. 6
9	Wemhoff case	FRG	Commission	length prev. detent.; length crim. proc.	viol. art. 5§3 Conv. no viol. art.6§1 of Conv.	27 June 68	MERITS: no viol. of Conv.	ECHR series A Vol. 7

Table 16.3 (Continued).

Serial number	Title of the case	State concerned	Initiator of proceedings before Court	Subject of case	Opinion of Commission	Date of judgement	Subject of judgement	Reference or state of proceedings
B. Individual Cases								
10	Neumeister case	Austria	Commission and Austria	length prev. detent.; length crim. proc.	viol. art. 5§3 Conv. viol. art. 6§1 Conv.	27 June 68 7 May 74	MERITS: viol. art. 5§3 Conv. no viol. art.6§1 Conv. art.58 Conv.	ECHR series A Vol. 6 ECHR series A Vol. 17
11	Stögmuller case	Austria	Commission and Austria	length prev. detent.	viol. art. 5§3 Conv.	10 Nov. 69	MERITS: viol. art.5§3 Conv.	ECHR series A Vol. 10
12	Matznetter case	Austria	Commission and Austria	length prev. detent.; appeal against lawfulness of detent.	viol. art. 5§3 Conv.	10 Nov. 69	MERITS: no viol. of Conv.	ECHR series A Vol. 9

13	Delcourt case	Belgium	Commission	role of Public Ministry before Court of Cassation	no viol. art.6§1 Conv.	17 Jan. 70	MERITS: viol. of Conv.	ECHR series A Vol. 11
14 to 16	DeWilde, Ooms and Versyp cases ("vagrancy" cases)	Belgium	Belgium	measures relating to vagrancy	viol. art. 4,5&4,8 Conv.	28 May 70 18 Nov. 70 18 June 71 10 March 72	role of Commission before Court Conv. MERITS: viol. art. 5&4 Conv. art.50 Conv.	ECHR series A Vol. 12 ECHR series A Vol. 14
17	Ringeisen case	Austria	Commission	length prev. detent.; length crim. proc.	viol. art 5§3 Conv.	16 Aug. 71 22 June 72 23 June 72	MERITS: viol. art 5§3 Conv. art.50 Conv. interpretation Judgement 22 June 72	ECHR series A Vol. 13 ECHR series A Vol. 15 ECHR series A Vol. 16

Table 16.3 (*Continued*).

Serial number	Title of the case	State concerned	Initiator of proceedings before Court	Subject of case	Opinion of Commission	Date of judgement	Subject of judgement	Reference or state of proceedings
B. Individual Cases								
18	Golder case	U.K.	U.K.	detainee refused authorization to consult lawyer	viol. art. 6§1 Conv. viol. art. 8 Conv.	21 Nov. 75	MERITS: viol. art. 6§1, Conv. 8	ECHR series A Vol. 18
19	Nat'l. Union Belgian Police case	Belgium	Commission	freedom of association	no viol. art.11 Conv.	27 Sept. 75	MERITS: no viol. of Conv.	ECHR series A Vol. 19
20 to 24	5 Netherlands military cases	Netherlands	Commission and Netherlands	military discipline	viol. art. 5§1 and 5§4	8 June 76	MERITS: viol. art. 5§1 and 6§1	ECHR series A Vol. 22
25	Svenska Lokmannaförbundet case	Sweden	Commission	freedom of association	no viol. of Conv.	6 Nov. 76	MERITS: no viol. of Conv.	ECHR series A Vol. 20

No.	Case	State	Referred by	Subject	Commission opinion	Date	Court decision	Reference
26	Schmidt and Dahlström case	Sweden	Commission	trade union rights	no viol. of Conv.	6 Nov. 76	MERITS: no viol. of Conv.	ECHR series A Vol. 21
27 to 29	Kjeldsen Busk-Madsen and Pedbersen cases	Denmark	Commission	law making sex education compulsory in public schools	no viol. of Conv.	7 Dec. 76	MERITS: no viol. of Conv.	ECHR series A Vol. 23
30	Handyside case	U.K.	Commission	freedom of expression	no Viol. of Conv.	7 Dec. 76	MERITS: no viol. of Conv.	ECHR series A Vol. 24
31	Tyrer case	U.K.	Commission	judicial corporal punishment	Viol. art.3 (degrading punishment)	25 April 78	MERITS: viol. art.3 Conv.	ECHR series A Vol. 26
32	König	FRG	FRG and subsequently the Commission	nature of administrative agencies	viol. art.6§1 Conv.	28 June 78	MERITS: viol. art.6§1	ECHR series A Vol. 27
						10 March 80	art.50	ECHR series A Vol. 36

Table 16.3 (*Continued*).

B. Individual Cases

Serial number	Title of the case	State concerned	Initiator of proceedings before Court	Subject of case	Opinion of Commission	Date of judgement	Subject of judgement	Reference or state of proceedings
33	Klass and others	FRG	Commission	wire-tapping	no viol. of Conv.	6 Sept. 78	MERITS: no viol. of Conv.	ECHR series A Vol. 28
34	Lue-dicke, Belka-cem, Koc.	FRG	FRG and subsequently the Commission	the cost of interpreting criminal proceedings	viol. art.6§3(e) Conv.	28 Nov. 78	MERITS: viol. art.6§3	ECHR series A Vol. 29
						10 March 80	art.50	ECHR series A Vol. 36
35	*Times*, News-papers, *Sunday Times*, Evans	U.K.	Commission	the right to publish information on a case pending before a court	viol. art.10 Conv.	26 April 79	MERITS: viol. art.10 Conv.	ECHR series A Vol. 30

532

No.	Case	Country	Applicant	Subject	Finding	Date	Merits	Reference
36	Marckx	Belgium	Commission	discrimination in inheritance against unmarried mothers and natural children	viol. art.8 and art.14 combined with art.8 Conv.	13 June 79	MERITS: viol. Conv.	ECHR series A Vol. 31
37	Winterwerp	Netherlands	Commission	internment in an asylum	viol. art.5§4 Conv.	24 Oct. 79	MERITS: viol. art.5§4	ECHR series A Vol. 33
38	Airey case	Ireland	Commission	deprivation of access to the courts in determination of civil rights	viol. art.6§1	9 Oct. 79	merits: viol art. 6§1 and art.8	ECHR series A Vol. 32
39	Schiesser case	Switzerland	Commission Switzerland	provisional detention	no viol. art.5§3	4 Dec. 79	MERITS: no viol. of Conv.	ECHR series A Vol. 34

Table 16.3 (*Continued*).

Serial number	Title of the case	State con-cerned	Initia-tor of proceed-ings before Court	Subject of case	Opinion of Commission	Date of judge-ment	Subject of judge-ment	Refer-ence or state of pro-ceed-ings
B. Individual Cases								
40	Dewer case	Belgium	Commis-sion	discipli-nary mea-sures	viol. art.6§1	27 Feb. 80	MERITS: viol. art. 6§1	ECHR series A Vol. 35
41	Artico case	Italy	Commis-sion	legal aid and law-fulness of de-tention	viol. art.6§3 (c)	13 May 80	MERITS: viol. art. 6§3(c)	ECHR series A Vol. 37
42	Guzzardi	Italy	Commis-sion	unfa-vorable condi-tions of confine-ment	viol. art.5 §1			Pending before the Court
43	Van Ooster-wijck	Belgium	Belgium and sub-sequently the Com-mission	refusal to amend civil status (trans-sexual)	viol. art.8,12			Pending before the court

44	Le Compte Van Leuven De Meyere cases	Belgium	Commission and Belgium	disciplinary proc. before the Council of the medical order; freedom of assoc.	Pending before the Court
45	Young and James case	U.K.	Commission	freedom of association	Pending before the Court
46	Webster case	U.K.	Commission	freedom of association	Pending before the Court
47	Dudgeon case	U.K.	Commission	private life (homosexual)	Pending before the Court

to apprise the organs of the Convention and in particular, the Commission, of any facts disclosed by the information he has received. This being so, the sanction of the right granted to the Secretary-General by article 57 can only be purely political, within the framework of the Statute of the Council of Europe (Statute, articles 3 and 8).

Article 57 was put into operation for the first time in October 1964, the subject of the request by the Secretary-General being all the substantive provisions of the Convention. It was used for the second time in July 1970 in connection with article 5, paragraph 5, of the Convention (right to compensation in the event of arbitrary arrest or detention). The third and last request to date, made in April 1975, concerned articles 8, 9, 10 and 11 of the Convention. It is to be noted that the findings of the first two "investigations" were communicated to the Consultative Assembly of the Council of Europe which made a critical evaluation of them in a report which was followed by a resolution which encouraged the Secretary-General to avail himself of article 57.

The first complete experiences of article 57 will no doubt be considered as disappointing. The right granted by article 57 to the Secretary-General has proved to be more a right to information than the authority to call in question the state of freedom in Europe. Could it have been otherwise? It was undoubtedly difficult for the Secretary-General to find a specific place in the apparently complete machinery for the legal protection of human rights instituted by the European Convention when it established a European Commission and Court of Human Rights.

At the very most the Secretary-General may have been able, on the basis of article 57 and by means of the central position which he occupies in the institutional structure of the Council of Europe, to promote a global conception of human rights in Europe that went beyond that which emerges from the Rome Convention. In this connection, there would probably be no obstacle to the Secretary-General, on the occasion of the yearly implementation of article 57, submitting to European public opinion a report which, in this field, could become the equivalent of the report on "the State of the Union" familiar to several federal States.

2. THE EUROPEAN SOCIAL CHARTER

According to the Special Message of the Committee of Ministers of the Council of Europe of 20 May 1954 announcing the beginning of work on a European Social Charter, the purpose of the latter was to determine the social objectives that Member States will seek to attain, and to guide the action of the Council of Europe in the social field. The Message also stated that the Charter would be *"the complement to the European Convention on Human Rights"* in that field. It is thus seen that, as regards the question of ensuring international protection for economic and social rights, the Council of Europe preferred to draw up a specific Convention; it would however have been perhaps possible to extend the protection ensured by the Convention on Human Rights to economic and social rights by means of additional Protocols.

There existed a precedent for the solution of two separate Conventions at the United Nations where, as has been seen above, two Covenants on human rights have been prepared. Moreover, there were several arguments in favour of such a solution. Thus, whereas civil and political rights are attributes of the human person, economic and social rights are claims that the individual can make on society. The first protect man's freedom; the second allow him to satisfy essential needs: food, housing and health. Thus, the first must be simply *respected* by the State which will refrain from interfering in any way with the exercise of those rights unless the necessities of social life make such interference unavoidable. It is not enough, however, for the second to be respected by the State: the State must, if not *realize* them, at least take responsibility for part of their realization. For the first, the State is the virtual enemy, that which most frequently impairs them. For the second, the State, instead of being the enemy, becomes the ally, sometimes the only ally.

Legal implementation likewise poses different problems: civil and political rights lend themselves without too much difficulty to application and judicial interpretation in the course of which the necessities of personal freedom and the imperatives of social life are carefully weighed, the balance tilting initially towards the side of the individual; economic and social rights, while not being absent in the courts, come before the courts only in the form of claims against the State and requests for protection addressed to the State.

These are some of the reasons which led the Council of Europe to follow the example of the United Nations. To these should be added a circumstantial reason: despite their political homogeneity which made it possible for a Convention for the protection of civil and political rights to be rapidly drawn up, the Member States of the Council of Europe are not at the same stage of economic development: in this regard one has only to compare the standard of living of the Scandinavian countries and the Balkan countries. The former may have been able to assume the costs resulting from the exercise of economic and social rights by everyone; for the latter, most of these rights could be, at most, objectives of a more or less long term social policy. These disparities account for the highly distinctive features of the machinery for the implementation of the rights included in the Social Charter.

It took a particularly long time to draw up the Social Charter, the preparatory work undertaken in 1954 being terminated only in 1961. Very early on the International Labour Organisation was associated with that work: in December 1958 a tripartite conference composed according to the principles of the ILO was even convened to consider the draft Charter prepared by the government experts.

The Social Charter was finally signed at Turin on 18 October 1961. It entered into force only on 26 February 1965. As of 1 January 1982, thirteen of the twenty-one Member States of the Council of Europe had ratified it:

Austria, Cyprus, Denmark, Federal Republic of Germany, France, Iceland, Ireland, Italy, Netherlands, Norway, Spain, Sweden and the United Kingdom.

(a). Rights protected by the Social Charter

The list of protected rights bears witness to the desire of the Member States of the Council of Europe to show their political unity in the social field while taking into account their *economic disparities*.

The Member States reveal their *political unity* by accepting, as the aim of a policy which they intend to pursue, "by all appropriate means, both national and international in character, the attainment of conditions in which the following rights and principles may be effectively realised": right to an occupation, right to just conditions of work, right to safe and healthy working conditions, right to fair remuneration, right to freedom of association, right to bargain collectively, right of children and young persons to protection, right of employed women to protection, right to vocational guidance, right to vocational training, right to health protection, right to social security, right to social and medical assistance, right to benefit from social welfare services, right of disabled persons to protection; right of the family to social, legal and economic protection, right of mothers and children to social and economic protection, right to work in a country other than one's own, right of migrant workers and their families to protection and assistance.

Under the terms of Part I of the Charter, these rights are first of all the *aims* of a policy common to all the Contracting States. At this stage, they consequently have no binding character in regard to those States or, more precisely, they are binding on them only as components of an overall policy in the social field.

However, the Social Charter is not merely a declaration of the principles of a social policy concerned with the *protection* of individuals. Part III of the Charter in fact returns, in 19 articles, to the different above-mentioned rights in order to give them, this time, a precise legal definition and content and consequently to define the scope of the undertakings of the Contracting States in regard to each of them. Among others, the right to an occupation of article 1 is defined in four paragraphs which constitute so many obligations for the Contracting States, the right to fair remuneration is defined in five paragraphs and the right of children and young people to protection in ten paragraphs.

In becoming Contracting Parties to the Social Charter, the Member States of the Council of Europe are not consequently and automatically bound by all the nineteen articles of Part II. A choice is available to them which allows the degree of their undertaking to be adjusted to their economic and social conditions. After affirming their unity, the Member States thus concern themselves with their *disparities*.

The choice offered, however, is not altogether free since it is exercised within what has been called the "double minimum floating nucleus".

Under article 20 of the Charter indeed, to become a Contracting Party, a State must undertake:

- to consider itself bound by at least five of seven articles of the Charter (articles 1, 5, 6, 12, 13, 16 and 19) which contain rights considered to be essential: right to an occupation, right to freedom of association, right to bargain collectively, right to social security, right to social and medical assistance, right of the family to social, legal and economic protection, right of migrant workers and their families to protection and assistance;
- to consider itself bound by an additional number of articles or numbered paragraphs, provided that the *total* number of articles and paragraphs thus accepted is not less than 10 articles (out of 19) or 45 numbered paragraphs (out of 68).

Whereas the aim of the inner nucleus (five rights out of seven), regardless of the combination selected, is to obtain protection for essential economic and social rights, the outer nucleus (ten rights out of nineteen) constitutes the beginning of protection for all economic and social rights. Despite its complexity which results in differences between the undertakings of the Contracting States, the system of the Social Charter has the advantage of being flexible, of being aligned to a reality made up of disparities and differences, and of leaving the door open to the future since each State is invited progressively to extend its undertakings.

(b). Implementation of the Social Charter

Like the European Convention on Human Rights, the Social Charter provides a machinery of implementation as a means of supervising the observance, by Contracting States, of their undertakings. Although it is not as effective in comparison with that of the Convention, the machinery of the Charter is just as complex.

(i). ORGAN OF IMPLEMENTATION OF THE CHARTER

Four organs have a role here, the first two being specific to the Social Charter which provides for their establishment, the two others being statutory organs of the Council of Europe. Furthermore, as will be seen, both the International Labour Office and international organizations of employers and workers have a role to play in the working of the Charter.

The Committee of Experts consists of not more than seven members appointed by the Committee of Ministers of the Council of Europe from a list of independent experts of the highest integrity and of recognized competence in international social questions. Proposed by the Contracting States, they are appointed for six years, a period sufficiently long for their independence not to suffer from any concern about re-election. The Social Charter provides no further particulars concerning the appointment procedure or the qualifications required of the candidates. These questions have been settled by the Committee of Ministers.

The Governmental Committee of the Social Charter is composed of one representative of each of the Contracting States; this is an organ which is the expression of governments: they alone decide on the term of office of the members of the Sub-Committee, define the positions that they shall adopt, etc.

The Consultative Assembly, which is one of the statutory organs of the Council of Europe, is composed of representatives of the Member States, elected by their parliaments or appointed according to a procedure determined by them. Although without power in that its competence is purely consultative, the Assembly is not without influence, insofar as it is a truly parliamentary organ, representing European public opinion within the peoples of the Member States. In this capacity the part it plays in the working of the Charter is such as to ensure that its observance is supervised by the people.

The Committee of Ministers, the organ which is competent to act within the Council of Europe, does not in fact possess, according to the Statute of the Council, any more than the power to make recommendations to Member States. The Social Charter does not modify the nature of its power since, as will be seen, only *recommendations* can be addressed by the Committee to the Contracting States. But the Charter has facilitated the exercise of that power and thereby no doubt increased its effectiveness: whereas, according to the Statute of the Council of Europe, recommendations to Member States must be unanimously adopted, only a majority of two-thirds is required for the Committee of Ministers to be able to make recommendations relating to the Social Charter.

(ii). PROCEDURE FOR THE IMPLEMENTATION OF THE SOCIAL CHARTER

The implementation procedure appears complex and has proved from experience to be fairly slow. It is entirely founded upon the reports of the Contracting States and consequently knows nothing of the machinery of State and individual complaints.

Thus, the Contracting States are obliged to submit to the Secretary-General of the Council of Europe, every two years, a report relating to the application of the provisions which they have accepted. Furthermore, the Committee of Ministers may request the Contracting States to submit, "at appropriate intervals", reports relating to the provisions which they have not accepted".[6] The system here is one which is clearly inspired by the International Labour Organisation. Copies of all reports must be sent to national organizations of employers and trade unions which are members of international organizations invited to be represented at meetings of the Governmental Committee.

These national organizations may make comments on the reports, which will be transmitted, if they so request, to the Secretary-General of the Council of Europe.

The national reports together with any comments forwarded by national organizations of employers and trade unions are examined by the Committee of Independent Experts in whose deliberations a representative of the International Labour Organisation may participate in a consultative capacity. Following this examination, which will lead to "conclusions" being formulated by the Committee of Experts, the reports and the said conclusions are submitted for examination to the Governmental Committee. That Committee does not sit alone: it invites no more than two international organizations of employers and no more than two international trade union organizations to send observers in a consultative capacity to its meetings. In addition, the Committee may—it is thus a possibility open to it and not an obligation as before—consult with no more than two representatives of international non-governmental organizations having consultative status with the Council of Europe on matters in which those organizations are "particularly qualified". The Governmental Committee, with this assistance, has to draw up, for the Committee of Ministers, a report containing its conclusions and append the report of the Committee of Experts. The Committee of Ministers also has before it the opinion of the Consultative Assembly concerning the report of the Committee of Experts which is communicated to it at the same time as to the Governmental Committee. It is to be noted that, even though the Assembly is expressly called upon to formulate an opinion only on the report of the Committee of Experts, and not on that of the Governmental Committee, in actual fact its opinion bears upon both reports at the same time.

Once in possession of the reports of the Contracting States, the reports of the Committee of Experts and the Governmental Committee and the views of the Consultative Assembly, the Committee of Ministers must express its opinion, that is to say ensure that the observance by the Contracting States of the provisions of the Social Charter is supervised. The Committee of Ministers, admirably informed as it is, is not competent to take decisions: it may merely make "to each Contracting Party any necessary recommendations". The outcome of this highly complex procedure thus appears fairly disappointing. Nevertheless, two facts point to its importance:

a) the Committee of Ministers may adopt its recommendations not unanimously but by a majority of two-thirds of the members entitled to sit on it (12 votes out of 18);

b) the recommendations are not *general*, but may be made to *each* of the Contracting States; consequently, individual sanction, although only of a purely moral character, nonetheless exists.

It should be pointed out that the Social Charter does not provide for cases where a Contracting State takes no account of the recommendations of the

Committee of Ministers. Perhaps recourse could then be had to the Statute of the Council of Europe which provides that a Member State that has seriously violated human rights and fundamental freedoms may be asked to withdraw from the Organization.

Six periods of supervision of the application of the European Social Charter have so far taken place; the seventh, which bears on the period 1981-1982 is still under way. From one period to another there has been a strengthening of the role of the ultimate organ of supervision, the Committee of Ministers, which no longer merely transmits critical reports to the Contracting States but now also calls the attention of States to the measures required for their legislation and practice to be in conformity with the obligations resulting from the Charter. The dialogue between the supervisory organs of the Charter and the governments of the States party to it is essentially founded upon the conclusions of the Committee of Experts, some of which, moreover, are challenged by the Governmental Committee. A genuine jurisprudence of European social law is thus being established, the originators of which are first of all the Committee of Experts and then the Governmental Committee of the Social Charter. But, above all, thanks to this regular application, several tangible measures have been taken, in order to provide better protection for economic and social rights in practically all of the Contracting States.

The Social Charter is thus tending to become what its authors wanted it to be: the complement to the European Convention on Human Rights.

NOTES

1. The provisions concerning them are analyzed above, Chapter 7, *supra*. Furthermore, in the tables in the present chapter a list is given of the most important cases, in which the organs of the Convention have interpreted and applied these provisions.

2. This provision has enabled the Cypriot member of the Commission to continue to hold office, although his term of office expired long ago. However, as there is no Cypriot delegation in the Assembly, no list of candidates could have been submitted to the Committee of Ministers.

3. See the "Rules adopted by the Committee of Ministers relating to Article 54 of the European Convention on Human Rights" (adopted in February 1976), in *Collected Texts. European Convention on Human Rights*, revised 30 January 1976, p. 507.

4. See the "Rules adopted by the Committee of Ministers for the application of Article 32 of the Convention", in *Collected Texts, European Convention on Human Rights*, August 1976, revised 30 January 1978, p. 501.

5. The United Kingdom also recognized the compulsory jurisdiction of the Court for some of the territories for whose international relations it has responsibility.

6. Such a decision was taken for the first time by the Committee of Ministers in January 1977.

17 The Organization of American States (OAS)

Héctor Gros Espiell

The Charter of the Organization of American States, signed at the 9th International Conference of American States (Bogotá, May 1948), contains several provisions relating to the fundamental rights of the human person. It is stated in the preamble that "the historic mission of America is to offer to man a land of liberty, and a favorable environment for the development of his personality and the realization of his just aspirations.[1]" In accordance with this mission, several of the principles reaffirmed by the American States relate to human rights. The latter are proclaimed to be "the fundamental rights of the individual without distinction as to race, nationality, creed or sex" and it is stipulated that "the solidarity of the American States and the high aims which are sought through it require the political organization of those States on the basis of the effective exercise of representative democracy"; it is stated that "social justice and social security are bases of lasting peace" and that "the education of peoples should be directed towards justice, freedom and peace," and the duty is imposed on States to respect human rights.[2] Similarly, articles 28, 29, 30 and 31 (Social and Cultural Standards) relate to human rights, but deal with the matter in the form of directives addressed to States which must recognize them and promote respect for them.

It is acknowledged in the Charter that the question of human rights is not subject exclusively to the internal jurisdiction of States and the possibility is envisaged of establishing legal provisions for their international protection. Despite the conciseness of the text, the Charter does not merely "proclaim" the rights of the individual but, in addition, it recognizes the duty of the State to respect them. Although not specifying the respective competences of its organs in regard to the protection of human rights—thus marking a step backwards in relation to the Charter of the United Nations—the Bogotá Charter represented, in America, a step towards the international recognition of human rights.

The conception of human rights as it emerged from the Charter was an integral conception, allowing for no form of discrimination, recognizing, alongside traditional civil and political rights, economic, social and cultural rights, and emphasizing that justice is the basis of lasting peace.

Institutionalized in 1948, the OAS marked the culmination of a process that began in 1889 at the time of the first Inter-American Conference. The Charter was the "consecration" of an international organization "established to achieve an order of peace and justice." The inter-American system was also integrated into the universal system of the United Nations as a regional agency.[3]

The principles proclaimed at Bogotá in the matter of human rights conformed to criteria which had been worked out throughout the course of development of Pan-Americanism. The affirmation, at the international level, of human rights in the inter-American system was the consequence of the recognition of the existence of an interdependent democracy in America.[4] At the Conference of Chapultepec in 1945, this idea was developed as follows: "The goal of the State is man's happiness in society. The interests of society must be harmonized with the rights of the individual. The American man cannot conceive of living without justice. Nor can he conceive of living without liberty".[5] And, the same Resolution, entitled "International protection of human rights", proclaimed the adherence of the American republics to the principles enshrined in international law for safeguarding the fundamental rights of man by advocating a system for the international protection of those rights. The Inter-American Juridical Committee was instructed to prepare a preliminary draft declaration of rights and the Governing Board of the Pan American Union was requested to convene a conference of jurists in order to approve this draft declaration as a convention.

Shortly afterwards, the Uruguayan note of 21 November 1945 initiated a vast debate on the question. Starting from the idea that it was necessary to protect human rights at the international level, it envisaged the problem by proposing that a system of multi-lateral intervention be studied. This was a mistake for, instead of suggesting the preparation of an international declaration and convention in which the means of protecting human rights would be established, it chose to propose a method which, on account of its vague and interventionist character, was inevitably to give rise to relentless opposition.[6]

The Inter-American Treaty of Reciprocal Assistance (Rio de Janeiro, 1947) affirmed that peace is founded "on the international recognition and protection of human rights and freedoms, on the indispensable well-being of the people, and on the effectiveness of democracy for the international realization of justice and security".[7]

At Bogotá, human rights were to find a place among the fundamental principles of the system. At the same time, in once again preparing the text relating to the principle of non-intervention, condemning both individual and multilateral intervention, the system for the protection of human rights as suggested in the note of November 1945 was rejected, in view of the fact that among the cases of collective action—a different concept from that of multilateral intervention—none was envisaged on the grounds of a violation of human rights.[8]

The principles proclaimed in article 5 of the Charter, far from constituting simple objectives laid down for the purpose of determining the conduct of the American States at the international level, are legally binding norms, that is to say, specific sources of duties for the American States.[9] True, the provisions of paragraph (j) of article 5 constitute norms which, to be fully and totally applied, need to be developed in other texts in which human rights would be listed and in which a system would be established by way of a convention, capable of affording effective protection for those rights; they nevertheless retain a legally binding character which is undeniable if they are considered in the light of article 13 of the Charter.

Despite the deep-seated divergencies in respect of the way in which the protection of human rights should be envisaged and which prevented any further progress being made in settling this question,[10] marking a step backwards in relation to the Chapultepec resolution (which had been in favour of "an international system of protection"), it was at Bogotá that the "American Declaration of the Rights and Duties of Man" was approved (Resolution XXX). This Declaration, approved some months before the adoption of the "Universal Declaration of Human Rights" by the United Nations, proclaimed in a broad and liberal text, the rights and duties of man. The rights of man were recognized as being "based upon attributes of his human personality," linked to duties, since "the fulfilment of duty by each individual is a prerequisite to the rights of all. It was stated that the rights of man are limited by the rights of others, by the security of all, and by the just demands of the general welfare and the advancement of democracy." It was declared that "the international protection of the rights of man should be the principal guide of an evolving American law" and that the list of rights established in the Declaration together with the guarantees given by the internal regimes of the states constitute "the initial system of protection considered by the American States as being suited to the present social and juridical conditions, not without a recognition on their part that they should increasingly strengthen that system in the international field as conditions become more favourable."[11] Resolution XXIX approved the "Inter-American Charter of Social Guarantees."[12] As economic and social rights had not been included in the Declaration, it was indispensable that a complementary text be established, for it was necessary to demand that democratic regimes respect political freedoms and the spirit and application of the postulates of social justice.[13] The Conference of Bogotá requested the Inter-American Juridical Committee to prepare the statutes of an Inter-American Court for the Protection of Human Rights (Resolution XXXI). In addition, two Conventions on the civil and political rights of women were adopted.

The years that followed were not marked by much progress. But this did not mean that the matter had been abandoned. The 10th Inter-American

Conference (Caracas, 1954) adopted Resolution XXVII which reaffirmed, systematically, all that had so far been achieved and took measures to encourage studies in comparative law and to ensure the dissemination of knowledge on this subject. In Resolution XXIX it was decided that the Council of the Organization would continue to study the jurisdictional aspects of the international protection of human rights with a view to examining the possibility of setting up an international Court.

At that time, the international situation of the American States was hardly conducive to a process allowing for much progress in this field. The Inter-American Juridical Committee observed, in addition, that the absence of positive law on the subject constituted an obstacle to the application of Resolution XXXI of the Bogotá Conference. For this reason it recommended that a Convention be prepared which, using the method adopted by the United Nations when they decided to prepare the Covenants on Human Rights, was to provide for the obligation to respect certain rights and establish an international system for their protection.

At the Meeting of Consultation of Washington (1951) Resolutions VII and IX were approved concerning the international protection of human rights and the improvement of economic, social and cultural levels. Several years were to elapse before the process got under way again, at the 5th Meeting of Consultation (Santiago, Chile, 1959). American law was ready for the establishment of an international system for the protection of human rights to be attempted. It was recognized from that time onwards that this subject was not solely a matter of the domestic jurisdiction of each State, that international regulations were possible and that the machinery of protection to be established by way of a Convention between the States did not constitute a violation of the sovereignty of those States.[14] To get beyond the stages already covered since 1948, the same approach had to be adopted as had governed the preparation of the American Declaration of the Rights and Duties of Man: a declaration together with a system of implementation solely at the level of municipal law constituted "the initial system of protection" to which an international system had to be joined which would foster the promotion and protection of human rights "as conditions become more favourable."

From the political point of view, the consequence of the repeated violations of human rights perpetrated by the Trujillo regime in the Dominican Republic and their external projection in the form of acts of intervention which endangered peace and security made it favourable for a new stage to be initiated in the process aimed at ensuring the international protection of human rights.[15] At the 5th Meeting of Consultation measures were taken towards the preparation of an American Convention on Human Rights. Seeking to set up a complementary system, the immediate creation of the Inter-American Commission on Human Rights was decided (Resolution VIII). The Declaration of Santiago, approved at the same Meeting, also listed in general terms the basic principles of Resolution VIII.[16]

Before considering the Inter-American Commission on Human Rights and the American Convention on Human Rights, I shall examine the amendments made by the Protocol of Buenos Aires of 27 February 1967 to the Bogotá Charter in regard to the question of human rights, with the exception of the two points already indicated, which will be dealt with separately.

Article 5 of the Charter, in which the American States reaffirmed the fundamental principles of the system, and which became article 3, was not modified. No change was made in paragraphs d, h, j and l. Nor was there any modification of article 13, which became article 16. But if one takes a look at the passages relating to economic standards (articles 26 and 27), social standards (articles 28 and 29) and cultural standards (articles 30 and 31) it is seen that a set of new provisions have been included which proclaim, at the international level, the economic, social and cultural rights which the State Members undertook to respect, guarantee and promote. They thus pledged themselves "to a united effort to ensure social justice in the Hemisphere" (art. 29), devoting themselves to that end to achieving the basic goals listed in article 31.

Convinced that "man can only achieve the full realization of his aspirations within a just social order" (art. 43), they decided to dedicate every effort to the application of the following principles:

"All human beings, without distinction as to race, sex, nationality creed or social condition, have a right to material well-being and to their spiritual development, under circumstances of liberty, dignity, equality of opportunity, and economic security;

Work is a right and a social duty, it gives dignity to the one who performs it, and it should be performed under conditions, including a system of fair wages, that ensure life, health, and a decent standard of living for the worker and his family, both during his working years and in his old age, or when any circumstance deprives him of the possibility of working;

Employers and workers, both rural and urban, have the right to strike, and recognition of the juridical personality of associations and the protection of their freedom and independence, all in accordance with applicable laws."

The Member States will exert the greatest efforts, in accordance with their constitutional processes, to ensure the effective exercise of the right to education and to ensure that the benefits of culture are available to the entire population, on the bases established in articles 47 and 48, among which the following deserve to be emphasized:

"Elementary education, compulsory for children of school age, shall also be offered to all others who can benefit from it. When provided by the State it shall be without charge;

Middle-level education shall be extended progressively to as much of the population as possible, with a view to social improvement...

Higher education shall be available to all...."

Thus the revised Charter of the OAS included a declaration of economic, social and cultural rights, but not a declaration of civil and political rights which were listed only in the American Declaration of the Rights and Duties of Man.

However, since the entry into force, in 1978, of the American Convention, civil and political rights have been covered by a new instrument which provides for a specific system of international protection. As for economic, social and cultural rights which, according to the "Pact of San José," are defined by the amended Charter, problems will continue to arise until the Member States have fulfilled their undertaking to adopt new internal provisions and to have recourse to international co-operation so as progressively to ensure that these rights are fully effective. Since the entry into force of the Protocol of Buenos Aires, the General Assembly has continued to deal with the question of human rights, in particular when it has had to consider the reports of the Inter-American Commission on Human Rights.[17]

The conception of the rights of the individual affirmed in the inter-American system starts off from the idea that man has rights which are inherent in his own nature, which predate the existence of the State and which are not the result of juridical attributions. Thus, municipal law and international law do not create rights but contribute, each in its own sphere, and in a harmonious manner, to their affirmation and protection. This is a conception which is directly bound up with democracy as a form assumed by the State and as a political and philosophical idea.

1. THE INTER-AMERICAN COMMISSION ON HUMAN RIGHTS

The 5th Meeting of Consultation of Ministers of Foreign Affairs created, by its Resolution VIII, an Inter-American Commission on Human Rights. This resolution originated from a feeling that the way had been paved in the hemisphere for the conclusion of an agreement. Consequently, it was stipulated that a Convention on Human Rights be prepared and, at the same time, that an Inter-American Commission on Human Rights be set up. The Commission was thus created by a resolution of a Meeting of Consultation as a complementary measure, which provided for the preparation of a draft Convention.

The Commission could not be a new organ of the Organization, for such an organ could be created only by the Inter-American Conference (art. 33) and not by a Meeting of Consultation of Ministers of Foreign Affairs (art. 39). Neither could it be a specialized organization (art.130), nor an organ of the Council. The competence of the Commission presented problems since, having been created by a simple resolution, the Commission could not be assigned the task of promoting respect for human rights in the broad sense; this would have been tantamount to giving it powers corresponding to those of the organs for the protection of human rights which were to be created by the Convention whose preparation had been ordered by Resolution VIII. These were the reasons for the reservations formulated by the delegation of Uruguay.

The Council of the Organization approved the Statute of the Commission in May and June 1960. This first text was immediately modified by the Council itself, so as to place the problem within the limits of the resolution providing for the creation of the Commission.[18] The Statute defined it as "an autonomous entity of the Organization of American States, the function of which is to promote respect for human rights" (art.1). It is stipulated that for the purpose of the Statute "human rights are understood to be those set forth in the American Declaration of the Rights and Duties of Man" (art.2). This provision gave to the American Declaration of 1948 a possibility of application which had been lacking until then and a specific scope which far exceeded the modest functions which had been envisaged at Bogotá.[19]

After dealing with the membership of the Commission (arts.3-8), the Statute assigned to it, in article 9, several specific powers for it to be able to carry out its function of promoting respect for human rights. The Statute dealt at the same time with matters relating to the Commission's headquarters, meetings, quorum, voting, Secretariat and amendments to the Statute. Once created, the Commission itself, in pursuance of its Statute, established its Regulations,[20] which opened the way to a possible expansion of its powers, particularly with regard to the procedure for considering communications.[21] The Commission endeavoured, unsuccessfully, to have its Statute amended so as to broaden its powers, particularly in respect of the examination of claims or communications. But the Council did not take action on its requests, despite the recommendation of the 8th Meeting of Consultation.[22]

It was the 2nd Special Inter-American Conference (November 1965) which decided, by its resolution XXII, originating with the Commission and in accordance with the opinion of the Secretary-General of the OAS himself,[23] to enlarge the sphere of competence of the Inter-American Commission on Human Rights along the lines mentioned previously. This resolution resulted in the Statute of the Commission being amended. In addition to certain amendments made for the purpose of making its working and administrative organization more effective (art.7A and 14A), article 9A was added to the Statute, giving the Commission additional functions and powers. What was involved was no longer merely promoting human rights in the strict sense. In addition, the Commission was to be given powers in the matter of supervision and control, assigning it responsibility for the examination and investigation of communications and complaints; henceforth, the Commission could request reports from Governments and submit to the Inter-American Conference or the Meeting of Consultation an annual report comprising a general statement and observations on matters covered in communications concerning which it had to verify whether the internal legal procedures and remedies of Member States had been duly applied and exhausted. The Commission thus became a body whose powers were complex and which related not only to the promotion, but also to the protection, of human rights.

Resolution XXII, by which the Inter-American Conference approved the new mandate of the Commission, removed the juridical flaw involved in its creation but did not completely eliminate the objection according to which a body invested with powers such as those assigned to the Commission should be created by a special convention. It was for this reason that several States abstained from voting, although favourable to the objectives of the international protection of human rights.[24] Thanks to these amendments to its Statute, the Commission was in a position to develop considerably its activities.

The Protocol of Buenos Aires relating to the amendment of the Charter of the OAS, resulting from a process marked by the 2nd Special Inter-American Conference, the Special Meeting of Panama and the 3rd Special Inter-American Conference of Buenos Aires,[25] fundamentally modified the Inter-American Commission on Human Rights, the existence and mandate of which it firmly established. The Commission became one of the organs through which the Organization would accomplish its purposes (art. 51, 3). Article 112, which provides for the existence of the Commission, assigned to it as its principal function "to promote the observance and protection of human rights and to serve as a consultative organ of the Organization in these matters." To this was added that "an inter-American convention on human rights shall determine the structure, competence and procedure of this Commission."

Most significantly, however, article 150 provided that, until the entry into force of the Inter-American Convention the existing Commission "shall keep vigilance over the observance of human rights." This provision made it possible to assert that the Commission's competence was not limited to promoting respect for human rights but also involved exercising a role of supervision and control since the Commission was entrusted with the examination of communications or complaints. Thus the enlarged powers of the Commission, decided at Rio de Janeiro in 1965, were regularized by means of a convention.[26]

Resolution VIII of the 5th Meeting of Consultation also established the composition, method of election, etc. of the Commission. These matters are also dealt with in the Statute of the Inter-American Commission on Human Rights adopted by the Ninth Ordinary Session of the General Assembly of the OAS in La Paz, Bolivia, in October 1979. Under the terms of the Statute, which took effect in November 1979, the seven members of the Commission are elected by secret ballot, in their personal capacity, by the Council of the Organization, from a list on which each Member State may propose three specialists as candidates. The members of the Commission must be nationals of the Member States of the Organization; they are elected for their high moral character and their recognized competence in the field of human rights. They represent all the Member States of the Organization and act in its name. They are elected for four years and may be re-elected only once. The Commission elects its Chairman and two Vice-Chairmen each of whom hold office for one year and who may be re-elected only once in each four-year period.

The permanent headquarters of the Commission is in Washington, D.C., but it may meet and discharge its duties in the territory of any American State when it so decides by an absolute majority of votes, and with the consent, or at the invitation, of the government concerned. As a transitory provision, the Regulations adopted by the Commission in 1967 shall apply until it adopts new regulations. However, in any event, a resolution adopted by the Permanent Council of the OAS in September 1978 provides that the Commission shall apply its *new* Statute and Regulations *only* to those states that have ratified the American Convention. Thus the pre-1979 arrangements will continue to apply to those OAS States which are not parties to the Convention.

The Secretariat services of the Commission are provided by a specialized functional unit of the General Secretariat of the OAS. The emoluments and travel expenses of the members of the Commission and the administrative expenses of the Secretariat are provided for in the budget of the Organization.

In carrying out its assignment of promoting respect for human rights, the Commission has the following functions and powers: to develop an awareness of human rights among the peoples of America; to encourage governments to promulgate progressive measures, within the framework of their domestic legislation, for the realization of human rights, and to adopt, in accordance with their constitutional precepts, appropriate measures to ensure the faithful observance of those rights; to prepare studies or reports; to urge the Governments of the Member States to supply it with information on the measures adopted by them in the field of human rights; to serve the OAS as an advisory body in respect of human rights.

Listed in article 9 of its Statute, these powers of the Commission result directly from its first function—the promotion of respect for human rights. They did not entail the attribution of any competence to take decisions concerning particular cases of violation of human rights or to examine communications or complaints relating to individual situations. But, in being assigned the function of making recommendations to governments for them to adopt progressive measures in favour of human rights within the framework of their domestic legislation and, in accordance with their constitutional precepts, appropriate measures to ensure the faithful observance of those rights, and in being given the possibility of requesting governments to supply it with information on the measures adopted by them in the field of human rights, a path was opened to the Commission which, if circumstances were favourable, made possible a juristic development such as to bring about an enlargement of its powers.

The revision of the Statute by Resolution XXII of the 2nd Special Inter-American Conference, which resulted in article 9 bis, remedied this situation. It made it possible for the Commission's powers to be enlarged and, in addi-

tion, enabled the problem to be centered not only on the rights declared by
the municipal law of the American States but also on the rights proclaimed in
the American Declaration of the Rights and Duties of Man.[27]

Thus, from 1965 onwards, the Commission, in addition to its initial powers,
was instructed: "To examine communications submitted to it and any other
available information; to address the government of any American State for
information deemed pertinent by the Commission; and to make recommendations when it deems this appropriate, with the objective of bringing about
more effective observance of fundamental human rights; to submit a report
annually to the Inter-American Conference or to the Meeting of Consultation
of Ministers of Foreign Affairs, which should include: a) a statement of progress achieved in realization of the goals set forth in the American Declaration; b) a statement of areas in which further steps are needed to give effect
to the human rights set forth in the American Declaration; and c) such observations as the Commission may deem appropriate on matters covered in the
communications submitted to it and in other information available to the
Commission."

In the exercise of its powers relating to communications submitted to it,
the Commission must first of all verify whether the internal remedies of each
State have been duly applied and exhausted. In examining the communication, it may apply to any American State to obtain information deemed pertinent by it. It may also make recommendations "with the objective of bringing
about more effective observance of fundamental human rights."

The Commission must also submit a report annually to the Inter-American
Conference or the Meeting of Consultation of Ministers of Foreign Affairs. In
this report it may call the attention of the supreme organ of the inter-American
system not only to the general situation of human rights in America and the
measures to be adopted for its improvement, but also to particular cases
covered by communications.

By means of its Regulations adopted in 1967, the Commission enlarged the
powers provided for by its Statute, particularly as regards "communications
or claims addressed to the Commission." It was not considered enough to
determine the formal conditions to be met by communications (art. 37) and
grounds for inadmissibility (art. 39), but it was also stipulated that communications must be addressed to the Commission within a reasonable period of
time, in the judgement of the Commission, from the date of occurrence of the
supposed violation (art. 40). Regulations were established concerning the
procedure to be followed: Examination of evidence and observation *in loco*
were provided for (art. 50), together with a special procedure for denunciations of the violation of those human rights which, provided for in the Declaration, are listed in Resolution XXII, 2, of the 2nd Special Inter-American
Conference. In this connection, it is stipulated that the occurrence of the
events on which information has been requested will be presumed to be
confirmed if the Government referred to has not supplied such information

within 180 days of the request, provided always, that the invalidity of the events denounced is not shown by other elements of proof, and on the understanding that the Commission may make an extension of the term of 180 days (art. 51).

In 1979 the General Assembly of the OAS approved the new Statute of the Commission. The new Statute incorporates important amendments to the preceding text, which were the outcome of the experience gained in the course of the Commission's work and the application of its previous Statute and Regulations, and also takes into account the implications of the entry into force of the Pact of San José and the need for distinguishing between the competence of the Commission as an organ of the inter-American system in respect of all the Member States of the OAS and the competence of the same Commission as an organ of the Pact of San José with reference to States Parties to it.

The Commission has realized an important achievement, the most outstanding aspects of which deserve to be emphasized. It has always understood its powers in the broadest sense and in the manner most suited for it to be able to exercise its functions with the greatest effectiveness. In promoting respect for human rights in America, it has carried out important work in developing a system of periodic information submitted by governments on civil, political, economic, social and cultural rights,[28] in disseminating information on problems relating to those rights, either through the preparation of studies,[29] the dissemination of texts, the organization of conferences, or through the creation of national commissions on human rights, the organization of seminars and competitions, the granting of scholarships, etc.

As a technical advisory body of the inter-American system in the field of human rights, the Commission has each year collected a substantial amount of information, and has made an extremely important contribution to the preparation of the American Convention on Human Rights and to that of the Draft Inter-American Convention on Freedom of Expression, Information and Investigation. In carrying out its task of obtaining information and in taking action in particular situations concerning several American States, the Commission has had to perform the difficult task of analyzing the situation regarding human rights in each of the Member States.[30]

Lastly, in examining the questions raised by individual communications and taking decisions in that connection, the Commission has developed an extremely interesting case-law which has made it possible for the provisions of its Statute and Regulations to be effectively applied.

The Commission has already examined many thousands of communications. Thus, for example, during 1978 it opened 1044 separate cases of alleged human rights violations. In accordance with its Statute (Art. 9(bis) c) the Commission's Annual Report contains observations only on cases which have been processed and examined during the period covered by the report, and in which a disregard for human rights has been confirmed and the appropriate recommendations have been made to the government concerned. Thus the 1978 report contained the Commission's observations relating to 37 cases involving 5 countries.[31]

In the case-law established by the Commission in examining communications, two points deserve to be stressed:[32]

a) the criterion according to which the prior exhaustion of domestic remedies must be taken to mean judicial remedies: the fact that a non-judicial remedy is pending does not prevent recourse to the Commission;[33] and

b) the distinction between particular cases and general cases: in general cases, the Commission may undertake an examination as to substance without it being necessary for domestic remedies to have been exhausted (art. 9A, para. 4).[34]

For over twenty years the Commission has accomplished important work. Its contribution to the promotion of respect for human rights and to the development of collective awareness of human rights is undeniable. The bulk of its work has not had any immediate impact on the observance of human rights in America and this is due to factors of a general nature which hinder and impede the full application of human rights in that continent. Moreover, its relentless and sustained action, although it has attracted the attention of specialists,[35] has not benefited from the support of the information media, and primarily the press. The peoples of America are still not aware at present of the work achieved by the Commission or of the possibilities afforded by its Statute for denouncing violations of human rights on the American continent and submitting relevant complaints.

Under its pre-1979 Statute the Commission has limited possibilities for action, particularly in regard to individual cases, in which complementary action by the OAS General Assembly is required. Moreover, the latter body was generally content, until recent years, merely to take note of the Commission's annual reports without taking any other action. This is no longer the case, however, as is exemplified by the resolution adopted by the Ninth Ordinary Session of the OAS General Assembly in October 1979 (OEA/Ser.P, AG/doc.1224/79). In its resolution, the General Assembly, *inter alia*, declared "that the practice of disappearance is an affront to the conscience of the hemisphere, and is totally contrary to our common traditional values and to the declarations and agreements signed by the American States" and endorsed "the Commission's recommendation for prompt clarification of the status of persons who have disappeared under circumstances described in the annual report." In addition to urging or appealing to particular governments to take action on human rights it required "the Commission to continue to monitor the exercise of human rights in Chile, Paraguay, and Uruguay, and to report thereon to the next regular session of the General Assembly."

It is also appropriate to mention that, in its 1977 annual report, the Commission recommended that a convention to make torture an international crime should be drafted. This was endorsed by the OAS General Assembly in 1978 (res. 368) and the draft subsequently prepared by the Commission was sent to the Inter-American Juridical Committee in 1980 for comments (OEA/Ser.G, CP/doc.1061/80).

The verdict on the work accomplished by the Commission is thus, in my opinion, a distinctly positive one. Its endeavours have been exemplary, particularly when one takes account of the limits within which it has been able to act and of the negative political factors which have influenced the OAS General Assembly. Overall the Commission has accomplished considerable work of great importance for the affirmation and observation of human rights in America.

2. THE AMERICAN CONVENTION ON HUMAN RIGHTS

Resolution VIII of the 5th Meeting of Consultation of Ministers of Foreign Affairs (Santiago, Chile, August 1959) recommended that the Inter-American Council of Jurists prepare a draft Convention on Human Rights together with a draft Convention on the creation of an Inter-American Court for the Protection of Human Rights and other suitable bodies to ensure the protection and observance of those rights.

At its 4th meeting held a few months later the Inter-American Council of Jurists performed this task and, on the basis of a text submitted by the delegation of Uruguay, it prepared a draft Convention which covered civil, political, economic, social and cultural rights and created, as bodies responsible for ensuring the observance of those rights, an Inter-American Commission on Human Rights and an Inter-American Court of Human Rights. However, as the 11th Inter-American Conference which was to examine the draft was not able to be held, it was not until 1965 that the prepared text was examined with a view to its being approved.

During this time the Inter-American Commission on Human Rights, also created at the 5th Meeting of Consultation by virtue of the same Resolution VIII, had started work and had expressed the wish that it be allowed to examine the draft Convention prepared by the Inter-American Council of Jurists.

At the 2nd Special Inter-American Conference, held at Rio de Janeiro (November 1965), which was instructed to study this question, the Governments of Chile and Uruguay submitted draft conventions to replace that prepared in 1959. The question was studied by the 4th Commission of the Conference. Under Resolution XXIV, the Santiago draft and the Chilean and Uruguayan drafts were submitted to the Council of the Organization so that it might, after hearing the Inter-American Commission on Human Rights and such other bodies and entities as it might deem desirable, make any amendments that it considered necessary to the original draft.

It was agreed that the draft would be submitted to the Governments to enable them to formulate observations and propose amendments and that subsequently the Council of the Organization would convene an Inter-American Specialized Conference to examine it. The draft was submitted to the Inter-American Commission on Human Rights which examined it thoroughly and formulated its opinion in two parts, approved on 21 October 1966 and 10 January 1967.[36] This opinion which went over the amendments proposed by the Commission was examined by the Council of the OAS. In accordance with the proposals of its Committee on Juridical-Political Affairs, the Council made a particular point of consulting governments as to whether the regional system should co-exist with the universal system, represented by the Covenants opened to signature in 1966 by the United Nations General Assembly.[37] After examining the observations received together with other elements on which to base its judgement, the Commission decided in favour of the possible co-existence of the two systems.[38]

Shortly afterwards the Council of the Organization adopted the new revised draft Convention, established by the Commission, as a working document intended for the Inter-American Specialized Conference and it transmitted the draft to the Governments for them to formulate observations and submit amendments .[39]

On receipt of the observations of several States[40], the Conference convened the special Conference in San José, Costa Rica from 7 to 22 November 1969 which prepared the text of the Convention. Once approved, it was signed on 22 November 1969 by twelve Latin American States.

The American Convention on Human Rights, the direct sources of which are the Santiago draft of 1959, the Chilean and Uruguayan drafts and the draft of the Inter-American Commission on Human Rights, is modeled, by way of these sources, on the American Declaration of the Rights and Duties of Man of 1948, the Universal Declaration of Human Rights of 1948, the Rome Convention of 1950, the case-law and practice of the organs created by that international instrument, and the United Nations Covenants on Civil and Political Rights and on Economic, Social and Cultural Rights.[41] But it follows a plan and adopts solutions which are very often specific to it. Although it refers frequently to the aforementioned sources, in numerous instances the Convention adopts formulae modeled on previous texts of the inter-American system or created in the course of the complex drafting process.

An Inter-American Convention was proposed between 1959 and 1965 when the adoption of the two Covenants on Human Rights by the United Nations seemed to be in difficulty. When, in 1966, the process was near completion and the two Covenants and the additional Protocol to the Covenant on Civil and Political Rights were opened for signature, the problem again arose as to whether it was necessary to prepare a regional instrument for the protection of human rights in the hemisphere, an instrument which, in the future, would have to co-exist with the universal Covenants, or whether, on the contrary, the regional draft should be abandoned.

After considering this question and consulting governments, the solution was that an American Convention would co-exist with the Covenants. Thus, two systems of protection provided for by Conventions could one day supplement each other, one regional, the other universal. These two systems were not intended necessarily to preclude each other and neither of them was meant to have a priority character: it was to be possible indeed to choose between the regional approach and the universal approach, taking into account the differences between the two systems.

The Preamble of the Convention contains certain affirmations which need to be stressed in order to situate that instrument and identify the ideological conceptions on which it is founded. The system of personal liberty and social justice which it is desired to consolidate is conceived of "within the framework of democratic institutions" and the affirmation, already contained in the American Declaration, is repeated: that the essential rights of man are not derived from one's being a national of a certain State, but are based upon attributes of the human personality, therefore justifying international protection of human rights complementing that provided by the internal law of the American States. Thus, the traditional American idea involves a system for the protection of rights which are inherent in the human personality, conceived of within the framework of a democratic system; this idea is fundamentally different from that serving as a basis for the United Nations Covenants, prepared with a view to their being applied in a universal system covering States whose philosophical, political, economic and social principles are different.[42]

Part I, entitled "State obligations and rights protected," consists of a first chapter which defines those obligations, a second chapter which lists the civil and political rights protected, a third chapter covering economic, social and cultural rights, a fourth chapter which deals with the suspension of guarantees, interpretation and application, and a final chapter which deals with the relationship between the rights and duties of man. Thus a single instrument covers both civil and political rights and economic, social and cultural rights.[43]

Part II deals with means of protection. Chapter VI lists the competent organs, the seventh is on the Inter-American Commission of Human Rights, the eighth on the Inter-American Court of Human Rights and the ninth on the provisions common to the two organs. Part III consists of two chapters which deal with general and transitory provisions.

The first two articles constitute the basis of the Convention. Article 1 provides for the obligation of the States Parties to respect the rights and freedoms recognized in the Convention and to ensure the free and full exercise of those rights and freedoms without any discrimination. This article derives from article 2 of the Covenant on Civil and Political Rights and from articles 1 and 14 of the Rome Convention. But the undertaking to ensure the equal right of all to the enjoyment of the civil and political rights set forth is not included in the Convention, as it is in the Covenant (art. 3). In practice, however, this difference may be considered to be non-existent since the principle of non-discrimination in the free and full exercise of rights is recognized (art. 1, 1), as is equality before the law (art. 14). Under article 2, the parties undertake, where the exercise of the rights set forth is not already ensured by domestic legislative provisions, to adopt such legislative or other measures as may be necessary to give effect to those rights. This provision has no equivalent either in the Covenant on Civil and Political Rights or in the Rome Convention.

It is provided that everyone has the right to simple, prompt and effective recourse for protection against acts that violate his or her fundamental rights (art. 25, 1). The States undertake to ensure that any person claiming such remedy shall have his rights determined by the competent authority provided for by the legal system of State, to develop the possibilities of judicial remedy and to ensure that the competent authorities shall enforce such remedies when granted (art. 25, 2).

It is specified that the term "person," referring to the beneficiary of the rights and freedoms guaranteed by the Convention, means every human being (art. 1, 2). Intended to guard against any possible problems of interpretation, this provision has no equivalent in the customary sources of the American Convention, although it can be contended that, both in the United Nations Covenants and in the Rome Convention, the solution is the same, except, in the latter instrument, in respect of the right to property, which, by virtue of Additional Protocol No. 1, is ensured for "every natural or legal person" (art. 1).

The rights set forth in chapter II are: the right to juridical personality, the right to life, the right to humane treatment, the prohibition of slavery and servitude, the right to personal liberty, the right to a fair trial, the principle of lawfulness and non-retroactivity, the right to compensation, the right to have one's honour and dignity protected, freedom of conscience and religion, freedom of thought and expression, the right of correction or reply, the right of assembly, freedom of association, the right to marry and to raise a family, the right to a name, the rights of the child, the right to a nationality, the right to private property, freedom of movement and residence, political rights, equality before the law and the right to judicial protection (arts. 4-25).

Generally speaking, the Convention itself determines the right which is covered by direct international protection. But in some cases, it recommends that specific action be taken in the framework of internal law, either to prohibit certain types of behaviour, or to adopt a particular norm or to settle a situation in a particular way (for instance, arts. 13, 5; 17, 5 and 21, 3).

The American Convention generally repeats the rights to be found in the Covenant on Civil and Political Rights and in the Rome Convention. There are a few differences, however, which deserve to be pointed out. Of these, mention should be made of the express recognition of the following:

a) the right of everyone to recognition as a person before the law (art.3);
b) the right to life, protected, in general, from the moment of conception (art. 4, 1)
c) the right of every person to be compensated when he has been sentenced by a final judgement through a miscarriage of justice (art. 10);
d) the right to have one's honour respected and one's dignity recognized (art. 11, 1);
e) the prohibition of prior censorship (art. 13, 2);
f) the right of correction or reply (art. 14);
g) the same rights granted to children born out of wedlock and those born in wedlock (art. 17, 5);
h) the right to a name (art. 18);
i) the right to seek and be granted asylum (art. 22, 7);[44]
j) the right of an alien not to be deported or returned to a country, regardless of whether or not it is his country of origin, if in that country his right to life or personal freedom is in danger of being violated because of his race, nationality, religion, social status or political opinions, and the prohibition of the collective expulsion of aliens (art. 22, 8 and 9).

Inclusion of the right to property is not wholly justified, for the view could be taken that the question falls within the competence of the national legislature.[45] As for the rest, in reality, at a time when what is called ideological pluralism has begun to be affirmed in the inter-American system (and there exist American States with varying and conflicting ideas in regard to the right to property), the inclusion of this provision could have created serious obstacles to the signing and ratification of the Convention by some States. It would perhaps have been preferable for there to have been a shorter and more simple list, centred on the protection of a few fundamental rights, for this might have facilitated the earlier entry into force of the text.

Despite the detailed character of the list of rights set forth, there are a few omissions. For instance, there is no reference to the right to self-determination, which may be considered not to be a right of the individual in the strict sense, but a right which is indispensable to the exercise of all other human rights (art. 1, International Covenant on Economic, Cultural and Social Rights and art. 1, International Covenant on Civil and Political Rights); the right of minorities is not recognized (art. 27, International Covenant on Civil and Political Rights), an issue which, in Latin America, in the case of indigenous populations, may be of particular importance.

Article 26 deals with economic, social and cultural rights. It makes do with stipulating that "the States Parties undertake to adopt measures, both internally and through international co-operation, especially those of an economic and technical nature, with a view to achieving progressively, by legislation or other appropriate means, the full realization of the rights implicit in the economic social, educational, scientific and cultural standards set forth in the

Charter of the Organization of American States as amended by the Protocol of Buenos Aires."

While recognizing the conceptual unity of all human rights, it is obvious that, on account of their specific characteristics, it is necessary to distinguish between civil and political rights and economic, social and cultural rights, in view of the fact that different systems of protection are required for these two categories of rights. In this connection, the approach adopted in the Convention was not the most appropriate.[46] First, because the articles of the Protocol of Buenos Aires relating to economic, social and cultural rights were not drafted for the purpose of ensuring protection for those rights, but in order to establish international co-operation in the economic, social and cultural spheres; on this account, such rights are only partially and incompletely listed. Second, because the method followed was bound to result in omissions. Thus, for instance, the right to freedom of association is recognized in the Protocol of Buenos Aires (art. 16) and also in the Convention (art. 43, c). On the other hand, certain rights which are included traditionally among economic and cultural rights, but which require a system of protection similar to that granted to civil and political rights, such as the right to strike (art. 43, e, of the Protocol of Buenos Aires), freedom of work and freedom of education, either are not included in the system of the Convention (such is the case for freedom of education and work) or do not benefit, as is the case for the right to strike which is indirectly recognized through the reference in article 26 to the Protocol of Buenos Aires, from a system of international protection corresponding to their nature.

As for economic, social and cultural rights, the States parties limit their undertaking to the adoption of internal measures and the establishment of international co-operation with a view to achieving progressively the full realization of those rights within the framework of available resources. Obviously, what was adopted was a cautious and, to a certain extent, restrictive criterion.[47]

As regards the international supervision of effective observance of those rights, it is stipulated solely that the Member States have the duty to submit to the Commission a copy of each of the reports which they must transmit annually to the Executive Committees of the Inter-American Economic and Social Council and the Inter-American Council for Education, Science and Culture (art. 42). In addition, since the Inter-American Commission on Human Rights is empowered to request information from governments (art. 41, d) it is possible to ensure a flow of communications to complement the annual reports mentioned in article 42.

The list of rights, established in the Convention may be expanded for the purpose of applying the system of international protection, as is provided in article 31, in accordance with the procedures established in articles 76 and 77. These provisions establish the possibility of amendments (art. 76) and additional protocols with a view to including other rights and freedoms in the Convention (art. 77).

Chapter IV contains provisions on the suspension of guarantees (art. 27), the federal clause (art. 28, 1), restrictions regarding interpretation (art. 29) and the scope of restrictions (art. 30).

As regards the suspension of guarantees, a provision which, under different titles, has often been used in America to violate human rights, article 27 establishes a specific and clearly restrictive system. It stipulates the sole cases where such measures can be taken, imposes a time-limit for their application, provides that such measures must not be inconsistent with other obligations under international law (paragraph 1) and that they must not be applied to a series of rights which are specifically identified (paragraph 2).

The federal clause is drafted in such a way that when a federal State is a party to the Convention, the constituent units of the federation must effectively observe, in the same way as the federal State, the rights set forth in the Convention (art. 28).

As for the restrictions regarding interpretation provided for in article 29, the purpose of these provisions is to guard against too restrictive or limitative an interpretation. The four cases dealt with include the prohibition against any interpretation whose result would be: to restrict the enjoyment of any right or freedom recognized by virtue of the laws of any State party or by virtue of another Convention to which that State is a party (paragraph b); to preclude other rights or guarantees inherent in the human personality or that are derived from representative democracy as a form of government (paragraph c); and to exclude or limit the effect that the American Declaration of the Rights and Duties of Man and other international acts of the same nature may have (paragraph d).

It is stipulated that the restrictions that, pursuant to the Convention, may be placed on the enjoyment or exercise of the rights and freedoms set forth therein may not be applied except in accordance with the laws enacted for reasons of general interest and solely for the purposes for which those laws have been provided, which is tantamount to affirming the principle of lawfulness while giving to the law alone the possibility of placing restrictions on fundamental rights. In addition, in recognizing the teleological principle according to which restrictive measures must be applied for the purpose of achieving the goal for which they have been provided, it is made possible to guard against the misuse of power.[48]

It is established that every person has responsibilities to his family, his community and mankind. The relationship between rights and duties is thus recognized (art. 32) and, by virtue of a principle whose implications are obvious for the interpretation of the recognized limits to the enjoyment and exercise of the rights set forth, it is provided that "the rights of each person are limited by the rights of others, by the security of all, and by the just demands of the general welfare, in a democratic society" (art. 32, 2).

The Convention establishes two organs with competence in matters relating to the fulfilment of the commitments made by the States parties:

a) the Inter-American Commission on Human Rights; and

b) the Inter-American Court of Human Rights.

In order that the Commission may watch over the promotion of the economic, social and cultural rights set forth in the amended Charter of Bogotá, it receives a copy of each report submitted by the States parties to the Executive Committees of the Inter-American Economic and Social Council and the Inter-American Council for Education, Science and Culture (art. 42). The States parties undertake to provide the Commission with such information as it may request of them as to the manner in which their domestic law ensures the effective application of any provisions of the Convention (art. 43).

By virtue of paragraph (f) of article 41, it has the task of taking action on petitions or communications, and articles 48 to 51 determine the procedure laid down for this purpose. Petitions or communications containing denunciations of violations of human rights committed by a State party may be submitted to the Commission by any person or group of persons or any non-governmental entity recognized in one or more Member States (art. 44). The right to individual recourse is thus recognized in that persons or groups of persons are treated as subjects of international law; this has been described as the most significant feature of the new American Convention.[49] What is involved here is a system contrary to the European system which directly provides any State party with the opportunity to take action against another State party in the event of a violation of the Rome Convention (art. 24), but which, on the other hand, makes the introduction of a petition by any person, group of persons or non-governmental organization dependent on the State concerned having declared that it recognizes the competence of the Commission to deal with individual petitions (art. 25). The American Convention also differs on this point from the system adopted by the United Nations. In the Covenant on Civil and Political Rights, in order for a State party to be able to submit communications to the Human Rights Committee alleging that another State party is not fulfilling its obligations, the latter must have made a declaration recognizing the competence of the Committee to receive and consider communications and the State submitting them must have made a like declaration in regard to itself (art. 41, 1). As for communications from individuals regarding violations of civil and political rights, these became possible only with the entry into force of the Optional Protocol to the Covenant on Civil and Political Rights, which provides for communications concerning a State party to the said Protocol from individuals subject to the jurisdiction of that State party (art. 1).

The American Convention also grants the opportunity to the States parties, if they so declare when they deposit their instruments of ratification or adherence, or at any later time, to recognize the competence of the Commission to deal with communications in which a State party alleges that another State party has violated the rights recognized by the Convention (art. 45). The Convention establishes the conditions of admissibility of communications (art. 46), which are generally those provided by international law. The text is more specific in this regard than that which determines the competence of the Inter-American Commission under its old (pre-1979) Statute. It includes paragraph (c) (which has no equivalent in the old Statute), in which it is stipulated that a petition is inadmissible if it is pending before another international procedure for settlement. Paragraph 2 of article 46 provides, for its part, that the provisions of paragraph 1 of the same article shall not be applicable when the domestic legislation of the State concerned does not afford due process of law for the protection of the right or rights violated, when the individual has been denied access to the remedies under domestic law or has been prevented from exhausting them, and when there has been unwarranted delay in rendering a final judgement under the aforementioned remedies. The existence side by side of the Optional Protocol to the United Nations Covenant on Civil and Political Rights and the Pact of San José raises important questions with regard to the co-ordination of the two systems, particularly in respect of procedures for individual communications.[50]

In the course of the procedure, the Commission may request information from the government of the State responsible for the alleged violation. Such information must be submitted within a reasonable period, to be determined in each case by the Commission. If the Commission decides to continue to consider the case, it proceeds to examine it as it merits; it may undertake a visit of enquiry and request all pertinent information. It places itself at the disposal of the parties concerned with a view to reaching a friendly settlement. If such a settlement is reached, it draws up a report which it transmits to the States concerned, which are not at liberty to publish it. If, within a period of three months, the matter has not been either settled or referred to the Court, the Commission may set forth its opinion accompanied by recommendations to the effect that the States should remedy the situation examined. When the prescribed period has expired, the Commission decides whether the State has taken adequate measures and whether to publish its report. This procedure is an extremely complex one.

The Court consists of seven judges of the highest moral, intellectual and juridical authority, elected in an individual capacity. The members of the Court cannot be members of the Commission, and vice versa. *Ad hoc* judges are provided for and their role defined (art. 55). The judges are elected by the General Assembly of the Organization. The Convention provides for the status of the judges, the organization and working of the Court, the quorum, the place where it has its seat, its secretariat and its Statute and Rules of Procedure (arts. 58, 59, 60).

The judges of the Court are elected by secret ballot, by an absolute majority of the States parties to the Convention, at the General Assembly of the Organization, from a list of up to three candidates nominated by each State party. Such candidates may be nationals of the State nominating them or nationals of another Member State of the OAS. If three candidates are nominated, at least one must be a national of a State other than the nominator (Art. 53). Judges are elected for six years and are eligible for re-election for one term (Art. 54). The Court is not an organ of the inter-American system, as the Commission is (Art. 51, paragraph (e) of the Revised OAS Charter), although the OAS Charter provides for the possibility of its existence without specifically mentioning it (Art. 51, last paragraph, and Art. 112). This means that it is competent only in the cases provided for in the Pact of San José in respect of American States Parties to that Pact.

The Commission takes part in hearings resulting from all cases brought before the Court (art. 57). In order for the Court to hear a case, it must make sure that the procedures before the Commission have been completed (art. 61, 2). Only the States parties to the Convention and the Commission have the right to submit a case to the Court (art. 61, 1). But as private persons or groups of persons may submit their complaints to the Commission, private individuals may therefore submit a case to the Court[51] by this indirect means. In the same way, a State may appear before the Court with regard to a matter previously examined by the Commission, by virtue of a request made by a State in accordance with article 45.

The competence of the Court as a decision-making body is left to the express choice of the States parties (art. 62). For the latter, it does not result from mere ratification of the Convention, but from a declaration which may be made at any time, unconditionally, on the condition of reciprocity, for a specified period, or for specific cases.[52] On the other hand, its competence as a consultative body (art. 64) regarding the Convention or any other treaty concerning the protection of human rights in the American States results directly from the Convention.[53]

When the Court, in the exercise of its functions pursuant to article 62, finds that there has been a violation of a right or freedom protected by the Convention, it rules that the injured party be ensured the enjoyment of the right or freedom violated and, if appropriate, that the consequences of the measure or situation that constituted the breach of such right or freedom be remedied and that fair compensation be paid to the injured party (art. 63).

It is worth emphasizing that in cases of extreme gravity or urgency, and when necessary to avoid irreparable damage to persons, the Court may adopt such provisional measures as it deems pertinent. With respect to a case not yet submitted to the Court, it may adopt such measures at the request of the Commission (art. 63, 2).[54]

The States parties undertake to comply with the judgement of the Court in any case to which they are parties; in addition, provisions are included concerning the execution in the country concerned of that part of a judgement that stipulates compensatory damages to the injured party (art. 68).

When the Pact of San José came into force, the Court, following a recommendation of the General Assembly of the OAS (Resolution 372), established itself in the capital of Costa Rica, in September 1978, and its judges were then elected in accordance with the procedure laid down in Article 81 and 82 of the Pact.[55] So far, the Court has not delivered any judgements or advisory opinions. The Court's Statute was adopted by the General Assembly of the OAS at its meeting in La Paz, Bolivia, in 1979.

The Convention also contains provisions relating to reservations,[56] amendments and denunciation.

It is open for signature and ratification by or adherence of any Member State of the OAS (art. 74, 1). In contradistinction with other international instruments, the period during which it remains open for signature is not stipulated, nor is there any indication as to when the process of adherence whereby a State may become a contracting party starts.

It entered into force as soon as eleven States had deposited their instruments of ratification or adherence (art. 74, 1).[57] This is a very large number if one takes into account what has already been said concerning the list of protected rights, if it is known that nineteen States took part in the Conference and that only twelve signed the Convention (El Salvador, Colombia, Ecuador, Honduras, Paraguay, Panama, Chile, Uruguay, Guatemala, Nicaragua, Venezuela and Costa Rica), if one bears in mind the declarations made in the Final Act by Argentina and Mexico.[58]

It was signed on 22 November 1969 by twelve States. One of them signed with reservations.[59] It was subsequently signed by various other States, including the United States of America, which, under the Carter administration, signed the Convention, departing from its traditional policy.[60] However, as of January 1982, the United States, along with Chile, Paraguay and Uruguay all of whom have signed, had not ratified the Pact of San José.

It has been ratified by seventeen American States to date. On 18 July 1978, having been ratified by eleven States, it came into force for those States (Colombia, Costa Rica, Dominican Republic, Ecuador, El Salvador, Grenada, Guatemala, Haiti, Honduras, Panama and Venezuela). Since that time the Convention, as of January 1982, has also been ratified by Peru, Nicaragua, Bolivia, Jamaica, Mexico and Barbados.

It should be mentioned that some of the most populous American States either have not signed the Convention or have not ratified it (Mexico, Brazil and Argentina). Although it is not inconceivable that further progress will shortly be made, especially perhaps in the case of the United States, Mexico or Brazil, the question is not easy, and the Pact will continue for an indefinite period to be a regional instrument only partially in force and covering only part of the American continent.

Under these circumstances, the limited hopes of any progress being achieved by the system for the international promotion and protection of human rights in America must be placed principally in the work of the present Inter-American Commission on Human Rights which, it is to be hoped will continue its positive action while increasing its prestige and affirming its competence.

3. THE INTER-AMERICAN COMMISSION ON WOMEN

International law has given particular attention to the status of women with a view to encouraging the elimination of all discrimination founded on sex. In 1923, at the 5th Inter-American Conference, it was recommended that future Conferences study "the means of abolishing the constitutional and legal incapacities of women, for the purpose of securing, in due course and by means of the development of adequate capacities, the consequent responsibilities and the same civil and political rights for women that are today enjoyed by men."

The question was raised again at the 6th Conference (Havana, 1928). At Montevideo, at the 7th Conference, the Convention on the Nationality of Women was adopted, which forbids "any distinction based on sex in the legislation or in the practice respecting nationality of the signatory States." At the 8th Conference in Lima (1938), resolution XX was approved, which provides for equal political treatment for women and men, equality as to civil status and larger possibilities of protection for women in work and as mothers. In 1948, the 9th Inter-American Conference adopted two Conventions: one on political rights and the other on civil rights of women.[61]

The Inter-American Commission of Women (CIM) was set up in 1928; it was instructed "to take charge of the preparation of juridical information and data of any other kind which may be deemed advisable to enable the Seventh International Conference of American States to take up consideration of the civil and political equality of women in the continent." It carried out the task entrusted to it and, at the 9th Conference, in 1948, was established on a permanent basis and was invited to work for "the extension of civil, political, economic and social rights to the women of America; to study their problems and propose means of solving them...."

The 10th Inter-American Conference (Caracas, 1954) modified the Statute of the Commission which had been adopted at the 9th Conference and incorporated the Commission in the inter-American system on a permanent basis. Its secretariat was to be attached to the General Secretariat of the OAS. The Agreement concluded by the Commission, as a specialized organization, with the Council of the OAS was signed on 16 June 1953. The seat of the Commission is the same as that of the Pan-American Union.

The Commission is composed of one delegate for each of the American States, appointed by the respective Government. It has an Executive Committee which is composed of the Chairman and the representatives of six countries elected for a period of two years.

There are also National Committees for Co-operation responsible for collaborating with the Titular Delegate in each country in the promotion of the Commission's aims and purposes. The Permanent Secretariat functions in the offices of the General Secretariat of the OAS.

In 1976, the CIM adopted a Regional Plan of Action for the Decade of Women in the Americas which emphasized six priority areas for action: (1)

integration of women into the rural economy; (2) participation of women in industrial urban development; (3) training of women for business activities within their traditional spheres of action; (4) legal equality of the sexes; (5) participation of women in development; and (6) projection of the image of modern woman in accordance with her full potential.[62]

At the 19th Assembly of Delegates in Washington, in 1978, the CIM adopted a wide range of resolutions dealing with, *inter alia*: the full integration of women into the process of agrarian reform; updating of current adoption laws and codes; the protection of women in prison; a study of the legal status of women; and the employment of women in the OAS.

In 1977, a Multinational Women's Center was established in Cordoba, Argentina under the auspices of the CIM, the Government of Argentina and the National University of Cordoba. Its stated objectives are: (1) to research the realities of women in the Americas, and to train them, no matter what their age, marital status or social position, to participate effectively and on an ongoing basis in the process of the integral development of the countries of the hemisphere; (2) to support the research, training, documentation and information programs of the Commission.[63]

At its Annual and Special Assemblies, held in turn in the different Member States, and on the occasion of its seminars, courses and various activities, the Commission has performed work which merits the highest praise. It has achieved success in many fields relating to the economic, social, cultural and political advancement of women. With regard to the political aspect, it should be mentioned that in 1928, when the Commission was established, only one American country recognized the right of women to vote. Today it is recognized by 26 States.

4. THE INTER-AMERICAN CHILDREN'S INSTITUTE

The Institute was created in 1927 under the name of the American International Institute for the Protection of Children, by virtue of a resolution approved by the 4th Child Congress (Santiago de Chile, 1924). The agreement between the Institute and the OAS was signed in 1949 and modified in 1962. The Institute is a specialized organization, enjoying technical autonomy, but is financially supported by the OAS; its secretariat is attached to the General Secretariat of the Organization. Its present Statute, modified in 1963 to be incorporated in the Agreement of 1962, assigns to it the task of promoting the study of the problems of motherhood, childhood, adolescence and the family in America and the adoption of such measures as may afford a solution to these problems.

The institute performs the task assigned to it through its Directing Council, the Pan-American Child Congress, which meets every four years, and its Bureau. The Director and the personnel of the Institute are appointed by the Secretary-General of the OAS. Its headquarters are in Montevideo. It has played a significant role in respect of the recognition and promotion of the rights of the child and the family, in particular through studies and proposals made with a view to modernizing and co-ordinating the relevant American laws. [64]

Conclusions

The first observation to be made about the inter-American system of human rights is the same as that suggested by consideration of Pan-Americanism. It stems from the fact that the system has two essentially different facets. On the one hand, the United States of America, an economic and social super-power, representing a political reality founded on the uninterrupted continuity of its constitutional system since Independence (which is reflected in the formal observance and the more or less effective legal protection of human rights) and, on the other hand, Latin America, divided and underdeveloped, politically unstable and presenting a political reality that tends, in general, but with exceptions, to deny the rights of the individual.

Even though the theoretical conception of human rights, the philosophical ideas on which they are founded, the role of the state and that of the international community in respect of those rights may be similar in the United States and in Latin America insofar as both share the same western outlook, in actual fact what is involved is two worlds; it is consequently extremely difficult to establish a joint system for the protection of human rights. It is also to be noted that the Inter-American Commission on Human Rights has so far, except in isolated cases, concerned itself almost exclusively with human rights in Latin America.

The second observation stems from the fact that during the last forty years, international law in the Americas has made progress at the normative level in proclaiming, promoting and protecting internationally the rights of the human person.

The Charter of Bogotá, the American Declaration of the Rights and Duties of Man, the Inter-American Charter of Social Guarantees, the Inter-American Commission on Human Rights, the Protocol of Buenos Aires and the Pact of San José have marked the most decisive stages in this process. But actual conditions have not kept abreast of these developments. While the system has advanced in theory, practical conditions in America in respect of human rights have made small progress. In Latin America, in the course of the last forty years, there has been a certain economic progress; it might also be said that public opinion is better informed and more critical, that there has been a rise in the standard of living and that the peoples of Latin America today rightly and irrefutably aspire to a situation in which their rights may be recognized and guaranteed. However, except in a few cases, human rights in Latin America today do not seem to be more respected than they were in 1948. Indeed, on the contrary, it is easy to find cases where there has been an obvious regression.

Things being what they are, one is obliged to note the sad fact that the force of those economic and political factors which have impeded progress and which have even led to a regression, has been greater and more decisive than the force which might have resulted from normative progress. However, one cannot on that account be absolutely pessimistic in the face of what has been achieved. The inter-American system for the promotion and protection of human rights could not, in itself, cause the *de facto* situation to change nor make practical conditions in the Americas develop along different lines. But what has been achieved has not been in vain. Without the progress accomplished by international law, the situation would be even more negative, for it cannot be denied that the juridical superstructure has an influence on the economic and social infrastructure and, in addition, that it has an impact at the level of the training of men's minds, reflected in an awareness which is of the utmost importance today. Normative progress has thus helped to produce and to advance an enlightened Latin American conscience, which demands with ever-increasing force that human rights be observed and respected. As a result, and on account also of the fact that Latin America has developed economically and has started to recover its natural resources, to affirm its international personality and to raise the standard of living of its peoples, the question of human rights is no longer simply a matter of juridical and academic rhetoric but is becoming a tangible feature of the real world.

The process of seeking to ensure respect for human rights cannot but continue. And as it does so, and as material conditions progressively improve, the international system for the protection of human rights and for the supervision of the observance of those rights in America has a positive part to play.

NOTES

1. Preamble, paragraph 1.
2. Article 5, paragraphs j, d, h, l and Article 13.
3. Charter of the OAS, Article A. Charter of the United Nations, Arts. 52-54.
4. International Conference of American States for the Maintenance of Peace, Buenos Aires, 1936; VIIIth International Conference of American States, Lima, 1938, resolutions XXVII, XXVIII, XXXVI and LXXII; Meeting of Consultation of Panama, 1939, resolution VII; Meeting of Consultation of Rio de Janeiro, 1942, resolution XVII. Reference may be made to other more remote antecedents, with the Convention on Asylum of 1928, a few decisions of the Conference of Montevideo of 1933 and a precedent from 1902 (Robert K. Goldman, *The Protection of Human Rights in the Americas: Past, Present and Future*, New York University, Center for International Studies, Vol. 5, No. 5, 1972, pp. 2-3); J.A. Cabranes, "The protection of human rights by the Organization of American States," *AJIL*, Vol. 62, 1968, p. 891 note 9.
5. Resolution XL.
6. *Paralelismo entre la democracia y la paz, Protección international de los derechos del hombre; acción colectiva en defensa de esos principios*, Ministry of Foreign Affairs, Montevideo, 1946; Diego Uribe Vargas, *Los derechos humanos y el sistema interamericano*, Madrid, 1972, pp. 281-301; Alberto Ulloa, La propuesta Rodriguez Larreta, *Revista Peruana*

de Derecho Internacional, 1945; Ramón Lopez Jimenez, *El principio de no intervención en America y la nota uruguaya,* Buenos Aires, 1947. It has been rightly noted that, owing to the profound historical roots of the principle of non-intervention in America, international protection has encountered great difficulties, and a long and difficult process was necessary for a system of international protection to be established (J.A. Cabranes, *op. cit.,* p. 889).

7. Preamble.

8. Antonio Gomez Robledo, *Idea y experiencia de América,* México, 1958, p. 233; Inter-American Juridical Committee, "Diferencia entre Intervención y Acción colectiva," *CIJ-8,* Washington, 1965.

9. Dardo Regules, *La lucha por la Justicia y por el Derecho,* Montevideo, 1949, pp. 18-31, 97-108. This criterion was upheld at some of the Inter-American meetings, as for instance by Uruguay, particularly between 1936 and 1966, but was not adopted. Concerning the interpretation of article 5, the position of the Inter-American Juridical Committee has not been as precise and clear as might be desired. See José Joaquín Caicedo Castillo, *El Panamericanismo,* Buenos Aires, pp. 364-365.

10. Karel Vasak, *La Commission interaméricaine des droits de l'homme,* Paris, 1968, p. 26; Dardo Regules, *La lucha por la justicia y por el Derecho,* Montevideo, 1949, pp. 97-108.

11. *The Organization of American States and Human Rights,* Washington, 1972, p. 560; Germán Fernandez del Castillo, La Declaracion Americana de Derechos y Deberes del Hombre," *México en la IX Conferencia Internacional Americana,* México, 1948, pp. 133-164. Carlos Garcia Bauer, *Los derechos humanos, preocupación universal,* Guatemala, 1966, pp. 111-112.

12. *The Organization of American States and Human Rights,* Washington, 1972 p. 572; Mario de la Cueva, "La Carta Internacional Americana de Garantias Sociales," *México en la IX Conferencia Internacional Americana,* México, 1948, pp. 185-196; Francisco de Ferrari, "Carta internacional Americana de Garantias Sociales, concordada con las disposiciones constitucionales, legales y reglamentarias vigentes en el Uruguay," *Derecho Laboral,* Montevideo, 1948, V.I., p. 186.

13. The Inter-American Juridical Committee had been requested to prepare the "American Declaration of the Rights and Duties of Man" and the "Inter-American Charter of Social Guarantees" by the Conference of Chapultepec (Resolution XL and LVIII). This task was only partly carried out by the Committee and had to be completed by a Commission of the Inter-American Conference.

14. *Simposio sobre el proyecto de Convención de Derechos Humanos de Santiago de Chile,* Faculty of Law and Social Sciences, Montevideo, 1959, pp. 19-24.

15. J. A. Cabranes, "Human Rights and Non-Intervention in the Inter-American System," *Michigan Law Review,* 1967, p. 1147; Robert K. Goldman, *The Protection of Human Rights in the Americas: Past, Present and Future,* New York University, Center for International Studies, Vol. 5, No. 2, 1972, p. 8.

16. Declaration of Santiago, Preamble, paragraph 4, and Declarations Nos. 4, 5, 6 and 7. See Resolutions III, IV, paragraphs 1 and 2; VIII and X.

17. Res. 53 of the 1st ordinary session of the General Assembly, "Promotion of the observance of human rights in the American States," 23/4/1971.

18. Statute of the Inter-American Commission on Human Rights, approved by the Council of the Organization on 25 May and 8 June 1960, OAS/Ser. L/V/11.26. This version includes the amendments introduced by resolution XXII of the 2nd Special Inter-American Conference and those approved by the Council on 24 April 1968. *The Organization of American States and Human Rights,* Washington, 1972, p. 600. On the occasion of the entry into force of the Protocol of Buenos Aires, it was possible to amend the Statute of the Commission (XXIIIrd Report, OAS/Ser. L/V/11.23, p. 44; XXIVth Report, OAS/Ser. L/V/11.24, pp. 40-43); it was finally decided not to do so (XXVIth Report, OAS/Ser. L/V/11.26, pp. 44-46).

19. Germán Fernandez del Castillo, "La Declaración Americana de Derechos y Deberes del Hombre," *México en la IX Conferencia Internacional Americana,* 1946, pp. 161-163.

20. OAS/Ser. L/V/11.17; *The Organization of American States and Human Rights*, Washington, 1972, p. 610.

21. Karel Vasak, *La Commission interaméricaine des droits de l'homme*, Paris, 1968, paragraph 114, p. 53.

22. Reports on the 1st, 3rd, 4th, 5th and 6th sessions. Karel Vasak, *op. cit.*, paragraphs 115-116, pp. 55-56.

23. José A. Mora, Fortalecimiento de Sistema Interamericano, 21 October 1964, 341-S-7009.

24. Karel Vasak, *op. cit.*, p. 140, note 3.

25. Karel Vasak, *op. cit.*, paragraphs 96-98, pp. 44-45.

26. See Thomas Buergenthal, "The revised OAS Charter and the protection of human rights," *AJIL*, 1975, Vol. 69, No. 4, pp. 828-836.

27. Resolution XII, paragraph 2, which refers to articles 1, 2, 3, 4, 18, 25 and 26 of the Declaration. Article 2 of the Statute already referred to the rights set forth in the Declaration. And article 10 referred to article XXVIII of the Declaration. Concerning the significance of this reference in respect of the legal force of the Declaration, see C. Garcia Bauer, *op. cit.*, pp. 113-116 and K. Vasak, *op. cit.*, pp. 61-62.

28 . Acuerdo de la Comisión (XXVI Periodo de Sesiones), OEA/Ser. L/V/11.26, p. 48.

29. See the studies published in *The Organization of American States and Human Rights*, 1969-1967, Washington, 1972; Luis Reque, "The Organization of American States and the protection of human rights;" *Anuario interamericano de derechos humanos*, 1968, Washington, 1973, p. 220. Justino Jiménez de Arechaga, "Primer informe acerca de la libertad sindical," OEA/Ser. L/V/11.24; Manuel Bianchi, "Los derechos humanos y el derecho de sufragio en América,"OEA/Ser. L/V/11.19; Durward V. Sandefer, "El derecho de petición," OEA/Ser. L/V/11.20; Mario Alzamora Valdez, "El derecho a la educación en la América latina," OEA/Ser. L/V/11.25, doc. 39; Gabino Fraga, "El agotamiento de los recursos internos previo a la acción internacional," OEA/Ser. L/V/11.28, doc. 19; Dunshee de Abranches, "El desarrollo de la ciencia y la tecnología y los derechos humanos," doc. 33-27, Rev. 1; Mario Alzamora Valdez, "Desarrollo de la ciencia y la tecnología y derechos humanos," doc. 29-27.

30. Thus for example reports have been prepared on: Cuba, Haiti and the Dominican Republic (all contained in *The Organization of American States and Human Rights, 1960-1967*, Washington 1972); Chile (OAS/Ser.L/V.II/34, doc. 19 (1974); ALG/doc. 795/77 (1977)); Nicaragua (OAS/Ser.L/V.II/45, doc. 16, rev. 1 (1978)); El Salvador, OAS/Ser.L/V.II/46, doc. 23, rev. 1 (1978)); Panama (OAS/Ser.L/V.II/44,doc. 38 (1978)); Uruguay (OAS/Ser.L/V.II/43, doc. 9 (1978)); and Paraguay (OAS/Ser.L/V.II/43, doc. 13 (1978)). For a thorough review of the fact-finding procedures applied by the Commission see Robert E. Norris "Observations In Loco: Practice and Procedure of the Inter-American Commission on Human Rights," *Texas International Law Journal*, Vol. 15, No. 1 (1980), pp. 46-95.

31. See OEA/Ser.L/V/11.47 doc. 13 rev.1, 23 June 1979, pp. 28-29.

32. In addition to those mentioned in footnotes 36 and 37 below, cf. the following: Presumption that the facts denounced have been proved by virtue of the defendant Government's failure to reply, for instance, Cases 1731 and 1741, XXXth Report, OAS/Ser. L/V/11.30, doc. 45, pp. 59 and 64; Case 1688, XXVIIIth Report, OAS/Ser. L/V/11.28, doc. 24, p. 32; Dismissal of a complaint concerning a situation that has been adjudged by a judicial decision against which no illegality had been alleged, Case 1752, XXXth Report, p. 50; Non-contentious appeal against the decisions of the Commission, Case 1683, XXXth Report, p. 13; Admissibility of communications despite the fact that another international procedure is pending, Case 1738, XXXth Report, p. 43.

33. Case 1697, XXVIIIth Session, OEA/Ser. L/V/11.28, doc. 24, § 26-41, pp. 8-13; Case 1684, pp. 14-21.

34. Case 1684, XXVIIIth Session, OEA/Ser. L/V/11.28, § 54-59, pp. 17-21. It was even envisaged to revise the Regulations to provide for this distinction (XXXth Report, OAS/Ser. L/V/11.30, doc. 45, p. 70).

35. Karel Vasak, *La Commission interaméricaine des droits de l'homme*, Paris, 1968; Robert K. Goldman, *The Protection of Human Rights in the Americas: Past, Present and Future*, New York, 1972; José A. Cabranes, "The Protection of Human Rights in the OAS," *AJIL*, Vol. 62, 1968; L. Ronald Scheman, "The Inter-American Commission on Human Rights," *AJIL*, Vol. 59, 1965, p. 335; Thomas and Thomas, "The Inter-American Commission on Human Rights," *Southwestern Law Journal*, 1965, p. 285; D. V. Sandefer, "Human Rights in the Inter-American System," *Howard Law Journal*, 1965, p. 508; William Korey, "The Key to Human Rights Implementation," *International Conciliation*, New York, 1968, No. 570, p. 45.

36. The texts of the Santiago draft, the drafts of the Governments of Chile and Uruguay, the amendments of the Commission and the final draft of the Convention are reproduced in: *Inter-American Yearbook on Human Rights 1968*, Washington, 1973; OEA/Ser.L/V11.15 and 16.

37. OEA/Ser.G.IV, 787, Rev. 3.(1967).

38. OEA/Ser.L/V/11.19,11 April 1968. This decision of the Commission was based on the report of C. A. Dunshee de Abranches, *Estudio comparativo entre los pactos de las Naciones Unidas sobre derechos civiles, políticos, económicos, sociales y culturales y los proyectos de Convención Americana sobre Derechos Humanos*, OEA/Ser.L/V/11.19, 4 April 1968. *Inter-American Yearbook on Human Rights*, 1968, Washington, 1973. A decision had already been taken in favour of the coexistence of the two systems, as is shown by Dunshee de Abranches, OEA/Ser.L/V/11.19, doc. 18 p. 18.

39. OEA/Ser. G/11, c-a-685, 2 October 1968; and OEA/Ser.G/IV, c-i-858 rev. 3.

40. OEA/Ser. L/V/11.22, doc. 10.

41. *Simposio sobre el proyecto de convención de derechos humanos de Santiago de Chile*, Montevideo, 1959; Council of Europe, "La Convention européenne des droits de l'homme et le projet de convention de Santiago" (H.64-8), Strasbourg, 1964; C. A. Dunshee de Abranches, "Estudio comparativo entre los pactos sobre derechos civiles, políticos, económicos, sociales y culturales y los proyectos de convención americana sobre derechos humanos," OEA/Ser. L/V/11.19, doc. 18; "Examen comparativo de los pactos internacionales de derechos humanos y el protocolo facultativo del Pacto internacional de derechos civiles y políticos, del CIJ y de las ennùedos approbadas por la CIDH," OEA/Ser. L/V/11.19, doc. 4, "Anotacien sobre el proyecto de convención interamericana de protección de derechos humanos," OEA/Ser. L/V/11.19. On the Convention in general, see: Carlos García Bauer. *La Convención Americana sobre Derechos Humanos. Estudios de Derecho Internacional. Homenaje al Profesor Miaja de la Muela*. T. I, pp. 521-553.

42. XXX Informe de la C.I.D.H., OEA/Ser.L/V/11.30, doc. 45, p. 4.

43. The question as to whether there should be one or two Conventions was examined at length; the present solution was adopted, not only on account of the conceptual unity of all human rights, but also for technical and even political reasons, since the ratification procedure was more simple in the case of a single Convention. Alberto Pérez Pérez, "Protección de los derechos humanos," *Anuario Uruguayo de Derechos Internacional*, II, 1963, p. 284; *Simposio sobre el Proyecto de Convención de Derechos Humanos de Santiago de Chile*, Montevideo, 1959, pp. 49-50; Daniel Hugo Martins, *Estado actual del Proyecto de Convención Americana sobre Derechos Humanos*, Montevideo, 1967, p. 10.

44. In America territorial asylum is governed by the Caracas Convention on Territorial Asylum (1954) and the Montevideo Treaties of 1889 and 1939. For diplomatic asylum, which is not referred to in the Pact of San José, see the Caracas Convention of 1954, the Montevideo Convention of 1933, the Havana Convention of 1928 and the Montevideo Treaties of 1889 and 1939.

45. The Covenant on Civil and Political Rights does not contain any reference to the right to property, nor does the Rome Convention. But in the latter case, the right to property was included in Additional Protocol No. 1. Although the text of the American Convention is modern in its formulation, it subordinates the right to the use and enjoyment of one's

property to the interest of society (art. 21, 1), it recommends that the legislature prohibit usury and any other form of exploitation of man by man (art. 21, 3) and ensures the international protection of the right to property solely to natural persons (art. 21. 2), in contrast with what is stipulated by article 1 of the first additional Protocol to the European Convention.

46. It was Dunshee de Abranches who recommended that economic, social and cultural rights should not be included in the Convention, OEA/Ser.L/V/11. 19, doc. 18, p. 42, and he was followed by the Commission. See a few other criticisms concerning this choice in Pedro Pablo Camargo, "The American Convention of Human Rights," *RDH/HJR*, Vol. III, 2, 1970, pp. 343-346.

47. Pedro Pablo Camargo, *op. cit.*

48. The source of this provision is article XXVIII of the American Declaration.

49. It is to be recalled that, as early as 1907, the Central American Court of Justice was competent to deal with individual requests. The creation of a jurisdictional organ of this type consequently has an early precedent in Latin America. Carlos García Bauer, *op. cit.*, pp. 230-264; Pedro Pablo Camargo, *La Protección juridica de los derechos humanos y la democracia en América*, México, 1960, pp. 29-31; Diego Uribe Vargas, *Los derechos humanos y el sistema interamericano*, Madrid, 1972, p. 310. Concerning the different solutions traditionally adopted in this connection by the European system and the Latin American system, see Karel Vasak, *op. cit.*, pp. 49 and 197.

50. Additional Protocol to the Covenant on Civil and Political Rights, art. 5a, Draft of the ICJ, art. 51; Draft of Commission 1 HR, art. 30, 1c; Rome Convention, art. 27b; ECOSOC Resolution 1503 (XLVIII) 6b, ii; Resolution 1 (XXIV) of the Sub-Commission on Prevention of Discrimination and Protection of Minorities, 4a. See M. E. Tardu, "The Protocol to the United Nations Covenant on Civil and Political Rights and the Inter-American System: A Study of Co-existing Petition Procedures," *AJIL*, vol. 70, no. 4, October 1976, pp. 778-801.

51. It is for this reason that I do not consider Camargo's criticism to be completely justified, *op. cit.*, p. 352.

52. The direct source of the Court's jurisdiction is the Rome Convention, in particular arts. 44, 45, 47 and 50.

53. In contrast with the European system in which this compulsory jurisdiction is established only in the second additional Protocol to the Convention (art. 1).

54. This rule does not exist in the European system. It was proposed by Costa Rica at the Conference (Doc. 83, Corr. 1, p. 6). See Luis Demetrio Tinoco, *El Tribunal Europeo de Derechos del Hombre y la Corte Interamericana de Derechos Humanos*, Anuario Hispano Luso Americano de Derecho Internacional, 5, 1979, p. 103.

55. The Judges elected to the Court are: Rodolfo Piza Escalante (Costa Rica); Thomas Buergenthal (United States and nominated by Costa Rica); Máximo Cisneros Sánchez (Peru); César Ordoñez Quintero (Colombia); Carlos Roberto Reina Idiáquez (Honduras); Miguel Rafael Urquía (El Salvador); and Huntley E. Monroe (Jamaica).

56. Article 75 which refers to the provisions of the Vienna Convention of 23 May 1969 was proposed by Uruguay at San José at the 3rd plenary session (Doc. 85, Corr. 1, p. 8). It provides for a much more liberal system of reservations than that of the draft of the Commission which authorized reservations only in the event of the text of the Convention conflicting with a constitutional precept (OAS/Ser./XVI/1.1, p. 121, art. 67).

57. This is a system similar to that of the Covenant on Civil and Political Rights (art. 48). The Vienna Convention on the Law of Treaties fixes a period for signature; after that period has expired, the procedure for adherence is possible (art. 81). The Rome Convention, on the other hand, refers to signature and ratification (art. 66). In other words, it is open indefinitely for signature and ratification.

58. The Convention was the subject of a reservation on the part of Uruguay and two declarations (Chile and Ecuador) concerning freedom of ratification. The Final Act of the Conference (OAS/Ser./XVI/1, 1 Doc. 70/Rev. 1, Corr. 1) contains three declarations. One of

them is restrictive (Argentina), another, on the other hand, is favourable as regards the compulsory jurisdiction of the Court (El Salvador), while the third consists of a reservation regarding article 27, 2, and an interpretation of article 48d, together with arguments in favour of the optional jurisdiction of the Court (Mexico). Robert K. Goldman, *The Protection of Human Rights in the Americas*, New York, 1972, pp. 36-42; Pedro Pablo Camargo, "The American Convention on Human Rights," *RDH/HRJ*, Vol. III, 1, 1970, pp. 353-356.

59. Mexico, which did not sign the Convention, made a partial reservation in the Final Act. The reservation formulated by Uruguay, relating to art. 23, 2, of the Convention, concerns article 82, 2, of the Uruguayan Constitution.

60. See Justino Jiménez de Arechaga: "La Convención Americana de Derechos Humanos y las posibilidades de su ratificación por los Estados Americanos," in *Revista de Derechos Humanos*, Vol. LV, No. 2-3, February-June 1974, Puerto Rico.

61. All these instruments are noted in Annex I of this book.

62. These areas, and the action taken with respect to them, are elaborated in CIM's 1980 report to the United Nations Commission on the Status of Women (E/CN.6/630).

63. *Ibid.*

64. *The Organization of American States and Human Rights*, Washington, 1972, pp. 80-82.

18 The League of Arab States*

B. Boutros-Ghali

The League of Arab States is the oldest of the numerous international organizations that were created at the time when the Second World War was drawing to its close; not only was it established before the United Nations, but it also predates all the European or Afro-Asian organizations. The League has undertaken a number of initiatives in the human rights field, including the establishment of a Permanent Arab Commission on Human Rights which first met in 1969. In addition, a draft Declaration for an Arab Charter of Human Rights was completed in 1971. Other initiatives in which representatives of the League of Arab States have participated include a May 1979 Symposium on Human Rights and Fundamental Freedoms in the Arab Homeland which adopted a Draft Arab Covenant on Human Rights.

INTRODUCTION: ESTABLISHMENT OF THE LEAGUE AND ITS RELATIONS WITH THE UNITED NATIONS

On 25 September 1944 a preliminary draft constitutional pact of the League was adopted, the Protocol of Alexandria, but it was not until 22 March 1945 that the Pact of the Arab League was finally accepted by the seven founding States: Jordan (then Transjordan), Syria, Iraq, Saudi-Arabia, Lebanon, Egypt and Yemen.[1] The purposes of the Pact were to strengthen relations between the Member States, to co-ordinate their political activities so as to achieve mutual collaboration, to safeguard their independence and to defend the interests of all the Arab countries.

The League comprises a Council which is its supreme organ and meets twice yearly in ordinary session. It has a permanent Secretariat whose headquarters are in Tunis and which is directed by a Secretary-General appointed by the Council. The League also includes several permanent special Committees, which merit our attention since the Arab Commis-

*Editor's note: This Chapter is a revised and updated version of the Chapter prepared for the earlier French edition of this book by B. Boutros-Ghali.

sion on Human Rights falls within this category. The six permanent committees, established in accordance with the 1945 Pact, deal with economic, communications, cultural, legal, social welfare and health matters. Subsequently, from time to time, new committees have been constituted and dissolved. These committees, which are composed of delegates from all the Member States, meet at the seat of the League or in any of the Arab capitals. They are convened by the Secretary-General and elect a Chairman for a period of two years. Their debates are not made public and their recommendations are adopted by a simple majority. Each committee prepares a co-operation programme in its respective field. These recommendations, resolutions and programmes must then be approved by the Council of the Arab League.

Although the Pact of the Arab League was adopted before the Charter of the United Nations, the Arab legislators provided, in two articles, both for collaboration with the future international organization and for amendments to the Pact to take account of new international obligations arising from the UN Charter. Even before the UN had been constituted, the Arab League had thus implicitly recognized the superior position of the new world organization and had declared its wish to work in harmony with it. The Joint Defence and Economic Co-operation Treaty adopted by the Arab States on 17 June 1950 contains several affirmations of its compatibility with the UN Charter (Preamble, art. 2, and art. 11 of the Treaty).

On 1 November 1950, the UN General Assembly, recognizing the League, invited its Secretary-General to take part in the sessions of the Assembly as an observer. Since that date the Secretary-General of the League has participated regularly in all the Assembly's sessions. In December 1954, the Arab League established permanent representation with the UN in New York and two years later, in Geneva. The two international organizations also co-operate with each other at the level of their Secretariats. It is in the context of this co-operation that the role played by the Arab League in promoting human rights should be considered.

1. THE REGIONAL ARAB COMMISSION ON HUMAN RIGHTS[2]

Co-operation between the Arab League and the United Nations on human rights was intensified when the Council of the Arab League adopted resolution 2259/46 by which it created a Special Commission to prepare an Arab contribution to Human Rights Year (1968). A few months later the Arab League adopted a further resolution creating a second Commission to study, in conjunction with the first, the application of the programmes established to celebrate Human Rights Year (res. 2304/46).

In December 1967, the views of the Secretary-General of the Arab League were sought by the UN on a proposal to create regional human rights commissions. In response the League endorsed the proposal on condition that: such a commission should be established within the framework of the permanent bodies of the Arab League; the League itself should determine the terms of its co-operation with the UN Commission on Human Rights; and a general congress, to which the regional commissions would be invited, would have the task of co-ordinating relations between those commissions and relevant organs of the UN and its specialized agencies.

In September 1968, the Council of the Arab League, after considering a draft prepared by the two special Commissions already referred to, adopted a resolution (2443/48) relating to the creation of a *Permanent Arab Commission on Human Rights*. Shortly afterwards, in December 1968, a Regional Conference on Human Rights was held in Beirut. The eight resolutions voted by that Conference were to serve as a background to the subsequent work of the projected Arab commission. They were primarily intended to safeguard human rights in the Arab territories occupied by Israel.

Consideration will now be given to the membership, procedures and principal activities of the Commission. It is to be noted, however, that although the Council of the League has regularly elected a Chairman for the Commission, no meetings have been held in recent years.

(a). Membership of the Commission

The membership of the Arab Commission on Human Rights conforms to that of all the other special committees previously created by the League of Arab States. It is composed of delegates of the Member States of the League together with the delegate of Palestine represented by the P.L.O. It adopts its resolutions by a simple majority.

(b). Procedures

The Rules of Procedure of the Arab Commission on Human Rights stipulate that each State may be represented by one or more delegates but that each may have only a single vote (article 2).

The role of the Secretariat-General of the League, also represented within the Commission, is that of an intermediary between the Commission and the Council of the League which studies the results of the work of the Commission and approves the drafts and agreements prepared by the Commission (art. 12). The Secretariat-General is also responsible for making the necessary contacts with Member States (art. 14). The Secretary of the Commission is an official of the Secretariat-General (art. 6).

The work of the Commission on Human Rights takes the form of drafts and agreements (art. 12) and its decisions are taken by a simple majority of the representatives present (art. 9).

(c). Work of the Commission

When the Commission held its first meeting in Cairo (March 1969), the after-effects of the Arab-Israeli conflict dominated the proceedings. At its second session (April 1969), the Commission established a work programme, the essential purposes of which were to call attention to the difficult position of the Arab population in the occupied territories and to promote respect for human rights in the Arab world. The Commission's activities were envisaged at three levels: the national level, the regional level and the world level.

At the national level, the Commission invited the Member States to form *national commissions* on human rights with a view to co-operating with the regional Commission in the framework of joint Arab action in the field of human rights (Resolution 10, Session II).

At the Arab regional level, the Commission proposed to co-ordinate the activities of the national commissions in the various Arab countries. It invited the Secretariat-General of the League to create a special department for human rights (Resolution 11, Session II; Resolution 7, Session V). The regional Commission had noted, in receiving the *ad hoc* group sent by the United Nations to investigate the position of the Arab population in the occupied territories, that it would be worthwhile creating an inter-Arab section in order to co-ordinate the efforts of the Arab States in this field and facilitate the task assigned to the UN *ad hoc* group.

At the world level, the underlying aim of the activities of the regional Commission is to appeal to humanitarian principles and to international law in order to arouse greater interest in the Arab cause. It is for this reason that the problems tackled by the Commission have centered around the following themes: the rights of combatants in the event of war or armed conflict in accordance with the provisions of the Geneva Conventions of 1949; the legitimacy of the struggle waged by the Palestinian Resistance (Resolution 6 of 10 July 1968); and the protection of holy places and archaeological sites in accordance with the principles established by international law (Resolution 8 of 10 July 1968).

In initially pursuing these objectives, the regional Commission made a sustained effort to achieve international co-operation at all levels with a view to rallying world public opinion to the Arab cause.

When an African Seminar was held in Cairo in 1969 under UN sponsorship to examine the question of the creation of an African Commission on Human Rights, the Arab Commission participated and paved the way for possible co-operation between itself and any future African Commission. The Arab Commission has also taken part in a variety of other human rights-related meetings and seminars organized by the UN. In addition, the League of Arab States has consistently been represented at sessions of the UN Human Rights Commission. Furthermore, when the Commission on Human Rights decided to set up an *ad hoc* Committee of Experts to investigate the position of the

Arab population in the occupied territories, the regional Commission made a point of placing at the disposal of that Committee all information likely to facilitate its task. A similar effort was made when a special committee, appointed by the General Assembly (res. 2443 (XXIII)(1968)), visited the Arab countries.

2. THE DRAFT DECLARATION FOR AN ARAB CHARTER OF HUMAN RIGHTS

Pursuant to the recommendation formulated at the Beirut Conference mentioned above, the regional Commission applied itself to the task of preparing an Arab Charter of Human Rights. At its fourth session, the Commission invited the Secretariat-General of the League to put the finishing touches to the draft Arab Charter and suggested that recourse be had to the experts of the United Nations to complete this task. A maximum period of six months was fixed for submission of the draft to the Member States.

In September 1970, the Council of the League set up a Committee of Experts to prepare a draft declaration (Resolution 2668/30). Meeting at the Secretariat-General of the League from April to July 1971, the Committee adopted a draft which was submitted to the Member States. While a number of States submitted comments on the draft, not all took the opportunity to do so.[3] It is thus to be regretted that in 1982, more than a decade after the completion of the first draft, no further progress has been achieved.

If the Universal Declaration of Human Rights is compared with the Arab draft, it is seen that the latter contains all the rights and freedoms proclaimed by the international community. The few specific features presented by the Arab draft consist in the more precise terms in which certain articles are set forth, dictated by regional considerations.

As a whole, the draft reflects at once a concern for continuity with the past, a desire to achieve Arab unity and lastly, a call for justice in respect of the Arab populations living in the occupied territories. This threefold objective gives the draft a specifically Arab regional character without, however, departing from the spirit of the Universal Declaration.

Overall, however, the activities of the Arab Commission on Human Rights seem to have been concerned more with international endeavours than with the problems of the different Member States of the League.

3. OTHER RELEVANT ACTIVITIES[4]

(a). The Commission on the Status of Arab Women

Another human rights-related regional body which is of significance in the present context is the Commission on the Status of Arab Women. The Commission is represented by an observer at meetings of the UN Commission on

the Status of Women and has, since 1951, generally presented a report on its
activities to the latter body. As an indication of the scope of its activities, the
1978 report of the Commission noted that the following were among the
issues dealt with: (a) family law in the Arab world, with attention to the
position of women and to the need to eliminate sex-based discrimination; (b)
education and the elimination of illiteracy; (c) the role of women, particularly
in rural areas, in national development; (d) the role of women in promoting
improved nutrition; and (e) the portrayal of women by the mass media.[5] The
1978 report also noted that the Council of the League of Arab States had
adopted an Arab Plan of Action relating to the status of women.

(b). The Baghdad Symposium

In May 1979 a Symposium on Human Rights and Fundamental Freedom in
the Arab Homeland was held in Baghdad, Iraq under the auspices of the
Union of Arab Jurists.[6] The symposium was attended by the representatives
of a wide range of organizations from the Arab world and it formulated a
number of recommendations. Amongst these was a decision to establish a
Standing Committee for the Defence of Human Rights and Fundamental
Freedoms in the Arab World to be composed of representatives of professional and peoples' organizations and other Arab personalities concerned
with human rights. The Committee's mandate was defined as being: (a) to
monitor the implementation of the recommendations of the Symposium, including efforts to persuade the Arab States to ratify the draft Arab Covenant
on Human Rights and Fundamental Freedoms, the implementation of whose
provisions it would likewise monitor; (b) to receive complaints from individuals and groups regarding violations of rights and freedoms; (c) to send
fact-finding missions to investigate violations of rights and freedoms in the
Arab States with a view to ascertaining the best ways and means to protect
and defend those rights and freedoms; and (d) to prepare annual reports on
the situation with regard to rights and freedoms in the Arab world for submission to Arab public opinion, Arab Governments and international bodies
concerned.

The Baghdad Symposium also: drafted an Arab Covenant on Human Rights
and Fundamental Freedoms to be submitted for comments to groups concerned with human rights in the Arab world; appealed to the Arab States to
ratify the International Covenants on Human Rights and a number of other
international human rights instruments; appealed to the League of Arab
States to activate its Standing Committee on Human Rights; reiterated the
right of the Palestinian Arab people to self-determination; and recommended
(1) that freedom of opinion and of the press in the Arab world be strengthened; (2) the adoption of measures to improve enjoyment of the rights to
freedom of movement, residence and work in the Arab world; and (3) the
abolition of special legislation, special courts and political detention particularly in the context of states of emergency.

On the subject of women's rights, the symposium noted "the distressing circumstances in which women in most Arab States find themselves" and recommended, *inter alia*, that efforts be made to abolish sex-based discrimination and to adopt legislation "that would allow women to enjoy their full political, civil and social rights." The symposium also emphasized the important role of non-governmental organizations in the promotion, protection and defence of human rights and the need to increase the teaching of human rights and humanitarian law in Arab educational institutions.

In conclusion it may be said that the Arab world is still dominated by the struggle for liberation rather than the pursuit of a policy of co-operation. The majority of Arab States has not, as of 1982, ratified the International Human Rights Covenants and none has ratified the Optional Protocol to the International Covenant on Civil and Political Rights. The Permanent Arab Commission on Human Rights has, like other organs of the League of Arab States, concentrated most of its efforts on the problems of human rights in the occupied territories, far more than on the problems of human rights within the territories of each Member State. Be that as it may, the interest shown by the Arab League as a whole and by each of the Arab States individually in the problems of human rights is a sign that the process of establishing a Pan-Arab legal system to protect the rights and freedoms of Arabs is under way. It will be difficult to reverse this process. In the future the struggle for peace, freedom, justice and development will take precedence over the struggle for national liberation, once the goal of the latter has been achieved.

NOTES

1. In 1980 the full membership of the League of Arab States consisted of: Algeria, Bahrain, Djibouti, Iraq, Jordon, Kuwait, Lebanon, Libyan Arab Jamahiriya, Mauritania, Morocco, Oman, Palestine, Qatar, Saudi Arabia, Somalia, Sudan, Syrian Arab Republic, Tunisia, United Arab Emirates, Arab Republic of Yemen and Peoples' Republic of Yemen.

2. See S.P. Marks, "La Commission Permanente Arabe des Droits de l'Homme," *RDH-HRJ*, Vol. III, pp. 101-108.

3. See generally the reports submitted by the League of Arab States to the UN Commission on Human Rights, including E/CN.4/1089 (1971); E/CN.4/1229 (1976); and E/CN.4/1283 (1977).

4. See generally: Moufid M. Chebab, "Droits de l'homme, universites et monde Arabe," in *L'enseignement des droits de l'homme* (Paris, Unesco, 1980) pp. 229-233; and A. H. Robertson, "The Permanent Arab Commission on Human Rights and the Proposed African Commission" in *Human Rights in the World* (Manchester University Press, 1973) pp. 140-158.

5. See E/CN.6/617 (1978).

6. The report was sent to the UN General Assembly in doc. A/C.3/34/11 (1979).

19 The Organization of African Unity (OAU)

Kéba M'Baye and Birame Ndiaye

1. HUMAN RIGHTS IN AFRICA by Kéba M'Baye

It is somewhat paradoxical to speak of "human rights in Africa" when, by their very nature, human rights concern each and every one of us, at one and the same time, without any consideration as to geographical location or adherence to a particular ideology.

In examining the situation in "dominated Africa," "traditional Africa" and "independent Africa," we shall see that each of these periods has its own characteristics and that, where human rights are concerned, the whole of Africa has been treated in a particular way.

(a). Human rights in dominated Africa

(i). UNIVERSALISM OF HUMAN RIGHTS?

The universal vocation of human rights led Leopold Sedar Senghor to caution the negotiators of the European Convention of 4 November 1950, Article 63 of which set the non-metropolitan territories outside the field of application of the new provisions. Senghor, then a member of the French Parliament, urged them to beware lest they prepare a Declaration of the Rights of "the European Man." Unfortunately, the ministerial organ of the Council did not feel it necessary to follow the recommendations of the deputy from Senegal, despite the preamble of the Universal Declaration of Human Rights which proclaims that all nations shall strive to secure the "universal and effective recognition and observance [of human rights], both among the peoples of Member States themselves and among the peoples of territories under their jurisdiction."

Related in this way, this event demonstrates that there is a natural tendency on the part of the western countries to consider human rights at the universal level only with a certain reluctance. And it is perhaps this which accounts for the lack of any systematic doctrine in this field. Such a tendency flies in the face of the very ideology of human rights; but, in the last analysis, is it not in keeping with the nature of things?

Since the Magna Carta, the different Declarations concerning rights and freedoms have been prepared by and for the societies to which their promoters belonged. Consequently, populations under foreign domination, and more particularly those of Africa, have always been prevented from benefiting unreservedly from the protection afforded by human rights rules. In the European "possessions" of Africa, the distinction between "citizens" on the one hand and "natives" on the other caused no account to be given to the principle of equality (and, at the same time, all the rules resulting from it), when non-citizens were concerned.

(ii). COLONIZATION AND HUMAN RIGHTS

Right to self-determination

Is not colonization in itself a denial of human rights? And is not the right of peoples to self-determination the first human right in that all the others are dependent on it? This is clearly recalled by the Law of Lagos.[1] For how can one justify the domination of one people by another without accepting in advance the inferiority of those dominated? As Jeanne Hersch has written,[2] "The colonialists' prime object was to go on exploiting their victims, and they justified their exploitation by an appeal to racial prejudice—the claim that those they were exploiting were intellectually inferior."

On the fallacious pretext of respecting "local traditions," the laws applied in the colonies were discriminatory. French nationality, for instance, was granted to everyone, citizens and natives, but only the former enjoyed public rights, in particular the right to vote (which, for Aristotle, constituted citizenship), at least until the law of 7 May 1946. The Universal Declaration of Human Rights itself neglected to mention the right to self-determination.

Public freedoms

In order to have access to public freedoms, it was necessary to enjoy civil and political rights, that is to say, to be recognized as a citizen. This rule applied in particular to public office in the French overseas territories prior to 1928. The indigenous population was allowed access to certain posts by a decree of 17 November 1928.[3]

Forced labour

The commandeering of "native" manpower was justified by the fact that "such manpower was needed for the first clearance operations and not enough workers presented themselves voluntarily, if there were any at all."[4] The French decree of 21 August 1930 authorized forced labour on two conditions: the goal pursued had to be in the public interest; and there had to be no means of obtaining voluntary labour. These conditions were, of course, soon invoked; there was no effective system for checking that they had been met. Moreover, it was easy for the settler who exploited the natives by availing himself of forced labour to demonstrate that those conditions had been satisfied. He was, however, not generally asked to do so.

International law itself was a party to these practices. Thus, the General Conference of the ILO at its 1930 session adopted a draft convention, declaring merely that forced labour should be suppressed within the shortest possible period, thus tacitly accepting its existence, which it subjected to "due regulation" and allowed "for public purposes." And yet, as has been recalled by Jean-Bernard Marie,[5] the ILO was in the vanguard of the struggle for human rights. Under Article 421 of the Treaty of Versailles, the Member States of the ILO undertook to apply to their "possessions" the Conventions adopted by them, subject to local conditions allowing of such an extension and with the reservation that the said Conventions may be modified to take account of local contingencies. When it is known that it was left to the colonizing State to interpret the notion of "local contingencies," it is immediately seen that this provision could not but remain a dead letter.

Human rights: a world programme?

Does it need to be stressed, finally, that the Declaration signed on 1 January 1942 in Washington, following on from the "four freedoms" of President Roosevelt and the "Atlantic Charter," essentially concerned those peoples who were at war against Nazism and consequently was of very small interest to Africa? It proclaimed that complete victory over their enemies was essential "to preserve human rights and justice in their own lands as well as in other lands." It is clear that the signatories of this Declaration were primarily concerned with bringing the Second World War to an honourable conclusion and with its consequences in their respective countries, leaving in the background the question of ensuring human rights and freedoms throughout the world.

The Universal Declaration of Human Rights of 1948 did not have the effect of putting an end to the discriminatory practices resulting from colonization. The Second World War had revealed a racism practised by white men against white men and, at the same time, the precarious nature of the rules established to protect human rights in the West.

Thus the measures taken at the time to prevent a return to the horrors of Hitlerism were closely bound up with the circumstances which had inspired them. Jeanne Hersch has rightly written: "The statement, in the preamble to the Constitution of Unesco, adopted in 1946, that the Second World War (the great and terrible war which has now ended) 'was a war made possible by the denial of the democratic principles of the dignity, equality and mutual respect of men and by the propagation, in their place, through ignorance and prejudice, of the doctrine of the inequality of men and races' does not refer primarily to colonialist racism, but to Hitlerian racialism."[6]

Furthermore, the African countries played but a minute part[7] in the preparation of the Universal Declaration. For a long time afterwards, it was not applicable to the nationals of those countries. Neither civil and political rights, nor economic, social and cultural rights were able to be applied to them without restrictions. And these restrictions were not necessitated either by respect for the right of others or by the safeguarding of public order, security or morals.

The principle of equality

The principle of equality before the law, although recognized by the Constitutions of the colonizing countries, was not applicable to those colonized. The French Constitution of 1946 provided (Article 80) that "all nationals of the overseas territories rank as citizens, by the same right as French nationals...." It then added, however, that "special laws shall establish the conditions under which they may exercise their rights as citizens." Despite Articles 81 and 82 which provided that nationals of the French Union ranked as citizens of the French Union, which ensured them of enjoyment of the rights and freedoms guaranteed by the Preamble of the Constitution, and that the special status which the new citizens were entitled to preserve could not, in any event, "constitute a ground for refusing or limiting the rights and freedoms guaranteed to French citizens," the application of these principles was far from being in conformity with their spirit.

Criminal proceedings

Until 1946, in the French colonies, particular penal legislation was applicable to the indigenous population, without any guarantee as to their security and safety. The punishments inflicted upon them were sometimes humiliating. Even today, in Namibia, men and even women are subjected to public flagellation, in violation of article 5 of the Universal Declaration, which prohibits cruel, inhuman and degrading punishment or treatment.

Migrations

The purpose of the restrictions placed on migrations by the regulations was to provide the agricultural settlers with low-cost labour, and they violated the principle of the right to freedom of movement. Freedom of expression was unrecognized, as was freedom of association. Participation in the conduct of public affairs was in reality but an illusion, since the indigenous population only exercised subordinate functions.

Free choice of employment

The political and social structures did not make the free choice of an occupation possible. The worker was not protected. In the French overseas territories it was necessary to wait until 1952 for there to be a Labour Code. Despite the vast progress thus achieved, the principle "equal work, equal pay" was not always respected.

The number of examples could be multiplied and each time it could be shown that the rules for the protection of human rights were not applied to colonized peoples. The normal consequence of such a situation has been that the peoples of Black Africa and Madagascar have always considered themselves to be completely alien to the principles and rules governing human rights. It was for this reason that, labouring under a feeling of frustration, their leaders in political or trade union organizations struggled above all to acquire equality and to be assimilated. Few of them were successful in shaking off the complex of inferiority which had been inculcated in them, in order to aspire to independence and to the affirmation of their own personalities.

In the majority of cases, independence was not the result of an armed struggle, but was granted in the framework of the decolonization campaign which was launched and supported immediately after the Second World War by the United Nations and the two super-powers (the United States and the Soviet Union).

(iii). THE CASE OF RHODESIA, SOUTH AFRICA AND NAMIBIA

The combined efforts of the United Nations, the OAU and the liberation movements led Portugal to liberate its former colonies: Guinea Bissau, Cape Verde, Mozambique and Angola. The problems of Namibia and South Africa remain, Zimbabwe (former Southern Rhodesia) having achieved independence. South Africa is responsible for the failure of the Geneva Conference on Namibian Independence.

South Africa, with its system of apartheid, maintains more than nineteen million Blacks, Coloured and Indians in a situation incompatible with the idea of human rights. Equality at birth is not recognized. Neither the right to life nor the right to freedom are considered to be fundamental rights. Obviously, all other rights are swept aside. A precise analysis of the situation in South Africa can be found in the reports drawn up by the *ad hoc* Group of Experts of the Commission on Human Rights since 1967.

In maintaining its presence in Namibia against the will of the international community, which has responsibility for the administration of that territory, South Africa has adopted a flagrantly unlawful attitude and, in addition, has extended apartheid to former South West Africa. This situation which has been imposed on Africa contrasts with the traditional rules which were in force on the continent before the arrival of the Whites. In pre-colonial Africa there existed a system of rights and fundamental freedoms which was adapted to the political and social situation of the period.

(b). Human rights in traditional Africa

(i). GENERAL REMARKS

In a communication presented by the World Veterans Federation on the occasion of the United Nations seminar held in Dakar from 8 to 22 February 1966, the following observation stands out: "How can a peasant from the bush appreciate freedom of expression, when the possibility of having modern fertilizers at his disposal would be much more valuable for him?"

This remark stems from a widespread idea which seems, *a priori*, to be justified. It brings out the fact that concern for effecting a radical change in, and improving, the quality of life clearly takes precedence over any desire to enjoy human rights and freedoms. Bread comes before roses. It might be concluded from this that, in societies which have not yet attained a certain level of satisfaction of their essential needs, men are not very worried about their rights and freedoms.

Such a conclusion would be a hasty and even false one in regard to traditional Africa. Admittedly, it is easy to meet needs in societies which are insufficiently developed, since those needs are reduced to the essential. In any event, pre-colonial Africa possessed a fitting system of rights and freedoms, although there was neither the recognition nor the clear formulation of such rights and freedoms as they are recognized, formulated and analyzed today. Nevertheless, it would be easy, in describing them as they were, to discover a definite kinship which undeniably links them to the present system of human rights. Those rights were recognized and protected. However, such recognition and protection must be understood in the context of the societies of yesteryear, split up and graded according to a hierarchy by the caste system and at the same time unified by mythical beliefs.

(ii). THE AFRICAN CONCEPTION OF LAW AND AFRICAN HUMANISM

Whereas modern man chooses between several types of society and shapes his law with the aim of achieving the object of his choice, in traditional African societies, the purpose of law is to maintain society in the state in which it has been transmitted by the elders, physically dead but still alive. "The dead are not dead," as the poet Birago Diop has said. Any contravention of that law leads to penalties which may consist in the elimination of the guilty person from the group. Thus, through "rejection," the head of a Malagasy family may exclude a child from the protection afforded by the tombs, and consequently by the family and the community.

The European conception of human rights, that is to say, a set of principles whose essential purpose is to be invoked by the individual against the group with which he is in conflict, is not met with in traditional Africa. In Africa, the individual, completely taken over by the archetype of the totem, the common ancestor or the protective genius, merges into the group. As has been pointed out by Professor Collomb,[8] living in Africa "means abandoning the right to be an individual, particular, competitive, selfish, aggressive, conquering being...in order to be with others, in peace and harmony with the living and the dead, with the natural environment and the spirits that people it or give life to it."

In traditional Africa, rights are inseparable from the idea of duty. They take the form of a rite which must be obeyed because it commands like a "categorical imperative." In this, they tie in, through their spiritualism, with the philosophy of Kant. The remark made by Jouon des Longrais in connection with Confucianist Asia may be applied to Africa which prefers the ideal of equality and freedom, "relations founded on attentive protection and respectful subordination."

If one bears in mind these features of African sociology, it becomes easy to single out a few fundamental rights as examples and demonstrate that they were well and truly recognized in traditional Africa. African society was both socialist and humanistic. It could not fail to have particular respect for man and for all that attaches to him, including his rights. This philosophy is expressed in the Woloff adage: "Nit moodi garab u nit" (man is man's cure) which Leopold Sedar Senghor never fails to recall. This form of humanism led to religious respect for others and the recognition of the rights and freedoms of everyone and of the entire group. We shall now review some of these rights and freedoms.

The right to life

On account of their traditional religious beliefs, Africans scrupulously respect life, even that of animals. Furthermore, life is not interrupted by death. It is the work of the gods and it is not in men's power to modify it or interrupt it. Children are taught that it is wrong to kill except in case of need: to feed oneself, to defend oneself, to make a sacrifice or to protect another life or a possession. Of course, these principles apply in particular to man.[9] The right to life requires not only that life be respected but also that it be maintained. Thus, not only is killing prohibited but it is also recommended to support life.

Freedom of expression

Freedom of expression was recognized in traditional Africa. However, it was exercised only in the framework of public or private institutions, in pursuance of the particular rules governing those institutions.

Religious freedom

Religious freedom was protected. It was exercised within the tribe or the ethnic group. And if it might not appear to be total within a single group or family, it was simply because beliefs were transmitted from parents to children, and the reverential respect due to elderly persons in fact left small room for any choice by the members of the same ethnic group.

Present-day Africa has retained this custom of respecting religious beliefs, as is borne out by the following words pronounced by the Senegalese deputy Galandou Diouf in 1936, on the occasion of the inauguration of the *Cathédrale du Souvenir africain* in Dakar. Addressing Cardinal Verdier, Galandou spoke as follows: "In inaugurating this church, your Eminence testifies to the bonds that link my country to the French motherland. Every morning, when dawn casts golden light upon the cathedral and the mosque, when, evening after evening, the imposing dome of the one and the delicate minarets of the other merge their shadows in the twilight, the sound of your bells and the chant of our muezzins will join together in inviting the faithful to pray to the Almighty on behalf of those whose memory must remain because they helped to create French Africa."

Freedom of association

Freedom of association was virtually total. Africans formed all kinds of groups among themselves. There were workers' associations which included cultural societies, admirably described by Zi-Kerbo. There were occult associations, associations formed for the purpose of entertainment, by age group, for games, etc.

Freedom of movement

Freedom of movement from one territory to another was a sacred principle which could be limited only by the insecurity of travel. The legendary hospitality of the Africans is but an outward sign of this freedom. Not only was the foreigner welcomed, but he was shown particular attention by the members of the host tribe; and the tokens of sympathy with which he was surrounded are evidence of the fact that man as such was recognized as having fundamental rights, as was the group to which he belonged, for, in the final analysis, such tokens were but the first gropings of the law of nations: respecting a foreigner means respecting the entity to which he belongs.

Foreigners were granted the right of asylum. Many examples are to be found in the history of Africa. Refugees were placed purely and simply on the same footing as autochthons. They were granted the right to settle, to possess a field,[10] to found a family, etc. No conditions had to be met to leave one's country or to return to it, or to settle elsewhere, either temporarily or for good.

The right to work

Work was both a right and a duty. In African society, which was structured along socialist lines, work was carried out principally for the benefit of the group, but also for the individual. In certain social units, the community-oriented character of which was more pronounced, the division of labour according to age made it possible to call on everyone so as to ensure, in the best conditions, the life and prosperity of all. Thus, in Gandoul (Sangomar Islands at the mouth of the Saloum in Senegal), the children watched over the fields and the livestock, the young people fished, the men cultivated the fields, the women prepared the meals and kept the houses and streets clean, while the old people wove the pagnes. Thus, everyone put his or her skills and industry at the disposal of the group.

The right to education

The right to education took the form of a duty to be borne by the community in order to make each child a fitting and useful element of the group. Education was the responsibility not only of parents but also of grandparents, brothers and sisters, uncles and aunts, cousins and even friends and neighbours. Everyone took an active part in the training and supervision of young men and women with a view to turning them into "good citizens."

Colonization disturbed the harmony of traditional society and changed the nature of the social relations on which it was founded by practising slave trade and forced labour and, in general, by denying the Africans the right to enjoy human rights and freedoms.

(c). Human rights in independent Africa

(i). CONSTITUTIONAL PRINCIPLES AND REALITY

It was reasonably to be expected that the former colonies, long prevented from enjoying public freedoms, would, once they had acceded to international sovereignty, set themselves up as passionate defenders of human rights.[11] It is a fact that, as soon as they were formed, the African States immediately became members of the United Nations and unreservedly accepted its principles and norms, in particular the provisions of the Charter of San Francisco and those of the Universal Declaration of Human Rights.

As has been observed by Lavroff and Peiser,[12] they then drew up constitutions and laws, adopting the terms of the Universal Declaration or referring to it. Some constitutions did not merely recall or quote the principles laid down by the principal documents relating to human rights. They defined, in special articles, public freedoms, thereby making them into provisions of positive law capable of being directly invoked in a court case. On the occasion of the Lagos Conference in 1961, El Hadji Sir Abubakar Tafawa Balewa emphasized this fact in respect of Nigeria.[13] On the invitation of the Nigerian Head of Government, the "Law of Lagos" stipulates that: "fundamental human rights, especially the right to personal liberty, should be written and entrenched in the Constitutions of all countries...."

However, things are quite different in reality. Looking beyond the phrases set down in these constitutions and laws, one discovers an Africa more concerned with achieving economic and social development and maintaining the stability of its government than with recognizing and promoting rights and freedoms. It is not to be denied that the myth of equality which haunted men's minds within the colonial entities survives at the international level. But what is claimed is the right to equality in the enjoyment of the wealth of the universe. Hence the pursuit of development for the sake of which all sacrifices are permissible.

(ii). THE OAU AND HUMAN RIGHTS

In this connection, the Organization of African Unity provides an eloquent illustration. At the opening of the Conference of Addis Ababa on 22 May 1963, Emperor Haile Selassie laid down in his introductory speech what were to be the true concerns of the African States: unity, non-interference and liberation. The Charter of the OAU provided at the outset for five specialized Commissions; but none of them were concerned either with human rights or even with legal matters. It is interesting to note this omission and to compare the attitude of the negotiators of Addis Ababa with that of the delegates of the San Francisco Conference who produced the Charter of the United Nations, in which a leading place is given to rights and freedoms.

An important event occured in Banjul (The Gambia) in January 1981: The Conference of Ministers of Justice of the OAU adopted a draft African Charter of Human and People's Rights. The Charter was subsequently adopted by the Thirty-seventh ordinary session of the Council of Ministers of the OAS and the OAS Assembly of Heads of States and Government, meeting in Nairobi, Kenya in June 1981. The full text of this Charter is reproduced as Part 3 of this chapter.

(iii). THE UN AND HUMAN RIGHTS

The place given by the UN Charter to the defense of human rights is perhaps to be accounted for by the keenness of the sad memories which had been left in the minds of the Europeans by the Second World War. Jean-Bernard Marie gives the following explanation:[14] "When on 25 April 1945 the United Nations Conference on International Organization opened, the end of the war was imminent and a new climate reigned at San Francisco. While the problem of security was a burning issue at Dumbarton Oaks, the immediate concerns of the 'United Nations' now were the organization of peace and economic and social co-operation. This more positive and open climate which reigned among the delegates to the Conference was to prove conducive to the new importance to be given to human rights in the Charter to be prepared."

(iv). THE SOCIOLOGY OF HUMAN RIGHTS IN CONTEMPORARY AFRICA

The Africans' concerns were quite different. Having long suffered from poverty, they wanted above all to make up for their economic backwardness, protect their fragile independence and help the other peoples of the continent to shake off the colonial yoke. This single-mindedness is revealed by the importance they accorded to commissions of an economic character. Once they had acquired independence, what they sought was improved well-being through an increase in the resources of each country. They reached a point where they neglected all that did not seem likely to consolidate their sovereignty and ensure their economic progress. What was involved here was a questionable conception, to say the least, of true economic and social development. Such development must necessarily include respect for the human person and the protection of his rights and freedoms. In assessing standards of living, the United Nations rightly take account of human freedoms.

Admittedly, during the first year of its existence, the OAU Assembly of Heads of State felt the need to create commissions for certain essential questions which had not been covered elsewhere by the existing organs.[15] Thus, a Commission of Jurists came into being at the same time as a Commission of Communications. But if one refers to the Lagos Conference of 1964, the occasion on which the idea was first put forward, it is seen that the purpose of the Commission of Jurists was not so much to act as an organ for the promotion and protection of human rights as to provide an instrument for legal research. Moreover, it was short-lived, and never properly came into being.

(v). THE FATE OF HUMAN RIGHTS

The attitude of the jurists

The African jurists, cautioned by their technical knowledge, eventually provided support for the attitude of the politicians which tended to relegate both human rights and any broad interpretation of the rules protecting them to the background. The first contact between African jurists took place in Lagos in January 1961 and the theme was "the rule of law." This was immediately after decolonization and one can detect, in the work of the Lagos Conference, a certain enthusiasm on the part of the Africans engaged, on behalf of their respective countries and of the continent as a whole, in the preparation of a coherent system for the recognition and protection of rights and freedoms. In their adherence to the principles and precepts laid down by the Universal Declaration of Human Rights, no false note was sounded.

The "Law of Lagos" unambiguously proclaims that "the Rule of Law is a dynamic concept which should be employed to safeguard and advance the will of the people and the political rights of the individual and to establish social, educational and cultural conditions under which the individual may achieve his dignity and realize his legitimate aspirations in all countries, whether dependent or independent." Admittedly, the Lagos Conference was attended only by jurists. But those jurists had done so with the approval of the national political authorities who had backed their participation in the Conference.

The attitude of the political authorities

After 1961, and once the first steps had been taken in the full exercise of national sovereignty, the political authorities responsible for the different states were faced with the hard facts of reality in the form of the countless difficulties which had arisen: the withdrawal of the subventions of the colonizing powers, the shrinking of the markets, the drop in world prices for raw materials, the spiralling prices of manufactured goods, lack of skilled labour and, above all, internal and external subversion.

This position of weakness, exploited by certain imperialist powers, created a permanent state of internal insecurity favourable to *coups d'état*, which have taken place in Africa at the average rate of two a year. Thus, the universal principles which are the foundation of human rights will still be seriously questioned. The idea of giving them a context compatible with economic and social development and with political stability quickly occurred to leading African statesmen. As Jean-Paul Masseron[15a] emphasized, "The leading states-men of Africa have a tendency to sacrifice individual liberties in order to safeguard national independence." Citing Lavroff and Peisen,[16] the author continues: "Development comes before liberty."

The same remark was made by M. Jéol:[17] "In the following years, however, national legislatures drafted new laws which considerably limit the scope of constitutional principles in this field." Thus, associations must not only be declared but they must also be authorized by the executive; meetings are severely controlled; the regime of political parties tends to favour the governmental party, which is often the only party; freedom of the press has severe restrictions; individual security is endangered by many emergency laws concerning State security. Property is severely limited in the "public interest" or the "national interest."

At the same time, the legislator made economic and social rights much more real through the progress of labour law and social security and the partial codification of civil law. Whereas the classical rights so prized in the "liberal" democracies are undergoing considerable restrictions for the benefit of State power, economic and social rights, on the other hand, are developing and it is to that development that the authors of African Constitutions no doubt refer when they describe their democracy as "social." Finally, it should be added that there exists a considerable gap between the letter of the law and its application by governments, which is practically beyond the control of the parliaments. Thus, judicial review as foreseen by African Constitutions takes on an increased importance.

No pretext was overlooked in order to "adapt" the interpretation of the Universal Declaration of Human Rights. Very few countries escaped this tendency, especially since the realities of other continents provided Africans with a rationalization for a clear conscience. As René Cassin[18] has emphasized, "No country, not even the most advanced, can pride itself on fulfilling all the Articles of the Declaration." Séan McBride, then Secretary-General of the International Commission of Jurists, wrote: "The evidence shows that the primacy of the rule of law is not fully respected throughout the world; our Commission must also direct its attention to areas of the world where it is too easily assumed that the rule of law prevails."

The African governments, which knew these facts, interpreted them in such a way as to justify the infringements required inevitably by the necessities of unity, prosperity and stability. The Declaration itself furnishes an excuse, first of all, in its Preamble which states that "this Universal Declaration of Human Rights" is proclaimed "as a standard of achievement" and then in its Article 29 which states: "Everyone has duties to the community in which alone the free and full development of his personality is possible." This prescription pleased them, as it conforms to the African conception of law.

Toward a new approach to the issue of human rights

At the Congress organized by the International Commission of Jurists in New Delhi in January 1959, it was specified that the rule of law is a "dynamic concept for the expansion and fulfillment of which jurists are primarily responsible and which should be employed not only to safeguard and advance the civil and political rights of the individual in a free society, but also to establish social, economic, educational and cultural conditions under which his legitimate aspirations and dignity may be realized."

The invitation to give fresh thought to the rule of law was quickly grasped by the Africans, who did not fail to create a sort of expanded legality on behalf of the general interest. Sékou Touré clearly expressed this idea when he wrote: "In our Republic personal liberty is viewed from the perspective of its practical usefulness for society."

Six years after Lagos, the International Commission of Jurists organized a conference of Francophone African jurists at Dakar in order to take stock of the situation. The final document of the conference, the "Declaration of Dakar," emphasized above all that there could not be any different interpretation where the dignity of man was concerned. It stipulated that the black man should respect the rule of law in the same way as the white man, since the fundamental demands of the rule of law were no different in Africa from what they were elsewhere. The jurists who met in Dakar were led to note, however, that in several fields, rights and freedoms were violated with more or less acceptable justification.

Freedom

Slavery, compulsory labour, the absence of trade union freedoms and freedom of the press provide an eloquent illustration of this. Although slavery has virtually disappeared in Africa, it continues to be tolerated in some of its forms. Thus, the institution of the "house captive" exists, by virtue of which the descendants of slaves retain their lowly status. They thus form a lower caste, generally despised and condemned, with few exceptions, to endogamy.

A decision taken by the Cadi de Thies (Senegal) on 20 July 1957 confirms this situation. The court had allowed the litigant to bring proof that the "*de cujus*" was his "common property," that is to say, his slave. A local notable corroborated the claims of the applicant, pointing out that his mother had purchased the mother of the "*de cujus*," without her freedom ever having been obtained. The Cadi decided that the applicant should inherit the assets left by the "*de cujus*" (his property), referring to local Islamic custom. This decision was reversed by a higher court in the interests of public order. It nonetheless provides an illustration of the survival of the institution of the "house captive."

The rule of law

The principle of lawfulness is not always respected in Africa. The judiciary, which guarantees that principle, is reduced to the rank of a "service." There is to be found in several speeches a statement to the effect that as the law is an expression of sovereign power, those invested with that power, that is to say, the people or its legitimate representatives, should be able to eliminate it. Sékou Touré defined Guinean law as "the product of our own manifold needs in that it expresses in the reality of its application the value of our civilization and in that it is in conformity with the object of our revolution." Speaking of the magistrates, he writes: "The magistrates...should embody and express the social morality of the nation, for each of their acts is interpreted by the people, not in accordance with a particular provision of the Penal Code or a particular consequence of the procedure, but solely in the light of its own social and spiritual conceptions and its political and moral aspirations."

In several countries the effect of there being a single party in power is that the decisions taken by that party are considered to be superior to laws and regulations. "No act of a public character," wrote Sékou Touré, "will be adopted in the future without the authorization of the Party." Almost all the constitutions allow the executive to take emergency measures as required by circumstances when institutions are threatened.

Freedom of employment

By and large, the public authorities consider that the principle of freedom of employment does not preclude the obligation to take part in work in the general interest. An ordinance issued in Mali provides that work is a duty. Thus, in the framework of civil obligations, human investment or work in the general interest, the citizens of the African countries are often invited to take part in what, in the absence of exceptional circumstances justifying it, may be regarded as compulsory labour. On this point, the jurists meeting in Dakar expressed their views as follows: "Freedom of employment may, in exceptional circumstances, be compatible with the obligation on the part of the citizen to perform work from which he shall derive fair profit."

This being so, everything depends on the way in which the notion of "exceptional circumstances" is understood. A restrictive interpretation, confined for instance to the obligation to provide assistance which weighs morally upon every individual living in society and according to which everyone's efforts must be mobilized when the life of the community is in imminent danger, is perfectly compatible with freedom of employment. Such an interpretation is subscribed to in certain long-established States including France.

However, the work of the Conference, and more particularly that of the first commission, provides grounds for affirming that the notion of "exceptional circumstances" must be given an interpretation which goes far beyond the limits determined by French law. In the minds of those participating in the Dakar Conference, the state of under-development should be considered to be a permanent exceptional circumstance.

This interpretation clearly emerges from the "Act of Dakar" which contains the following statement: "Once free from their implications inherited from the colonial past, the fundamental demands of the rule of law appear clearly to be no different in Africa from those accepted elsewhere." This cryptic statement discreetly conceals the idea of a state of permanent emergency which, as long as it lasts, justifies certain violations of the principle of the rule of law. It is to be noted that the time at which the effects of the colonial past may be reasonably considered to have become exhausted was not specified, and indeed it would appear that it is for each individual State to decide.

Freedom of association

As far as freedom of association is concerned, it must be recognized that it is difficult for it to exist in countries where an institutional or *de facto* single or unified party system has been imposed. In Africa the single party system is the general rule. This system, however, is a prerequisite for the exercise of many other rights and, in particular, the right to take part in political activities in one's own country. Just as, with a few exceptions, including Senegal, there are no opposition parties, trade unions must give their allegiance to the party in power. On this point, it is to the merit of the Dakar Declaration that it does not mince its words: "The worker's freedoms and rights are but illusory if they are not supported by a free trade union movement." It even goes so far as to define the "free trade union," specifying that it is "a trade union in no way controlled by the public authorities and open to all those who fulfil its conditions for membership."

The right to strike

The right to strike is generally recognized, but it is regulated in such a way that it scarcely exists, given that in most countries the exercise of that right is subject to the government authorities not adopting a solution of conciliation in regard to collective disputes. Any strike that occurs despite a decision to adopt a solution of conciliation becomes unlawful with all the consequences which may arise from such a situation.

Criminal proceedings

The safety of citizens is rarely guaranteed. The individual is inadequately protected against arbitrariness on the part of the Administration. There do not always exist regulations governing the taking into custody of detained persons. When they do exist, the rules and provisions of the codes and laws are often violated with impunity by the authorities of the police administration. By means of administrative internment and house arrest, even outside periods of disturbance, unwelcome political rivals can be isolated, and those who are subjected to such measures are seldom allowed the assistance of counsel. The political authorities distrust common law tribunals and often set up *ad hoc* courts to sit in judgment on acts already committed; this is a form of violation of the principle *"nullum crimen sine lege."* The first Commission of the Dakar Conference in 1967 even accepted that the creation of emergency courts should be envisaged insofar as they are warranted by the situation.

The right to freedom of movement

The African States have found it necessary, in order to guard against the brain drain and the building up of a Black proletariat in Europe, the source of countless difficulties in bilateral relations, to place restrictions on the movements of their nationals.

Freedom of the press

In Africa, freedom of information does not exist to any greater extent than that of association. This state of affairs is a serious handicap to the free exercise of democracy. The press is often reduced to its simplest expression. In many countries there exists only one daily newspaper, and it is controlled by the party in power. If any other newspapers exist, they do not escape this pressure. As has been said by Mr. Madeira Keita, "There can be no question of neutral journalism in Africa."[19]

Development and human rights

Thus, the African governments appear clearly to have sacrificed rights and freedoms for the sake of development and political stability. This situation can be explained and even justified. In mobilizing the masses in order to secure economic and social development, everyone's attention is directed exclusively towards the prospect of improved standards of living. Inaction or idleness thus come to be regarded as an infraction and the exercise of certain freedoms, even in the absence of any abuse, as an attack on public order.

It may be noted however, that several recent conferences in Africa have sought to explore the difficult issues involved in the relationship between respect for human rights and the quest for development. In July 1978 a Colloquium on Human Rights and Economic Development in Francophone Africa was held in Butare, Rwanda. In the course of the colloquium, considerable attention was paid to the need for a new international economic order and the colloquium concluded that a more equitable distribution of the world's economic power was essential to achieve economic development and to guarantee human rights. Since the protection of the economic rights of the individual depends ultimately on the economic development of the society as a whole, the colloquium assumed that the right to development itself must be held to be a fundamental human right implicit in the guarantee of individual economic and social rights.

The Colloquium also emphasized concepts of human rights in traditional African societies and the necessity of ensuring that this traditional respect for human rights be continued in the modern African state. It was not accepted that "human rights" was an alien notion in Africa; rather, the principle of individual rights within the framework of the legitimate concerns of the community has long been a part of African life.[20]

At a subsequent conference on "Development and Human Rights" organized by the International Commission of Jurists and the Association Sénégalaise d'Etudes et de Recherches, and held in Dakar in September 1978, conclusions were adopted which, *inter alia*, called for: "the establishment, at the Pan-African level, of a Convention on Human Rights; the creation of sub-regional institutes of human rights for their promotion by information documentation, research and the awakening of public opinion; the creation of one or several Inter-African Commissions on Human Rights composed of independent judges authorised to examine complaints concerning the violations of human rights; and the creation within African States of mass organizations capable of effectively defending human rights."[21]

Judicial organs

The judicial organs have not acquired sufficient maturity for them to be able to carry out their natural functions in complete independence. Moreover, the control of the judiciary by the executive is leading, finally, to the gradual abandonment of the rule of the separation of powers.

The citizens themselves do not help to ensure that the administration of justice is improved. Even where recourse exists against the abuse of power, it is very seldom used. The Africans consider a trial to be always subjective and everyone has the feeling, in attacking a decision, that they are attacking the authority responsible for it, and generally the latter reacts in the same way. The Administration itself refuses, in some cases, to apply the decisions of the courts until such time as a "more comprehensive" judicial organ reaches a verdict, or pending a change in the law by a legislative organ which obeys the instructions of the party and of the government.

It is perhaps this which accounts for the suspicion with which the African leaders view jurisdictional bodies, particularly when they are international in character. It is undoubtedly this which underlies the delay in the adoption of an African convention on human rights. The idea was first broached at the Lagos Conference, thanks to the insistence of Karel Vasak. The law of Lagos declares in paragraph 4: "In order to give full effect to the Universal Declaration of Human Rights of 1948, this Conference invites the African governments to study the possibility of adopting an African Convention of Human Rights in such a manner that the Conclusions of this Conference will be safeguarded by the creation of a court of appropriate jurisdiction and that recourse thereto be made available for all persons under the jurisdiction of the signatory States." However, as noted in Part 2 of this Chapter, it was only in 1979 that the OAU first initiated concrete steps in this direction.

Similarly, the *ombudsman* institution has scarcely met with much success. Only Mauritius (Constitution of 1968), Tanzania (Constitution of 1965) and Zambia (Constitution of 1973) have set up and put into operation genuine systems of supervision of the *ombudsman* variety. And except for Senegal, few African States have set up a permanent committee on human rights. It is also noteworthy that, in January 1979, the cornerstone was laid for the Dakar Institute of Human Rights and Peace, the first human rights institute on the African continent.

Private bodies

Associations working for the public good which could assist in establishing a better legal system are not tolerated. And yet they might at least have been able to popularize the means of struggling against arbitrariness and to ensure, even directly, if necessary, the defense of their members' interests.

Conclusion

The restrictions placed on the recognition of human rights and on the application of the rules governing them are certainly not peculiar to underdevelopment. History reveals that the non-universalistic conception of human rights has long prevailed, and still prevails, in Africa. This conception has been used to challenge the "human" aspects of those rights or to question whether they are truly rights in the legal sense. In the past, and still today, the universal application of human rights has been denied by dehumanizing peoples, races and groups. Such was the fate of the slaves, the colonized peoples, the Indians and the Blacks. Even today the colour of one's skin can prevent one from having the right to "human dignity."

In addition, at any time, in any place, those organs entrusted with the responsibility of government are seen to benefit, on certain occasions, from a margin of discretion which escapes all control and by virtue of which some of their acts, since they are directly attached to their functions, are, *a priori*, considered to be legitimate. This tolerance has given rise to the well-known theories concerning discretionary powers, acts of government and exceptional circumstances.

What is more, even in homogeneous societies where the universalism of the concept "man" is not contested, the scope of human rights is limited according to the period and circumstances. Generally this is a reflection of the level of the society concerned and of the ideology of those in power, but sometimes it reveals simply a state of crisis.

And Africa, in fact, is undergoing a crisis. For this reason, one should not despair either of its leaders or of its people. In the long run, they will tend asymptotically towards that ideal common to all mankind: the Universal Declaration of Human Rights.

2. THE PLACE OF HUMAN RIGHTS IN THE CHARTER OF THE ORGANIZATION OF AFRICAN UNITY by Birame Ndiaye

The Charter of the Organization of African Unity (OAU) does not appear to attach a particular significance to human rights although they are referred to in several articles. However, this approach cannot readily be criticized, in view of the the fact that the constitutional instruments of the other regional organizations and the United Nations also contain relatively few references to human rights. In general, the tasks of constructing a system for the promotion and perhaps also for the protection of human rights has been performed by means of organizational practice, sometimes backed by a binding legal instrument. In the case of the OAU, however, most of the efforts of that Organization which represents the African continent have focused upon the right of peoples to self-determination and the struggle against racial discrimination. It is only since 1979 that serious efforts have been undertaken by the OAU itself to establish a formal human rights machinery.

There is no doubt that exercise of the right of peoples to self-determination, guaranteed by Article 1, paragraph 1 of both Human Rights Covenants, is a prerequisite for the implementation of human rights. As J. Salmon has written,[22] "The genuine and fundamental problem, however, was that there can be no question of human rights for those who belong to a people which is subjugated and which is refused the right to be itself." And Salmon adds: "Whatever the case, recent developments, texts such as resolution 1514 (XV) on decolonization and resolution 2625 (XXV) on friendly relations make it undeniable today that the right of peoples to self-determination is recognized as a right and forms a part of international law." The idea had previously been explored by Chaumont.[23] He cogently concluded as follows: "It is not by chance that in the resolutions of the United Nations General Assembly the right of peoples to self-determination is set forth as the first set of rights. The corollary to this idea is that man should not feel himself to be an alien or estranged in his own community, in which alone (according to Article 29 of the Universal Declaration) the free and full development of his personality is possible. In other words, a people is but an inert mass unless it is composed of individuals in the sense of Article 29." There is a profound bond between the nations, the people and the individual person. It is this which makes it necessary to proclaim the right of peoples to self-determination and, at the same time, to prohibit racial discrimination. Those who framed the Addis Ababa Charter learned from this lesson; it has been taken into consideration by the OAU in its practice.

Was it right, however, for the Organization of African Unity to have this dualistic and hierarchical conception which created legal obligations in respect of the right of peoples to self-determination and to the prohibition of racial discrimination, but which, after formally recognizing other rights, made its Member States solely responsible for their implementation. Whatever the answer, the days of OAU neglect of the broader human rights picture appear to be over. In addition to actions taken by the Organization in the late 1970s in relation to specific human rights problems, the Assembly of Heads of State and Government of the OAU decided in July 1979 to organize as soon as possible an expert meeting "to prepare a preliminary draft of an 'African Charter on Human and Peoples' Rights' providing, *inter alia*, for the establishment of bodies to promote and protect human and peoples' rights."[24] The same meeting also adopted a Declaration on the Rights and Welfare of the African Child.[25] These initiatives are examined further below.

(a). A global but formal recognition of human rights

There was hardly any mention of "human rights" in the Ethiopian draft[26] of 17 May 1963 which was preferred to the Ghanaian draft and which served as a basis for discussion. The Ethiopian draft made do, first of all, with a reference to the Charter of the United Nations in paragraph 5 of its preamble which stated: "Convinced that the Charter of the United Nations, to the principles of which we reaffirm our adherence, affords a sound basis for peaceful and positive co-operation among States...." Then, in Article 43, it dealt with the problem of the compatibility of the OAU and the UN. According to this article, the Member States agree that none of the provisions of the Charter shall be understood or interpreted as impairing the undertakings or other rights and obligations contracted by the Member States of the Organization of African Unity by virtue of the Charter of the United Nations.

No doubt the text submitted by the Government of the Negus contained general and vague provision which could be interpreted as establishing human rights in whole or in part. This is true for instance of paragraphs 3, 4 and 5 of the preamble:

"Firmly resolved to safeguard the hard-won independence as well as the sovereignty and territorial integrity of our States and to fight against neo-colonialism in all its forms, including political and economic intervention,

"Dedicated to the total liberation of those African territories which are still under foreign domination,

"Noting the express desire of the African peoples and governments to achieve improved living conditions for the peoples of Africa, through the triumph of freedom...."

It is also true of Article 1, paragraph 1, which deals with the purposes of the Organization:

"To co-ordinate and intensify their collaboration and efforts to achieve improved living conditions for the peoples of Africa."

Mention might also be made of Article 17 of the same draft, which states: "The essential purpose of the Commission shall be to increase economic and social well-being by means of effective and close co-operation between them."

Nevertheless, it was necessary to wait for the Charter drafted by the Special Sub-Committee of Ministers of Foreign Affairs of the Summit Conference for human rights to be expressly established once and for all.[27]

(i). GLOBAL RECOGNITION OF HUMAN RIGHTS

From that time onwards human rights were established as a result both of the provisions of the preamble of the Charter and of the purposes and principles defined therein. Moreover, the stipulations are formulated in such flexible terms as to allow for the global recognition of human rights.

The contribution of the Preamble of the Charter

The preamble of the Charter no longer contains simply a reference to the constitutional text of the UN. It also mentions the Universal Declaration of Human Rights as the principles to which the States parties reaffirm their adherence. For those States, the Charter of the United Nations and the Universal Declaration of Human Rights "provide a solid foundation for peaceful and positive co-operation" among them.

From earlier paragraphs, couched in too general terms, the intention of those who framed the Addis Ababa Charter to recognize human rights could be inferred. In the first paragraph, it is written that "it is the inalienable right of all people to control their own destiny"; in the second, it is stated that "freedom, equality, justice and dignity are essential objectives for the achievement of the legitimate aspirations of the African peoples." In the third, *denique tandem*, is established, for the Member States, the "responsibility to harness the natural and human resources" of the continent "for the total advancement of our peoples in spheres of human endeavour."

However, use of the expression would constitute an abuse of language if recognition of human rights resulted solely from the provisions of the preamble. It is to be noted in fact that the preambles of both internal and international constitutional acts often have the hidden function of allowing for the reconciliation of divergent and even seemingly irreconcilable conceptions. In the case of the preamble of the French Constitution of 1946, Burdeau,[28] in his Treaty on political science, recalled that "compromise proved to be doubly necessary: on the one hand, between those who supported the liberal ideas of 1789, who would have been content to make a few minor changes in the august text without altering its spirit, and those who wished to give the Declaration a more pronounced progressive character and, on the other hand, between those who regarded the rights set forth as having an absolute character and who consequently wished to protect them against any interference on the part of the legislature, and the Marxists who, contending that they had a relative character, sought to prevent those rights from being paralyzed by imperative texts." The UN, notwithstanding the provisions of its preamble, did not fail to seek more operative instruments by proceeding to draft the Universal Declaration of Human Rights. Moreover, the shortcomings of that instrument, related to both its legal nature and to its content, were to make it necessary to prepare the two Covenants, together with other instruments. In other words, rights may be enshrined in a preamble but not effectively established. In the case of the OAU, the formulations noted earlier give no indication of any desire on the part of those who drafted them to create a rule of positive law. This is important, for as Burdeau has written,[29] "Declarations, preambles and ideological provisions of constitutions can no longer today be considered as each forming a whole, the parts of which, without distinction, have the same legal force. A distinction must be made between that which is a rule of positive law and that which is a programme or directive.... Texts of this kind have the character of positive law on account of the fact that for them to be applied, they do not require any change to be made in existing law; they record a legal situation the content of which immediately imposes itself...." It is certain that such characteristics are presented by the provisions of the preamble and those of the Universal Declaration or the Charter to which the preamble under consideration refers only very generally.

The fact remains that the stipulations of the preamble of the Addis Ababa Charter expressed an ideological function which respects human rights. Moreover, they do not exist in isolation but are supported by those contained in the paragraphs regarding the purposes and principles of the Organization.

Human rights according to the purposes set forth in the Charter

The purposes assigned to the OAU by its Member States contain an explicit reference to human rights, as does the preamble of the Charter, in the form of a mention of the Universal Declaration. According to Article II, paragraph c), one of the purposes of the Organization shall be "to promote international co-operation, having due regard to the Charter of the United Nations and the Universal Declaration of Human Rights." Paragraph b) of the same article provides that one of its purposes shall be "to co-ordinate and intensify their co-operation and efforts to achieve a better life for the peoples of Africa." Paragraph d) outlaws colonialism. While it might seem to be clearly established that the OAU intended to make it an obligation for its members to protect human rights as guaranteed by the UN Charter and especially those set forth in the Universal Declaration, this is far from being so. For, without requiring that the Member States ensure the protection of human rights in order that they be admitted as members of the club, it seems that the Charter of the OAU would have wanted to make the assurance of such protection the basis and justification (paragraph b) of their co-operation. However, it is difficult to see how the implementation of human rights can be laid down as a basis for international co-operation without first of all making it into a condition of admission, a sort of entrance fee. It is a fact, however, that the inclusion of human rights under the heading "purposes" does not entail any obligation on the part of the Member States to implement them.

As F. Borella has written,[30] "These purposes define the powers of the Organization which are formulated restrictively, thus proving, if proof were needed, that the dogma of State sovereignty was not called in question at Addis Ababa. The Organization is competent to co-ordinate and harmonize the general policies of its Member States, in particular in the following spheres: Article II[31] then lists all the activities of a modern State, except in respect of the central nucleus of the concept of State (constitutional and administrative organization, law and police)." As is seen, this "central nucleus" relates to a large extent to human rights. The fact that it is excluded confirms that tendency on the part of Third World countries in general to continue to honour the dogma of sovereignty, at least in its positive aspects. The allusion made here to human rights is no doubt of greater value than that of a clause of style; it cannot be reduced to a simple reference to the Universal Declaration, and it cannot be regarded as entailing an obligation for the Member States. If it could be, it would have been included among the legal and political principles which the Member States undertook to implement in accordance with Article VI of the Charter which states: "The Member States pledge themselves to observe scrupulously the principles enumerated in Article III of the present Charter."

Human rights in the principles set forth in the Charter

Not only is there no mention of human rights in the principles set forth, apart from the right of peoples to self-determination, but neither is there mention of the question of co-operation among States. However, the rule of non-interference is vigorously affirmed, as is easily understandable, for, as Borella has written,[32] account must be taken of the "fragility of the African States, the artificial character of which must be camouflaged by the permanent affirmation that they exist and that they possess exclusive jurisdiction over their populations and their territories." But it goes without saying that one does not promote the protection of human rights while laying emphasis on the exclusive domain of control of each separate State.

The right of peoples to self-determination is confirmed by the provisions enumerating the principles of the Organization of African Unity. But at the same time a dualistic conception emerges: on the one hand, the right of peoples to self-determination and, on the other hand, all other human rights. This conception is not founded solely on the fact that the implementation of the right of peoples to self-determination is a prerequisite for the protection of human rights, rather it assigns importance only to that right.

The conception of the OAU Charter in the matter of human rights is not only dualistic but also preferential and selective, for whereas the Member States are obliged to respect the right of peoples to self-determination, no such obligation exists in respect of other human rights. It is obvious that such a conception exonerates the Member States of the OAU from any international obligation in regard to the implementation of those rights. Moreover, this interpretation is supported by the fact that the Charter does not provide for any system for the promotion or protection of human rights. As a result, recognition of human rights in general is purely formal.

(ii). FORMAL RECOGNITION OF HUMAN RIGHTS

It is no doubt desirable for a constitutional text not to be too rich in details: sparing as it is in this respect, the Charter of the OAU conforms to the established rules. All the same, it precisely lays down the purposes and principles of the Organization and rigorously describes its institutions. Article XX of the Charter, concerning the specialized Commissions, contains no mention of a commission on human rights. The list which it provides, however, is not exhaustive. Consequently, the omission is not irreversible even though, as it stands, one may regret the political character of the commissions under Article XXI.

The economy of Article XX

Under the terms of Article XX, "The Assembly shall establish such Specialized Commissions as it may deem necessary, including the following: 1. Economic and Social Commission; 2. Educational and Cultural Commission; 3. Health, Sanitation and Nutrition Commission; 4. Defense Commission; 5. Scientific, Technical and Research Commission."

Of course, the fact that this initial list did not include a commission on human rights is still of significance as regards the wishes of the African States. Article 68 of the Charter of the United Nations is formulated in more general terms: "The Economic and Social Council shall set up commissions in economic and social fields and for the promotion of human rights, and such other commissions as may be required for the performance of its functions." It bears witness to greater consideration for human rights. All the same, the breach opened by Article XX of the Charter of the OAU could have provided a means of making up for that omission. It is revealing, however, that none of the amendments relating to Article XX have given rise to the establishment of a commission on human rights. On the basis of Article XX, a Conference of Heads of State established two new commissions in 1964: 1.the Commission of Jurists (resolution AHG/4-1); 2.the Commission of Communications (resolution AHG/20-1).

Moreover, these new specialized commissions were short-lived. In 1966 the Conference of Heads of State and Government decided to dissolve the Commission of Jurists and to reduce the number of Specialized Commissions from six to three, viz: 1.the Economic and Social Commission, incorporating the Commission of Communications; 2.the Educational, Scientific, Cultural and Health Commission, incorporating three former Commissions: the Educational and Cultural Commission, the Health, Sanitation and Nutrition Commission and, lastly, the Scientific, Technical and Research Commission; 3.the Defense Commission which retains its original structure without change.[33] In addition, the Conference decided to adopt a recommendation by virtue of which the Specialized Commissions must meet once every two years.

The political character of the prescribed commissions

Article XXI which provides for the membership of the Specialized Commissions prescribed in Article XX imposes a political character on them. "Each Specialized Commission referred to in Article XX shall be composed of the Ministers concerned or other Ministers or Plenipotentiaries designated by the governments of the Member States."

The tendency to give greater legal value to human rights cannot, however, be maintained nor have all the anticipated effects unless competent organs are established, for purposes either of promotion or protection, composed of independent persons, chosen on the basis of their qualifications. This requirement must be met if the interests of an organization are to take precedence over those of its Member States. For while the relations between law and politics are inextricable at the domestic level, they are even closer and more intense at the international level.

And, while the relations between international law and politics are, as a general rule, deep-seated, they are even more so when human rights are involved. There is in fact a quantitative and qualitative relationship between the superstructure of a State and the human rights which it will accept to guarantee at the international level, so deep-seated is the relationship between States and human rights. This being so, there is a pressing need to remove the political character of international bodies specializing in human rights. And the least that can be said is that those who established the Charter of the Organization of African Unity, without perhaps giving any particular thought to it, placed an obstacle in the way.

(b). The human rights practice of the OAU

In almost two decades of existence the nature and extent of the OAU's concern for human rights have steadily evolved. For the first fifteen years or so of its existence it did not appear to have been unduly concerned with human rights except when denouncing the violation of such rights in the former Portuguese colonial territories, Rhodesia, Namibia and the Union of South Africa.

No doubt the Charter of the Organization provided small incentive for it to do so. However, international organizations are governed by their own dynamics. Their practices are almost never in conformity with their constitutional texts. Any revision of those texts is too fraught with political implications and, on this account, very seldom occurs.

It is a fact today—and this is corroborated by the Opinion of the International Court of Justice regarding the expenditures of the United Nations and Article 5 of the Vienna Convention on the Law of Treaties—that an international organization, by virtue of its practice, defines rules of common law. It is to be deduced from this that the wording adopted corresponds to a concern not to be confined to what is contained in the constitutional act, but also to take into account that which has emerged from practice.

In the original version of the present chapter, written in 1976, the present writer observed that "the practice of the OAU has proved to be even less inspired than its Charter. Expressing it metaphorically, one might say that it honours the pedestal but does not care about the statue, which is passed over in complete silence: not a single resolution, not a single recommendation, not a single declaration."

Writing in 1981 it is possible to distinguish two facets of the evolution of the OAU's human rights efforts. In the first place, the Organization has taken a number of steps to bring the practice of *apartheid* to an end once and for all. To that end: resolutions have been adopted, manifestos have been issued, an institute has been established, a Committee of Liberation has been set up and co-operation with the UN with regard to the situation in southern Africa has been extensive.[34] In the second place, the OAU has begun the process of establishing a Human Rights Commission and of adopting a comprehensive human rights charter.

(i). HUMAN RIGHTS: A MEANS OF CALLING THE COLONIAL POWERS TO TASK

Human rights undoubtedly constitute at present an effective weapon against colonialism—especially when the colonizing power has not taken the precaution of providing for assimilation, when that power openly establishes and supports apartheid.

All the former French, British and Portuguese-speaking colonial territories in Africa are now subjects of international law. The major part of Africa is independent or is recognized to be worthy of freedom. The Declaration on the Granting of Independence to Colonial Countries and Peoples eloquently reflects international law in the matter. The main point of it is the solemn proclamation of "the necessity of bringing to a speedy and unconditional end colonialism in all its forms and manifestations...The subjection of peoples to alien subjugation, domination and exploitation constitutes a denial of fundamental human rights, is contrary to the Charter of the United Nations and is an impediment to the promotion of world peace and co-operation. All peoples have the right to self-determination...."

This declaration is supported by a series of pre-existing or subsequent instruments, of varying legal force, but all with the goal of unconditionally condemning colonization as a system of relations between peoples. Such is also the goal of the Charter, or at least of its first article, devoted to the purposes of the Organization; and of the first articles of the Covenants on Human Rights, and the Declaration on Friendly Relations. To challenge a State on the basis of these documents is to seek, with much likelihood of success, to submit it to universal censure. And the Portugal of Salazar and Caetano understood this very well when they tried to conceal the colonial status of Portugal's African provinces. The Republic of South Africa, no doubt falsely but not without malice, rejects all charges that it has any colonial designs in Namibia.

Admittedly, calling the colonial powers to task in the name of human rights is a judicious way of using the ways and means afforded by contemporary international law to put an end to colonialism in Africa. In this, the practice of the OAU is constant. Moreover, in order to give added force to that practice, the OAU has established certain structures.

"At their first historic meeting in Addis Ababa in 1963," writes the Administrative Secretary-General,[35] "one of the first acts of the Heads of State and Government was to give material expression to their concern for the total liberation of the continent by establishing the Co-ordination Committee for the Liberation Movement of Africa to co-ordinate and harmonize the struggle of national liberation movements and to direct and co-ordinate assistance to the freedom fighters in order to allow them to recover their confiscated independence and sovereignty." This Committee, endowed with a special fund, is the subject of special attention. In 1969 again, the Conference of Heads of State and Government decided to designate a Committee to study the terms of reference, structure and composition of the Co-ordination Committee for the Liberation Movement of Africa.[36]

The activities of the Organization of African Unity in respect of the struggle against colonialism led it at the same time to concern itself with refugees, the number of whom was attaining alarming proportions. In Africa, the refugee phenomenon was not linked exclusively to the national liberation struggles in South Africa, Rhodesia, Angola, Mozambique, Guinea-Bissau and South West Africa. As is rightly pointed out by the Administrative Secretary-General, it is also linked to the "internal crises undergone by certain independent African States."[37] Nevertheless, the struggle against colonialism in Africa is one of the causes of the phenomenon. The OAU set up, in February 1964, an *ad hoc* commission whose recommendations in this field constitute the Charter of the Organization.

In regard to these developments, one can consequently agree with Borella[38] when he writes: "The liquidation of colonialism in Africa is probably the best known substantial principle of African law. The application of this principle has been one of the most important tasks of the OAU, through its Liberation Committee.... The questions of Southern Rhodesia (Zimbabwe), the Union of South Africa, and Namibia (South West Africa) are regularly included on the agenda of the Council and of the Conference." It is to be added that this principle is founded on the absolute incompatibility which exists between colonialism and respect for human rights.

At the same time as fighting colonialism, and still in the name of human rights, the OAU has also made intense efforts to eradicate the policy of *apartheid* from the continent.

Forcing States to abandon the policy of apartheid in the name of human rights

It is no doubt easier, or at least less dangerous, to combat colonialism in the name of, and with the assistance of, human rights than to combat *apartheid* by virtue of, and with the aid of, those same rights. Can one ever be sure that one has swept in front of one's own door, as Voltaire recommended? Virally[39] has wisely pointed out that "ensuring that the rights established on behalf of individuals are respected will appear to be an abstract and hardly attractive objective to a government, especially when it runs the risk of jeopardizing its good relations with another government. To this will be added an elementary rule of prudence: the government under attack can always retaliate and, in turn, accuse its accuser of the same crime as that for which it is being reproached." Nevertheless, the Organization of African Unity has embarked on this path, but not without first of all taking certain precautions. In adopting the Lusaka Manifesto, the Addis Ababa Organization managed to protect not only its left flank but also its right flank. This particularly well-drafted Manifesto was adopted by the Heads of State and Government of East and Central Africa meeting in conference at Lusaka from 14 to 15 April 1969. It was to meet with tremendous success. At the 24th session of the UN General Assembly, the Manifesto was adopted (113 for, 2 abstentions, 2 against: South Africa and Portugal).

In this text of world importance, the African States renewed their faith in human rights: "By this Manifesto we wish to make clear, beyond all shadow of doubt, our acceptance of the belief that all men are equal and have equal rights to human dignity and respect, regardless of colour, race, religion or sex. We believe that all men have the right and duty to participate as equal members of the society, in their own government. We do not accept that any individual or group has any right to govern any other group of sane adults, without their consent. . . ." By this Manifesto they rejected, in the name of human rights, all forms of discrimination resulting from the system of *apartheid*.

Moreover, the Lusaka Manifesto achieved more than one purpose since, in addition to the above proclamation, it eliminated the charge of anti-racist racism on the part of the Africans; above all, it did a splendid job of demolishing all the excuses founded on the non-implementation of human rights by the Africans themselves. By a masterly stroke, the African States declared as follows in the text: "We recognize that at any one time there will be, within every society, failures in the implementation of these ideals. We recognize that for the sake of order in human affairs, there may be transitional arrangements while a transformation from group inequalities to individual equality is being effected. But we affirm that without an acceptance of these ideals—without a commitment to these principles of human equality and self-determination—there can be no basis for peace and justice in the world. None of us would claim that within our own States we have achieved that perfect social, economic and political organization which would ensure a reasonable standard of living for all our people and establish individual security against avoidable hardship or miscarriage of justice." This wonderful passage expresses an unassailable theory of the international implementation of human rights, and of the necessity to modulate the content of these rights, once one steps out of the natural framework of their protection, namely the States. It thus enabled the African States to secure a condemnation of the policy of *apartheid*, in the name of human rights, even though they themselves are a long way from fully meeting the requirements of these rights.

Nevertheless, and even though, for very good reasons, the positions of those who support *apartheid* have been continuously and irreversibly undermined, the fact remains that those in favour of such a policy do not fail to point out that if African workers continue to go to South Africa, it is because the atmosphere there is not so infernal as, or at least no more infernal than, it is elsewhere. Whatever the case, Africans must show greater respect for the rights of Africans, if they wish to preserve their international prestige.

(ii). THE PRESENT CONCEPTION OF THE OAU IN THE MATTER OF HUMAN RIGHTS

Until recently the OAU's practice in the matter of human rights has been clearly inadequate. Admittedly, to have contributed, to a small extent, to the liberation of the colonized African territories, is in itself an invaluable achievement; without such liberation, the implementation of human rights is an illusion for colonized peoples. Similarly, it is clear that the policy of *apartheid*, regardless of how it is justified, is the very denial of all the rights of the Black peoples of South Africa and Namibia. And to have helped, by using human rights as a means of calling the colonial powers to task, to discredit such a policy, is again to have facilitated the realization of those rights in regions where they were particularly suppressed.

However, one cannot justifiably claim to base one's relations on the effective implementation of human rights by a neighbouring State if, at the domestic level, insofar as one's means permit, those same rights have not been provided with the necessary guarantees. One is not necessarily exempt from blame simply because one is neither a colonizer nor a segregationist. It is not enough to liberate all peoples from all forms of internal and external domination. Liberation for all peoples and for man himself from all the constraints to which human rights may be subjected must be ensured.

In reality, however, and without there being any need to compare the G.N.P. of the Republic of South Africa with that of the Member States of the OAU, or to confuse the colonial status of certain Africans with that of the African States, and even less to confuse the political systems of those States with *apartheid*, the fact remains that violations of identical rights are committed equally in the colonial territories and the States practising segregation and in the African States.

However, in relation to the promotion of human rights in Africa as a whole, recent developments have occured which are of major significance. In addition to the achievement of independence by Zimbabwe in 1980 and the disappearance of several dictatorial regimes in the late 1970's, the OAU itself has acknowledged the need for comprehensive, institutionalized machinery to give effect to "the firm attachment of the Member States of the Organization of African Unity to the promotion of respect for and protection of Human and Peoples' Rights."[40] For this purpose the Assembly of Heads of State and Government decided in 1979 to organize a meeting of highly-qualified experts to prepare a preliminary draft of an African Charter on Human and Peoples' Rights.[41] At the Group's first meeting in Dakar, a detailed draft containing 64 articles was prepared. In addition to enumerating a wide range of traditional civil, political, economic, social and cultural rights the draft places strong emphasis on collective rights such as: the right of peoples to self-determination; the right of colonized or oppressed peoples to free themselves from the bonds of domination by resorting to any means recognized by the international community; the right to development; the right to national and international peace and security; and the right to a generally satisfactory environment favourable to their development.[42]

This draft has subsequently been considered by two further meetings of the group held in Banjul, The Gambia. In June 1980 the OAU Council of Ministers urged the group to complete its work in time for a final draft to be submitted to the Assembly of Heads of State and Government, which adopted it in June 1981.[43]

Also at its 1979 meeting the Assembly adopted a Declaration on the Rights and Welfare of the African Child. The 12 paragraph Declaration provides, *inter alia*, that Member States of the OAU should: review their current legal codes and provisions relating to the rights of children; thoroughly examine cultural legacies and practices that are harmful to normal growth and development of the child; formulate and implement programmes in the field of health, nutrition and education as part of national development plans with a view to making these services universally accessible to all children within the shortest possible time; give priority to the most deprived and vulnerable children, paying particular attention to disabled children in the expansion of essential services; and expand day-care facilities with priority to the most needy and economically disadvantaged families. Other provisions of the Declaration relate to: the needs of refugee and displaced children; the importance of participation in the planning and management of basic services programmes for children; and the need to preserve and develop African arts, languages and culture.

Another major development was the holding, in Monrovia in September 1979, of a UN Seminar on the Establishment of Regional Commissions on Human Rights with Special Reference to Africa. The seminar, in which the OAU participated actively, adopted the "Monrovia proposal for the setting up of an African Commission on Human rights."[44] The proposal, which contained a possible model for an African commission on human rights, was submitted, through the UN Secretary-General, to the OAU for consideration.

The reaction of other States

The credibility of the OAU in the matter of human rights may be expected to decline to a considerable extent if the discrepancy between the rights continually proclaimed and honoured in words and the rights effectively protected persists. Those other States which are at present outlawed by international society will then escape, in whole or in part, from universal censure.

The reaction of the nationals of the Member States of the OAU

Although citizens are often unaware of the real factors which determine foreign policy, the ways in which that policy is justified always influences their reactions, be it positively or negatively. Since, for a long time now, they have been learning to follow the example of their leaders, the nationals of the Member States of the OAU could become particularly keen to preserve their rights.

Taking into consideration both reactions within States and reactions outside them, there are grounds for thinking that radical changes are now in the making in respect of the promotion and protection of human rights in Africa.

NOTES

1. *Journal of the International Commission of Jurists*, 1961, Vol. III, No. 1, p. 9.
2. "The concept of race," *Diogenes*, 1967, No. 59, p. 117.
3. Rolland et Lampue, *Précis de droit des pays d'outre-mer*, p. 275.
4. *Ibid.*, p. 271.
5. Jean-Bernard Marie, *La Commission des droits de l'homme de l'ONU*, Pédone, Paris, 1975, p. 9.
6. "The concept of race," *Diogenes*, 1967, No. 59, p. 117.
7. Only two black African countries were members of the international community at that time.
8. Fortieth Francophone Medical Congress, Dakar, 1975.
9. The right to life was protected not only by the prohibition against killing but also by the obligation to provide those who did not have any means of subsistence with that which was necessary to ensure their survival.
10. Roman quiritarian property, as far as land and livestock were concerned, was generally unknown in Africa. Such property belonged to the community.
11. Karel Vasak, "Les droits de l'homme et l'Afrique," *Revue belge de droit international*, 1967, No. 2, pp. 459-478.
12. *Les constitutions africaines*, Vol. I, p. 18 and Vol. II, p. 30, Pédone, Paris
13. "...We felt that this was a subject of such tremendous importance that the human rights should not be left hidden here and there in a legal maze, and we insisted on having a special chapter of our Constitution devoted to the exposition of those fundamental human rights."
14. Jean-Bernard Marie, *op. cit.*, p. 22.
15. Jon Woronoff, *Organizing African Unity*, The Scarecrow Press Inc., 1970, p. 169.
15a. Jean-Paul Masseron, *Le pouvoir et la justice en Afrique noire francophone et à Madagascar*, Pédone, Paris, 1966, p. 43.
16. *Les constitutions africaines, op. cit.*
17. "Droit public africain," *Cahiers de l'IIAP*, Paris, 1967, p. 107.
18. *Unesco Courier*, January 1968.
19. Quoted by Jean-Paul Masseron, *Le pouvoir et la justice en Afrique noire francophone et à Madagascar*, Pédone, Paris, 1966, p. 42.
20. See H. Hannum, "The Butare Colloquium on Human Rights and Economic Development in Francophone Africa: A Summary and Analysis," *Universal Human Rights*, Vol. 1, No. 2, 1979, pp. 63-88.
21. See *Revue Sénégalaise de Droit*, Numéro spècial, December 1977, No. 22, (1978), 255p.

22. J. Salmon, "Rapport sur le droit des peuples à disposer d'eux-mêmes," *Annales de la Faculté de droit et des sciences éconòmiques de Reims*, 1974, published by the ASERJ, p. 268.

23. Ch. Chaumont, Cours général de droit international public, 1970, *RCADI*, 1970, Vol. I, p. 412.

24. AHG/Dec.115 (XVI), para. 2. See UN doc. A/34/552 (1979), Annex II, pp. 92-93.

25. AHG/ST.4 (XVI). See UN doc. A/34/552 (1979), Annex II, pp. 81-83.

26. "Ethopia, Draft Charter of the Organization of African States," Com. I/17 May 1963. *Acts of the Summit Conference of Independent African States*, Vol. I, Section 1, Addis Ababa, May 1963.

27. *Acts of the Summit Conference of Independent African States*, Vol. I, Section 1, Addis Ababa, Confidential summit, CIAS/COM/report 1-24 May 1963, p. 8.

28. G. Burdeau, *Traité de science politique*, 2nd edition, LGDJ, Paris, Vol. IV, *Le statut du pouvoir dans l'Etat*, p. 135.

29. G. Burdeau, *op. cit.*, p. 134.

30. François Borella, "Organisations internationales régionales," *Le régionalisme africain*, 1964, *AFDI*, p. 854.

31. Art. II. 1. The Organization shall have the following purposes:
   (a) to promote the unity and solidarity of the African States;
   (b) to co-ordinate and intensify their co-operation and efforts to achieve a better life for the peoples of Africa;
   (c) to defend their sovereignty, their territorial integrity and independence;
   (d) to eradicate all forms of colonialism from Africa;
   (e) to promote international co-operation, having due regard to the Charter of the United Nations and the Universal Declaration of Human Rights.
      2. To these ends, the Member States shall co-ordinate and harmonize their general policies, especially in the following fields;
   (a) political and diplomatic co-operation;
   (b) economic co-operation, including transport and communications;
   (c) educational and cultural co-operation;
   (d) health, sanitation and nutritional co-operation;
   (e) scientific and technical co-operation;
   (f) co-operation for defense and security.

32. F. Borella, "Le système juridique de l'OUA," *AFDI*, 1971, p. 236.

33. See OAU doc. CM/272 (1968) (Part I) para. 32. The same document notes the irregularity with which meetings of the various Specialized Commissions occurred in the early years of their existence.

34. With regard to the latter see UN doc. A/35/446 (1980).

35. Introductory note to the report of the Administrative Secretary-General to the ninth regular session of the Conference of Heads of State and Government, Rabat, June 1972, p. 38.

36. Conference of Heads of State and Government, sixth regular session, Addis Ababa, September 1969, AHG/Dec. 36 (VI).

37. Introductory note to the report of the Administrative Secretary-General to the ninth regular session of the Conference of Heads of State and Government, Rabat, 1972, p. 64.

38. Borella, "Le système juridique de l'OUA," *AFDI*, pp. 244-245.

39. Virally, "L'accès des particuliers à une instance internationale: la protection des droits de l'homme dans le cadre européen," *Mémoires publiés par la Faculté de droit de Genève*, n° 20, 4ème journée juridique, 10 Octobre 1964, p. 75.

40. Resolution of the OAU Council of Ministers, CM/Res. 792 (XXV)(1980). See UN doc. A/35/463, Annex I, p. 39.

41. AHG/Dec. 115 (XVI). See UN doc. A/34/552 (1979), Annex II, pp. 92-93.

42. See OAU doc. CAB/LEG/67/3/Rev.1 (1979), reprinted in *Bulletin of Peace Proposals* (Oslo), Vol 11, No. 4, 1980; and OAU doc. CM/1068 (XXV)(1980).
43. CM/Res. 792 (XXXV) *op. cit.*.
44. UN doc. ST/HR/SER.A/4 (1979), Annex I, pp. 17-20.

3. AFRICAN CHARTER ON HUMAN AND PEOPLES' RIGHTS

PREAMBLE

The African States members of the Organization of African Unity, parties to the present Convention entitled "African Charter on Human and Peoples' Rights,"

Recalling Decision 115 (XVI) of the Assembly of Heads of State and Government at its Sixteenth Ordinary Session held in Monrovia, Liberia, from 17 to 20 July 1979 on the preparation of "a preliminary draft on an African Charter on Human and Peoples' Rights providing *inter alia* for the establishment of bodies to promote and protect human and peoples' rights";

Considering the Charter of the Organization of African Unity, which stipulates that "freedom, equality, justice and dignity are essential objectives for the achievement of the legitimate aspirations of the African peoples";

Reaffirming the pledge they solemnly made in Article 2 of the said Charter to eradicate all forms of colonialism from Africa, to co-ordinate and intensify their co-operation and efforts to achieve a better life for the peoples of Africa and to promote international co-operation having due regard to the Charter of the United Nations and the Universal Declaration of Human Rights;

Taking into consideration the virtues of their historical tradition and the values of African civilization which should inspire and characterize their reflection on the concept of human and peoples' rights;

Recognizing on the one hand, that fundamental human rights stem from the attributes of human beings, which justifies their international protection and on the other hand that the reality and respect of peoples rights should necessarily guarantee human rights;

Considering that the enjoyment of rights and freedoms also implies the performance of duties on the part of everyone;

Convinced that it is henceforth essential to pay a particular attention to the right to development and that civil and political rights cannot be dissociated from economic, social and cultural rights in their conception as well as universality and that the satisfaction of economic, social and cultural rights is a guarantee for the enjoyment of civil and political rights;

Conscious of their duty to achieve the total liberation of Africa, the peoples of which are still struggling for their dignity and genuine independence, and undertaking to eliminate colonialism, neo-colonialism, apartheid, zionism and to dismantle aggressive foreign military bases and all forms of discrimination, particularly those based on race, ethnic group, colour, sex, language, religion or political opinions;

Reaffirming their adherence to the principles of human and peoples' rights and freedoms contained in the declarations, conventions and other instruments adopted by the Organization of African Unity, the Movement of Non-Aligned Countries and the United Nations;

Firmly convinced of their duty to promote and protect human and peoples' rights and freedoms taking into account the importance traditionally attached to these rights and freedoms in Africa;

HAVE AGREED AS FOLLOWS:

PART I - RIGHTS AND DUTIES

CHAPTER I

HUMAN AND PEOPLES' RIGHTS

ARTICLE 1
The Member States of the Organization of African Unity parties to the present Charter shall recognize the rights, duties and freedoms enshrined in this Charter and shall undertake to adopt legislative or other measures to give effect to them.

ARTICLE 2
Every individual shall be entitled to the enjoyment of the rights and freedoms recognized and guaranteed in the present Charter without distinction of any kind such as race, ethnic group, colour, sex, language, religion, political or any other opinion, national and social origin, fortune, birth or other status.

ARTICLE 3
1. Every individual shall be equal before the law.
2. Every individual shall be entitled to equal protection of the law.

ARTICLE 4

Human beings are inviolable. Every human being shall be entitled to respect for his life and the integrity of his person. No one may be arbitrarily deprived of this right.

ARTICLE 5

Every individual shall have the right to the respect of the dignity inherent in a human being and to the recognition of his legal status. All forms of exploitation and degradation of man particularly slavery, slave trade, torture, cruel, inhuman or degrading punishment and treatment shall be prohibited.

ARTICLE 6

Every individual shall have the right to liberty and to the security of his person. No one may be deprived of his freedom except for reasons and conditions previously laid down by law. In particular, no one may be arbitrarily arrested or detained.

ARTICLE 7

1. Every individual shall have the right to have his cause heard. This comprises:
   a) The right to an appeal to competent national organs against acts violating his fundamental rights as recognized and guaranteed by conventions, laws, regulations and customs in force;
   b) the right to be presumed innocent until proved guilty by a competent court or tribunal;
   c) the right to defence, including the right to be defended by counsel of his choice;
   d) the right to be tried within a reasonable time by an impartial court or tribunal.

2. No one may be condemned for an act or omission which did not constitute a legally punishable offence at the time it was committed. No penalty may be inflicted for an offence for which no provision was made at the time it was committed. Punishment is personal and can be imposed only on the offender.

ARTICLE 8

Freedom of conscience, the profession and free practice of religion shall be guaranteed. No one may, subject to law and order, be submitted to measures restricting the exercise of these freedoms.

ARTICLE 9

1. Every individual shall have the right to receive information.

2. Every individual shall have the right to express and disseminate his opinions within the law.

ARTICLE 10

1. Every individual shall have the right to free association provided that he abides by the law.

2. Subject to the obligation of solidarity provided for in Article 29 no one may be compelled to join an association.

ARTICLE 11

Every individual shall have the right to assemble freely with others. The exercise of this right shall be subject only to necessary restrictions provided for by law in particular those enacted in the interest of national security, the safety, health, ethics and rights and freedoms of others.

ARTICLE 12

1. Every individual shall have the right to freedom of movement and residence within the borders of a State provided he abides by the law.

2. Every individual shall have the right to leave any country including his own, and to return to his country. This right may only be subject to restrictions, provided for by law for the protection of national security, law and order, public health or morality.

3. Every individual shall have the right, when persecuted, to seek and obtain asylum in other countries in accordance with the laws of those countries and international conventions.

4. A non-national legally admitted in a territory of a State Party to the present Charter, may only be expelled from it by virtue of a decision taken in accordance with the law.

5. The mass expulsion of non-nationals shall be prohibited. Mass expulsion shall be that which is aimed at national, racial, ethnic or religious groups.

ARTICLE 13

1. Every citizen shall have the right to participate freely in the government of his country, either directly or through freely chosen representatives in accordance with the provisions of the law.

2. Every citizen shall have the right of equal access to the public service of his country.

3. Every individual shall have the right of access to public property and services in strict equality of all persons before the law.

ARTICLE 14

The right to property shall be guaranteed. It may only be encroached upon in the interest of public need or in the general interest of the community and in accordance with the provisions of appropriate laws.

ARTICLE 15

Every individual shall have the right to work under equitable and satisfactory conditions, and shall receive equal pay for equal work.

ARTICLE 16

1. Every individual shall have the right to enjoy the best attainable state of physical and mental health.

2. States Parties to the present Charter shall take the necessary measures to protect the health of their people and to ensure that they receive medical attention when they are sick.

ARTICLE 17

1. Every individual shall have the right to education.

2. Every individual may freely, take part in the cultural life of his community.

3. The promotion and protection of morals and traditional values recognized by the community shall be the duty of the State.

ARTICLE 18

1. The family shall be the natural unit and basis of society. It shall be protected by the State which shall take care of its physical and moral health .

2. The State shall have the duty to assist the family which is the custodian of morals and traditional values recognized by the community.

3. The State shall ensure the elimination of every discrimination against women and also ensure the protection of the rights of the woman and the child as stipulated in international declarations and conventions.

4. The aged and the disabled shall also have the right to special measures of protection in keeping with their physical or moral needs.

ARTICLE 19

All peoples shall be equal; they shall enjoy the same respect and shall have the same rights. Nothing shall justify the domination of a people by another.

ARTICLE 20

1. All peoples shall have the right to existence. They shall have the unquestionable and inalienable right to self-determination. They shall freely determine their political status and shall pursue their economic and social development according to the policy they have freely chosen.

2. Colonize or oppressed peoples shall have the right to free themselves from the bonds of domination by resorting to any means recognized by the international community.

3. All peoples shall have the right to the assistance of the States parties to the present Charter in their liberation struggle against foreign domination, be it political, economic or cultural.

ARTICLE 21

1. All peoples shall freely dispose of their wealth and natural resources. This right shall be exercised in the exclusive interest of the people. In no case shall a people be deprived of it.

2. In case of spoliation the dispossessed people shall have the right to the lawful recovery of its property as well as to an adequate compensation.

3. The free disposal of wealth and natural resources shall be exercised without prejudice to the obligation of promoting international economic cooperation based on mutual respect, equitable exchange and the principles of international law.

4. States parties to the present Charter shall individually and collectively exercise the right to free disposal of their wealth and natural resources with a view to strengthening African unity and solidarity.

5. States parties to the present Charter shall undertake to eliminate all forms of foreign economic exploitation particularly that practised by international monopolies so as to enable their peoples to fully benefit from the advantages derived from their national resources.

ARTICLE 22

1. All peoples shall have the right to their economic, social and cultural development with due regard to their freedom and identity and in the equal enjoyment of the common heritage of mankind.

2. States shall have the duty, individually or collectively, to ensure the exercise of the right to development.

ARTICLE 23

1. All peoples shall have the right to national and international peace and security. The principles of solidarity and friendly relations implicitly affirmed by the Charter of the United Nations and reaffirmed by that of the Organization of African Unity shall govern relations between States.

2. For the purpose of strengthening peace, solidarity and friendly relations, States parties to the present charter shall ensure that:
   (a) any individual enjoying the right of asylum under Article 12 of the present Charter shall not engage in subversive activities against his country of origin or any other State party to the present Charter;
   (b) their territories shall not be used as bases for subversive or terrorist activities against the people of any other State party to the present Charter.

ARTICLE 24

All peoples shall have the right to a general satisfactory environment favourable to their development.

ARTICLE 25

States parties to the present Charter shall have the duty to promote and ensure through teaching, education and publication, the respect of the rights and freedoms contained in the present Charter and to see to it that these freedoms and rights as well as corresponding obligations and duties are understood.

ARTICLE 26

States parties to the present Charter shall have the duty to guarantee the independence of the Courts and shall allow the establishment and improvement of appropriate national institutions entrusted with the promotion and protection of the rights and freedoms guaranteed by the present Charter.

CHAPTER II

DUTIES

ARTICLE 27

1. Every individual shall have duties towards his family and society, the State and other legally recognized communities and the international community.

2. The rights and freedoms of each individual shall be exercised with due regard to the rights of others, collective security, morality and common interest.

ARTICLE 28

Every individual shall have the duty to respect and consider his fellow beings without discrimination, and to maintain relations aimed at promoting, safeguarding and reinforcing mutual respect and tolerance.

ARTICLE 29

The individual shall also have the duty:

1. To preserve the harmonious development of the family and to work for the cohesion and respect of the family; to respect his parents at all times, to maintain them in case of need;

2. To serve his national community by placing his physical and intellectual abilities at its services;

3. Not to compromise the security of the State whose national or resident he is;

4. To preserve and strengthen social and national solidarity, particularly when the latter is threatened;

5. To preserve and strengthen the national independence and the territorial integrity of his country and to contribute to its defence in accordance with the law;

6. To work to the best of his abilities and competence, and to pay taxes imposed by law in the interest of the society;

7. To preserve and strengthen positive African cultural values in his relations with other members of the society, in the spirit of tolerance, dialogue and consultation and, in general, to contribute to the promotion of the moral well being of society;

8. To contribute to the best of his abilities, at all times and at all levels to the promotion and achievement of African unity.

PART II - MEASURES OF SAFEGUARD

CHAPTER I

ESTABLISHMENT AND ORGANIZATION OF THE AFRICAN COMMISSION ON HUMAN AND PEOPLES' RIGHTS

ARTICLE 30

An African Commission on Human and Peoples' Rights, hereinafter called "the Commission," shall be established within the Organization of African Unity to promote human and peoples' rights and ensure their protection in Africa.

ARTICLE 31

1. The Commission shall consist of eleven members chosen from amongst African personalities of the highest reputation, known for their high morality, integrity, impartiality and competence in matters of human and peoples' rights; particular consideration being given to persons having legal experience.

2. The members of the Commission shall serve in their personal capacity.

ARTICLE 32

The Commission shall not include more than one national of the same State.

ARTICLE 33

The members of the Commission shall be elected by secret ballot by the Assembly of Heads of State and Government, from a list of persons nominated by the States parties to the present charter.

ARTICLE 34

Each State party to the present Charter may not nominate more than two candidates. The candidates must have the nationality of one of the States parties to the present Charter. When two candidates are nominated by a State, one of them may not be a national of that State.

ARTICLE 35

1. The Secretary-General of the Organization of African Unity shall invite States parties to the present Charter at least four months before the elections to nominate candidates;

2. The Secretary-General of the Organization of African Unity shall make an alphabetical list of the persons thus nominated and communicate it to the Heads of State and Government at least one month before the elections.

ARTICLE 36

The members of the Commission shall be elected for a six year period and shall be eligible for re-election. However, the term of office of four of the members elected at the first election shall terminate after two years and the term of three others, at the end of four years.

ARTICLE 37

Immediately after the first election, the Chairman of the Assembly of Heads of State and Government of the Organization of African Unity shall draw lots to decide the names of those members referred to in Article 36.

ARTICLE 38

After their election, the members of the Commission shall make a solemn declaration to discharge their duties impartially and faithfully.

ARTICLE 39

1. In case of death or resignation of a member of the Commission, the Chairman of the Commission shall immediately inform the Secretary-General of the Organization of African Unity, who shall declare the seat vacant from the date of death or from the date on which the resignation takes effect.

2. If, in the unanimous opinion of other members of the Commission, a member has stopped discharging his duties for any reason other than a temporary absence, the Chairman of the Commission shall inform the Secretary General of the Organization of African Unity, who shall then declare the seat vacant.

3. In each of the cases anticipated above, the Assembly of Heads of State and Government shall replace the member whose seat became vacant for the remaining period of his term unless the period is less than six months.

ARTICLE 40

Every member of the Commission shall be in office until the date his successor assumes office.

ARTICLE 41

The Secretary-General of the Organization of African Unity shall appoint the Secretary of the Commission. He shall also provide the staff and services necessary for the effective discharge of the duties of the Commission. The Organization of African Unity shall bear the cost of the staff and services.

ARTICLE 42

1. The Commission shall elect its Chairman and Vice Chairman for a two-year period. They shall be eligible for re-election.

2. The Commission shall lay down its rules of procedure.

3. Seven members shall form the quorum.

4. In case of an equality of votes, the Chairman shall have a casting vote.

5. The Secretary-General may attend the meetings of the Commission. He shall neither participate in deliberations nor shall he be entitled to vote. The Chairman of the Commission may, however, invite him to speak.

ARTICLE 43

In discharging their duties, members of the Commission shall enjoy diplomatic Privileges and Immunities provided for in the General Convention on the Privileges and Immunities of the Organization of African Unity.

ARTICLE 44

Provisions shall be made for the emoluments and allowances of the members of the Commission in the Regular Budget of the Organization of African Unity.

CHAPTER II

MANDATE OF THE COMMISSION

ARTICLE 45

The functions of the Commission shall be:

1. To promote Human and Peoples' Rights and in particular:

   a) to collect documents, undertake studies and researches on African problems in the field of human and peoples' rights, organize seminars, symposia and conferences, disseminate information, encourage national and local institutions concerned with human and peoples' rights, and should the case arise, give its views or make recommendations to Governments.

   b) to formulate and lay down, principles and rules aimed at solving legal problems relating to human and peoples' rights and fundamental freedoms upon which African Governments may base their legislations.

   c) co-operate with other African and international institutions concerned with the promotion and protection of human and and peoples' rights.

2. Ensure the protection of human and peoples' rights under conditions laid down by the present Charter.

3. Interpret all the provisions of the present Charter at the request of a State party, an institution of the OAU or an African organization recognized by the OAU.

4. Perform any other tasks which may be entrusted to it by the Assembly of Heads of State and Government.

CHAPTER III

PROCEDURE OF THE COMMISSION

ARTICLE 46

The Commission may resort to any appropriate method of investigation; it may hear from the Secretary-General of the Organization of African Unity or any other person capable of enlightening it.

COMMUNICATION FROM STATES

ARTICLE 47

If a State party to the present Charter has good reasons to believe that another State party to this Charter has violated the provisions of the Charter, it may draw, by written communication, the attention of that State to the matter. This communication shall also be addressed to the Secretary-General of the OAU and to the Chairman of the Commission. Within three months of the receipt of the communication, the State to which the communication is addressed shall give the enquiring State, written explanation or statement elucidating the matter. This should include as much as possible relevant information relating to the laws and rules of procedure applied and applicable and the redress already given or course of action available.

ARTICLE 48

If within three months from the date on which the original communication is received by the State to which it is addressed the issue is not settled to the satisfaction of the two States involved through bilateral negotiation or by any other peaceful procedure, either State shall have the right to submit the matter to the Commission through the Chairman and shall notify the other States involved.

ARTICLE 49

Notwithstanding the provisions of Article 47, if a State party to the present Charter considers that another State party has violated the provisions of the Charter, it may refer the matter directly to the Commission by addressing a communication to the Chairman, to the Secretary-General of the Organization of African Unity and the State concerned.

ARTICLE 50

The Commission can only deal with a matter submitted to it after making sure that all local remedies, if they exist, have been exhausted, unless it is obvious to the Commission that the procedure of exhaustion of these remedies would be unduly prolonged.

ARTICLE 51

1. The Commission may ask the States concerned to provide it with all relevant information.
2. When the Commission is considering the matter, States concerned may be represented before it and submit written or oral representations.

ARTICLE 52

After having obtained from the States concerned and from other sources all the information it deems necessary and after having tried all appropriate means to reach an amicable solution based on the respect of Human and Peoples' Rights, the Commission shall prepare, within a reasonable period of time from the notification referred to in Article 48, a report stating the facts and its findings. This report shall be sent to the States concerned and communicated to the Assembly of Heads of State and Government.

ARTICLE 53

While transmitting its report, the Commission may make to the Assembly of Heads of State and Government such recommendations as it deems useful.

ARTICLE 54

The Commission shall submit to each Ordinary Session of the Assembly of Heads of State and Government a report on its activities.

OTHER COMMUNICATIONS

ARTICLE 55

1. Before each Session, the Secretary of the Commission shall make a list of the communications other than those of States parties to the present Charter and transmit them to the Members of the Commission, who shall indicate which communications should be considered by the Commission.

2. A communication shall be considered by the Commission if a simple majority of its members so decide.

ARTICLE 56

Communications relating to human and peoples' rights referred to in Article 55 received by the Commission, shall be considered if they:

1. indicate their authors even if the latter request anonymity,

2. are compatible with the Charter of the Organization of African Unity or with the present Charter,

3. are not written in disparaging or insulting language directed against the State concerned and its institutions or to the Organization of African Unity,

4. are not based exclusively on news disseminated through the mass media,

5. are sent after exhausting local remedies, if any, unless it is obvious that this procedure is unduly prolonged,

6. are submitted within a reasonable period from the time local remedies are exhausted or from the date the Commission is seized of the matter, and

7. do not deal with cases which have been settled by these States involved in accordance with the principles of the Charter of the United Nations, or the Charter of the Organization of African Unity or the provisions of the present Charter.

ARTICLE 57

Prior to any substantive consideration, all communications shall be brought to the knowledge of the State concerned by the Chairman of the Commission.

ARTICLE 58

1. When it appears after deliberations of the Commission that one or more communications apparently relate to special cases which reveal the existence of a series of serious or massive violations of human and peoples' rights, the Commission shall draw the attention of the Assembly of Heads of State and Government to these special cases.

2. The Assembly of Heads of State and Government may then request the Commission to undertake an in-depth study of these cases and make a factual report, accompanied by its finding and recommendations.

3. A case of emergency duly noticed by the Commission shall be submitted by the latter to the Chairman of the Assembly of Heads of State and Government who may request an in-depth study.

ARTICLE 59

1. All measures taken within the provisions of the present Chapter shall remain confidential until such a time as the Assembly of Heads of State and Government shall otherwise decide.

2. However, the report shall be published by the Chairman of the Commission upon the decision of the Assembly of Heads of State and Government.

3. The report on the activities of the Commission shall be published by its Chairman after it has been considered by the Assembly of Heads of State and Government.

CHAPTER IV

APPLICABLE PRINCIPLES

ARTICLE 60

The Commission shall draw from international law on human and peoples' rights, particularly from the provisions of various African instruments on human and peoples' rights, the Charter of the United Nations, the Charter of the Organization of African Unity, the Universal Declaration of Human Rights, other instruments adopted by the United Nations and by African countries in the field of human and peoples' rights as well as from the provisions of various instruments adopted within the Specialised Agencies of the United Nations of which the parties to the present Charter are members.

ARTICLE 61

The Commission shall also take into consideration, as subsidiary measures to determine the principles of law, other general or special international conventions, laying down rules expressly recognized by Member States of the Organization of African Unity, African practices consistent with international norms on human and peoples' rights, customs generally accepted as law, general principles of law recognized by African States as well as legal precedents and doctrine.

ARTICLE 62

Each State party shall undertake to submit every two years, from the date the present Charter comes into force, a report on the legislative or other measures taken with a view to giving effect to the rights and freedoms recognized and guaranteed by the present Charter.

ARTICLE 63

1. The present Charter shall be open to signature, ratification or adherence of the Member States of the Organization of African Unity.

2. The instruments of ratification or adherence to the present Charter shall be deposited with the Secretary-General of the Organization of African Unity.

3. The present Charter shall come into force three months after the reception by the Secretary-General of the instruments of ratification or adherence of a simple majority of the Member States of the Organization of African Unity.

PART III - GENERAL PROVISIONS

ARTICLE 64

1. After the coming into force of the present Charter, members of the Commission shall be elected in accordance with the relevant Articles of the present Charter.

2. The Secretary-General of the Organization of African Unity shall convene the first meeting of the Commission at the Headquarters of the Organization within three months of the constitution of the Commission. Thereafter, the Commission shall be convened by its Chairman whenever necessary but at least once a year.

ARTICLE 65

For each of the States that will ratify or adhere to the present Charter after its coming into force, the Charter shall take effect three months after the date of the deposit by that State of its instrument of ratification or adherence.

ARTICLE 66

Special protocols or agreements may, if necessary, supplement the provisions of the present Charter.

ARTICLE 67

The Secretary-General of the Organization of African Unity shall inform Member States of the Organization of the deposit of each instrument of ratification or adherence.

ARTICLE 68

The present Charter may be amended if a State party makes a written request to that effect to the Secretary-General of the Organization of African Unity. The Assembly of Heads of State and Government may only consider the draft amendment after all the States parties have been duly informed of it and the Commission has given its opinion on it at the request of the sponsoring State. The amendment shall be approved by a simple majority of the States parties. It shall come into force for each State which has accepted it in accordance with its constitutional procedure three months after the Secretary-General has received notice of the acceptance.

20 The Socialist Countries and Human Rights

Vladimir Kartashkin

1. THE SOCIALIST CONCEPT OF HUMAN RIGHTS

(a). The law of the socialist countries and human rights

The socialist concept of human rights does not reject the idea of inalienable natural human and citizens' rights. But the Marxist-Leninist theory deduces human rights not from the "nature" of man but from the position of an individual in the society and, above all, in the process of public production. It proceeds from the premise that social opportunities and rights are not inherent in the nature of man and do not constitute some sort of natural attributes. Rights and freedoms of individuals in any State are materially stipulated and depend on socio-economic, political and other conditions of the development of society, its achievements and progress.

Karl Marx and Friedrich Engels defined law as the will of the dominating class raised to the level of law, as determined by material conditions of life.[1] Applied to human rights, this definition means that the State cannot guarantee the realization of the rights whose real ensurance is not prepared by the course of the economic development of a given society. Human rights mature deep inside the socio-economic structure of the State and are a product of its development. Their fundamental source is the material conditions of society's life. It goes without saying that the State may proclaim any rights and freedoms but it cannot implement them unless appropriate material prerequisites exist.

Of course, economic relations cannot by themselves engender either legal prescriptions or any human rights and freedoms. They only create conditions and prerequisites for the emergence of these or those legal ideas and views which are then recognized legislatively. The question as to what rights and freedoms are to be granted to an individual and to what extent they are to be realized depends on the interests of the dominating class, its political, economic and social requirements. This means that the institution of human rights and freedoms has a clearly defined class nature. Freedom of personality, democracy, law, justice—all these notions serve as instruments of the implementation of the dominating class's policy, a form of the expression of its interests. Not only do the civil and political rights have a class nature, but this is equally true of the socio-economic rights.

Pointing out the necessity of class evaluation of the social process, V.I. Lenin wrote that people have always been and will always be silly victims of deceit and self-deceit in politics until they learn to disclose the interests of these or those classes behind any moral, religious, political, social phrases, statements and promises.[2] Thus the socialist theory of human rights proceeds from the premise that human rights and freedoms are of a class and political nature and are materially determined by the economic conditions of the society's development.

Scientists of socialist countries subdivide law into objective law—the existing legislation of a country—and subjective law—specific rights, obligations and opportunities which emerge within the limits of the legislation concerning the participants in legal relations.[3] The socialist theory of State and law recognizes that all citizens' rights are subjective, that is, personal and inalienable rights guaranteed by the conditions of the society's life.

Under socialism all citizens are granted broad rights and freedoms which permit them to participate in the administration of State affairs, in economic and cultural construction, to enjoy all social benefits, to develop their abilities and talents. The Programme of the Communist Party of the Soviet Union stresses that the goal of socialism is an increasingly full satisfaction of material and cultural requirements of the people through permanent development and improvement of public production.[4]

The abolition of private ownership of the means of production and elimination of exploitation of man by man and the radical transformation of political and public life created the necessary conditions for ensuring a broad complex of rights and freedoms under socialism. The rights and freedoms recognized in the Covenants on Human Rights and other international instruments have not only been proclaimed in the constitutions of socialist countries and other legislative acts but were also really ensured through the creation of social and material conditions and provisions of concrete means open to the citizens for the realization of their rights.

The socialist concept of human rights proceeds from the unity and indissolubility of rights and obligations of citizens. The constitutions of socialist countries recognize the rights and freedoms of citizens, as a rule, in one chapter under the title of "Fundamental rights and freedoms of citizens." The constitutional obligations are established not only in the interests of the society and State, but above all, in the interests of every citizen individually. For example, the eight-grade primary education in most of the socialist countries is not only a right but also an obligation of everyone. Accordingly, the sending of children to school is not only a moral right but an obligation of the parents and failure to comply with it may entail measures of public censure or even administrative responsibility. Similarly, the right to work includes an obligation for everyone to work and to maintain the discipline of work. This right and obligation pursues the aim of ensuring the constant growth of production and the improvement of the well-being of every citizen.

A right written into law always reflects at least bilateral links between subjects. The right of one person always corresponds to an active or passive obligation of other persons. Every citizen may dispose of the right recognized by law only with the assistance and help of other persons, State bodies and public organizations. Therefore the constitutional rights of citizens correspond to obligations of States whose juridical expression is manifested as guarantees written into the law, that is, conditions and means which the socialist State provides to its citizens for the implementation of their rights. Thus the right to work recognized by law engenders for the State an obligation to provide to every citizen employment which corresponds to his abilities, knowledge and skill. The right to education is ensured by its being free of charge, by the development of all forms and kinds of education and by a system of State scholarships and stipends.

Under socialism human rights are viewed in direct connection with the freedom of personality, and the attainment of real freedom is related, first of all, to the liberation of labour from the domination of capital and the elimination of exploitation of the working people. The socialist concept of human rights proceeds from the premise that a genuine manifestation of freedom in society is possible only under the conditions of the liberation of man from all forms of exploitation. The Programme of the Communist Party of the Soviet Union stresses that Soviet society ensures the real freedom of personality. The highest manifestation of this freedom is the liberation of man from exploitation. Here there is genuine social justice.[5] The political freedoms—freedom of the press, of expression, of assembly—are interpreted from class positions as conditions of the consolidation of the working people and the spread of socialist ideology which rules out the "freedom" of anti-socialist propaganda, the freedom to organize counter-revolutionary forces against the fundamentals of socialism.

Freedom in a society is created by the socio-political system of the State. The rules of law only formally recognize and protect it. The freedom of the individual is understood as freedom of man in a society, State, collectivity, and not as freedom from them. Man lives in a certain collectivity, and he cannot be fully independent of it. Therefore, everyone should compare his behaviour with the interests and requirements of the whole society.

Personal freedom should be differentiated from personal arbitrariness which disregards the interests of the society as a whole and hence the interests of the collectivity. To avoid the transformation of freedom into its opposite—arbitrariness—it is necessary to promote responsible behaviour in every individual, that is, a behaviour co-ordinated with the requirements of the law and public morals.

The freedom of expression recognized in the constitutions of socialist countries, for example, does not mean an unlimited freedom of statements harmful both to individuals and the society as a whole. Under socialism, law prohibits the spread of slanderous information, which smears individual citizens, and legislatively prohibits propaganda of war, spread of ideas based on racism and provoking racial discrimination, etc. In a general form the notion of freedom of personality is expressed, for example, in Article 38 of the Constitution of the Socialist Republic of Vietnam which states that no one may use democratic rights and freedoms to the detriment of the interests of the State and the people.

The following principles underline the rights and freedoms of citizens in socialist countries: unity and combination of personal and public interests; universal accessibility of rights and incontestable nature of obligations; equality of citizens; and guaranteed rights and freedoms.

The principle of the unity and combination of personal and public interests belongs to the guiding and fundamental ideas of socialism. In some socialist countries, this idea was recognized in the constitutions and thus became a general binding legal rule. The Constitution of Czechoslovakia of 1960 stipulates that in a society of the working people, where exploitation of man by man has been eliminated, the development and the interests of its every member are co-ordinated with the development and the interests of the entire society. Rights, freedoms and obligations of citizens thus serve the free and comprehensive development of personality and simultaneously the consolidation and strengthening of the socialist society (p. 1, Art. 19).

One should not conclude from the principal of the unity and combination of personal and public interests that under socialism the interests of the society and the individual always coincide. Contradictions appear between them as a result of the clash of interests of the society as a whole with the interests of individuals (individualism, consumerism, hooliganism, etc.). Contradictions may emerge from the bureaucratic attitudes of officials of the State machinery towards their duties. These contradictions are overcome by the elimination of their causes and constant improvement of State policies.

Universal accessibility of rights and incontestable nature of obligations mean that under socialism every citizen, who has reached a legally established age and fulfilled other conditions prescribed by law, has an actual and a real opportunity to avail himself of all rights and has corresponding obligations. This principle rules out any privileges for some citizens and additional obligations for others. It also means that no one may evade his obligations unless this is provided for by law.

The idea of universal accessibility lies at the basis of such rights, as, for example, the right to work, to education, to social security, etc. In most of the socialist countries, for instance, everyone is guaranteed accessible, free and qualified medical assistance. No citizen in need of such assistance may be denied it. Denial of such rights or their limitation is possible only in cases provided for by law.

Equality of citizens is part of the fundamental basis of the legal status of citizens under socialism. The content of socialist equality is expressed in the equal position of all members of society in respect to the means of production, in their equal liberation from all forms of exploitation and oppression, in equal opportunity to work, to take part in the administration of State and public affairs, as well as to enjoy all rights and freedoms recognized by the law. Equality of rights and obligations of all citizens in all walks of life is expressed in their equality regardless of their social origin, property status, class affiliation, in equality of men and women, as well as in equality of citizens regardless of their racial or national origin. Equality of citizens in socialist countries is guaranteed by law. Article 76, for instance, of the Constitution of the Mongolian People's Republic states that the citizens of the MPR have equal rights regardless of sex, racial and national affiliation, faith, social origin and status. Legislation of socialist countries provides for criminal responsibility for any direct or indirect limitation of the rights of citizens or, on the contrary, the establishment of preferences for citizens depending on their racial and national affiliation.

Guaranteed rights and freedoms are expressed in the fact that socialist countries have firm legal guarantees which ensure the protection of the rights and freedoms of citizens and safeguard against their violation. Administrative legislation in socialist countries determines the rights and obligations of officials and administrative organs at different levels in such a way that their activity would best facilitate an effective realization of the rights and freedoms of citizens and protect them from encroachments. State institutions are responsible for the damage inflicted upon citizens by incorrect acts of officials, and such damage done to the property of citizens is to be restituted fully.

A major role in the protection of the rights of citizens is played by organs of control and supervision—party control, popular control, procurator's supervision and judicial control. Supervision of strict compliance with law, both by institutions and organizations and by officials and individual citizens, is entrusted in socialist countries to organs of the Procurator's department which perform their functions independently of any local organs. As an organ exercising the highest control over the implementation of laws, the Procurator's office also takes steps for the elimination of violations in criminal and civil legal proceedings.

The exercise of supervision of strict compliance with the law and the adoption of steps for the elimination of violations are the main content of the activity of the Procurator's office. Having established a violation, the Procurator's office takes steps for its elimination by submitting proposals for consideration by other organs of the State (judiciary organs, administrative bodies, courts of law). These proposals are necessarily examined by the State organs and officials, and decisions are taken on them.

The Procurator's office has broad powers in protecting political labour, housing, property and other rights of citizens. According to Article 41 of the Criminal and Procedural Code of the Russian Federation, the Procurator may take up a case at any stage in court if it is demanded by the protection of state or public interests or rights and interests of citizens protected by law. For example, any citizen of the USSR may send to the Procurator an application or complaint regarding a violation of the law or of his rights. These complaints have to be considered within one month. In case of the establishment of a fact of violation of law, the Procurator is under obligation to achieve the full restoration of the citizen's rights and punishment of persons who violated the law. Officials and citizens who commit criminal offences are subjected to criminal proceedings by the Procurator.

The institution of appeal is one of the main guarantees of the observation of the rights and freedoms of citizens. In the USSR, for example, any citizen may appeal against actions of any official or any institution which violate or encroach upon his personal rights and interests. The Decree of the Presidium of the USSR Supreme Soviet of 12 April 1968, "On the order of considering proposals, applications and complaints of citizens," has determined: the order of lodging complaints in the Soviet Union; time limits for their examination; control over the implementation of decisions taken on the application of citizens; and responsibility of officials for the violation of the established order of the examination of complaints.

The level of the development of the rights and freedoms of citizens in socialist countries is not limited. The process of extending the real content and economic assurance of the rights, their legal safeguards, protection and defence will continue.

(b). The socialist countries and the protection of international human rights

In some respects international life today is characterized by a turn from confrontation to a relaxation of international tensions, and by the reorganization of the entire system of international relations on the basis of the principles of peaceful co-existence, the observance of which is becoming a norm of relations among States with different social systems. The establishment and consolidation of peaceful, good-neighbourly relations among countries is inseparable from the expansion of their co-operation in promoting and ensuring observance of fundamental human rights and freedoms.

Having proclaimed the principle of respect for human rights and freedoms and outlawed the use of force between States, the UN Charter has thereby recorded in modern international law the right to peace as a fundamental right of every human being. Fundamental rights and freedoms can be secured only in conditions of peace and peaceful co-existence. The right to peace is an inalienable right of everyone on earth. The ideal of a free human personality relieved of fear and want may be realized only in conditions of peace and peaceful co-existence among States. This is a necessary condition for securing for everyone economic, social, cultural, civil and political rights.

Co-operation among States in promoting and encouraging respect for human rights and in achieving other aims of the UN must be based, according to Article 2 of the Charter, on the observance of its principles. This means that co-operation of States in the field of human rights must be combined with unfailing observance of the principles of sovereign equality of States and non-interference in the affairs which are essentially within their domestic jurisdiction.

The report of the Subcommittee I/1/A of the San Francisco Conference, which discussed paragraph 3 of Article 1 of the UN Charter, pointed out that the ensurance and direct protection of human rights and fundamental freedoms is the internal affair of every State. For this reason, the Subcommittee did not accept proposals to the effect that paragraph 3 of Article 1 should speak not of "promoting and encouraging respect for human rights and for fundamental freedoms," but of "protecting" them.[6]

The volume of human rights, their real content and guarantees are determined in the final analysis by the character of the social and economic system of a State. It is therefore only natural that the volume of rights and freedoms granted to the individual is different in member countries of the UN. Depending on the social and economic conditions and the extent of the realization of human rights and freedoms, each State regulates their volume and introduces definite guarantees. Proclamation of rights unsupported by appropriate internal State measures is largely an empty formality.

The participants in the European Security Conference in Helsinki, formulating the principle of sovereign equality and respect of rights inherent in sovereignty, reached a fundamental understanding to "respect each other's right freely to choose and develop its political, social, economic and cultural systems, as well as its right to determine its laws and regulations." In this way, a formulation was given of an important norm of international law pledging the States to build their mutual relations on the basis of respect for both the laws and administrative regulations of each other. It goes without saying that in establishing their laws and administrative regulations, States must act according to their juridical obligations assumed under international agreements. The Conference on Security and Co-operation in Europe reaffirmed the most important thesis of modern international law to the effect that the immediate settlement of questions of the legal regulation of human rights and freedoms lies within the domestic jurisdiction of States.

The UN Charter, as well as the post-war agreements in the field of human rights, refer the direct provision and protection of human rights and freedoms exclusively to the domestic jurisdiction of the States. They speak not about "international protection" of human rights but of promotion of international co-operation with the aim of encouraging universal respect for, and observance of, human rights and freedoms (Art. 1 and Art. 55 of the Charter).

These questions are regulated in the Charter differently with respect to trust and non-self-governing territories. The provisions of the UN Charter on matters constituting the domestic jurisdiction of States do not apply to the colonial system based on suppression of sovereignty and seizure of foreign territories. The problems relating to non-self-governing and trust territories are of an international character and do not belong to the domestic jurisdiction of the colonial powers.[7] The UN Charter places on the colonial powers the obligation "to promote to the utmost... the well-being of the inhabitants" of these territories, to ensure their social advancement, "their just treatment and their protection against abuses, to assist them in the progressive development of their free political institutions" (paragraphs "a" and "b," Article 73) and also "to encourage respect for human rights and for fundamental freedoms for all without distinction as to race, sex, language or religion" (paragraph "c," Article 76). Chapters XI and XII of the UN Charter oblige the colonial powers to submit to the UN information on the non-self-governing and trust territories and the Trusteeship Council is empowered to "accept petitions and examine them" and also to "provide for periodic visits to the respective trust territories." The Special Committee on the Situation with regard to Implementation of the Declaration on Granting Independence to Colonial Countries and Peoples, set up by a decision of the UN General Assembly in 1961, also has the powers to examine petitions, to receive petitioners, to receive information and visit respective territories.[8] The Trusteeship Council and Special Committee regularly examine at their sessions petitions, many of which concern violations by the colonial powers of the rights and freedoms of the peoples of dependent territories. These questions are also dealt with by the Committee on the Elimination of Racial Discrimination in accordance with Article 15 of the International Convention on the Elimination of All Forms of Racial Discrimination.

The UN Charter and resolutions and agreements adopted by the United Nations Organization not only place on the colonial powers the obligation to promote respect for human rights and their observance on non-self-governing and trust territories, but also established a system of direct international control over their activities. It is therefore fully justified to speak of international protection of human rights with reference to colonial and dependent peoples.

International protection of human rights is also implemented through the application of Chapter VII of the UN Charter. According to paragraph 7 of Article 2 of the Charter, the principle of non-interference in matters which are essentially within the domestic jurisdiction of any State does not affect the application of enforcement measures in line with Chapter VII of the Charter.

The report of the Subcommittee I/1/A at the San Francisco Conference pointed out that if "rights and freedoms were grievously outraged so as to create conditions which threaten peace or to obstruct the application of provisions of the Charter, they cease to be the sole concern of each State."[9] In this case the UN can apply enforcement measures against the State which by its actions is jeopardizing peace and international security. The UN has repeatedly discussed the question of enforcement measures against countries where flagrant violations of human rights and freedoms created a threat to peace and international security. The UN General Assembly has often qualified the *apartheid* policy pursued by the Republic of South Africa as a crime against humanity and recommended the use of sanctions against this country. The Convention on the Prevention and Punishment of the Crime of Genocide adopted in 1948 provides for a whole complex of international measures to cut short this crime. The Convention on the Suppression and Punishment of the Crime of *Apartheid*, adopted in 1973 by the UN General Assembly, qualifies *apartheid* as a crime and provides for international criminal responsibility for it.

Consequently, violation of human rights perpetrated on a mass scale and endangering peace and international security or representing gross negation of the aims and principles of the UN Charter is not the exclusive concern of the State pursuing such policy and gives the UN the right to apply enforcement measures. It is equally clear that if a State perpetrates actions qualified by international law as international crimes or international offences such actions are not the internal affair of the State concerned.

In pursuance of the provisions of the UN Charter, a number of international agreements and conventions on human rights have been adopted within the framework of the United Nations Organization. Some of them provide for the establishment of special committees, one of whose functions is, in particular, to examine reports of participating States on measures taken by them to implement assumed obligations.

In literature on international law, there is a widely-held view that these committees are organs in charge of the implementation of the given agreements.[10] The use of the term "implementation" implies that such organs have the functions for the practical realization of agreements by means available to them. The term "implementation" is defined in the dictionaries as carrying into effect according to a definite procedure[11] or as ensuring practical effect and actual fulfillment by concrete measures.[12] Many experts in international law give a similar interpretation of the powers of the so-called implementation organs, believing that they possess the functions of direct implementation of human rights and their protection. They claim that implementation of human rights should be effected not by the States, but by a special international mechanism.[13] Only a few individual scholars adhere to correct positions on these questions and hold the view that implementation of human rights is the internal affair of States.[14]

We are convinced that theoretically and practically it is more proper to speak not about implementation organs but about an international mechanism with functions of control over fulfilment of adopted agreements. In international law the concept of control is used mainly to denote methods of verification of fulfilment of obligations assumed by States. As regards human rights, forms of control and the principles of their functioning are determined by the UN Charter and decisions of the United Nations Organization and international agreements. Under the most widespread form of control, the States submit information to the General Secretary of the UN or to a specially instituted organ concerning maintenance of specific rights.

Under the Covenants, the Economic and Social Council is empowered to make recommendations of a "general nature" only, on the information submitted by the participating States. The Human Rights Committee, established in keeping with the Covenant on Civil and Political Rights, is likewise empowered, after examining reports of States on the implementation of obligations assumed under the Covenant, to make comments of a "general" character only. "General recommendations" on reports of the States parties to the Covenant, on measures taken by them to fulfil the obligations assumed by them are also made by the Committee on the Elimination of Racial Discrimination set up in accordance with the International Convention on the Elimination of All Forms of Racial Discrimination.

The expressions "general recommendations" and observations of a "general nature" signify that the appropriate bodies of the UN, when examining reports of States, have no right to make concrete recommendations on specific measures to be taken to implement particular human rights and freedoms. The elaboration and implementation of such measures is the internal affair of States.

International control over the activity of States in securing human rights and freedoms must be exercised with strict observance of their sovereignty and non-interference in their internal affairs. Only on this basis is it possible to ensure effective operation of the entire system of international control. Making recommendations of a general character, the UN has no power to address them to particular States, since both the direct elaboration of concrete measures and their realization are matters of domestic jurisdiction of States. Exceptions to this general rule are justified only when they concern the application of Chapters VI and VII of the UN Charter with reference to trust and non-self-governing territories and also in cases when international crimes are committed.

This practice has become fairly widespread in the UN with special groups being set up to study concrete situations and to investigate the cases of gross, mass and systematic violations of human rights, including the policy of racial discrimination and *apartheid* in colonial and dependent countries and also on territories occupied as a result of aggression.

Special organs may be formed by the UN to investigate violations of human rights by fascist and militarist dictatorships. The legality of formation of such organs rests on the fact that the policy pursued by military-fascist dictatorships negates the aims and principles of the UN Charter and is accompanied by mass and systematic violations of elementary human rights and freedoms. This is why the Commission on Human Rights in 1975 formed an *ad hoc* working group of five members to investigate the situation in the field of human rights existing in Chile by visiting the country and collecting oral and written evidence from all appropriate sources (Res. 8 (XXXI)).

There are diverse forms of control over the fulfilment by States of their obligations to promote respect of human rights and freedoms and their observance. They depend on whether control is applied with reference to sovereign States or to the activities of metropolitan powers on colonial territories. In a number of cases it may also be determined by the character of violations of human rights and freedoms.

The institution by the UN of special bodies with the functions of direct control is rightful only in strictly defined and concrete situations in cases of flagrant violations of human rights representing negation of the aims and principles of the UN Charter or constituting an international crime, by way of application of Chapters VI and VII of the UN Charter, and also in cases of systematic, mass and gross violations of human rights and freedoms in colonial and dependent countries and in territories occupied by an aggressor.

The institution of special organs in other situations to examine questions related to human rights inevitably lends an unlawful orientation to their activity which assumes the character of interference in the internal affairs of States. The many years' experience of discussion of questions of human rights in the UN has clearly demonstrated that a well thought out and legitimate activity of a control mechanism based on the UN Charter and universally recognized principles of international law is of paramount importance for effective functioning of the entire system of relations among States in this field.

International relations are developing today in conditions of relaxation of tension among States and a mounting struggle against the policy of aggression, fascism, colonialism, genocide, apartheid, racialism and other gross and mass violations of fundamental human rights and freedoms. The deepening of the process of international détente and extension of good neighbour relations among States with different social and economic systems are inseparably bound up with the elimination of gross and massive violations of human rights which are still fairly extensive. International co-operation of States in the field of human rights should be aimed, first of all, at combating mass and gross violations of rights and freedoms committed as a result of policies of aggression, fascism, colonialism, genocide, apartheid and racialism. The elimination of hotbeds of international tension and development of normal relations between States is a most important prerequisite for the observance of human rights and freedoms.

Unless aggressive wars, fascism, colonialism, genocide, apartheid and racism are eliminated, elementary human rights and freedoms cannot be ensured. Struggle against these international delicts is the only radical way of deepening co-operation of States in promoting respect for human rights and their observance. There are still many untapped reserves and potentialities here. The growth of co-operation of States in eliminating mass and gross violations of human rights rests on a firm base of international law. The most gross and mass violations of fundamental human rights and freedoms representing a special danger to universal peace and international security are treated by modern international law as international crimes. This is reflected in a number of international documents according to which the concept "international crime" includes crimes against humanity and crimes against international law.

Article 6 of the Charter of the International War Tribunal in Nuremberg includes three types of crimes against mankind in the category of international crimes—crimes against peace, war crimes and crimes against humanity:

Crimes against peace, namely: the planning, preparation, unleashing or waging of an aggressive war or war in violation of international treaties, agreements or assurances, or participation in a common plan or conspiracy pursuing one of the above mentioned actions;

War crimes, namely: violation of the laws or customs of war. These violations include the killing, torturing or withdrawal for enslavement or other purposes of the civil population of occupied territories, the killing or torturing of prisoners of war or persons at sea; killing of hostages; plunder of public or private property; senseless destruction of towns or villages; devastation unjustified by military necessity and other crimes;

Crimes against humanity, namely: killings, annihilation, subjugation, deportation and other cruelties perpetrated against civilian populations before or during war, or persecution for political, racial or religious motives with the aim of committing a crime or in connection with any crime subject to the jurisdiction of the Tribunal, irrespective of whether these actions constituted a violation of the law of the country concerned or not.

All these crimes involve violation of elementary human rights and freedoms.

Aggression is incompatible with the principle of respect for, and observance of, human rights. It signifies complete negation of practically the entire complex of rights fixed in the Covenants on Human Rights and other international instruments. To the right of peoples to self-determination, the right of every individual to life, liberty and security of person, to just and favourable working conditions, to the highest attainable standard of physical and mental health and other rights, the aggressor opposes his domination through appropriation of natural wealth and resources of peoples inhabiting occupied territories, terror, repression, violence and killing. The removal of war from the life of society and the development of mutual relations between States on the basis of the principles of peaceful coexistence are the most important prerequisites and the necessary conditions for the observance of human rights and freedoms.

The Convention on the Prevention and Punishment of the Crime of Genocide refers to the category of international crimes of which genocide, according to Article I of the Convention, is a crime under international law. The Convention on the Non-Applicability of the Statutory Limitations to War Crimes and Crimes against Humanity treats as international crimes, war crimes, crimes against humanity, eviction as a result of armed attack or occupation and inhuman acts which are the consequences of the policy of *apartheid*, and also crimes of genocide (Article I). *Apartheid* is also qualified as a crime violating the principles of international law in the Convention on the Suppression and Punishment of the Crime of *Apartheid* (Article I).

International documents adopted within the framework of the·UN refer to international crimes against peace, war crimes, crimes against humanity, crimes of genocide and *apartheid* and the policy and practice of racial segregation and discrimination similar to it.

The separation of international crimes from the category of international delicts is justified by their particularly dangerous character for peace and international security. International crimes are also specific in that they are usually committed not by private individuals but by officials acting on behalf of a State. Therefore the perpetration of an international crime should lead not only to the criminal responsibility of the culprits, but also to the responsibility under international law of the State on whose behalf they acted.

In contrast to international crimes we must distinguish international offences which take the form of violations of the operative norms and principles of international law. These offences resulting in violations of human rights and freedoms include the policy of fascism, colonialism and racial discrimination. Fascism is the total negation of human rights and freedoms. Resorting to crude violence as a means of achieving power, Nazi and fascist forces consciously use terror to suppress opposition and bolster their power. Fascist parties and groupings use democracy merely as a stepping stone to power and then they abolish it, establishing a regime of terror and cynical and outright negation of legality. For many years the UN has examined the question of measures to be taken against Nazism and racial intolerance. In a number of its resolutions the General Assembly has qualified Nazism as an ideology based on terror and racial intolerance and representing a gross violation of human rights and fundamental freedoms and also the aims and principles of the UN Charter (Resolutions 2331 (XXII), 2433 (XXIII), 2545 (XXIV), 2713 (XXV), 2839 (XXVI)). In these resolutions, the General Assembly urgently appealed to all States to put an end to the dissemination of such ideology and practice.

Colonialism, too, is incompatible with the principle of respect for, and observance of, fundamental human rights and freedoms recorded in the UN Charter. The Declaration on the Granting of Independence to Colonial Countries and Peoples emphasizes that "the subjection of peoples to alien subjugation, domination and exploitation constitutes a denial of fundamental human rights, is contrary to the Charter of the United Nations and is an impediment to the promotion of world peace and co-operation." The Declaration states that "all peoples have the right to self-determination; by virtue of that right they freely determine their political status and freely pursue their economic, social and cultural development." It stresses that "inadequacy of political, economic, social or educational preparedness should never serve as a pretext for delaying independence." The Declaration calls on all the States to observe strictly and faithfully the provisions of the UN Charter and the Universal Declaration of Human Rights. One of the fundamental ideas of the Declaration is that colonialism is a negation of fundamental human rights and freedoms. Only when they implement the right to self-determination and achieve independence can the peoples of colonial and dependent territories win complete respect for, and observance of, their rights and freedoms.

Modern international law also qualifies as unlawful racial discrimination, prohibiting it in any form and manifestation. The development of inter-State co-operation in ensuring human rights and freedoms is inseparable from the elimination of these mass and gross violations which result from the policies of aggression, fascism and Nazism, colonialism, genocide, *apartheid* and racism. A cardinal way of international protection of human rights lies through liquidation of these violations. As regards the direct provision of rights for every individual, this is a prerogative of the State, not of the international community. Further perfection of the forms and methods of international co-operation in the field of human rights will depend on the extension of the process of relaxation of tensions and its materialization and, as a consequence thereof, growth of trust among States with different social systems.

2. CO-OPERATION AMONG SOCIALIST COUNTRIES IN THE FIELD OF HUMAN RIGHTS

The socialist concept of human rights does not reject the idea of regional protection of human rights but posits that steps taken on a regional scale should be based on the strict observance of the UN Charter and the universally recognized principles of international law. Activities of regional organizations should promote the realization of the aims and principles of the United Nations and facilitate the implementation of its decisions in the sphere of human rights.

Some international law experts are concerned lest the division of the world into regions should weaken the forces of the international community in the elaboration and realization of specific measures aimed at safeguarding human rights. They believe that, in the present conditions of the existence of the United Nations, regional organizations are incapable of achieving any major success in this field.[15] According to them, efforts should be concentrated, first of all, on the elaboration of a specific procedure for safeguarding human rights within the UN framework.[16]

Socialist countries, on their part, proceed from the premise that in the specific conditions of the construction of socialism and communism the best form of co-operation among them in all fields of relations are bilateral and multilateral agreements.[17] Scholars of socialist countries believe that individuals are not subjects of international law. According to them, the recognition of the international legal capacity of individuals leads to undermining of state sovereignty and to interference with domestic affairs of States.[18]

According to this concept, every individual is under the jurisdiction of the State in whose territory he resides and to whose law and order he submits. It is not an individual who operates in the world arena but the State as a sovereign political entity which has its own will, as distinct from the will of individual citizens. This is the will of the dominating class in a given society. It is obvious that both the State and its organs operate in international relations as duly authorized persons. Acting in this capacity, an individual acquires rights not for himself but for the State which bears international law responsibility for his actions. In concluding an international treaty which provides for certain rights to individuals, the State assumes the responsibility to provide such rights to persons under its jurisdiction.

Each State party to a treaty, in the implementation of its international obligation, takes legislative and other adequate internal measures. Specific application of these measures is wholly under the domestic competence of the States. International agreements do not grant any rights directly to individuals. These agreements only place the States under obligation to ensure certain rules of behaviour by individuals and to grant them certain rights.

Under socialism, States perform their functions exclusively in the interests of their citizens. Every citizen has at his disposal a number of national facilities for the protection of his rights and interests. Therefore, according to the socialist concept of human rights, there is no need to establish special regional organizations for the protection of individuals' rights in the countries which are in the process of constructing socialism and communism. This protection is ensured both by domestic facilities and through the development of bilateral and multilateral co-operation among the socialist countries.

Socialist States have concluded a number of treaties on legal assistance in civil, family and criminal cases. In accordance with these agreements, citizens of one contracting party enjoy in the territory of another country the same legal protection as the local citizens with respect to their personal and property rights. These treaties regulate problems of the family, marriage, establishment and contestation of parenthood, guardianship, trusteeship, adoption, inheritance, etc.[19]

Direct protection of the rights and interests of the citizens of one socialist country in the territory of another is effected by consular missions. They are established by the conclusion of appropriate consular conventions. Since 1957, socialist countries have concluded among themselves a large number of such conventions either for an indefinite period or for the period of five years with subsequent automatic prolongation for another five years. The convention may be denounced by any of the contracting parties. In this case it becomes invalid upon the expiry of the six-month period, after one of the parties has notified the other of its wish to withdraw from it.

The main function of the consular missions is to protect the rights and interests of their State and their citizens. The consul represents his country in his consular region and performs mainly administrative and legal functions. In the exercise of their duties, the consuls may address representations to the local authorities of the consular region on the occasion of the violation of rights and interests of the citizens of the country which had appointed the consul. He may also represent his citizens in the courts of law of the host country.[20]

Relations among socialist countries after the Second World War emerged and developed as the relations of political co-operation which in many respects determined the scope and nature of their economic, cultural and other ties. Although the agreements in the political and economic fields do not directly concern problems of human rights, their implementation and observance by the contracting parties has direct importance for the ensurance of economic, social and other rights of citizens of socialist countries.

In the political field, socialist countries have concluded a number of treaties of friendship, co-operation and mutual assistance. Presently, over thirty such treaties are in force. Although these treaties are of a general political nature, the obligations of the contracting parties cover also other spheres of their relations—economic and cultural. For example, the Treaty of Friendship, Co-operation and Mutual Assistance, concluded on 12 May 1967 between the USSR and Bulgaria, contains obligations of the contracting parties to develop economic, scientific and technical co-operation, as well as ties in the field of education, health, literature, arts, press, cinema, radio and television (Art. 2-3). The Treaty of Friendship, Co-operation and Mutual Assistance signed in 1961 between the Socialist Republic of Vietnam and the Mongolian People's Republic states that the Parties shall conclude individual agreements in the economic and cultural fields (Art. 2-3).

The multilateral Warsaw Treaty of Friendship, Co-operation and Mutual Assistance, concluded on 14 May 1955 by Albania, Bulgaria, Hungary, the German Democratic Republic, Poland, Rumania, USSR and Czechoslovakia, did not abolish obligations following from bilateral treaties, but rather supplemented them. Article 8 of the Warsaw Treaty notes that the contracting parties will act in the spirit of friendship and co-operation with the purpose of the further development and consolidation of economic and cultural ties among them. After the conclusion of the Warsaw Treaty, the socialist countries continued the practice of concluding bilateral treaties of friendship, co-operation and mutual assistance. These treaties laid the basis for a broad development of economic and cultural relations among socialist countries.

In the first post-war years economic ties among socialist countries were developing on a bilateral basis. At a later stage these bilateral forms began to be supplemented by multilateral agreements of an economic nature. The beginning of such multilateral co-operation was laid by the establishment in 1949 of the Council for Mutual Economic Assistance whose founding members were Bulgaria, Hungary, Poland, Rumania, USSR and Czechoslovakia.[21] The purpose of the establishment of the Council for Mutual Economic Assistance, as noted in Article 1, paragraph 1 of its Charter, is to promote: the acceleration of economic and technological progress in the CMEA Member States; the level of industrialization of countries with less developed economies; continuous growth or productivity of labour; and the continuous improvement of the well-being of the peoples of the CMEA Member States.

The drawing closer of the levels of economic development of the CMEA Member States through the achievement of levels of the most advanced socialist countries and raising on this basis the material status and well-being of every member of the society facilitates the real ensurance of such fundamental rights of the working people as the right to work, to an adequate standard of living and continuous improvement of its conditions.

The activities of the Council for Mutual Assistance are based on the principle of sovereign equality of all member countries (Article I, paragraph 2, of the CMEA Charter). The Council is authorized to pass only recommendations on all matters of economic, scientific and technical co-operation (Article IV, paragraph 1). Decisions are adopted only on procedural and organizational matters (Article IV, paragraph 2). In 1971 the CMEA member countries adopted the Comprehensive Programme of socialist economic integration. This programme determines the principles, aims, ways and means of economic integration and envisages the gradual drawing together and levelling of economic development of these countries. The implementation of the programme will facilitate the fullest realization of a broad complex of socio-economic rights provided in the International Covenant on Economic, Social and Cultural Rights.

In past years co-operation in the field of social security, including social insurance, has been broadly developed among the socialist countries. Several inter-governmental agreements have been concluded, extending the provisions of social security legislation applicable to citizens of one socialist State to citizens of other socialist countries who reside in its territory. The agreement between the USSR and Bulgaria on social security of 11 December 1959 envisages the extension of its provisions to all aspects of social security of citizens which will be established by legislation of the contracting parties (Article 1). According to the agreement, citizens of one contracting party who permanently reside in the territory of another contracting party are equal to the citizens of the other contracting party in all matters of social security including medical assistance and labour relations.

Article 4 stipulates that in granting pensions and benefits full account is taken of the length of service in the territories of both contracting parties.

According to Article 8, temporary disability benefits, child allowances, maternity and confinement benefits and benefits at childbirth are determined and paid by the competent authorities of the contracting parties in whose territory a given citizen is residing, and in accordance with the legislation of that country. Mutual payments between the contracting parties are not made (Article 12).

Similar provisions can be found in other agreements concluded between socialist countries in the field of social security. Cultural co-operation among socialist countries has been considerably developed. The socialist countries proceed from the premise that international cultural co-operation is one of the most important conditions of the development of contemporary science and culture which facilitates the fullest ensurance of the right of everyone to free participation in cultural life. This co-operation lays an important role in mutual enrichment of national cultures. Agreements on cultural and scientific co-operation in the post-war period have been concluded at different times between all socialist countries.

The types and forms of co-operation among socialist countries in the field of culture and science are diverse. For example, the agreement between the USSR and Hungary of 1968 requires each State to familiarize regularly their working people with the people's life in the other country (Article 2). The agreement contains the obligation to encourage teaching in higher and other educational establishments of the language, literature, history and geography of the other country, as well as to spread information about it (Article 5). Much attention is paid to the question of co-operation in the field of press, cinema, radio and television. The agreements on cultural co-operation provide for the establishment of permanent mixed commissions or committees, as well as annual meetings of representatives of the parties for the elaboration and examination of the progress of the implementation of plans of co-operation.

Matters of co-operation in the field of education occupy a place of importance in the inter-governmental agreements on cultural co-operation. They are also regulated by bilateral agreements between the USSR and other socialist countries on the training of the citizens of these countries in the USSR's higher educational institutes and by bilateral agreements on conditions of mutual acceptance of students and post-graduates in the higher educational establishments and scientific research institutes.

The less developed socialist countries receive great assistance from the more developed socialist countries in the sphere of training specialists in higher education. For example, in 1978 several tens of thousands of students, post-graduates and probationers from socialist countries studied in the Soviet Union. From the Socialist Republic of Vietnam alone, seven thousand students studied in the USSR. All expenses connected with education, including transportation to the place of study, travel inside the country, provision of lodging and free medical assistance are covered by the host country.

Thus bilateral and multilateral agreements concluded between the socialist countries in different fields of their relations have a direct bearing on the ensurance of human rights. The realization of these agreements facilitates the fullest ensurance of a broad complex of civil, economic, social and cultural rights of citizens of socialist countries.

NOTES

1. K. Marx and F. Engels, *Manifest Kommunisticheskoj Partii*, Soch., t. 4, izd. 2-e, Gospolitizdat, Moskva, 1955, str. 443 (Communist Party Manifesto, Collection of Works, Vol. 4, Second Edition, State Political Publishing House, Moscow, 1955, p. 443).

2. V.I. Lenin, *Poln. sobr. soch.*, izd 5-e, t. 23, str. 47, Gospolitizdat, 1961 god. (V.I. Lenin, Complete Works, Fifth Edition, Vol. 23, p. 47, State Political Publishing House, 1961).

3. I. Szabo, *Sotsialisticheskoye pravo*, Moskva, Izdaniye "Progress," 1964, str. 316 (I. Szabo, Socialist Law, Moscow, "Progress" Publishing House, 1964, p. 316); N.I. Matuzov, *Lichnost. Prava. Democratiya*, Saratov, 1972, str. 12-48 (N.I. Matuzov, Personality Rights. Democracy, Saratov, 1972, pp. 12-48).

4. *Programma Kommunisticheskoj Partii Sovetskogo Sojuza*, Politizdat, 1973 str. 15 (Programme of the Communist Party of the Soviet Union, Political Publishing House, 1973, p. 15).

5. *Programma Kommunisticheskoj Partii Sovetskogo Sojuza*, Politizdat, 1973, str. 16 (Programme of the Communist Party of the Soviet Union, Political Publishing House, 1973, p. 16).

6. See *Documents of the United Nations Conference on International Organization*, Vol. VI, London-New York, 1945, p. 705.

7. G.N. Morozov, *Organizatsiya Obyedinennyh Natsii*, Moskva, 1962, str. 171-179 (United Nations Organization, Moscow, 1962, pp. 171-179).

8. UN doc. A/AC/109 (1962).

9. *Documents of the United Nations Conference on International Organization*, Vol. VI, London-New York, p. 705.

10. See McDougal and C. Bebr, "Human Rights in the United Nations," *AJIL*, Vol. 58, No. 3, 1964, pp. 603-641; "Proceedings of the American Society of International Law at its Sixty-Fourth Annual Meeting," *AJIL*, Vol. 64, No. 4, 1970, pp. 110-119, 123-125. See also, for example, V. Chkhikvadze, "Narody otvergayut rasizm" (Peoples Reject Racism), *Mezhdunarodnaya zhizn*, No. 5, 1966, pp. 70-77; Y.A. Ostrovsky, *OON i prava cheloveka*, Moskva, 1968, str. 108-115 (The UN and Human Rights, Moscow, 1968, pp. 108-115).

11. *The Random House Dictionary of the English Language*, New York, 1968, p. 667.

12. Webster's *Third New International Dictionary*, Massachusetts, 1966, pp. 1134-1135.

13. H. Lauterpacht, *International Law and Human Rights*, New York, Praeger, 1950, pp. 221-229; McDougal and C. Bebr, *op. cit.*, pp. 603-641; A. Robertson, *The International Protection of Human Rights*, Nottingham, 1970, pp. 6-11.

14. *AJIL*, Vol. 64, No. 4, 1970, pp. 123-125.

15. *Human Rights in National and International Law*, edited by A.H. Robertson, Manchester, University Press,1968, pp. 355-356.

16. John P. Humphrey, "The International Law of Human Rights in the Middle Twentieth Century," in *The Present State of International Law and Other Essays*, edited by Maarten Bos, Kluwer, The Netherlands, 1973, pp. 75-105.

17. *Mezhdunarodnoye pravo v otnosheniyah mezhdu sotsialisticheskimi gosudarstvami. Kurs mezhdunarodnogo prava*, Tom VI, Moskva, 1973 (International Law in the Relations among Socialist States. A Course in International Law, Vol. VI, Moscow, 1973).

18. *Kurs mezhdunarodnogo prava*, Moskva, Tom I, str. 161-166 (A Course in International Law, Moscow, Vol. I, pp. 161-166).

19. *Dogovori ob okazanii pravovoi pomoshchi po grazhdanskim, semeinym i ugolovnym delam, zakliuchenniye SSSR s drugimi sotsialisticheskimi stranami*, redaktor M.D. Grishin, Moskva, 1973 (Treaties on Legal Protection in Civil, Family and Criminal Cases concluded by the USSR with Other Socialist States, edited by M.D. Grishin, Moscow, 1973).

20. For more detail, see: *Mezhdunarodno-pravoviye formi sotrudnichestva sotsialisticheskih stran*, redaktor V.M. Shurshalov, Moskva, 1962, str. 412-458 (International Law Forms of Co-operation among Socialist Countries, edited by V.M. Shurshalov, Moscow, 1962, pp. 412-458).

21. Presently, the German Democratic Republic, Cuba, Mongolia, and the Socialist Republic of Vietnam are also Member States of the Council for Mutual Economic Assistance.

21 Asia[1] and Human Rights

Hiroko Yamane

"I learnt from my illiterate but wise mother that all rights to be deserved and preserved came from duty well done. Thus the very right to live accrues to us only when we do the duty of citizenship of the world. From this one fundamental statement, perhaps it is easy enough to define the duties of Man and Woman and correlate every right to some corresponding duty to be first performed. Every other right can be shown to be a usurpation hardly worth fighting for."

(M.K. Gandhi)

It is apparent that the subject "Asia and Human Rights" has certain misleading connotations: it conveys the idea that Asia is a regional entity with a particular "Asian" approach to human rights. In fact, there is no basis in geographical proximity to make Asian nations a continent in the same way as Europe or Africa are considered. Asia is a conglomeration of countries with radically different social structures, and diverse religious, philosophical and cultural traditions; their political ideologies, legal systems, and degrees of economic development vary greatly; and, above all, there is no shared historical past even from the times of colonialism. Most research on human rights problems in Asia has, therefore, been national rather than regional.

Yet, there are clearly valid reasons to reflect on "Asia and Human Rights" and to undertake studies on the subject. The first reason is that the countries of Asia display certain essential similarities which facilitate the making of comparisons. These similarities are the result of two sets of factors. First, Asian countries are characterized by vast populations, with forms of highly complex civilizations and social organizations that were in existence long before the reception of Western laws and legal concepts, and which could hinder to a certain extent the acceptance of the idea of human rights. Secondly, the socio-economic and demographic conditions, which prevail in some Asian countries at least, are conducive to regional co-operation as these countries strive for economic development. It is important to note that this latter factor has considerably influenced the view and interpretation of human rights by Asian political leaders and economic planners.

The second reason for studying Asia and human rights is the need to look at a series of important questions raised by efforts to promote respect for human rights in Asia: (1) to what extent is the concept of human rights peculiar to the Western philosophical tradition and a product of specific political and socio-economic settings? (2) how compatible is it with the ageless beliefs, institutions and social practices of the peoples of Asia? and (3) if the means to protect human rights developed in response to European concern with the individual in his relationship to the State, what means are appropriate for the protection of human rights, in situations where neither the "individual" nor the "State" constitute solid institutional realities? In sum, if the concept of human rights is inherently Western, its implantation in Asia might be considered as an infringement on the cultural rights of the peoples of Asia.

Nevertheless, despite some resistance to what are viewed as alien concepts or approaches, there are increasingly powerful forces at work within the region which favour the protection and promotion of human rights. Regional co-operation in this field might come to play a larger role in the future. At the same time, consideration of these forces and the struggles they generate reveals some of the problems which may arise in seeking to implement human rights standards in non-Western cultural settings.

This short chapter on "Asia and Human Rights" will indicate: (1) that Asia, which has always been confronted with classical human rights problems of poverty, hunger, unemployment, deprivation of certain civil and political liberties, and minority problems and which today faces new and "emerging" problems of human rights, generated in part by the activities of transnational corporations and by growing environmental pollution problems, constitutes a rich source for reflection on the new dimensions of human rights, new forms of violations of human rights, and new ways and means to combat these problems; (2) that the struggle for human rights is universal, despite the different cultural expressions it may take; (3) that what is needed is a real effort to raise the consciousness of the people at large so that human rights cease to be essentially a preoccupation of the elite and attain their full potential significance for all sectors of society; and (4) that in the Asian region, where rapid economic growth has been accompanied by a radical social transformation in a short span of time, so-called "collective" rights are basically a problem of individual rights, in the sense that no collective realization is possible without the assurance of basic individual rights; otherwise, realization of such collective rights would remain at the level of authoritarian undertakings that would not awaken people's consciousness of their rights and fundamental freedoms. The Asian experience reinforces the concept of the "indivisibility" of human rights by showing that it is not possible to allocate, *a priori*, priority to certain categories of human rights, or to propose particular stages for the promotion of human rights, according to the degree of development of a society.

1. EVOLUTION OF THE APPROACH TO HUMAN RIGHTS PROBLEMS

(a). The spirit of the 1960s

"... It is, perhaps, not by accident that affluent countries of the world came to believe in and practice democracy. We... who belong to the other side, i.e. that of the underdeveloped countries, also believe in democracy, not because it is believed in by the Western world, but because we realize that the dignity of man, in fact the survival of the human spirit, is only possible when a government is freely elected by the people of a country.

It is also well to remember, however, that to the teeming millions of Asia and Africa, things like freedom and indeed even human dignity itself are only of academic interest...For them—and they account for the overwhelming majority of the human race—the central problem...is the problem of getting enough to eat...(and) the satisfaction of hunger alone is a worthwhile achievement for the foreseeable future. In their case, if totalitarianism can deliver the goods, i.e.satisfy their hunger, nothing else really matters, not even the loss of political and civil liberties which they have not known in any case...The main thing is to fill the stomach first."

(Statement by an Asian Minister, February 1964)[2]

The most striking characteristic of the approach to human rights problems in Asia in the 1960s was the assumption that the attitudes of Asian countries to human rights are, in general, identical with those of developing countries, as a whole. This was the view expressed at the Seminar on Human Rights in Developing Countries[3] organized by the United Nations in Kabul from 12-25 May 1964. At the seminar, which gathered together Asian government officials, law professors and eminent journalists, a significant controversy arose concerning the extent which human rights were dependent upon the standard of living and the level of economic development. Some maintained that implementation of plans for economic development might, at times, necessitate restrictions upon the exercise of certain human rights. Others opposed this view by asserting that the State should never lose sight of the fact that the purpose of such planning should be to benefit the individual and that, in discharging its functions, the State should not infringe upon the basic freedoms of the individual. Nevertheless, the main focus of discussion at the seminar was that the failure to achieve socio-economic rights was the main obstacle to ensuring respect for other human rights. For this reason, the concept of the "welfare state" was considered to be of particular importance to developing countries.

At the same seminar, it was also stressed that human rights could not be fully implemented without a stable system of government and a body of public officials discharging their duties with fairness and impartiality. In this regard, some pointed out that the prevalence in certain countries of an authoritarian attitude on the part of parents, school teachers and the administration tended to inhibit the development of free criticism and to prevent people from claiming or respecting human rights. The seminar pointed out also that an excessive concern for the internal and external security of the State might motivate unnecessary restrictions on human rights. In addition, the possibility of establishing regional implementation machinery following the model of the European Convention of Human Rights was discussed at the seminar.

About the same time, the International Commission of Jurists (ICJ) held a South-East Asian and Pacific Conference of Jurists in Bangkok, Thailand (15-19 February 1965).[4] In discussing the factors undermining the rule of law in South-East Asia, the Conference pointed out that the national movements which culminated in the obtaining of independence and the introduction of Western democratic institutions had broken down because the achievement of economic and social goals through the path of democracy was too slow. Other factors considered to be hindrances to the realization of human rights included: the lack of technical skills, absence of proper planning, inefficiency and corruption in the administrative services, shortage of capital, inadequacy of foreign aid, political interference in the sphere of administrative and technical decisions, and the population explosion.

The Conference also discussed the possibility of establishing an Asian regional convention on human rights, and examined two other proposals for regional Conventions on Human Rights which were under active consideration at the time: the Inter-American Draft Convention on Human Rights adopted by the Organization of American States; and the Central-American Draft Convention on Human Rights which was sponsored by the Organization "Freedom through Law."

It is significant that the idea of drawing up an Asian Convention on Human Rights was accepted favorably both at the United Nations seminar in Kabul and at the ICJ Conference in Bangkok, especially by most of the lawyers participating. However, it is evident that the weakness of such a proposal resides in the disinterest manifested by Asian governments. Moreover, the absence of effective regional inter-governmental political or socio-economic institutions, constitutes a fundamental drawback to such a project.

A further example of concern with the universality of human rights and with the link between development and human rights during the 1960s was the Round Table organized by Unesco at Oxford, United Kingdom, from 11 to 19 November 1965.[5] This Round Table examined (a) different philosophical and religious traditions and human rights, and (b) socio-economic conditions facilitating or hindering the exercise of human rights. The Round Table aimed at seeking the means to implement, in different societies, the articles of the Universal Declaration of Human Rights.[6] Judaeo-Christian traditions, Islam, Hinduism, Buddhism, and other Asian traditions, as well as traditional African philosophies, Western liberalism, Marxism and "negritude" were examined to assess how different value systems affect the action of individuals and States and to facilitate the reconciliation of these values and those advanced by the Universal Declaration of Human Rights. It is a truism that this latter, at least up to article 21, reflects the individualistic value system which grew out of the Judaeo Christian tradition and the rise of capitalism in Europe since the 17th century. It is also evident that the full implementation of these civil and political rights requires a society which has yet to emerge, even in the West. The problem for the realization of human rights in actual practice in other parts of the world is compounded by the presence of social and cultural norms which appear to be contrary to the ideals contained in the Universal Declaration of Human Rights.

All religions and cultural traditions are responses to specific social conditions and results of various quests for achieving the ideals of equality, fraternity and justice. However, the Round Table pointed out that certain practices stemming from traditional social values can hinder the exercise of human rights. Among those which are particularly relevant to the Asian experience are the following:

—the existence of rigid social hierarchies, determining social functions according to social category or cast. In Confucianism, for example, differences in birth, wealth, race, sex and language create conditions for different treatment. In Hinduism, the law (dharma) sets forth the duties which each man must fulfill if he wishes to avoid losing caste or has any concern for the afterworld. These duties vary according to the status of each person and his age; they are especially demanding for those of a superior social caste.
—the pursuit of certain family and tribal practices which treat rights and duties from the viewpoint of role obligation in accordance with one's status in the family or clan.
—the encouragement of submissive attitudes towards political and social authorities, especially toward the State, and
—the idea that the well-being of the community takes priority over that of the individual and that loyalty in personal relations is of the utmost importance.

Underlying many such ideas is the notion that "rights" are defined and granted *ad libidum* by the authorities.

It is undeniable that certain traditional behaviour patterns make more difficult the effective exercise of human rights as defined, for example, in the Universal Declaration of Human Rights. To the extent that these behaviour patterns are more or less widespread in the Asian region, the implementation of human rights is problematic to say the least. The psychological security which is provided by traditional conceptions of community and human relations could be used to exclude people from participating in the processes of political decision-making and development.

Thus the spirit of the 1960s, insofar as scholars, diplomats and international organizations gave any consideration to the matter of human rights in Asia, seems to have been characterized by two contradictory trends: optimism concerning the importation of Western models, on the one hand, and awareness of the obstacles created by traditional cultural and social patterns and by acute under-development, on the other. The economic dimension was to become predominant in the 1970s.

(b). The impact of Asian economic "take-off" on respect for human rights

"Two justifications for authoritarianism in Asian developing countries are currently fashionable and I find I must say a word on this.

One is that Asian societies are authoritarian and paternalistic and so need governments that are also authoritarian and paternalistic; that Asia's hungry masses are too concerned with filling their stomachs to concern themselves with civil liberties and political freedoms; that the Asian conception of freedom differs from that of the West; that, in short, Asians are not fit for human rights. Well, the first justification is racist nonsense—and I will say no more than that. The second is a lie: authoritarianism is not needed for development; what it is needed for is to maintain the *status quo*.[7]

Development and ideally also planning for development express the desire for a rationally pursued programme for the realization of all-embracing and comprehensive well-being. The experience of two development decades of the United Nations forces one to admit that the programmes and pronouncements of governments and political parties have little permanent impact on socio-economic reality, which seems to follow its own logic to a large extent, regardless of the wishes of the planners, although the planners themselves might also be at fault in failing to implement the objectives of the development decades.

Some examples of economic trends in Asia may illustrate this experience. Starting with a labour-intensive type of economy, Japan launched its economic expansion in the 1960s and achieved a technology-intensive economy. Later, the Republic of Korea and Singapore followed a similar pattern of economic growth. India has joined the group of big industrial powers, although it suffers from the problems of income distribution and over-population. Admitting the validity of the wide-spread scepticism as to the value of growth in GNP as an indicator of economic well-being (i.e. problems of income distribution, non-economic factors determining quality of life, etc.), a particular type of rapid economic growth is transforming the environment as well as the mode of living of the inhabitants in many parts of Asia.[8] In most countries, average household income has substantially increased.[9]

If during the 1960s, realization of human rights was claimed by some to depend on the achievement of rapid economic development, one may wonder what human rights implications should be drawn from the rapid socio-economic transformation of the 1970s. Either the human rights situation should already have improved very substantially or be about to do so, or it must be conceded that much more is involved in the realization of human rights than rapidly increasing overall economic growth rates.

The state of human rights in Asia

(i). THE RATIFICATION OF INTERNATIONAL INSTRUMENTS

Asian governments continue to show a degree of reluctance to be actively engaged in human rights issues, especially at the international level. Although the record of ratification of international instruments is not the best indicator of a country's concern for international promotion and protection of human rights, it does provide some guide.

As the table of ratification on page 000 shows, only India, Japan, Sri Lanka and Mongolia have ratified both the International Covenant on Civil and Political Rights and the International Covenant on Economic, Social and Cultural Rights. The Philippines has ratified the latter only. No Asian country has ratified the optional protocol, as of 1 January 1982.

Another indication is provided by the extent to which countries of the Asian region have ratified international labour conventions as adopted by the ILO. A survey undertaken by the ILO in 1980 indicated that, on the whole "the ratification pace for Asia remains slower, and the regional average . . . is lower than corresponding figures for other regions."[10] This position is also reflected in the number of Asian ratifications of certain of the Conventions which are categorized by the ILO as relating to basic human rights. Thus for example the most widely accepted ILO standards among those concerning basic human rights are the two Conventions relating to forced labour: the Forced Labour Convention, 1930, (N° 29) and the Abolition of Forced Labour Convention 1957 (N° 105). As regards the first of these, the rate of ratification by Asian countries is comparable to that of the general ILO membership, while the rate is noticeably lower (by some 25%) for the second Convention. Similarly, while the Right to Organize and Collective Bargaining Convention 1949 (N° 98) has been ratified by a majority of Asian countries, the Freedom of Association and Protection of the Right to Organize Convention 1948 (N° 87) has been ratified by only one third of the Asian countries.

(ii). THE HUMAN RIGHTS SITUATION

In terms of civil and political human rights the situation in Asia is perhaps neither better nor worse than in other developing regions. While no authoritative assessment can be provided it is relevant to note that the 1980 annual report of Amnesty International makes specific reference to "the vast scale of political imprisonment in Asia—which usually takes the form of detention without trial—."[11] In some instances, according to the report, political prisoners are detained for many years in re-education camps on the grounds that the release of such prisoners would constitute a threat to the security of the state. The phenomenon of the "disappearance" of political prisoners in certain Asian countries was also noted in the report. A variety of other problems has also been experienced in Asia in recent years.

It is, however, in the field of economic, social and cultural rights that the human rights situation in Asia is most tragic. Poverty is rampant in a number of Asian countries. On the basis of World Bank statistics and analyses, almost 800 million human beings throughout the world lived in abject poverty in 1974. They subsisted in conditions of malnutrition, disease, illiteracy and squalor beneath any reasonable standard of human decency. Of that total 580 million

(74 per cent) were in Asia (excluding China). As a recent ILO report concludes, "global poverty is thus disproportionately Asian poverty. Using the total Asian population (excluding China) as the base, about half (53 per cent) of the population existed in absolute poverty in 1974."[12] The outlook for the future, in terms of the realization of economic, social and cultural rights, is equally distressing. Thus, according to the ILO "there are ominous indications that Asian poverty will remain massive throughout the 1980s."

Secondly, the rise of the average standard of living did not necessarily lead to the improvement of respect for human rights. At the same time, the problems of poverty, hunger, unemployment and underemployment still prevail in large sections of the population and have disastrous consequences for human rights. The press in most Asian countries is subject to some form of government pressure or to the strict self-restraint of journalists. In addition, legislative and administrative measures to curtail the right to liberty and security of persons and the right to a fair trial were adopted and the imposition of martial law and the consequent suspension of legal safeguards occured in several cases. These measures were usually attributed to the need to overcome extreme political and ideological tensions.

While these perennial human rights problems remain of major concern,[13] new types of human rights problems have emerged as a result of rapid economic expansion. The following two issues are indicative of their scope and nature:

(a) environmental pollution affecting massive numbers of people;

(b) effects of the activities of multinational corporations on the implementation of human rights, such as the right of peoples to self-determination and to permanent sovereignty over natural resources, and the right to cultural identity.

The scope of the present chapter is unfortunately limited to non-socialist countries, due to the radically different approach of the socialist countries to human rights and development and to the lack of sufficient data.

Pollution

Regarding environmental pollution, the Asian experience shows:

(i) The difficulties which arise in reconciling the economic objective of rapid growth and promotion of the right to health, particularly in densely populated countries; (ii) the importance of the right to freedom of expression, and the press, freedom of association in solving problems through solidarity and the victims of violations who are not readily identifiable; (iii) the possibilities of establishing judicial means to oppose the violation of human rights by private entities including private enterprises which constitute the third power next to the State and individuals. In Japan, for example, the Basic Law for Environmental Pollution Control[14] of 1967 made it possible to sue private enterprises on civil grounds, and the Criminal Act concerning Environmental Pollution of 1970, made it possible to charge private enterprises as well as the Government with criminal offences, wherever their responsibility is involved. Since the late 1960s the protection of victims of pollution has become possible through a firmly established legal procedure, imposing joint obligations upon the State and private enterprises.[15] In countries where the expansion of private enterprise is viewed as a factor promoting welfare and progress, these types of measures constitute an indispensable tool for checks and balances in the development process.

Pollution is not only a problem for economically developed societies. It also affects profoundly the life of people in developing countries in a process of rapid industrialization. In countries where fundamental individual rights are not ensured and where masses of people live in perpetual poverty and fear, it is difficult to expect environmental awareness and action to take the same form as in richer countries. Monitoring pollution, identifying the causes, and taking appropriate action against the polluting agents relies largely upon the exercise of such individual rights as freedom of the press, expression, association and the right to assembly.[16] Solidarity of the victims (usually only the victims have the right to complain under existing institutions) is possible only when individuals are free from fear. Only then will participation of all people in the decisions that affect their lives be possible.

Transnational corporations

Other chapters in this textbook dwell on the provisions of the Charter of the United Nations which define the objectives of the Organization in the fields of economic and social progress and respect for fundamental human rights.[17] These objectives and the means to be used to obtain them were progressively given greater precision in individual documents such as the programmes for the United Nations Development Decades,[18] the New International Economic Order,[19] and the Declaration on Social Progress and Development,[20] and constitute a framework of principles for judging the conduct of States, intergovernmental organizations and other entities.

Special status is given in these instruments to the rights of peoples to self-determination and to permanent sovereignty over natural resources, which are set out in greater detail in other documents.[21] By virtue of the former right, peoples "freely determine their political status and freely pursue their economic, social and cultural development."[22]

More recently, Article 1 of the Charter of Economic Rights and Duties of States[23] affirms that: "Every State has the sovereign and inalienable right to choose its economic system as well as its political, cultural and social systems in accordance with the will of its people, without outside interference, coercion or threat in any form whatsoever."

Article 2, paragraph 2, stipulates that the laws and regulations of the State concerned are authoritative in regard to foreign investment, the "activities of transnational corporations," and in determining the compensation to be paid in the event of nationalization, expropriation or transfer of ownership of foreign property.[24]

In fact, the international community has become increasingly concerned about the impact of transnational corporations on the exercise of human rights, especially in developing countries[25] where the institutional framework often does not allow a sufficient guarantee of host countries protection of their natural and human resources. In 1974, the UN General Assembly called for the formulation, adoption and implementation of an "international code of conduct for transnational corporations,"[26] a responsibility which was subsequently entrusted to the Commission on Transnational Corporations[27] which, in turn, set up an Intergovernmental Working Group to prepare a draft code. In November 1977, the Governing Body of the International Labour Organisation adopted the Tripartite Declaration of Principles concerning Multinational Enterprises and Social Policy.[28] Other regional organizations and non-governmental organizations have also elaborated general codes of conduct for transnationals.[29]

Much more study[30] needs to be undertaken to assess the benefits and costs of the effects of multinationals, taking into consideration the specific conditions prevailing in each host country. In some Asian States, no less than elsewhere, abuses of their power by transnationals have emerged as important human rights problems, as they tend to undermine the conditions conducive to the promotion and protection of various human rights. For example, certain dangerous industrial processes and products[31] (chemical drugs and nuclear waste), which have been banned abroad, are sometimes introduced due to the inability of host governments to undertake the necessary tests or gather the relevant technical data; inappropriate exploitation of land and natural resources chases away the peasant or particular ethnic groups whose legal status of ownership was ill-defined; destruction of the traditional community life of certain tribes which have existed outside the modernization process,[32] and use of particular forms of labour. Thus, even where benefits of transnationals generally asserted by the orthodox school of economics i.e., possibility of technology transfer, rise of productivity, generally higher wage rate compared to local wages, and rise of employment levels, are actually achieved they are often more than offset by practices which amount to, or facilitate human rights violations. It may be noted that these problems will not generally give rise to specific legal action by governments against the corporations since the former are generally disposed or obliged to encourage the activities of the latter. Thus in many respects it is possible to attribute the adverse consequences of TNC's activities to the internal political and socio-economic structures of the host countries.

The above new human rights issues are not peculiar to Asia, but are common to all industrializing countries swept by a process of rapid socio-economic change. In Asia, however, the institutional mechanisms for the defence of the rights of individuals in the face of this process of social change was particularly weak for the following reasons:

(a) Before the rapid economic expansion, Asian societies were essentially traditional, although certain Western liberal thinking permeated intellectual life and Western legal systems and concepts were adopted. However, the idea of individual rights was not firmly implanted, since people continued to identify law with moral duties.[33]

(b) Economic growth was made possible by channelling intelligence, discipline, and the work ethic of the masses into economic activities. However economic development does not in itself open up the possibility of enjoying individual liberty and human rights.

(c) Economic expansion in Asia was not accompanied by the establishment of institutions for the defence of human rights. Legal systems which can be used for this purpose are generally not at the disposal of the masses. In certain countries where the independence of the judiciary and other human rights safeguards are not guaranteed, the response of the people often takes the form of subversion which, in turn, engenders fear on the part of those in power, who, in turn, strengthen their repressive apparatus. The institutional safeguards for human rights are thus eroded in this vicious circle.

2. VARIOUS VIEWS AND TYPES OF ACTION FOR THE PROMOTION AND PROTECTION OF HUMAN RIGHTS IN ASIA: OLD AND NEW

Does the present situation in Asia leave any hope for the future of human rights in the region? While the dialectics between human rights and socio-economic conditions, as well as between human rights and traditional values complicate the process, there is nevertheless a marked trend towards improved implementation of human rights in Asian countries. First of all, their implementation is not completely determined by the prerequisite physical conditions. Secondly, traditional values can be used creatively to find new ways and imaginative means for realizing human dignity and rights. The aspirations of people for life, liberty and security are universal, no matter what moral, cultural and political constraints are imposed upon them. Various methods for the promotion and protection of human rights in Asia have been adopted. These vary according to the specific nature of the human rights problems concerned, the institutional restraints which operate and the sociological background of those who fight for human rights (types of education, cultural values, social status, etc.). The two main approaches which have emerged are the use of legal or quasi-legal remedies and political activism.

Legal remedies

The first approach aims at the protection of human rights through normal judicial remedies. Recourse to judicial remedies is increasingly common especially in countries where the independence of the judiciary is guaranteed. With sufficient respect for the spirit of the law on the part of legislators, decision-makers and adjudicators, this approach is a useful technique for protecting the rights of individuals, even under certain emergency measures. In areas where poverty and illiteracy prevail, free legal aid groups play a crucial role in helping the people to resort to legal remedies. The number of these legal clinic services is increasing in South and South-East Asia.[34]

Quasi-legal remedies

Normal judicial remedies can be supplemented by a network of non-legal remedies. The strength of the latter is that those who are culturally and morally inhibited about taking formal legal action can obtain justice by seeking a friendly settlement. In a culture alien to the action of militant assertion of individual rights, and where non-conflictual human relations are important, these provide for reconciliatory measures which attempt to satisfy individual dignity (basic motivation) without destroying the idea of the harmony of the community (cultural values). An example of the means by which such remedies may be pursued is the existence of the institution of an ombudsman in Hong Kong, India (State of Maharastra), Japan (City of Yokohama) and Nepal.

A similar institution but on a much larger scale, is the Civil Liberties Bureau within the Ministry of Justice in Japan.[35] These bodies have no powers to prosecute, but they are able to take action with regard to a wide range of human rights infringements, by public officials or by private individuals or organizations. The sponsorship by the Ministry of Justice also makes it easier for an authority-minded people to express their human rights problems.

Human Rights Activism

An alternative to the use of legal and quasi-legal approaches, is the adoption of a more activist, even militant approach to voicing human rights complaints. Such a response has been used on occasion by, *inter alia*, trade unions and other types of pressure groups, religious missionary movements, and political parties. In countries where the judiciary lacks independence, especially in constitutional matters, and adopts an extensive interpretation of the principle of national security, the role played by these activist organizations is important. They can be particularly effective in areas of challenge to the enjoyment of human rights where a purely legal and formalistic conception of justice does not get to the heart of the problem. This is often the case in matters relating to the activities of transnationals, destruction of the environment or the perpetuation of gross inequities in income and wealth distribution. It is in this connection that the idea of "people's rights" has developed in Asia as elsewhere. If a community is subject to domination (examples may include an oppressed minority or a country existing under a neo-colonialist yoke), not only are the human rights of the individual violated, but so too are those of the "people," the collectivity. Advocates of "people's rights" generally differentiate these two dimensions in the struggle for human rights: the rights of the individual and the rights of peoples.[36] Although these dimensions are interrelated, they stress the importance of the liberation of oppressed communities and the achievement of social transformation as a prerequisite to respect for individual rights. They reject the slogan of "economic development" imposed from above: without the implementation of people's and individual rights, "development" will remain merely an ideology for legitimizing the *status quo*. The idea of people's rights is thus a militant expression of those who side with the masses of people whose human rights concerns cannot be dealt with only through legal or quasi legal remedies.

These different approaches and movements operating in Asia are not mutually exclusive. Depending on the nature of the problems, they reinforce each other. It is important to indicate that activists generally agree that, whatever the nature of human rights dealt with, the promotion and protection of human rights in Asia depends on the degree to which they succeed in awakening the individual consciousness. Only individual awareness can free people from all forms of ideology, values or ideas which seek to justify the dominance of power and the use of fear. If some of them advocate "people's rights," it is not necessarily only to highlight the collectivity: it is a concept which leads inevitably to the realization of individual rights as both a beginning and an end.

3. POSSIBILITIES OF REGIONAL CO-OPERATION FOR THE PROMOTION AND PROTECTION OF HUMAN RIGHTS IN ASIA

"It is not enough to rely upon emotional commitments to human rights. The time for generalities has long since passed, the time now is for specifics."[37]

The above overview of the approaches to human rights in Asia is far from comprehensive in terms of both the geographical coverage and of the issues examined. There are important human rights issues in the region which this chapter has neglected: for example, women's status and refugee problems. The increasingly diversified situation in Asia does not allow any hurriedly made synthesis for the whole of Asia.

The question of Asian regional co-operation in the field of human rights is difficult because of the extreme diversity of situations. Several countries are reluctant to apply uniform criteria for judging the situation of all the Asian countries, given the different political institutions, levels of economic development, legal traditions, and cultural heritage of each country. Unlike the European Convention on Human Rights which was made possible by a relative homogeneity of political institutions, a common conception of the respect of human rights and the will for European integration by the Member States,[38] Asian countries have fewer common denominators for establishing a regional mechanism for the protection of human rights.

Overview of existing regional institutions in Asia

The development of institutions for regional co-operation in Asia reflects the complexity of geo-political interests which divide rather than unite the Asian countries. Approximately four types of co-operation have developed in Asia: (i) co-operation to combat colonialism and neo-colonialism represented by the non-aligned movement; (ii) military treaty organization such as the SEATO;[39] (iii) political and/or economic co-operation such as the Association of South East Asian Nations (ASEAN)[40] and the Asian Development Bank;[41] and (iv) UN related regional organizations such as the ESCAP.[42]

Other forms of regional or sub-regional co-operation are of a specific and limited character and have little potential for developing into institutions for the promotion of human rights objectives.

In the Asian region, where development is the primary concern of governments, ESCAP plays an important role in regional co-operation. In its efforts to provide information, to undertake research and to train staff, ESCAP could in the future incorporate the subject of human rights as an integral part of its activities.[43]

Prospects for institutionalized co-operation in the field of human rights

The absence of a regional institution having a general competence (like the OAU and OAS) and the absence of the will for regional integration makes it difficult for Asia to establish a regional institution for the promotion and protection of human rights.

A regional seminar of Member States[44] of the Asian region, which will consider appropriate arrangements for the promotion and protection of human rights, will be convened by the Secretary-General of the United Nations in 1982. This initiative could be of crucial importance in formulating an original solution, adapted to the Asian reality.

Other initiatives for co-operation for the protection and promotion of human rights in Asia have come rather from private organizations of lawyers, university professors, and human rights militants, as well as religious groups.[45] One such example of the role of a non-governmental initiative in establishing regional co-operation for the protection and promotion of human rights was the action by the Asia and Pacific branch of Amnesty International in holding in September 1976 its First Pacific Regional Conference in Tozanso, Japan.[46] The conference discussed the possibility of setting up regional machinery to provide protection from violations of human rights. Another example is the Permanent Standing Committee on Human Rights created in August 1979 within Lawasia. Lawasia is a professional association of Asian and Western Pacific lawyers (private lawyers, government lawyers, judges and law teachers), formed in August 1966 at a Conference called by the Law Council of Australia, in Canberra. The association comprises Asian and Pacific countries (Australia,

Fiji, Hong Kong, India, Indonesia, Japan, Republic of Korea, Malaysia, Nepal, New Zealand, Papua-New Guinea, Philippines, Singapore, Sri Lanka, Thailand). The objectives of the Standing Committee are:

(i) to work towards the establishment of a Centre or Centres for Human Rights in the region, for the promotion, propagation and protection of human rights in the region, by research, education, the use of mass media and the publication of literature concerning human rights, and by other means;

(ii) to initiate, as a matter of priority, steps towards the ultimate establishment of an Asian Commission for Human Rights in the region;

(iii) to take steps towards the implementation of the principles of the Universal Declaration of Human Rights in specific form within the region;

(iv) to promote, by education and publicity, awareness of human rights among the members;

(v) to prepare and publish reports on matters affecting human rights within the region;

(vi) to urge the ratification of the International Covenants on Human Rights by governments within the region, and to work towards adherence to other UN instruments in the field of human rights including those concerning law enforcement and refugees;

(vii) to safeguard the independence and freedom of judges and lawyers in the discharge of their duties in matters concerning human rights.

This effort is in the spirit of the guidelines elaborated at the UN Seminar on the establishment of Regional Commissions on Human Rights, with special reference to Africa (Monrovia, Liberia, 10-21 September 1979) and also responds to General Assembly Resolution 34/171 of 17 December 1979 which calls for suitable regional arrangements for the promotion and protection of human rights. In addition it constitutes a useful follow-up activity to the Unesco International Congress for the Teaching of Human Rights (Vienna, Austria, 12-16 September 1981).

The weakness of the project lies in the fact that the initiative is purely non-governmental. It is also a project formulated primarily by lawyers educated in the West. The adoption of Western models, particularly that of the European Convention on Human Rights as already proposed by organizations like the International Council of Jurists[47] would be poorly suited to operate in the vast and complex reality of Asia.

Conclusion

On the basis of the foregoing survey of Asian experience in the field of human rights, the following points can be made;

(i) Economic, social and cultural rights are interdependent with civil and political rights; the full enjoyment of one set depends on the enjoyment of the other. This point is reaffirmed in UN General Assembly Resolution 32/130[48] which enumerates the guiding concepts for future UN work in the field of human rights. The Asian experiences bear witness to the indivisibility and interdependence of human rights.

(ii) The situation of every country, with respect to human rights, is different in a variety of ways. This warns us against all assumptions as to the existence of general panaceas.

(iii) The diversity of national situations renders all measurement of human rights performance according to uniform criteria, illusory or misleading in Asia. For example, income distribution can be an economic indicator of the conditions facilitating the observance of human rights, but a perfectly egalitarian society in the economic sense does not necessarily mean a high degree of human rights implementation.

(iv) Action to promote and protect human rights should vary from one country to another according to its particular situation, but it should always take into account the indivisibility of human rights. Asia offers a rich terrain for a new synthesis in this regard.

The Asian experience also shows that the aspiration for self-respect, self-expression, independence and a better life is universal and that the fight against the abuse of power is a constant factor in Asian reality. It is undeniable that the concept of human rights as expressed in the Universal Declaration of Human Rights is increasingly inspiring the mind and action of those who work toward these objectives. The philosophical foundations of these movements can diverge, but the underlying aspirations are common.

It is true that the Western ways and means of protecting human rights are not ideally adapted to Asian cultural values and institutions. This is specially true in the societies where the concern for the community is much greater than the concern for the individual. If belonging to a collectivity takes overriding importance, there are real difficulties and psychological inhibitions in affirming the rights of the individual on a priority basis. If such is the case, the solution is not to impose a Western model of human rights protection, but to formulate original ways and means of ensuring human rights adapted to each situation. Above all the education of people enables them to develop fully their self-respect and to liberate them from the fear of power and authority must be a fundamental element in any attempt to make human rights institutions functional and effective.

Society is not immutable, nor are cultural values. It would be an error to consider the conflicts between human rights and cultural values statically. Much more creative endeavours are needed to develop appropriate institutions for human rights promotion and protection in Asia.

NOTES

1. For the purpose of this chapter, we are using historical, cultural and political criteria to define the Asian region. It excludes the countries of Western Asia, Arab Slate, the Pacific and Oceania, and includes Afghanistan, Bangladesh, Bhutan, Burma, China, India, Indonesia,

Japan, Kampuchea, Malaysia, Mongolia, Nepal, Pakistan, Philippines, Republic of Korea, Democratic Republic of Korea, Singapore, Sri Lanka, Thailand and Vietnam.

2. International Commission of Jurists "The Dynamic Aspects of the Rule of Law in the Modern Age." Report on the proceedings of the South-East Asian and Pacific Conference of Jurists, Bangkok, Thailand, February 1965, p. 13.

3. UN Document ST/TAO/HR/21

4. Ibid.

5. Some of the working papers from this Round Table are reproduced in *International Social Science Journal*, Vol. XVIII, no. 1, 1966, Unesco, Paris.

6. On the question of philosophical and cultural bases of human rights, see *Human Rights: Comments and Interpretations: A Symposium*, edited by Unesco with an Introduction by Jacques Maritain, Greenwood Press, Westport, Connecticut, 1949.

7. Former Senator, José W. Diokno, untitled lecture, International Council of Amnesty International, Cambridge, 21 September 1978, pp. 11-12, mimeo.

8. Data on this subject may be found in the table showing variation in volume of GNP in UN *Statistical Yearbook*, 1979. The increase in GNP in most Asian countries was above 6.0% (Burma +6.70%, China +7.0%, Japan +6.00%, Korea, People's Democratic Republic +8.10%, Korea, Rep. of, +7.40%, Malaysia +7.50%, Pakistan +6.00%, Singapore +9.20%, Thailand +6.60%) which is higher than in most countries in the world.

9. *Statistical Yearbook*, United Nations Economic and Social Commission for Asia and the Pacific (ESCAP) 1979.

10. *Application of ILO standards*, Report of the Director General, Report 1 (Part 2) to the ILO Ninth Regional Conference, Manila 1980 (Geneva, ILO, 1980).

11. *Amnesty International Report 1980* (London, 1980) pp. 173-175.

12. *Asian Development in the 1980s: Growth, Employment and Working Conditions*; Report of the Director-General, Ninth Asian Regional Conference, Manila, December 1980 (Geneva, ILO, 1980).

13. Most reporting and writing on Asia and human rights stresses the perennial human rights problems. See for example: "Human Rights Problems in Asia" by L. Kadirgamar, in *Summaries of Lectures of the Sixth Study Session*, July 1975, International Institute of Human Rights; *Amnesty International Reports*; Minority Rights Group's Report; *Country Reports on Human Rights Practices* submitted to the Committee on International Relations, U.S. House of Representatives and Committee on Foreign Relations, U.S. Senate by the Department of State.

14. It is significant that in Japanese law, as in English common law, environmental pollution is called public nuisance (Ko-gai) to give it a public character even if the pollution is caused by private enterprises.

15. The most prominent instances of the application of this legislation concern diseases caused by mercury (Minamata) and certain pharmaceutical products (Sumon). *Jurist* No. 458 (Special issue on Environmental Pollution), August 1970, *Jurist* No. 548 (Special issue on Human Rights and Medicine), November 1973, Tokyo, Yuhikaku.

16. The right to demonstration (which is not exactly the equivalent of the right to assembly), although it has been used extensively in the anti-pollution movement, is not explicitly included in the Universal Declaration of Human Rights.

17. See Charter of the United Nations, Art.1, 55 and 56. as discussed particularly in Chapters 5, 8, 10.

18. First Decade, General Assembly resolution 1710 (XVI); Second Decade, General Assembly resolution 2626 (XXV); Third Decade, General Assembly resolution 35/56 Annex I.

19. General Assembly resolutions 3201 (S-VI) and 3202 (S-VI) of 1 May 1974.

20. General Assembly resolution 2542 (XXIV) of 11 December 1961.

21. See: Declaration on the Granting of Independence to Colonial Countries and Peoples (General Assembly resolution 1514 (XV) of 14 December 1960) and the resolution on Perma-

nent Sovereignty of Natural Resources (General Assembly resolution 1803 (XVII) of 14
December 1962.)

22. Resolution 1514 paragraph 2.

23. General Assembly Resolution 3281 (XXIX) Dec. 12, 1974, UN Doc. A/9631 (1975).

24. Ibid.

25. Transnationals concentrate their activities in developed countries. 40% of their direct
investment is in four countries (Canada, USA, Federal Republic of Germany, UK) with only
one quarter of their investments in developing countries. Transnational Corporations in
World Development: a Re-examination. United Nations Publication, Sales No. E. 78. II A.
5., para. 125 et seq.

26. General Assembly resolution 3020 (S-VI) of 1 May 1974.

27. Economic and Social Council Resolution 1913 (LVII) of 5 December 1974. This resolution was adopted by 48 States (12 African, 11 Asian, 10 Latin American, 5 Eastern European,
10 Western European and others).

28. The Tripartite Declaration recognizes the substantial benefits which multinational
enterprises can make to development as well as the potential abuses of their power and has
adopted a progressive view of its purpose which is to: "Encourage the positive contribution
which multinational enterprises can make to economic and social progress and to minimize
and resolve the difficulties to which their various operations may give rise taking into account
the United Nations resolutions advocating the Establishment of a New International Economic Order."

29. *Guidelines for Multinational Enterprises* and the procedures on those guidelines
adopted in 1976 by OECD (OECD publication *International Investment and Multinational
Enterprises*, Paris 1976); the International Chamber of Commerce adopted in 1972 "Guidelines for International Investment" (Paris 1972) and in 1975 the International Confederation
of Free Trade Unions adopted its "Multinational Charter" (Brussels, 1975) Parliamentary
Assembly of the Council of Europe, resolution 639 (1976), IME (76), annex II, calls upon
corporations to "respect human rights in all countries in which they operate." The Foreign
Ministers of the European Economic Community in September 1977 agreed to a voluntary
code of conduct for enterprises based in EEC countries with subsidiaries, affiliates or
representative offices in South Africa.

30. Unesco has carried out the following studies: *The Impact of Transnational Book
Publishing on Intellectual Knowledge in Less Developed Countries*, by K. B. Smith; Report
on *Methodology for Measuring the Impact of Advertising by Transnational Tourism Corporations on Socio-cultural Values in the Developing Countries*, by M. Brigaud Robert; Report
on *Methodology for Research into the Influence of Transnational Corporations on the
Educational Systems of Developing Countries* by A. Cartapanis, W. Experton and J. L.
Fuguet; *The Cultural Impact of Multinational Corporations in Singapore* by K. P. Wong.

31. Several industrial countries allow hazardous products or substances that they have
banned or restricted for domestic use to be freely exported to other countries. There have
been several well-documented incidents of the export of banned consumer products, pesti-
cides, and toxic chemicals, contaminated food, ineffective or dangerous drugs, and toxic
chemical wastes. (See *Exports of Hazardous Products: Hearings before the Subcommittee on
International Economic Policy and Trade of the Committee on Foreign Affairs, U.S. House
of Representatives, 96th Cong., 2nd sess. (1980)* and C. Medawar, *Injury or Insult: An
Inquiry into the Marketing and Advertising of British Food and Drug Products in the Third
World* (1979). Concerned by this problem, the General Assembly at its thirty-fourth session
on 17 December 1979, addressed this practice by adopting a resolution urging that countries
exchange information on banned hazardous chemicals and unsafe pharmaceutical products
and discourage, in consultation with importing countries, their exportation. It requested that
the Secretary-General submit a report on the subject to the next session of the General
Assembly and appealed to all United Nations organs, organizations and bodies concerned to
assist in the Secretary-General's report. (General Assembly resolution 34/173, 17 December

1979). See document E/CN.4/NGO/310, 19 January 1981 (Commission on Human Rights, 37th session) *"The export of dangerous products and substances; human rights implications."*

32. See for example, Report submitted to the UN Centre on Transnational Corporations (CTC) and Economic and Social Commission for Asia and the Pacific (ESCAP) by the Third World Studies Centre, University of the Philippines, 1979. Bibliography on the subject is compiled by ESCAP Library "Transnational Corporations: a select bibliography with partial focus on the ESCAP region," N.Y. 1979 (ESCAP/LIB/SER.D/1).

33. Masami, Ito, "The problems of human rights in Asian traditions," paper submitted at the Unesco Round Table on Human Rights, Oxford, *supra.*

34. Legal assistance services are active in India, Indonesia, Malaysia and the Philippines related to the International Legal Aid Association.

35. The Civil Liberties Bureau, created in 1948, functions through Civil Liberties Commissioners. Appointed by a process of representative selection, they are volunteers who must meet requirements of moral character and basic knowledge of human rights. In 1979, Japan counted over 10,500 Commissioners throughout the country. Over a half of the cases annually submitted (6,000 to 10,000 cases) are settled.

36. See, for example, the speech made by an Asian lawyer at the Sixth Conference of Lawasia (Colombo, Sri Lanka, 27 to 30 August 1979) in which he said "...there is complementarity—between the rights of the people and the rights of individuals: indeed unless rights are recognized in the people as a community, the rights of individuals would not be secure, for there would then be neither legal nor moral basis for the right to revolution against tyranny and oppression, whether by a government installed by external colonialism or one born of internal colonialism."

37. Report of the discussion session on International Institutions for the Protection of Human Rights, 6th Lawasia Conference.

38. See the preamble of the European Convention of Human Rights, discussed in chapter 16.

39. The Manila Pact of 8 September 1954 created the South East Asia Treaty Organization (Parties: Australia, France, New Zealand, Philippines, Thailand, U.K., U.S.A.).

40. The ASEAN, created in 1967 (Indonesia, Malaysia, Philippines, Singapore, Thailand) was a significant start in promoting sub-regional co-operation.

41. The Asian Development Bank was created in Manila in 1966 in support of the development objectives of the developing member countries (DMCs) of the Asian and Pacific region. As of January 1982, the Member States count 43, including the ESCAP countries and those outside Asia and Pacific region. Apart from lending activities, the Bank administers technical assistance and a Training Programme on Development Banking for the Region. See Asian Development Bank: Annual Report 1979.

42. United Nations Economic and Social Commission for Asia and the Pacific serves 2.4 billion people (in 1979), or more than 55 per cent of the world's population. The ESCAP region extends from Iran in the west to Mongolia in the north, Japan in the north-east and the Cook Islands in the south-east. To assist Member Countries in solving their economic and social problems, ESCAP has developed programmes at three levels: at the regional level, to combat region-wide problems; at the sub-regional level; and at the country level, by assisting individual Governments in planning and implementing balanced development programmes. Although ESCAP does not itself provide capital resources, it has helped to establish institutions to attract funds for regional and subregional projects, which, in turn supply development aid.

43. This would accord with the approach adopted in the "Declaration on Social Progress and Development" proclaimed by the General Assembly of the United Nations on 11 December 1969 (Resolution 2542 (XXIV)).

44. United Nations General Assembly Resolution 35/197.

45. These movements are mostly Christian (Churches' Commission on International Affairs (World Council of Churches), World Student Christian Federation, Christian Confer-

ence on Asia (Asia Pacific) and Centre for the Progress of Peoples) but recently Islam reformists became actively concerned by human rights (for example Muslim youth movement ABIM in Malaysia).

46. *Report of the First Pacific Regional Conference of Amnesty International*, ICM/September 1976, NS 132/76.

47. See Bangkok, "The Dynamic Aspect of the Rule of Law in the Modern Age" supra.

48. Resolution of the General Assembly at its Thirty-second Regular Session (20 September-21 December 1977).

22 Toward a Specific International Human Rights Law

Karel Vasak

It hardly needs to be said that *municipal law* is characterized by the existence, within the framework of the State, of political power which assumes the threefold function of defining the rules of life in society (legislative function), ensuring that they are applied (executive function) and providing a means of dealing with any disputes that might arise (judicial function). It is a *law of integration and subordination* which gives rise to a single legal system, the subjects of which, both active and passive, are subordinated to the power of the State.

International law, for its part, is characterized by the existence of sovereign States: as has often been said, it is a *law of co-ordination* seeking to become a *law of co-operation* among States, by means, in particular, of international organizations at the world or regional level.

The *international rules of human rights* do not have the characteristics of the law of subordination since, like all rules of general international law, they are developed in the framework of an international community whose prime characteristic is the existence of sovereign States. But those rules do not come under, or rather, do not come solely under the law of co-ordination and co-operation. Their object is precisely defined: they give rise to a *law of protection* since, by virtue of all its norms and all its institutions, this law is intended to ensure the individual of the enjoyment and observance of a number of values considered to be common to the entire international community.

More than thirty years after the Universal Declaration of Human Rights, this law for the protection of the human being may legitimately claim to be an autonomous branch of international human rights law. The foregoing pages clearly show the extent to which it has been developed and made more precise and the wealth of its actual content and connotations. The application of the norms which give expression to that law raises particular problems, as has been noted, and this is gradually bringing us to call into question certain traditional categories and solutions of general international law, such as the principle of reciprocity or the notion of conciliation, and to modify the methods of interpretation of those rules, if not to reconsider all the solutions which one is tempted, at first sight, to borrow from the law of nations.[1]

For, being a law of protection, international human rights law will naturally seek to establish a legal system for the protection of the individual in international law. But its specificity does not necessarily consist in the fact that it provides an unambiguous solution to that question, which has always been hotly debated, of the individual's standing as a subject of international law. This question may in fact be said to be immaterial to international human rights law which seeks to achieve its purpose—the protection of the individual—by means of rules, procedures and institutions which do not necessarily call into question the traditional structures of international law, and first of all the predominant place of the State as a subject of international law. Defined in this way, the specificity of international human rights law will appear both at the level of its norms and at the level of their implementation.

(a). Specificity at the level of norms

International human rights law is an ideological law

International human rights law directly acknowledges its ideological character, but in so doing, it aspires to express an ideology which is common to all mankind. Admittedly, some will endeavour to demonstrate that this law is of Western origin and that it in fact expresses the needs for protection felt by a minority which is able to afford the luxury of exercising all human rights. In actual fact, human rights by no means reflect the historical conditions of a particular society, for the values which they express are to be found, in one form or another, in all political, social and religious doctrines. It is here that mention should be made of the work of Unesco and, in particular, the admirable volume, *The Birthright of Man*, which reveals the community of interests expressed by human rights.[2] Other works of the same kind are currently being carried out in respect of the various streams of religious thinking;[3] but it already seems clear that human rights form a genuine heritage common to all religions and that, on this account, they are capable of providing a common language for all Churches, thereby helping to reconcile them.

Being an ideological law, international human rights law is consequently an unstable law in a process of constant change. How can one fail to note in this connection the deep-seated aspirations of the peoples of the United Nations to ensure that, to the human rights already guaranteed, be added rights of which there was not even any mention ten years ago, namely the right to a healthy environment and the rights to peace and development *inter alia*? We might also note the demand for men and women to be granted the right freely and consciously to determine the size of their families and the spacing of the births of their children.[4]

International human rights law is a derived law

While the direct source of international human rights law is the Universal Declaration of Human Rights, it in fact derives from national law, in contrast with the law of nations which, so far as its main rules are concerned, is an original law owing nothing to national law. The fact that international human rights law thus derives from national law is but the direct consequence of its ideological character. There is a very pronounced filiation between the Covenant on Civil and Political Rights and the French Declaration of the Rights of Man and of the Citizen of 1789 and the American Declarations. There is also an obvious relationship between the Covenant on Economic, Social and Cultural Rights and the Mexican Constitution of 1917 and a whole series of other constitutional texts adopted after the First World War, including several instruments of Soviet constitutional law.

It does not follow, however, that the law with which we are concerned here is dependent on national laws. The right of men and women to determine the number and spacing of their offspring was first formulated and proclaimed at the international level before being legally incorporated into the various national laws. It is even possible that, for reasons of contingency, this right will never be able to be enshrined as such in most municipal laws, although it will be proclaimed at the international level.

Being in the main a law derived from national laws, international human rights law is playing, and increasingly frequently will continue to play, a unifying role without enabling the various national laws regarding human rights to be reconciled, harmonized and integrated within it. The unifying effect produced in regard to the various national laws of the States parties to the European Convention on Human Rights by the provisions of that Convention provides too many illustrations of this fact for it to be possible to refer to them all. But it is particularly interesting to note that in the case of the right to the proper administration of justice, Article 6 of the Rome Convention accelerated, if it did not cause, the process whereby States with inquisitorial procedures, and those with accusatorial procedures, have brought their practices more into line with each other. The same is true of the duration of provisional detention which, under Article 5, paragraph 3, of the Rome Convention, should not exceed what is considered to be a "reasonable" time, a notion which is vague but which, in the actual legislative practice of the States parties to the Convention, tends in ordinary cases to correspond to six months.

The unifying effect of international human rights law, curiously enough, may even relegate to the background the political intentions specific to the draftsmen of human rights treaties: conceived as an instrument of *political unification* in respect of the European democracies, the Rome Convention has been transformed, as a result of the copious case-law of its organs, into an instrument ensuring the *unification of the legal systems* governing human rights in the contracting States. Some may regret the weakening of the ideological character specific to the European Convention, but this was in fact inevitable, as its provisions indeed expressed the common values of all mankind, and not values peculiar to the community of European States.

International human rights law is a minimum law

Being derived from municipal law, international human rights law consequently relates to a field which is continuing to be developed thanks to the
action of the legislative, governmental and judicial authorities of the different
States. The international conventions on human rights clearly foresaw this
situation, for they contain a provision which, constituting a true "most-favoured-
individual clause," makes international human rights law a minimum law.
Article 5, paragraph 2, of the International Covenant on Civil and Political
Rights of 1966 provides, for instance: "There shall be no restriction upon or
derogation from any of the fundamental human rights recognized or existing
in any State party to the present Convention pursuant to law, conventions,
regulations or custom on the pretext that the present Convention does not
recognize such rights or that it recognizes them to a lesser extent."[5] This
clause authorizes and makes sacrosanct, in terms of the Covenant, any national and international protection of human rights greater than that provided for by the Covenant itself. Does it, however, prohibit a State or group
of States from limiting such protection, provided, of course, that the degree
of protection still ensured is at least as great as that provided for by the
Convention, the latter being an irreducible minimum? The problem has been
raised in exactly these terms in connection with a similar provision before the
ILO Committee responsible for considering a complaint concerning non-
observance of an international labour convention. That Committee considered that the provision did not impose upon a State the obligation to maintain
in force provisions establishing more exacting norms than those provided for
by the Convention.[6]

International human rights law is an objective law

A distinction is usually made between law-treaties and contract-treaties.
International human rights law, which is primarily a written law, since it is
embodied mainly in the fifty or so conventions referred to above, is fundamentally at variance with all idea of contract and, on this account, tends as
far as possible to ignore the principle of reciprocity so characteristic of general international law.

The European Commission of Human Rights made no mistake about this
when, in its decision relating to the *Austria v. Italy* case, it vigorously
emphasized the objective character of international human rights law:[7]

"Whereas it clearly appears...that the purpose of the High Contracting
Parties in concluding the Convention was not to concede to each other *reciprocal* rights and obligations in pursuance of their individual national interests, but to realize the aims and ideals of the Council of Europe, as expressed
in its Statute, and to establish a *common public order of the free democracies
of Europe* with the object of safeguarding their common heritage of political
traditions, ideals, freedoms and the rule of law..."

Whereas, therefore, in becoming a Party to the Convention, a State undertakes, vis-à-vis the other High Contracting Parties, to secure the rights and freedoms defined in Section I to every person within its jurisdiction, regardless of his or her nationality or status; whereas, in short, it undertakes to secure those rights and freedoms not only to its own nationals and those of other High Contracting Parties, but also to nationals of States not parties to the Convention and to stateless persons, as the Commission itself has expressly recognized in previous decisions; whereas it follows that the obligations undertaken by the High Contracting Parties in the Convention are essentially of an *objective character*, being designed rather to *protect the fundamental rights of individual human beings from infringement by any of the High Contracting Parties than to create subjective and reciprocal rights for the High Contracting Parties themselves. . . .*"

The objective character of international human rights law does not signify, however, that the principle of reciprocity is completely excluded from the field under consideration. Such is the case in respect of the conditions under which human rights can be enjoyed. But, so far as the conditions of exercise of those same rights are concerned, that principle could probably be brought to bear, provided, however, that the minimum standard represented by international human rights law is not endangered. Consequently, there is nothing to prevent States from allowing the nationals of certain other States to benefit, on a basis of reciprocity, from more liberal conditions of exercise of their human rights than those generally applicable, provided that human rights as such are respected.[8]

The principle of reciprocity may also be included among the conditions governing the procedures of international human rights organs: thus, for instance, the compulsory jurisdiction of the European Court of Human Rights may be recognized by the contracting States, on the condition that such recognition is reciprocal. It is to be noted that this condition is expressly authorized by the Convention; if such were not the case, its legitimacy could be held in doubt, given the very purpose of international human rights law.[9]

(b). Specificity at the level of the implementation of norms

In *general international law*, international action in the broad sense of the term can be initiated by States in all circumstances, provided that their nationals are involved; it may also be initiated by non-governmental organizations and by the individual, but only in exceptional circumstances. International action relates systematically to the individual, since what is involved in *international human rights law* is more respect for human rights than settling inter-State disputes, although expressed in typical international law terminology.

There is nothing exceptional, *a priori*, in the fact that a State can initiate proceedings against another contracting State respecting the observance of conventions on human rights; but the fact that a State can do so *on behalf of individuals who are not its nationals* illustrates the fact that international human rights law is designed to protect persons without distinction, particularly as to nationality. However, the international treaties on human rights do not unanimously recognize that the State has the right *ipso jure* to take action in the framework of the specific procedures provided for by them. Thus, Article 41 of the Covenant on Civil and Political Rights declares that the competence of the Human Rights Committee to receive and consider communications from one contracting State against another contracting State is optional, whereas Article 24 of the European Convention on Human Rights stipulates in this connection that the jurisdiction of the European Convention on Human Rights is compulsory.

The specific procedures provided for by the human rights treaties do not, however, preclude the traditional procedures for settlement existing in international law; but the proceedings will then take place within the traditional framework of international law in which it is a question of settling a dispute arising from the interpretation or application of the human rights treaty (see, for instance, Article 44 of the International Covenant on Civil and Political Rights).[10]

Action by *non-governmental organizations* is, in most of the treaties on human rights, placed on the same footing as action undertaken by individuals (see, for instance, Article 25 of the European Convention on Human Rights). It is almost always optional in character in the sense that the State concerned must expressly agree to the international human rights organ being competent to receive complaints against it.

A separate place must be reserved for action initiated in the framework of the *International Labour Organisation* by organizations of employers or trade unions or on the initiative of delegates of workers or employers to the International Labour Conference. The Constitution of the ILO (Article 24) expressly provides for the possibility for associations of employers or workers to make a *representation* against a State which, in the opinion of the association, "has failed to secure in any respect the effective observance within its jurisdiction of any Convention to which it is a party"; the Governing Body remains in charge of the procedure to be followed. Similarly, in the case of a *complaint* (Articles 26 to 29 and 31 to 34 of the Constitution of the ILO) and in the case of the special procedure concerning the protection of trade union rights, if the procedure is initiated by the delegates of employers or workers to the Conference or by trade union organizations, at a certain stage that procedure is thoroughly examined by the Governing Body which then has, in effect, to assume responsibility for it. As a result, the "proceedings" in each of these cases will be instituted not so much by the non-governmental organizations against the State concerned as by the International Labour Organisation against that same State. Once again, the objective and constitutional character of human rights is clearly to be seen.

As far as the *individual* is concerned, he has, in my opinion, acquired once and for all the right to set in motion the machinery for the implementation of international human rights law. The individual's right of international action is always exercised by means of the *right of petition* which, while not a human right, is now the means employed for the international implementation of human rights.

The right of petition has a protective significance which varies according to its legal nature. Simplifying matters, four categories of petitions relating to human rights can be distinguished:

Petitions which are merely *gracious remedies of a humanitarian character*, insofar as the applicant can, at the very most, expect a reply from the State against which the complaint has been lodged. Such petitions are provided for by the American Declaration of the Rights and Duties of Man of 1948, in its Article 24: "Every person has the right to submit respectful petitions to any competent authority, for reasons of either general or private interest, and the right to obtain a prompt decision thereon." The United Nations receives each year some tens of thousands of such petitions and, for a long time, they were examined in accordance with the provisions of Resolution 728 F (XXVIII) of the Economic and Social Council, the "examination" consisting merely in the communication of summaries of such petitions to the State concerned and, confidentially, to the Commission on Human Rights;

Petitions which, being appeals at law, are *acts which institute legal proceedings*: mention may be made here, by way of example, of the applications addressed to the European Commission of Human Rights in accordance with Article 25 of the Rome Convention, and those to be brought before the Inter-American Commission on Human Rights once the Convention of San José has entered into force;

Petitions which, not being true appeals at law; nevertheless provide a means of instituting *proceedings of a mixed, administrative, judicial and diplomatic character*: into this category should be placed, for instance, the petitions addressed to the Inter-American Commission on Human Rights which, concerning certain limitatively listed human rights, are examined in accordance with the so-called "special" procedure[11] and, probably, the individual communications brought in accordance with the International Convention on the Elimination of All Forms of Racial Discrimination (Article 14) and the Optional Protocol to the Covenant on Civil and Political Rights;

Petitions which, after being deemed to be admissible, become so many *sources of information* on the general situation in respect of human rights in the State concerned: these include, for instance, petitions examined by the Inter-American Commission on Human Rights in accordance with the so-called "ordinary" procedure,[12] together with communications coming within the framework of ECOSOC Resolution 1503 (XLVIII).

From the point of view of general international law, the foregoing solutions appear heretical since they do not make it possible to give a definitive answer to the question whether the individual is a subject of international law. However, as was noted earlier, since international human rights law is a law of protection, it matters little whether the entity to be protected—the individual—has any standing as a subject of the rules of law, provided that means exist whereby he may reassert his human rights. This analysis is particularly well illustrated by the example of the inter-American system for the protection of human rights since, as set up in 1959, the right of individual petition to the Inter-American Commission on Human Rights is exercised *ipso jure*, without the Commission having considered it necessary to request the State concerned to recognize its competence to receive and consider individual petitions. The same is true of the American Convention on Human Rights since the individual's right to bring an application before the Commission, initiating in this case proceedings at law, is exercised *ipso jure*, whereas before a State can exercise its right to act against another State, it must first of all expressly recognize the competence of the Commission. Has the individual, for all that, become a subject of international law in his own right? It may legitimately be doubted, even given the existence of such institutional machinery; what is certain, however, is that he now has means of protection at his disposal in the inter-American system.

Thus, while it avails itself of categories and notions borrowed from general international law, international human rights law generally assigns to them a specific significance and bearing. This specificity stems from the fact that it is a law of protection since it is calculated to guarantee for the individual certain values common to the whole of mankind.

Should one seek, however, to sever the links between general international law and international human rights law? Nothing would be more dangerous. The latter can function only on the basis of the former, for the very reason that it must take account of that reality which is constituted by States; but it is also in the interest of the former to allow its categories which are often all too State-influenced to be open to human considerations derived from international human rights law: human rights will thus become a means of permanently challenging general international law.

When all is said and done, the marriage between the two is a marriage of reason which touches the essence of human existence: for deep in *every* human being resides the eternal and irrepressible desire for freedom and equality, the desire to be human, that is a brother or sister for all one's fellow human beings.

NOTES

1. K. Vasak, "Le droit international des droits de l'homme," *RCADI*, 1976, Vol. 174, p. 374 *et seq.*

2. *The Birthright of Man*, a selection of texts prepared under the direction of Jeanne Hersch, Paris, Unesco, 1968, 591 pages.

3. See: the McGill Symposium of March 1974 on "Judaism and Human Rights"; the reports prepared by the Saudi Arabian Grand Ulemas on "Human Rights in Islam"; the Montreal Symposium of December 1973 on "The Catholic Church and Human Rights"; the particularly abundant work of the World Council of Churches, and primarily the St. Polten Consultation of October 1974; and the Final Report of a Meeting of Experts on the Place of Human Rights in Cultural and Religious Traditions, Bangkok, December 1980, Unesco doc. SS.79/CONF.607/10 (1980).

4. Cf. Proclamation of Teheran, 1968, para. 16.

5. See also Article 23b of the American Convention on Human Rights and Article 60 of the European Convention on Human Rights.

6. See the Report of the Committee set up under Article 26 of the Constitution of the ILO to examine the observance by Chile of Convention No. 1 and Convention No. 111 (provisional edition, p. 22). This report refers to other views which have been expressed along the same lines.

7. *ECHR Yearbook*, Vol. IV, p. 139 *et seq.*

8. The question arises above all, and increasingly often now, in the framework of a group of States achieving a measure of alignment, and even unification, as is the case of the European Communities.

9. See the very pertinent ideas developed in connection with the reciprocity clause by Vincenzo Starace: "La juridiction obligatoire de la Cour européenne des droits de l'homme" in *Les clauses facultatives de la Convention européenne des droits de l'homme*, p. 225 *et seq.*

10. See also A.C. Kiss, "La Convention européenne des droits de l'homme et le système de garantie du droit international public" in *La protection internationale des droits de l'homme dans le cadre européen*, Paris, 1961, p. 239 *et seq.*

11. See K. Vasak, *La Commission interaméricaine des droits de l'homme*, Paris, Pédone, 1968, Chapter VII. See also *supra*, Chapter 17.

12. See K. Vasak, *op. cit.*, Chapter VI. See also *supra*, Chapter 17.

Annex I

Chart of Ratification

Note: The Chart of Ratification is contained in the back pocket of the book.

Annex II

Figures

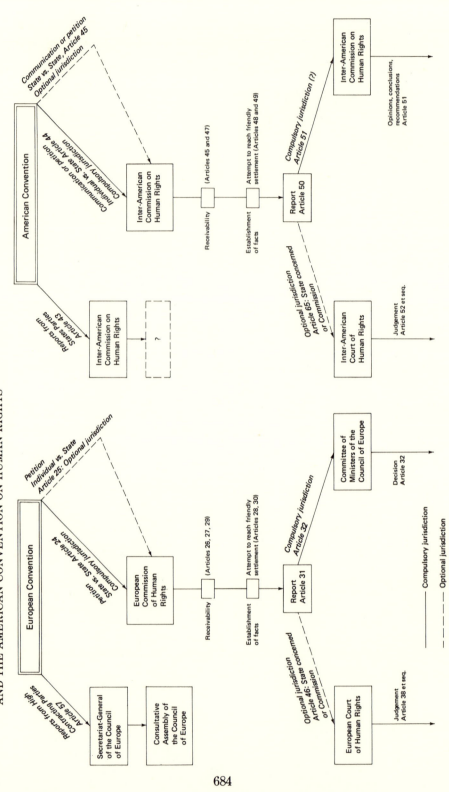

FIGURE 1. COMPARATIVE SCHEMA OF THE IMPLEMENTATION MACHINERY OF THE EUROPEAN CONVENTION AND THE AMERICAN CONVENTION ON HUMAN RIGHTS

684

FIGURE 2. SCHEMA OF THE IMPLEMENTATION MACHINERY OF THE
INTERNATIONAL COVENANT ON CIVIL AND POLITICAL RIGHTS

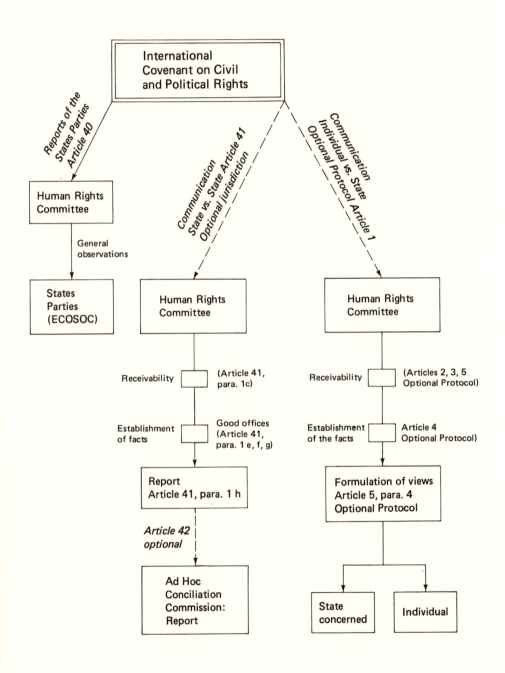

FIGURE 3. COMPARATIVE SCHEMA OF THE IMPLEMENTATION MACHINERY
OF THE EUROPEAN SOCIAL CHARTER AND THE INTERNATIONAL
COVENANT ON ECONOMIC, SOCIAL AND CULTURAL RIGHTS

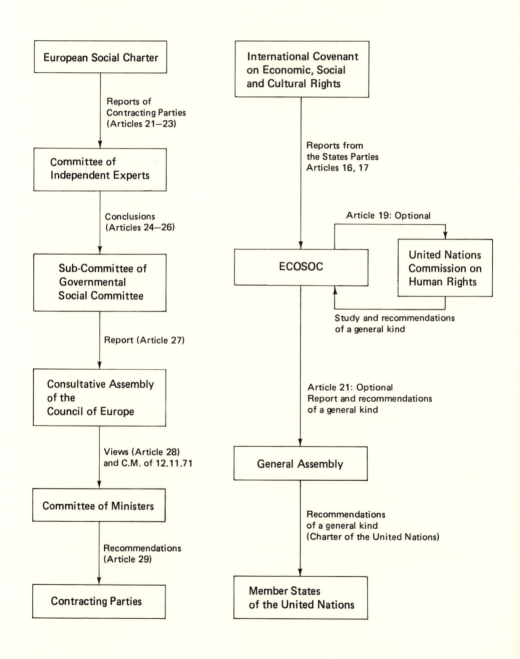

Annex III

Selected Bibliography on International Human Rights Law

This bibliography does not include references to works which deal with specific human rights situations in, or the policies of, particular countries.

I. *Documentary Sources*

A. Compilations of Documents

BROWNLIE, Ian (Ed.). *Basic Documents on Human Rights*. London/New York, Oxford University Press, 1981, 505 p.

CHAFEE, Zechariah. *Documents on fundamental human rights, the Anglo-American tradition*. New York, Atheneum, 1963. 2 vol.

Collection of International Instruments concerning Refugees. 2nd ed., Office of the United Nations High Commissioner for Refugees, Geneva, 1979, 335 p.

COUNCIL OF EUROPE. *European Convention on Human Rights. Collected Texts*. Strasbourg, Council of Europe, 1975, 914 p.

————. *Human Rights in International Law: Basic Texts*. Strasbourg, Doc. H(78)4, 144 p.

Declaraciones de derechos sociales. Selección de Felipe Remolina. 1. ed. México, Ediciones del V. Congreso Interamericano de Derecho del Trabajo y de la Seguridad Social, 1974, 108 p.

Derechos Humanos, Declaraciones, Pactos y Convenios Internacionales. Arzobispado de Santiago—Vicaria de la Solidaridad, Santiago de Chile, 1978, 150 p.

DRAGOSEI, Italo e Francesco. *I diritti dell'uomo*. Naples, Editore Alberto Marotta, 1969, 657 p.

HERVADA, Javier, and ZUMAQUERO, Jose. *Textos Internacionales de Derechos Humanos*. Ediciones Universidad de Navarra, Pamplona, 1978, 1012 p.

The International Bill of Human Rights. New York, United Nations, 1978 (OPI/598), 42 p.

JOYCE, J.A. (ed.). *Human Rights: International Documents*. Dobbs Ferry, N.Y., Oceana, 1979, 3 vol., 1707 p.

LAQUEUR, W., and RUBIN, B. (Eds.). *The Human Rights Reader*. Philadelphia, Temple University Press, 1979, 375 p.

ORGANIZATION OF AMERICAN STATES. *Inter-American Commission on Human Rights. Basic documents*. Washington, D.C., PAU, 1960, 30 p.

PECES-BARBA, M. *Textos básicos sobre derechos humanos*. Madrid, 1973.

PERRUCHOUD, Richard. *Les résolutions des Conférences internationales de la Croix-Rouge*. Geneva, Institut Henry-Dunant, 1979, 469 p.

ROSENNE, Shabtai. *Documents on the International Court of Justice*. Leyden, Sijthoff, 1974, 391 p.

SOHN, Louis, and BUERGENTHAL, Thomas. *Basic documents on the international protection of human rights*. Indianapolis, Ind., Bobbs-Merrill Co., 1973, 244 p.

TOMAN, Jiri. *Index of the Geneva Conventions for the Protection of War Victims of 12 August 1949*. Leyden, Sijthoff, 1973, 194 p.

TORRELL, Maurice, and BAUDOIN, Renée. *Les droits de l'homme et les libertés publiques par les textes*. Montréal, Presses de l'Université du Québec, 1972, 387 p.

TRUYOL, Antonio. *Los derechos humanos. Declaraciones y convenciones internacionales*. Madrid, Edit. Tecnos, 1968, 71, 160 p.

UNITED NATIONS. *Human Rights: A compilation of international instru-*

ments of the United Nations. New York, United Nations, 1978, 106 p. (Sales No. E.78.XIV.2).

VASAK, Karel. *La protection internationale des droits de l'homme dans le cadre des organisations régionales.* Paris, La Documentation française, Déc. 1973, 64 p. (Documents d'études. Droit international public, nos. 305 et 306.)

———. La protection internationale des droits de l'homme. Vingt-cinquième anniversaire de la Déclaration universelle. Paris, la Documentation fran-çaise, 30 Nov. 1973, 60 p. (Problèmes politiques et sociaux, n° 203-204).

B. Documents and Publications of International and Regional Organizations

1. United Nations

Assistance to Racist Regimes in Southern Africa: Impact on the Enjoyment of Human Rights, by A. Khalifa, New York, 1979 (Sales No. E.79.XIV.3).

Bulletin of Human Rights, published quarterly in four languages by the UN Division of Human Rights, Geneva.

COMMISSION ON HUMAN RIGHTS, Reports on the sessions. Supplements to the Official Records of the Economic and Social Council. Sessions, years and UN doc. nos. as follows: 1, 1947, E/259; 2, 1947, E/600; 3, 1948, E/800; 4, 1949, E/1315; 5, 1949, E/1371; 6, 1950, E/1681; 7, 1951, E/1992; 8, 1951, E/2256; 9, 1952, E/2447; 10, 1954, E/2573; 11, 1955, E/2731; 12, 1956, E/2844; 13, 1957, E/2970/Rev. 1; 14, 1958, E/3088; 15, 1959, E/3229; 16, 1960, E/3335; 17, 1961, E/3456; 18, 1962, E/3616/Rev.1; 19, 1963, E/3743; 20, 1964, E/3873; 21, 1965, E/4024; 22, 1966, E/4184; 23, 1967, E/4322; 24, 1968, E/4475; 25, 1969, E/4621; 26, 1970, E/4816; 27, 1971, E/4949; 28, 1972, E/5113; 29, 1973, E/5625; 30, 1974, E/5464; 31, 1975, E/5635; 32, 1976, E/5768; 33, 1977, E/5927; 34, 1978, E/1978/34; 35, 1979, E/1979/36; 36, 1980, E/1980/13; 37, 1981, E/1981/25.

COMMITTEE ON THE ELIMINATION OF RACIAL DISCRIMINATION, *Reports,* Supplements to the Official Records of the General Assembly. Sessions, years and UN doc. nos. as follows: 1 and 2, 1970, A/8027; 3 and 4, 1971, A/8418; 5 and 6, 1972, A/8718; 7 and 8, 1973, A/9018; 9 and 10, 1974, A/9618; 11 and 12, 1975, A/10018; 13 and 14, 1976, A/31/18; 15 and 16, 1977, A/32/18; 17 and 18, 1978, A/33/18; 19 and 20, 1979, A/34/18; 21 and 22, 1980, A/35/18; 23 and 24, 1981, A/36/18.

Committee on the Elimination of Racial Discrimination and the Progress made Towards the Achievement of the Objectives of the International Conven-tion on the Elimination of All Forms of Racial Discrimination, New York, 1979 (Sales No.E.79.XIV.4).

COMMISSION ON THE STATUS OF WOMEN, *Reports* on the sessions. Sup-plements to the Official Records of the Economic and Social Council. Ses-sions, years and UN doc. nos. since 1970 as follows: 23, 1970, E/4831; 24, 1972, E/5109; 25, 1974, E/5451; 26, 1976, E/5909; 27, 1978, E/1978/32/Rev.1; 28, 1980, E/1980/15.

Definition and Classification of Minorities, New York, 1950 (Sales No.1950.XIV.3), 51 p.

Draft International Covenants on Human Rights: Annotation Prepared by the Secretary-General, Doc.A/2929 (1955).

Exploitation of Child Labour, Final Report submitted by Mr. Abdelwahab Bouhdiba, Special Rapporteur to the Sub-Commission on Prevention of Discrimination and Protection of Minorities, Doc. E/CN.4/Sub.2/479 (1981).

Exploitation of Labour through Illicit and Clandestine Trafficking, Study by Mrs. Halima Embarek Warzazi, Special Rapporteur of the Sub-Commission on Prevention of Discrimination and Protection of Minorities, Doc. E/CN.4/Sub.2/L.640 (1975).

Final Act of the International Conference on Human Rights. Teheran, 22 April-13 May 1968. New York, 1968, (Sales No. E.68.XIV.2), 64 p.

Handbook on Procedures and Criteria for Determining Refugee Status, Office of the United Nations High Commissioner for Refugees, Geneva, 1979, 93 p.

HUMAN RIGHTS COMMITTEE, *Reports*, Supplements to the Official Records of the General Assembly. Sessions, years and UN doc. nos. as follows: 1 and 2, 1977, A/32/44; 3, 4 and 5, 1978, A/33/40; 6 and 7, 1979, A/34/40; 8, 9 and 10, 1980, A/35/40; 11, 12 and 13, 1981, A/36/40.

Human Rights: 50 Questions and Answers on Human Rights and on UN Activities for the Promotion of Human Rights. New York, 1980 (DPI/646).

Human Rights International Instruments, Signatures, Ratifications, Accessions etc., issued annually by the United Nations, 1981 edition Doc. no. ST/HR/4/Rev.3.

The International Dimensions of the Right to Development as a Human Right in relation with Other Human Rights based on International Co-operation, including the Right to Peace, taking into account the Requirements of the New International Economic Order and the Fundamental Human Needs, Report of the Secretary-General, Doc. E/CN.4/1334 (1979).

International Provisions Protecting the Human Rights of Non-Citizens. Study by Baroness Elles, New York, 1980 (Sales No. E.80.XIV.2), 63 p.

National institutions for the promotion and protection of human rights: Report of the Secretary-General. Doc. A/36/440 (1981).

Parental Rights and Duties, including Guardianship. Report by the Secretary-General, New York, 1968 (Sales No. E.68.XIV.3).

Present international conditions and human rights: Report of the Secretary-General, Doc. A/36/462 (1981).

Protection of minorities: Special protective measures of an international character for ethnic, religious or linguistic groups. New York, 1967 (Sales No. E.67.XIV.3).

Questions and answers on human rights. New York, 1980. (OPI/493).

Racial discrimination (revised, updated version). Study by Hernán Santa Cruz, New York, 1977 (Sales No. E.76.XIV.2), 284 p.

The realization of economic, social and cultural rights: problems, policies, progress, by Manouchehr Ganji, New York, 1975 (Sales No. E.75.XIV.2), 326 p.

The regional and national dimensions of the right to development as a human rights: Study by the Secretary General. Docs. E/CN.4/1421 (1980) and E/CN.4/1488 (1981).

Report of the Working Group on Enforced or Involuntary Disappearances of Persons. Docs. E/CN.4/1435 (1981) and E/CN.4/1492 (1982).

Report of the World Conference of the International Women's Year, Mexico City, 19 June-2 July 1975. New York, 1976 (Sales No. E.76.XIV.1).

Report of the World Conference of the United Nations Decade for Women: Equality, Development and Peace, Copenhagen, 14 to 30 July 1980. New York, 1980 (Sales No. E.80.XIV.3).

Report of the World Conference to Combat Racism and Racial Discrimination, Geneva, 14-25 August 1978. New York, 1979 (Sales No. E.79.XIV.2).

Report on slavery, by Mohamed Awad, New York, 1967 (Sales No. E.67.XIV.2).

Reports of the Sessional Working Group of ECOSOC on Implementation of the International Covenant on Economic, Social and Cultural Rights. Docs. E/1979/54 (1979); E/1980/60 (1980); E.1981/64 (1981).

Reports prepared by the Secretary-General, since 1976, on Human Rights and Scientific and Technological Developments. Docs. E/CN.4/1172 & Adds., 1194, 1195, 1196, 1198, 1199 & Add., 1233, 1234, 1235 & Add., 1236, 1237, 1276 and 1306.

The Right to Self-Determination: Historical and Current Development on the Basis of United Nations Instruments, by Aureliu Cristescu, New York, 1981 (Sales No. E.80.XIV.3).

The Right to Self-Determination: Implementation of United Nations Resolutions, by Hector Gros Espiell, New York, 1980 (Sales No. E.1979.XIV.5).

Round Table of University Professors and Directors of Race Relations Institutions on the Teaching of Problems of Racial Discrimination, Geneva, 1979. New York, 1979 (Doc. No. ST/HR/SER. A/5).

Seminar on National and Local Institutions for the Promotion and Protection of Human Rights, Geneva, 18-29 September 1978. New York, 1978 (Doc. No. ST/HR/SER.A/2).

Seminar on Political, Economic, Cultural and Other Factors Underlying Situations leading to Racism including a Survey of the Increase or Decline of Racism and Racial Discrimination, Nairobi, 19-30 May 1980. New York, 1980 (Doc. ST/HR/SER.A/7).

Seminar on Recourse Procedures Available to Victims of Racial Discrimination and Activities to be Undertaken at the Regional Level, Geneva, 9-20 July 1979. New York, 1979 (Doc. No. ST/HR/SER.A/3).

Seminar on the Effects of the Existing Unjust International Economic Order on the Economies of the Developing Countries and the Obstacle that this represents for the Implementation of Human Rights and Fundamental Freedoms, Geneva, 30 June-11 July 1980. New York, 1980 (Doc. ST/HR/SER.A/8).

Seminar on the Establishment of Regional Commissions on Human Rights with Special Reference to Africa, Monrovia, Liberia, 10-21 September 1979. New York, 1979 (Doc. No. ST/HR/SER.A/4).

Seminar on the Relations that Exist between Human Rights, Peace and Development, New York, 3-14 August 1981. New York, 1981 (Doc. ST/HR/SER. A/10).

The status of the unmarried mother: law and practice. Report of the Secretary-General. New York, 1970 (Sales No. E.71.IV.4).

Study of Discrimination against Persons Born out of Wedlock, by Vieno Voitto Saario, New York, 1968 (Sales No.68.XIV.3).

Study of discrimination in education, by Charles D. Ammoun, New York, 1957 (Sales No. E.57.XIV.3), 182 p.

Study of discrimination in respect of the right of everyone to leave any country, including his own, and to return to his own country, by José Inglés, New York, 1963 (Sales No. E.64.XIV.2), 122 p.

Study of discrimination in the matter of political rights, by Hernán Santa Cruz, New York, 1963 (Sales No. E.63.XIV.2).

Study of Discrimination in the Matter of Religious Rights and Practices, New York, 1960 (Sales No.60.XIV.2).

Study of equality in the administration of justice, by Mohamed Ahmed Abu Rennat, New York, 1971 (Sales No. E.71.XIV.3).

Study of the implications for human rights of recent developments concerning situations known as states of siege or emergency: Progress report by Mrs. N. Questiaux, Special Rapporteur of the Sub-Commission on Prevention of Discrimination and Protection of Minorities, Doc. E/CN.4/Sub.2/490.

Study on the Independence and Impartiality of the Judiciary, Jurors and Assessors and the Independence of Lawyers, Progress Report by Mr. L.M. Singhvi, Special Rapporteur of the Sub-Commission on Prevention of Discrimination and Protection of Minorities, Doc. E/CN.4/Sub.2/481, & Add. 1.

Study of the Individual's Duties to the Community and the Limitations of Human Rights and Freedoms under Article 29 of the Universal Declaration of Human Rights, Final Report by Mrs. Erica-Irene A. Daes, Special Rapporteur of the Sub-Commission on Prevention of Discrimination and Protection of Minorities, Doc. E/CN.4/Sub.2/432 (1979).

Study on the New International Economic Order and the Promotion of Human Rights, Progress Report by Mr. Raúl Ferrero, Special Rapporteur of the Sub-Commission on Prevention of Discrimination and Protection of Minorities, Doc. E/CN.4/Sub.2/477 (1981).

Study of the Problem of Discrimination against Indigenous Populations, Final Report submitted by the Special Rapporteur, Mr. José R. Martínez Cobo, Doc. E/CN.4/Sub.2/476 and Adds. 1-6 (1981) (Study incomplete).

Study of the Question of the Prevention and Punishment of the Crime of Genocide, Study prepared by Mr. Nicodème Ruhashyankiko, Special Rapporteur of the Sub-Commission on Prevention of Discrimination and Protection of Minorities, Doc. E/CN.4/Sub.2/416 (1978).

Study of the right of everyone to be free from arbitrary arrest, detention and exile. New York, 1964 (Sales No. E.65.XIV.2).

Study on the Rights of Persons Belonging to Ethnic, Religious and Linguistic Minorities, by F. Capotorti, New York, 1979 (Sales No. E.78.XIV.1).

Study on ways and means of insuring the implementation of international instruments such as the International Convention on the Suppression and Punishment of the Crime of Apartheid, including the establishment of the international jurisdiction envisaged by the Convention. Doc.E/CN.4/1426 (1981).

SUB-COMMISSION ON PREVENTION OF DISCRIMINATION AND PROTECTION OF MINORITIES, *Reports* according to session, year and UN doc. nos. as follows: 23, 1970, E/CN.4/1040; 24, 1971, E/CN.4/1970; 25, 1972, E/CN.4/1101; 26, 1973, E/CN.4/1128; 27, 1974, E/CN.4/1160; 28, 1975, E/CN. 4/1180; 29, 1976, E/CN.4/1218; 30, 1977, E/CN.4/1261; 31, 1978, E/CN.4/1296; 32, 1979, E/CN.4/1350; 33, 1980, E/CN.4/1413; 34, 1981, E/CN.4/1512.

The Suppression of Slavery. New York, 1951 (Sales No.1951.XIV.2), 83 p.

Symposium on the Exploitation of Blacks in South Africa and Namibia and on Prison Conditions in South African Jails, Maseru, Lesotho, 17-22 July, 1978. Geneva, 1978 (Doc. No. ST/HR/SER.A/1).

Symposium on the Role of the Police in the Protection of Human Rights, The Hague, 14-25 April 1980. New York, 1980 (Doc. ST/HR/SER.A/6).

United Nations Action in the Field of Human Rights. New York, 1974 (Sales No.E.74.XIV.2) and revised edition, 1980 (Sales No. E.79.XIV.6).

The United Nations and Human Rights. New York, 1978 (Sales No.E.78.I.18), 166 p.

Yearbook on Human Rights. New York, Vol. 1, 1946. Issued annually until 1972 and since then every two years (Sales No. E.XIV.1).

2. International Labour Organisation

Abolition of forced labour: General survey of the reports relating to the Forced Labour Convention, 1930 (No. 29) and the Abolition of Forced Labour Convention, 1957 (No. 105). International Labour Conference, 65th Session, Geneva, 1979, Report III (Part 4B), 101 p.

Chart of ratifications. Published as of 1 January each year.

Comparative analysis of the international covenants on human rights and international labour conventions and recommendations, Official Bulletin 1969, No. 2, pp. 181-216.

Conventions and Recommendations adopted by the International Labour Conference, 1919-66, xvi, 1176 p. Conventions and Recommendations adopted since 1966 are printed in the ILO *Official Bulletin.*

Discrimination in employment and occupation: standards and policy statements adopted under the auspices of the ILO. Geneva, ILO, 1967, 56 p.

Employment of women with family responsibilities: General survey of the reports relating to the Employment (Women with Family Responsibilities) Recommendation, 1965 (No. 123). International Labour Conference, 64th Session, Geneva, 1978, Report III (Part 4B), iv, 68 p.

Equality in respect of employment under legislation and other national standards. Geneva, ILO, 1967, 135 p.

Equality of opportunities and equal treatment for men and women workers: Workers with family responsibilities. International Labour Conference, 66th Session, Geneva, 1980, Report VI(1), 69 p.

Equality of opportunity and treatment for women workers. International Labour Conference, 60th session, Geneva, ILO, 1975, Report VIII, 124 p.

Fighting discrimination in employment and occupation. A worker's education manual. 2nd imprint. Geneva, ILO, 1975.

Freedom by dialogue: Economic development by social progress: The ILO contribution. Report of the Director-General, Part 1, International Labour Conference, 56th Session, Geneva, 1971, 54 p.

Freedom of association and collective bargaining. General survey on the reports relating to the Convention on Freedom of Association and Protection of the Right to Organise, 1948 (No. 87) and the Convention on the Right to Organise and Collective Bargaining, 1949 (No. 98). International Labour Conference, 58th session, Geneva, ILO, 1973, Report III (Part 4B), 94 p.

Freedom of association. Digest of decisions of the Freedom of Association Committee of the governing body of ILO. 2nd rev. ed., Geneva, ILO, 1976, 180 p.

General survey on the Reports relating to the Discrimination (Employment and Occupation) Convention and Recommendation, 1958. International Labour Conference, 56th session, Geneva, ILO, Report III (Part 4B), 1972.

General survey on the Reports relating to the Employment Policy Convention and Recommendation, 1964. International Labour Conference, 57th session, Geneva, ILO, Report III (Part 4B), 1972.

The ILO and human rights. Report presented by the International Labour Organisation to the International Conference on Human Rights, 1968, Geneva, ILO, 1968, 118 p.

ILO principles, standards and procedures concerning freedom of association. 1978, 25 p.

The impact of international labour Conventions and Recommendations. 1976, vi, 104 p.

The International Labour Code, 1951. A systematic arrangement of the Conventions and Recommendations adopted by the International Labour Conference, 1919-51, with appendices embodying other standards of social policy framed by or with the co-operation of the International Labour Organisation 1919-51, 1952, 2 vol.

International labour standards. Public information booklet, 1978, 48 p.

International labour standards. A workers' education manual. 1978, 98 p.

Making work more human. Working conditions and environment. Report of the Director-General, Geneva, ILO, 1975, 122 p.

Manual on procedures relating to international labour Conventions and Recommendations. 1975, iv, 29 p.

Minimum Age: General Survey by the Committee of Experts on the Application of Conventions and Recommendations. International Labour Conference, 67th Session, Geneva, 1981, Report III (Part 4B), 214 p.

Poverty and minimum living standards: the role of the ILO. International Labour Conference, 54th session, Geneva, ILO, 1970, Report I (Part 1), 122 p.

Reports by the Committee of Experts on the Application of Conventions and Recommendations of the International Labour Organisation on progress in achieving observance of the provisions of articles 6 to 9 of the International Covenant on Economic, Social and Cultural Rights. UN docs: E/1978/27 (1978), E/1979/33 (1979) and E/1980/35 (1980).

Reports of the Committee of Experts on the Application of Conventions and Recommendations. General report and observations concerning particular countries. Submitted each year to the International Labour Conferences as Report III (Part 4A).

Termination of employment. General survey on the Reports relating to the termination of employment recommendation, 1963 (No. 119). International Labour Conference, 59th session, Geneva, ILO, Report III (Part 4B), 1974.

Trade union rights and their relation to civil liberties. International Labour Conference, 54th session, Geneva, ILO, Report VII, 1970.

3. United Nations Educational, Scientific and Cultural Organization

Activities of Unesco in connection with the promotion of human rights. Paris, Unesco, 1968.

Apartheid: Its effects on education, science, culture and information. 2nd ed. revised, Paris, Unesco, 1972.

ARCINIEGAS, Germán. *La culture, droit de l'homme.* Liège, Sciences et lettres. Paris, Librairie du Recueil Sirey, n.d., 51 p. (Droits de l'homme, 4).

Birthright of man. A selection of texts prepared under the direction of Jeanne Hersch. Paris, Unesco, 1968, 591 p.

BOK, Bart. "Freedom of science," in *Freedom and culture,* London, Wingate, 1950, 270 p.

Bulletin for the Teaching of Human Rights. Paris, Unesco, Vol. 1, No. 1 issued December 1980. To be published biannually.

Cultural rights as human rights. Paris, Unesco, 1970, 125 p. (Studies and documents on cultural policies).

Final report of a Colloquium on the New Human Rights: The "Rights of Solidarity", Mexico City, 12-15 August 1980, Doc. SS-80/CONF.806/12 (1980).

Final Report of an Expert Meeting on Human Rights, Human Needs and the Establishment of a New International Economic Order, Paris, 19-23 June 1978, Doc. SS.78/CONF.630/12 (1978).

Final Report of a Meeting of Experts on the Place of Human Rights in Cultural and Religious Traditions, Bangkok, 3-7 December 1979, Doc. SS.79/CONF. 607/10 (1980).

Four statements on the race question. Paris, Unesco, 1969, 56 p.

Freedom and culture. Introduction by Julian Huxley. London, Wingate, 1950, 270 p. Reprinted by Books Libraries Press, Freeport, N.Y., 1971.

Human Rights Aspects of Population Programmes: With Special Reference to Human Rights Law. Paris, Unesco, 1977, 154 p.

Human rights. Comments and interpretations. A symposium edited by Unesco with an introduction by Jacques Maritain. London, Wingate, 1949, 288 p.

Human rights studies in universities. Report prepared with the financial assistance of Unesco, under the direction of Karel Vasak, by T.E. McCarthy, J.B. Marie, S.P. Marks and L. Sirois. Paris, Unesco, 1972 (mimeographed). Published in French in *Revue des droits de l'homme/Human rights journal,* Vol. VI, No. 1, 1973.

Illiteracy and human rights. Published on the occasion of the International Year for Human Rights. Paris, Unesco, 1968, 15 p.

Implementation of the Recommendation concerning education for international understanding, co-operation and peace and education relating to human rights and fundamental freedoms. Report of a meeting of experts held Unesco House, Paris, 15-19 March 1976. Paris, Unesco, 1976.

INTERNATIONAL FEDERATION OF SOCIETIES OF PHILOSOPHY. *Enquête sur la liberté.* Published with the assistance of Unesco. Paris, Hermann, 1953, iv, 375 p. (Actualités scientifiques et industrielles, 1199).

JUVIGNY, Pierre. *The fight against discrimination: towards equality in education.* Paris, Unesco, 1962, 2nd ed. 1965.

KIDD, Sheila. *Some suggestions on teaching about human rights*. Paris, Unesco, 1968, 155 p. Contribution to the International Human Rights Year (1968).

LEVIN, Leah. *Human Rights: Questions and Answers*, Paris, Unesco, 1981, 86 p.

Meeting of experts on the ethical problems posed by recent progress in biology. Varna, Bulgaria, 24-27 June 1975. Final report. Paris, Unesco, 30 September 1975 (SHC/5/CONF.605/21).

MIALARET, Gaston (Ed.). *The Child's Right to Education*. Paris, Unesco, 1979, 258 p.

MORRIS, Ben. *Some Aspects of Professional Freedom of Teachers*. Lausanne, Unesco, 1977, 213 p.

PIAGET, Jean. *Le droit à l'éducation dans le monde actuel*. Liège, Sciences et lettres. Paris, Librairie du Recueil Sirey, n.d., 57 p. (Droits de l'homme, 1).

Race as news. Paris, Unesco, 1974, 173 p.

Race, science and society. Edited and introduced by Leo Kuper. Paris, Unesco/ George Allen and Unwin, 1975, 365 p.

Reports of the Committee on Conventions and Recommendations on the reports of States on the implementation of the Convention against Discrimination in Education: 1st report, 1968, Doc.15C/11; 2nd report, 1972, Doc.17C/15; 3rd report, 1978, Doc.20C/40 and 1980, Doc.21C/27.

Rights and responsibilities of youth. Paris, Unesco, 1972 (Educational studies and documents, 6).

"Science, technology and the law," *Impact of science on society*, Vol. XXI, No. 3, July-September 1971. Paris, Unesco.

Some Suggestions on Teaching about Human Rights. Paris, Unesco, 1968, 155 p.

Study of the procedures which should be followed in the examination of cases and questions which might be submitted to Unesco concerning the exercise of human rights in the spheres of its competence, in order to make it more effective. Unesco, Executive Board, 102nd session. Paris, 7 April 1977 (Doc. 102/EX/19).

The Teaching of human rights. (Proceedings of the International Congress on the Teaching of Human Rights, Sept. 1978, Vienna). Paris, Unesco, 1980, 274 p.

Les Textes Normatifs de l'Unesco. Paris, 1980, loose-leaf edition.

"Unesco's contribution to peace and its tasks with respect to the promotion of human rights and the elimination of colonialism and racialism", General Conference Docs. 20C/14 (1978) and 21C/14 (1980).

UNESCO Secretariat. "Unesco and the Challenges of Today and Tomorrow: Universal Affirmation of Human Rights", in Ramcharan (Ed.), *Human Rights, op. cit.*

The Universal Declaration of Human Rights. A guide for teachers. Paris, Unesco, 1951, 87 p. (Towards world understanding, 8).

Women, education, equality: a decade of experiment. Paris, Unesco, 1975, 109 p.

World Problems in the Classroom: A Teacher's Guide to Some United Nations Tasks. Paris, Unesco, 1973, rev. ed. 1981.

ZAVALA, Silvio. *The defence of human rights in Latin America (XVIth-XVIIIth centuries)*. Paris, Unesco, 1964, 65 p. (Race and Society).

4. World Health Organization

"Development of codes of medical ethics", containing, *inter alia*, in an Annex, a draft Body of Principles prepared by the Council for International Organizations of Medical Sciences and entitled "Principles of medical ethics relevant to the role of health personnel in the protection of persons against torture and other cruel, inhuman or degrading treatment or punishment", UN Doc. A/34/273 (1979).

Health Aspects of Human Rights with Special Reference to Developments in Biology and Medicine. Geneva, WHO, 1976, 48 p.

Medical Experimentation and the Protection of Human Rights. Proceedings of the 12th CIOMS Round Table Conference, Cascais, Portugal, 1978, N. Howard-Jones and Z. Bankowski (Eds.), Geneva, WHO, 1980, 249 p.

Protection of Human Rights in the Light of Scientific and Technological Progress in Biology and Medicine. Proceedings of the 8th CIOMS Round Table Conference, S. Btesh (Ed.), Geneva, WHO, 1974, 384 p.

Use of Human Tissues and Organs for Therapeutic Purposes: A Survey of Existing Legislation. Geneva, WHO, 1969, 19 p.

W.H.O., Report to the UN Economic and Social Council on the rights covered by Article 12 of the International Covenant on Economic, Social and Cultural Rights, UN Doc.E/1980/4 (1980).

5. Food and Agriculture Organization of the United Nations

A Right to Food. A Selection from Speeches by Addeke H. Boerma, Director-General of FAO 1968-1975, Rome, FAO, 1976, 177 p.

6. Council of Europe

Activities of the Council of Europe in the field of human rights. Annual report of the Secretary-General. Strasbourg, Council of Europe.

"Adhesion des communautés à la Convention Européenne des droits de l'homme: memorandum de la Commission", *Bulletin des Communautés Européennes*, supplement no. 2, 1979, pp. 1-21.

Bibliography relating to the European Convention on Human Rights. Strasbourg, 1978, 4th ed., 173 p.

Case-law topics/Sujets de jurisprudence: 1. Human rights in prison (1971). 2. Family life (1971). 3. Bringing an application before the European Commission of Human Rights (1972). 4. Human rights and their limitations (1971). Strasbourg, Council of Europe.

COUNCIL OF EUROPE. *Collected Edition of the "Travaux Préparatoires" of the European Convention on Human Rights.* The Hague, Martinus Nijhoff, 8 Vols. 1981-.

―――. *Human Rights Files No. 5: Conditions of Detention and the European Convention on Human Rights and Fundamental Freedoms.* Strasbourg, 1981, 37 p.

―――. *Decisions and Reports of the European Commission of Human Rights.* Strasbourg, 1980, 256 p.

Digest of case-law relating to European Convention on human rights (1955-1967). Heule, Belgium, éditions U.G.A., 1970, 523 p.

European Commission of Human Rights: Annual Review. Published annually.

European Convention on Human Rights: National aspects. Strasbourg, Council of Europe, 1975.

European Court of Human Rights. Series of publications. Series A: Judgements and decisions; series B: Pleadings, oral arguments, documents.

Explanatory report on the additional protocol to the European Convention on Extradition. Strasbourg, Council of Europe, 1975.

Human rights: Problems arising from the co-existence of the United Nations Covenants on Human Rights and the European Convention on Human Rights; differences as regards the rights guaranteed. Report of the Committee of experts on human rights to the Committee of Ministers. Strasbourg, Council of Europe, 1970, Doc. H(70)7, 93 p.

Implementation of article 57 of the European Convention on Human Rights. (Replies of governments to the Secretary-General's enquiry relating to the implementation of articles 8, 9, 10 and 11 of the European Convention on Human Rights). Memorandum prepared by the Directorate of human rights. Strasbourg, Council of Europe, 1976.

Implementation of the Final Act of the Conference on Security and Co-operation in Europe. Council of Europe Parliamentary Assembly, Doc.AS/Inf(77)9, Strasbourg, 1977, 195 p.

Mass communications media and human rights. Strasbourg, Council of Europe, 1970. 31 p.

OPSAHL, Torkel. *Substantive Rights.* Report presented to a Colloquy on The European Convention on Human Rights in Relation to Other International Instruments for the Protection of Human Rights, Council of Europe Doc.H/Coll.(78)8, Strasbourg, 1978, 53 p.

Parliamentary Conference on Human Rights, Vienna, 1971. Working papers. Strasbourg, Council of Europe, 1971.

Reports on the 25th anniversary of the Universal Declaration and the 20th anniversary of the European Convention on Human Rights. Strasbourg, Council of Europe, 1973.

The right to strike: its scope and limitations. Strasbourg, Council of Europe, 1973.

Stock-taking on the European Convention on Human Rights. European Commission on Human Rights, Strasbourg, 1979, 146 p.

Yearbook of the European Convention on Human Rights. The Hague, Nijhoff, Vol. 1, 1958/1959, published annually.

7. Organization of American States

Annual Report of the Inter-American Commission on Human Rights. Washington D.C., OAS, 1978 report issued in doc. OEA/Ser.L/V/11.47/13rev.1 (1979); 1979-1980 report issued in doc. OEA/Ser.G/CP/doc.1110/80 (1980).

Annuario interamericano de derechos humanos/Inter-American yearbook on human rights. Washington, D.C., OAS, General Secretariat, 1969-1970 (1976).

Comparative study of the International Covenant on Human Rights together with the Optional Protocol to the International Covenant on Civil and Political Rights adopted by the U.N. (December 1966), the draft Convention on Human Rights of the Inter-American Council of Jurists (fourth meeting, 1959), and the text of the amendments to the IACJ draft adopted by the Inter-American Commission on Human Rights (October 1966 and January 1967). Washington, D.C., OAS, 1968.

Conferencia especializada inter-americana sobre derechos humanos. San José, Costa Rica, 7-22 de noviembre de 1969. Actas y documentos. Washington, D.C., OAS, 1973, 534 p.

Estudio sobre la relación jurídica entre el respeto de los derechos humanos y el ejercicio de la democracía. Washington, D.C., OAS, 1960, 39 p.

Handbook of existing rules pertaining to human rights. Washington, D.C., OAS, 1979, 75 p.

Human rights and representative democracy. Washington, D.C., OAS, 1965, 15 p.

Human rights in the American States. Study prepared in accordance with resolution XXVII of the 10th Inter-American Conference. Preliminary ed. Washington, D.C., OAS, 1960, 226 p.

INTER-AMERICAN COMMISSION OF WOMEN. SPECIAL COMMITTEE FOR STUDIES AND RECOMMENDATIONS FOR THE WORLD CONFERENCE OF INTERNATIONAL WOMEN'S YEAR. *Final report, committee meeting results, basic documents.* Washington, D.C., OAS, 1975, 296 p.

Statute of the Inter-American Commission on Human Rights, OAS doc. OEA/Ser.P, AG/Com.1/doc.22/79 rev.2 (1979).

Statute of the Inter-American Court of Human Rights, OAS doc. OEA/Ser.P, AG/doc.1196/rev.1 (1979).

8. Non-Governmental Organizations

AMNESTY INTERNATIONAL. *The Death Penalty.* London, Amnesty International Publications, 1979, 209 p.

——. *Report*, published annually, 1978, 320 p.; 1979, 220 p.; 1980, 408 p.; 1981, 426 p.

——. *Report on Torture.* London, G. Duckworth Ltd., 1973.

ANTI-SLAVERY SOCIETY. *Human Rights and Development Working Papers.* Published occasionally, London.

CENTRE FOR THE INDEPENDENCE OF JUDGES AND LAWYERS. *CIJL Bulletin*, Geneva.

CHALLIS, James, and ELLIMAN, David, in association with the ANTI-SLAVERY SOCIETY. *Child Workers Today.* Quartermaine, Sunbury, U.K., 1979, 170 p.

Derechos humanos en las zonas rurales. Report of a seminar organized by the International Commission of Jurists and the Latin-American Council for Law and Development, Bogota, September 1979, Bogota, Sociedad Ediciones Internacionales, 1979, 306 p.

Development, Human Rights and the Rule of Law. Report of a Conference Held in The Hague on 27 April—1 May 1981, convened by the International Commission of Jurists, Oxford, Pergamon, 1981, 237 p.

FAWCETT, James. *The International Protection of Minorities.* London, 1979, Minority Rights Group report No. 41, 20 p.

FONSECA, G. DA. *How to file complaints of human rights violations: a practi-*

cal guide to inter-governmental procedures. Geneva, World Council of Churches, 1975, 152 p.

FRIEDMAN, Julian, and WISEBERG, Laurie. *Teaching Human Rights.* Washington, D.C., Human Rights Internet, 1981, 134 p.

GARLING, M. (Ed.). *The Human Rights Handbook: A Guide to British and American International Human Rights Organizations.* New York, Facts on File, 1979, 299 p.

GAUTIER, J-J; MACDERMOT, N.; MARTIN, E.; and VARGAS, F. de. *Torture: How to Make the International Convention Effective.* Geneva, International Commission of Jurists and Swiss Committee against Torture, 1979, 46 p.

GREENFIELD, Richard. *Research Manual on Human Rights.* Washington, D.C., Human Rights Internet, 1982.

Human Rights and Development: Report of a Seminar on Human Rights and their Promotion in the Caribbean. Barbados, September 1977, organised by the International Commission of Jurists and the Organisation of Commonwealth Caribbean Bar Association, Bridgetown, The Cedar Press, 1978, 190 p.

Human Rights Directory: Latin America, Africa, Asia. Washington, D.C., Human Rights Internet, 1980, 244 p.

Human Rights in a One-Party State. International Seminar on Human Rights, their Protection and the Rule of Law in a One-Party State, convened by the International Commission of Jurists, London, Search Press, 1978, 133 p.

HUMAN RIGHTS INTERNET REPORTER, Washington, D.C., published every two months except during July/August, Vol. 1, 1976. Until Vol. 6 (Fall 1980) the Reporter was titled the *HRI Newsletter.*

HUMAN RIGHTS INTERNET and MCPL EDUCATION FUND. *Human Rights Directory 1979.* Washington, D.C., 1979, 155 p.

Index on Censorship (London). Published every two months.

INTERNATIONAL COMMISSION OF JURISTS. *The Review* (Geneva). Quarterly.

———. *ICJ Newsletter, Quarterly Report.*

———. *The Rule of Law and Human Rights.* Geneva, 1966, 83 p.

INTERNATIONAL COMMITTEE OF THE RED CROSS. *International Review of the Red Cross.* Geneva, published every two months.

INTERNATIONAL INSTITUTE OF HUMANITARIAN LAW. *Human rights as the basis of of international humanitarian law.* Proceedings of the International Conference on Humanitarian Law, San Remo, Italy, 24-27 September 1970. Lugano-Bellinzona, Switzerland, Instituto Editoriale Ticinese, 385 p.

INTERNATIONAL LEAGUE FOR HUMAN RIGHTS. *Annual Review.* New York.

INTERNATIONAL YOUTH AND STUDENT MOVEMENT FOR THE UNITED NATIONS. *Political Conscience: War Resistance as a Human Right.* Geneva, ISMUN, 1978, 32 p.

North American Human Rights Directory. Washington, D.C., Human Rights Internet, 1980, 182 p.

"Numéro spécial relatif au colloque de Dakar sur le développement et les droits de l'homme", organisé par l'Association Sénégalaise d'Etudes et de Recherches Juridiques et la Commission Internationale de Juristes, September 1978, *Revue Sénégalaise de Droit*, December 1977, No. 22, 255 p.

PALLEY, Claire. *Constitutional Law and Minorities*. London, 1978, Minority Rights Group report No. 36, 20 p.

PICTET, J. *Humanitarian Law and the Protection of War Victims*. Leyden, A.W. Sijthoff, Geneva, Institut Henry-Dunant, 1975.

———. *The principles of international humanitarian law*. Geneva, International Red Cross Committee, 1967, 66 p.

RED CROSS. *The Geneva Conventions of 12 August 1949*. Commentary published under the General Editorship of Jean S. Pictet, Vol. I-IV, Geneva, 1952-1960.

———. *International Red Cross Handbook*, 2nd edition, 1971.

SOUZA, Frances d'. *The Refugee Dilemma: International Recognition and Acceptance*. London, 1980, Minority Rights Group report No. 43, 19 p.

TAJFEL, Henri. *The Social Psychology of Minorities*. London, 1978, Minority Rights Group report No. 38, 20 p.

WHITE, Helen C., and CAZAMIAN, Madeleino. *Human rights: the task before us*. London, International Federation of University Women, n.d., 100 p.

WORLD PEACE THROUGH LAW CENTER. *The law and refugees*. Washington, D.C., The Center, 1976, 45 p.

———. *The ratification of international human rights treaties: a report of the Committee on Human Rights*. Washington, D.C., World Association of Lawyers, 1976, 78 p.

II. *Analytical Works*

A. General Works and Articles

ACKERMAN, Steven. "Torture and Other Forms of Cruel and Unusual Punishment in International Law", *Vanderbilt Journal of Transnational Law*, Vol. 11, 1978, pp. 653-707.

AIT-AHMED, Hocine. *L'Afro-fascisme: les droits de l'homme dans la Charte et la pratique de l'Organisation de l'unité africaine*. Paris, L'Harmattan, 1980, 437 p.

AJAMI, F. "Human Rights and World Order Politics", *Alternatives* (New Delhi), Vol. 3, 1978, pp. 351-83.

AL-'AILI, 'Abd-el-hakim. Houqouq al-insan filshari'a al-islamiyya (Human Rights in Islamic Law). *Assyassat ad-dawliyya*, Cairo, No. 39, January 1975, pp. 20-27.

AL-ASFAHANI, Nabih. Mawqif al-djami 'a al-'Arabiyya min houqouq al-insan (The position of the Arab League on human rights). *Assyassat ad-dawliyya*, Cairo, No. 39, January 1975, pp. 28-33.

ALDRICH, George H. "New Life for the Laws of War", *American Journal of International Law*, Vol. 75, No. 4, 1981, pp. 764-83.

ALEXANDER, Yonah, and FRIEDLANDER, Robert (Eds.). *Self-Determination: National Regional and Global Dimensions*. Boulder, Westview Press, 1981, 371 p.

ALSTON, Philip. "Human Rights and Basic Needs: A Critical Assessment",
    Revue des droits de l'homme/Human rights journal (Paris), Vol. XII, No.
    1-2, 1979, pp. 19-67.
————. "Human Rights and the New International Development Strategy", *Bul-
    letin of Peace Proposals* (Oslo), Vol. 10, No. 3, 1979, pp. 281-90.
————. "Linking Trade and Human Rights", *German Yearbook of International
    Law* (Berlin, FRG), Vol. 23, 1980, pp. 126-58.
————. "Peace as a Human Right", *Bulletin of Peace Proposals* (Oslo) Vol. 11,
    No. 4, 1980, pp. 319-30.
————. "Prevention Versus Cure as a Human Rights Strategy", in *Development,
    Human Rights and the Rule of Law, op. cit.*, pp. 31-108.
AMERICAN ACADEMY OF POLITICAL AND SOCIAL SCIENCE. *Essen-
    tial Human Rights*. Philadelphia, 1946, 196 p.
ANDREWS, J.A. (Ed.). *Human Rights in Criminal Procedure: A Comparative
    Study*. The Hague, Martinus Nijhoff, 1981, 475 p.
ANTALFFY, György. "On Human Rights", *Hungarian Law Review* (Budapest),
    No. 1/2, 1978, pp. 5-34.
ARANGIO-RUIZ, Gaetano. "Human Rights and Non-Intervention in the Helsinki
    Final Act", *Recueil des cours*, (Hague Academy of International Law), IV,
    Vol. 157, 1977, pp. 195-331.
ARANGUREN, J.L. et al. *Los Derechos Humanos*, "Cuaderno Cienia Nueva",
    Madrid, 1968.
ASBECK, F.M. *The Universal Declaration of Human Rights and its predeces-
    sors*. Leyden, 1949.
ASHOOR, Yadh ben. "Islam and International Humanitarian Law", *International
    Review of the Red Cross* (Geneva), March-April 1980, No. 215, pp. 59-69.
AURENCHE, Guy. *L'aujourd'hui des droits de l'homme*. Paris, Nouvelle Cité,
    1980, 265 p.
BAMMATE, N. "Le destin et la liberté selon l'Islam", *L'âge nouveau* (Paris), n°
    66, Octobre 1951.
BARTOLOMEI, Donato Massimo. *La protezione dei diritti umani nell'ordinamento
    internazionale*. Rome, Soc. ed. del Foro italiano, 1958, 116 p.
BELLO, Emmanuel. "Shared Legal Concepts between African Customary Norms
    and International Conventions on Humanitarian Law", *Indian Journal of
    International Law*, Vol. 21, 1981, pp. 79-95.
BIANCHI GUNDIAN, Manuel. *La paz y los derechos humanos*. Santiago de
    Chile, Editorial Andres Bello, 1969, 92 p.
BILDER, Richard B. "Rethinking international human rights: some basic ques-
    tions", *Revue des droits de l'homme/Human rights journal* (Paris), Vol.
    II, No. 4, 1969, pp. 557-608.
BISSELL, J. "Negotiations by International Bodies and the Protection of Human
    Rights", *Columbia Journal of Transnational Law*, Vol. 7, 1968, pp.
    90-134.
BLISHCHENKO, I.P. "The Impact of the International Economic Order on
    Human Rights in Developing Countries", *Bulletin of Peace Proposals* (Oslo),
    Vol. 11, No. 4, 1980, pp. 375-86.
BOLTE, Paul Emile. *Les droits de l'homme et la papauté contemporaine*. Synthèse
    et textes. Montréal, Editions Fides, 1975, 428 p. (La pensée chrétienne).

BOSON, Gerson de BRITTO MELLO. *Internacionalizacao dos direitos do homen.* 1. ed. São Paulo, Sugestões Literaarias, 1972, 134 p.

BOSSUYT, Marc. *L'interdiction de la discrimination dans le droit international des droits de l'homme.* Brussels, E. Bruylant, 1976, 262 p.

————. "The Direct Applicability of International Instruments on Human Rights", *Revue belge de droit international* (Brussels), Vol. 15, 1980, pp. 317-44.

BOTHE, M.; PARTSCH, K.; and SOLF, W. *New Rules for Victims of Armed Conflicts.* The Hague, Martinus Nijhoff, 1981, 1100 p.

BOUTROS-GHALI, B. Al-aqualiyyat wa houqouq al-insan fil-fiqh al-dawli (Minorities and human rights in international legislation). *Assyassat ad-dawliyya* (Cairo), No. 39, January 1975, pp. 10-20.

BOVEN, Theodoor C. Van. De volkenrechtelijke bescherming van de godsdienstvrijheid. Editions Van Gorcum, 1977, 305 p.

————. "Fact-finding in the sphere of human rights", *Israel Yearbook on Human Rights* (Tel Aviv), Vol. 3, 1973, pp. 93-117.

————. "Human Rights and the New International Order", *Bulletin of Peace Proposals* (Oslo), Vol. 11, No. 4, 1980, pp. 369-74.

————. "Some remarks on special problems relating to human rights in developing countries", *Revue des droits de l'homme/Human rights journal* (Paris), Vol. III, No. 3, 1970, pp. 383-96.

BRANCHU, Françoise. *Le problème des minorités en droit international depuis la seconde guerre mondiale.* Lyons, Impr. Bosc Frères, 1959, 253 p.

BRUEGEL, J.W. "A neglected field: the protection of minorities", *Revue des droits de l'homme/Human rights journal* (Paris), Vol. IV, 1971, No. 2-3, pp. 413-42.

BRUNET, René. *La garantie internationale des droits de l'homme d'après la Charte de San Francisco.* Geneva, C. Grasset, 1947, 383 p., bibliography.

BUERGENTHAL, Thomas (Ed.). *Human Rights, International Law and the Helsinki Accords.* Montclair; Allanheld, Osmun and Co., and New York; Universe Books, 1977, under the auspices of the American Society of International Law, 203 p.

————. "International and regional human rights law and institutions: some examples of their interactions", *Texas International Law Journal* (Austin, Tex.), Vol. 12, No. 2 and 3, 1977, pp. 321-30.

————. "The right to receive information across national boundaries", in ASPEN INSTITUTE FOR HUMANISTIC STUDIES, *Control of the direct broadcast satellite: values in conflict,* 1974, pp. 73-84.

————, and TORNEY, Judith V. *International human rights and international education.* Washington, D.C., U.S. National Commission for Unesco, 1976, 211 p.

BURROWS, Noreen. "The Promotion of Women's Rights by the European Economic Community", *Common Market Law Review* (Leyden), Vol. 17, No. 2, 1980, pp. 191-209.

CALOGEROPOULOS-STRATIS, Aristidis. *Droit humanitaire et droits de l'homme.* The Hague, Martinus Nijhoff, 1981, 264 p.

————. *Le droit des peuples à disposer d'eux-mêmes.* Brussels, E. Bruylant, 1973, 388 p.

CAMARGO, Pedro Pablo. "L' "amparo" au Mexique et en Amérique latine comme instrument de protection des droits de l'homme", *Revue des droits de l'homme/Human rights journal* (Paris), vol. I, n° 3, 1968, pp. 332-62.

———. *Problemática mundial de los derechos humanos*. Bogotá, Universidad la Gran Colombia, 1974, 378 p., bibliography.

———. *La protección jurídica de los derechos humanos y la democracia en América: los derechos humanos y el derecho internacional*. México, Edit. Excelsior, 1960, 481 p.

———. "The right to judicial protection: "amparo" and other Latin American remedies for the protection of human rights", *Lawyers of the Americas* (Coral Gables, Fla.), Vol. 2, No. 2, 1971, pp. 191-230.

CAREY, John. *International protection of human rights*. Dobbs Ferry, N.Y., Oceana, 1968, 116 p.

———. "Procedures for international protection of human rights", *Iowa Law Review* (Iowa City, Iowa), Vol. 53, October 1967, pp. 291-324.

CARILLO SALCEDO, J.A. "Derecho al desarrollo como derecho de la persona humana", *Revista española de derecho internacional* (Madrid), Vol. 25, 1972, pp. 119-25.

CASCAJO CASTRO, José-Luís et al. *Los derechos humanos: significación, estatuto jurídico y sistema*. Sevilla, Secretariado de Publicacione de la Universidad de Sevilla, 1979, 332 p.

CASSESE, Antonio. "The Approach of the Helsinki Declaration to Human Rights", *Vanderbilt Journal of Transnational Law*, Vol. 13, 1980, pp. 275-91.

———. (Ed.). *The New Humanitarian Law of Armed Conflict*. Dobbs Ferry, N.Y., Oceana, 1979, 501 p.

———, and JOUVE, Edmond (Eds.). *Pour un droit des peuples: esśais sur la déclaration d'Alger*. Paris, Berger-Levrault, 1978, 220 p.

CASSIN, René."La Déclaration universelle et la mise en oeuvre des droits de l'homme", *Recueil des cours* (Hague Academy of International Law), 1951, pp. 241-367.

———. "De la place faite aux devoirs de l'individu dans la Déclaration universelle des droits de l'homme", *Mélanges Modinos*, Paris, 1968, pp. 479-88.

———. "Science and human rights", *Impact of science on society* (Paris, Unesco), Vol. XXII, No. 4, October-December 1972, pp. 329-39.

CASTÁN TOBEÑAS, José. *Los derechos del hombre*. 2nd ed. Madrid, Reus, 1976. 200 p.

CASTBERG, Frede. "Natural law and human rights", *Revue des droits de l'homme/Human rights journal* (Paris), Vol. I, No. 1, 1968, pp. 14-40.

CENTRE DE DROIT INTERNATIONAL DE L'INSTITUT DE SOCIOLOGIE DE L'UNIVERSITE LIBRE DE BRUXELLES. *Droit humanitaire et conflits armées*. Editions de l'Université de Bruxelles, 1976, 296 p.

CENTRE D'ETUDES EUROPEENNES, UNIVERSITE CATHOLIQUE DE LOUVAIN, DEPARTEMENT DES DROITS DE L'HOMME. 1er colloque: *Les droits de l'homme et les personnes morales*. Brussels, E. Bruylant, 1970, 166 p.; 2e colloque: *Vers une protection efficace des droits économiques et sociaux*. Louvain, Vander, 1973, 209 p.

CHALIDZE, Valery. "The Humanitarian Provisions of the Helsinki Accord: A Critique of their Significance", *Vanderbilt Journal of Transnational Law*, Vol. 13, 1980, pp. 429-50.

CHALMERS, Donald. "Human rights and what is reasonably justifiable in a democratic society", *Melanesian Law Journal* (Australia), Vol. 3, April 1975, p. 92.

CHATTERJEE, S.K., "Terrorism and Certain Legal Aspects of Human Rights", *International Relations* (London), Vol. VI, No. 5, 1980, pp. 749-68.

CHEN, Lung-chu. "Self-determination as a human right", in *Toward world order and human dignity*, New York, Free Press, 1976, pp. 198-261.

CHERNICHENKO, S.V. Bor'ba s narushenijami prav cheloveka i mezhdunarodnye protsedury (Struggle against violations of human rights and the international procedures). *Sovetskoy gosudarstvo i pravo* (Moscow), No. 1, 1980, pp. 91-99.

CHKHIKVADZE, V. "Armed Conflict and Human Rights", *International Affairs* (Moscow), Vol. 11, 1979, pp. 43-51.

————. *Sotsialisticheskij gumanizm i prava cheloveka (Socialist humanism and human rights), Moscow, 1978.*

———. *"Human Rights and Non-Interference with the Internal Affairs of State", International Affairs* (Moscow), 2 November 1978, pp. 22-30.

CHONCHOL, Jacques. "The Declaration on Human Rights and the Right to Development: The Gap between Proposal and Reality", in *Development, Human Rights and the Rule of Law, op. cit.*, pp. 109-20.

CHOSSUDOVSKY, M. "The Political Economy of Human Rights", *Bulletin of Peace Proposals* (Oslo), Vol. 10, 1979, pp. 172-78.

CLAUDE, Richard Pierre (Ed.). *Comparative human rights.* Baltimore, Md., Johns Hopkins University Press, 1976, 410 p.

COHN, Haim A. "The right and duty of resistance", *Revue des droits de l'homme/Human rights journal* (Paris), Vol. I, No. 4, 1968, pp. 491-517.

COLONNESE, Louis M. (Ed.). *Human rights and the liberation of man in the Americas.* Notre Dame, Ind., University of Notre Dame Press, 1970, 278 p.

COMMISSION INTERNATIONALE DES JURISTES. "L'incidence des réalisations technologiques sur le droit à la vie privée", *Revue internationale des sciences sociales* (Paris, Unesco), vol. XXIV, n° 3, 1972, pp. 441-53.

COULSON, N.J. "The state and the individual in Islamic law", *The International and Comparative Law Quarterly* (London), Vol. 6, No. 1, 1957, pp. 49-60.

CRANSTON, Maurice. *What are human rights?* London, Bodley Head, 1973, 170 p.

CUADRA, Hector. *La proyección internacional de los derechos humanos.* 1st ed., México, UNAM, Instituto de Investigaciones Jurídicas, 1970, 308 p.

DELBRUCK, Jost. *Die Rassenfrage als Problem des Völkerrechts und nationaler Rechtsordnungen.* Frankfurt, Athenäum, 1971, 324 p., bibliography.

Development, Human Rights and the Rule of Law: Report of a Conference held in The Hague on 27 April—1 May 1981 convened by the International Commission of Jurists, Oxford, Pergamon Press, 1981, 237 p.

DIALLO, Issa ben Yacine. *Les réfugiés en Afrique: de la conception à l'application d'un instrument juridique de protection.* Vienna, Universitäts Veregsbuchhandlung GES MBH, 1974, 239 p.

DIAS, Clarence J. "Realizing the Right to Development: The Importance of

Legal Resources", in *Development, Human Rights and the Rule of Law*, *op. cit.*, pp. 187-98.

DIMITRIJEVIC, Vojin. "The Place of Helsinki on the Long Road to Human Rights", *Vanderbilt Journal of Transnational Law*, Vol. 13, 1980, pp. 253-73.

DINSTEIN, Y. "Human Rights: The Quest for Concretization", *Israel Yearbook on Human Rights* (Tel Aviv), Vol. 1, 1971, pp. 13-28.

———. "Science, Technology and Human Rights", *Dalhousie Law Journal*, Vol. 5, 1979, pp. 155-68.

———. "The New Geneva Protocols: A Step Forward or Backward?", *The Yearbook of World Affairs* 1979 (London), Vol. 33, pp. 265-83.

DIREITO, Carlos Alberto Menezes. *O Estado moderno e a proteção dos direitos de homen*. Rio de Janeiro, Freitas Bastos, 1968, 245 p., bibliography.

DOMB, I. "Jus Cogens and Human Rights", *Israel Yearbook on Human Rights* (Tel Aviv), Vol. 6, 1976, pp. 104-21.

———. "Who is a 'Victim' of a Violation of Human Rights?", *Israel Yearbook on Human Rights* (Tel Aviv), Vol. 5, 1975, pp. 181-201.

DOMINGUEZ, Jorge I., and RODLEY, Nigel. *Human rights and international relations*. New York, McGraw-Hill, 1976, 160 p.

DOMINGUEZ, J.I.; RODLEY, N.S.; WOOD, B.; and FALK, R. *Enhancing Global Human Rights*, 1980's Project/Council on Foreign Relations, New York, McGraw-Hill, 1979, 270 p.

DOWRICK, F.E. (Ed.). *Human Rights: Problems, Perspectives and Texts*. Farnborough, England, Saxon House, 1979, 223 p.

DRAPER, G.I.A.D. "The Geneva Conventions of 1949", *Recueil des cours* (Hague Academy of International Law), Vol. 1, 1965, pp. 63-162.

———. "The relationship between the human rights regime and the law of armed conflict", *Israel Yearbook on Human Rights* (Tel Aviv), Vol. 1, 1971, pp. 191-207.

Les droits de l'homme: droits collectifs ou droits individuels: actes du Colloque de Strasbourg des 13 et 14 mars 1979. Paris, Librairie générale de droit et de jurisprudence, 1980, 220 p.

DROST, Pieter N. *The crime of state: penal protection for fundamental freedoms of persons and peoples*. 1. Humanicide. 2. Genocide. Leyden, Sijthoff, 1959, 2 vol.

———. *Human rights as legal rights. The realization of individual human rights in positive international law*. Leyden, Sijthoff, 1965, 272 p.

DUCHACEK, Ivo D. *Rights and liberties in the world today: Constitutional promise and reality*. Santa Barbara, Calif., ABC-CLIO, 1973, 269 p.

DUNSHEE DE ABRANCHES, Carlos A. *Proteção internacional dos direitos humanos*. Rio de Janeiro, Freitas Bastos, 1964, 159 p., bibliography.

DUPUY, René-Jean (Ed.). *The Right to Health as a Human Right*. Papers of a workshop of the Hague Academy of International Law and the United Nations University, The Hague, 27-29 July 1978, Sijthoff and Noordhoff, 1979.

———. *The Right to Development at the International Level*. Papers of a workshop of the Hague Academy of International Law and the United Nations University, The Hague, 16-18 October 1979, Sijthoff and Noordhoff, 1980.

EIDE, Asbjørn. "Choosing the Paths to Development: National Options and International Regulation. The Implications for Human Rights", *Bulletin of Peace Proposals* (Oslo), Vol. 11, No. 4, 1980, pp. 349-60.

———. "Human rights and non-intervention in the all-European system", *Bulletin of Peace Proposals* (Oslo), Vol. 8, No. 3, 1977, pp. 209-15.

———, and SHOU, August (Eds.). *International Protection of Human Rights. Proceedings of the Seventh Nobel Symposium.* Oslo, 25-27 September 1967, Almquist and Wiksell, 1968.

ELIAN, George. *The Principle of Sovereignty over Natural Resources.* Alphen aan den Rijn, Sijthoff and Noordhoff, 1979, 238 p.

ERMACORA, Felix. Menschenrechte in der sich wandelnden Welt. Vienna, Verlag der österreichischen Akademie der Wissenschaften, 1974, 629 p.

———. "International enquiry commissions in the field of human rights", *Revue des droits de l'homme/Human rights journal* (Paris), Vol. I, No. 2, 1968, pp. 180-218.

———. "Partiality and impartiality of human rights inquiry commissions of international organizations", *René Cassin amicorum discipulorumque liber I*, Paris, 1969, pp. 64-74.

ESIEMOKHAI, Emmanuel Omoh. "Towards Adequate Defence of Human Rights in Africa", *Indian Journal of International Law*, Vol. 21, 1981, pp. 141-48.

ESPIRITU, A.C. "Keeping Human Life Human: Altering Structures of Power, Economic Benefits and Institutions", in *Development, Human Rights and the Rule of Law, op. cit.*, pp. 175-80.

EVERTS, Philip. "Some Notes on the Connection between Disarmament and Human Rights", *Bulletin of Peace Proposals* (Oslo), Vol. 12, No. 3, 1981, pp. 271-76.

EZE, Osita C. "Les droits de l'homme et le sous-développement", *Revue des droits de l'homme/Human rights journal* (Paris) Vol. XII, No. 1-2, 1979, pp. 5-18.

EZEJIOFOR, G. *Protection of human rights under law.* London, 1964.

FALCONER, Alan (Ed.). *Understanding Human Rights: An Interdisciplinary and Interfaith Study.* Dublin, Irish School of Ecumenics, 1980, 242 p.

FALK, Richard. "Comparative Protection of Human Rights in Capitalist and Socialist Third World Countries", *Universal Human Rights* (New York), Vol. 1, No. 2, 1979.

———. *Human Rights and State Sovereignty.* New York, Holmes and Meier, 1981, 251 p.

———. "Militarization and human rights in the third world", *Bulletin of Peace Proposals* (Oslo), Vol. 8, No. 3, 1977, pp. 220-32.

FENSTERHEIM, G. David. "Toward an International Law of Human Rights Based upon the Mutual Expectations of States", *Virginia Journal of International Law*, Vol. 21, No. 1, 1980, pp. 185-210.

FERENCZ, Benjamin. *An International Criminal Court: A Step Toward World Peace.* 2 Vols., Dobbs Ferry, N.Y., Oceana, 1980, 673 p.

FERGUSON, Clyde. "Global Human Rights: Challenges and Prospects", *Denver Journal of International Law and Policy*, Vol. 8, 1979, pp. 367-77.

FLATHMAN, R. *The Practice of Rights.* London, Cambridge University Press, 1976, 250 p.

FONSECA, Glenda DA, and VILLAPANDO, Waldo. *Defensa de los derechos humanos.* Ed. Tierra Nueva SRL, 1976, 271 p.

FORSYTHE, David P. "Political prisoners: the law and politics of protection", *Vanderbilt Journal of Transnational Law* (Nashville, Tenn.), Vol. 9, Spring 1976, pp. 295-322.

——, and WISEBERG, L. "Human Rights Protection: A Research Agenda", *Universal Human Rights* (New York), Vol. 1, No. 4, 1979, pp. 1-24.

FRAENKEL, Jack R.; CARTER, Margaret; and REARDON, Betty. *The struggle for human rights: a question of values.* New York, Random House, 1975, 71 p.

FRANCK, Thomas M., and FAIRLEY, H. Scott, "Procedural Due Process in Human Rights Fact-Finding by International Agencies", *American Journal of International Law* (Washington, D.C.), Vol. 74, No. 2, 1980, pp. 308-45.

FREYMOND, J. "Human Rights and Foreign Policy", in Ramcharan (Ed.), *Human Rights, op. cit.*

GALTUNG, Johan. "What Kind of Development and What Kind of Law?", in *Development, Human Rights and the Rule of Law, op. cit.*, pp. 121-30.

——, and WIRAK, Anders. "Human needs and human rights: a theoretical approach", *Bulletin of Peace Proposals* (Oslo), Vol. 8, No. 3, 1977, pp. 251-58.

GANJI, Manouchechr. *International protection of human rights.* Geneva, Librairie E. Droz, 1962, 317 p.

GARBO, Gunnar. "Freedom of the press: media structure and control", *Bulletin of Peace Proposals* (Oslo), Vol. 8, No. 3, 1977, pp. 233-35.

GARCIA-AMADOR, F.V. *Recent Codification of the Law of State Responsibility for Injuries to Aliens.* Alphen aan den Rijn, Sijhtoff and Noordhoff, 1974, 416 p.

GARCIA BAUER, Carlos. *Los derechos humanos, preoccupación universal.* Guatemala, Editorial universitaria, 1960, 532 p.

GARCIA RAMIREZ, Sergio. *Los derechos humanos y el derecho penal.* México, Sepsetentas, 1976, 205 p.

GARIBALDI, Oscar M. "General limitations on human rights: the principle of legality", *Harvard International Law Journal* (Cambridge, Mass.), Vol. 17, Summer 1976, pp. 503-57.

GARNICK, L., and TWITCHETT, C.C. "Human Rights and a Successor to the Lomé Convention", *International Relations* (London), Vol. 6, 1979, pp. 540-57.

GAZZALI, Muhammad al-. *Human Rights in the Teaching of Islam.* Cairo, al Makhtabat al-Tjariyah, 1962 (in Arabic).

GLASER, Kurt, and POSSONY, Stefan. *Victims of Politics: The State of Human Rights.* New York, Columbia University Press, 1979, 614 p.

GOLSONG, Heribert. "Implementation of international protection of human rights", *Recueil des cours* (Hague Academy of International Law), Vol. III, 1963, pp. 1-151.

GOODE, William J. "Family patterns and human rights", *International Social Science Journal* (Paris, Unesco), Vol. XVIII, No. 1, 1966, pp. 45-60.

GORMLEY, W. Paul. *Human Rights and Environment: The Need for International Co-operation.* Leyden, Sijhtoff, 1976, 274 p.

GOTESKY, Rubin, and LASZLO, Ervin. *Human dignity. This century and the next.* Gordon and Breach, Science Publishers, 1970, 380 p.

GOTLIEB, Allan (Ed.). *Human Rights, Federalism and Minorities*, Toronto, Canadian Institute of International Affairs, 1970, 268 p.

GRAEFRATH, B. "Against Cold War—For Promotion of Human Rights", *GDR Committee for Human Rights, Bulletin No.3/1978* (Berlin), pp. 3-25.

———. "A Necessary Dispute on the Contents of the Peoples' Right to Self-Determination: Rejection of an Old Concept in a New Guise", *GDR Committee for Human Rights Bulletin* No. 1/1981, Berlin, pp. 11-25.

———. "On the 6th Version of the Proposal for a High Commissioner for Human Rights", *GDR Committee for Human Rights, Bulletin No. 4/1978* (Berlin), pp. 26-42.

———. "The Socialist States and International Co-operation in the Field of Human Rights", *GDR Committee for Human Rights, Bulletin No. 2/1979* (Berlin), pp. 38-53.

GRAHL-MADSEN, Atle. *The Status of Refugees in International Law.* 2 vol., Leyden, Sijthoff, 499 p. + 482 p.

———. *Territorial Asylum.* Stockholm, 1980, 230 p.

GREEN, L.C. "Derogation of Human Rights in Emergency Situations", *Canadian Yearbook of International Law*, Vol. 16, 1978, pp. 92-115.

GREEN, Reginald. "Basic Human Rights/Needs: Some Problems of Categorical Translation and Unification", *The Review of the International Commission of Jurists* (Geneva), No. 27, December 1981, pp. 53-58.

GREENSPAN, Morris. "The protection of human rights in time of warfare", *Israel Yearbook on Human Rights* (Tel Aviv), Vol. 1, 1971, pp. 228-45.

GROS ESPIELL, Hector, "The Evolving Concept of Human Rights—Western, Socialist and Third World Approaches", in *Rights: Thirty Years after the Universal Declaration*, Ramcharan (Ed.), *Human Rights, op. cit.*

GRUBER, H. "Co-operative Movement and Human Rights", *GDR Committee for Human Rights, Bulletin No. 3/1978* (Berlin), pp. 34-40.

GUILHAUDIS, Jean-François. *Le droit des peuples à disposer d'eux-mêmes.* Grenoble, Presses Universitaires de Grenoble, 1976, 226 p.

GURADZE, H. Der Stand der Menschenrechte im Völkerrecht. Göttingen, 1956.

GUZMÁN CARRASCO, M.A. *No intervención y protección internacional de los derechos humanos.* Quito (Ecuador) Editorial Universitaria, 1963, 414 p.

HAKKIK, Mohammad al-. "Some aspects of democracy in Islamic community life", *Islamic Literature*, Vol. XVI, No. 2, 1970, pp. 49-57, Vol. XVI, No. 3, 1970, pp. 39-48.

HAKSAR, Urmila. *Minority protection and international bill of human rights.* Bombay, Allied Publishers, 1974, 181 p.

HALÁSZ, Jójsef. *Socialist Concept of Human Rights.* Budapest, Akadémiai Kiadó, 1966, 309 p.

HAMBURGER, Ernest. "Droits de l'homme et relations internationales", *Recueil des cours* (Hague Academy of International Law), No. 97, 1959, pp. 293-429.

HANEY, G. "Man's Right to Humanity", *GDR Committee for Human Rights Bulletin No.1/1981* (Berlin), pp. 3-10.

HANNIKAINEN, L., Human Rights and Non-Intervention in the Final Act of the CSCE", *GDR Committee for Human Rights Bulletin No.1/1980* (Berlin), pp. 50-63.

HARTMAN, Joan F. "Derogation from Human Rights Treaties in Public Emergencies", *Harvard International Law Journal*, Vol. 22, 1981, pp. 1-52.

HARTUNG, Fritz. Die Entwicklung der Menschen- und Bürgerrechte von 1776 bis zur Gegenwart. 3 erw. Aufl. Göttingen, Musterschmidt, 1964, 184 p., bibliography.

HENKIN, Alice (Ed.). *Human Dignity: The Internationalization of Human Rights*. New York, Aspen Institute/Oceana/Sijthoff and Noordhoff, 1979, 203 p.

HENKIN, Louis. *The Rights of Man Today*. Boulder, Colo., Westview Press, 1978, 173 p.

HERCZDGH, G. "Problems of international humanitarian law requiring a solution", (In Hungarian). *Allam-es Jogtudomàny* (Budapest), Vol. 19, p. 239.

HIGGINS, Rosalyn. "Derogations under Human Rights Treaties", *British Yearbook of International Law 1976-1977* (London), pp. 281-320.

HIRSZOWICZ, Maria. "The Marxist approach to human rights", *International Social Science Journal.* (Paris, Unesco), Vol. XVIII, No. 1, 1966, pp. 13-24.

HOLCOMBE, Arthur N. *Human Rights in the Modern World*. New York, New York University Press, 1948, 162 p.

HOSKEN, Fran. "Women's Human Rights: Towards a Definition", *Human Rights Quarterly*, Vol. 3, No. 2, 1981, pp. 1-10.

HÜBNER, Gallo, and JORGE, Iván. *Panorama de los derechos humanos*. Santiago de Chile, Andrés Bello, 1973, 268 p., bibliography.

"Humanitarian Law and the Protection of Man". Special issue of *Annals of International Studies* (Geneva), Vol. 8, 1977, 171 p.

Human rights in perspective. Papers presented at the Round-table Meeting on Human Rights, held at Oxford, United Kingdom, from 11 to 19 November 1965. *International Social Science Journal* (Paris, Unesco), Vol. XVIII, No. 1, 1966, pp. 7-96.

Human Rights: Protection of the Individual under International Law. South Hackensack, N.J., Rothman, 1970, 286 p.

HUMPHREY, John. "The International Law of Human Rights in the Middle Twentieth Century", in *The Present State of International Law and Other Essays*, Maarten Bos (Ed.), (Deventer, Kluwer, 1973), pp. 75-105.

IMBERT, P-H. "Reservations and Human Rights Conventions", *The Human Rights Review* (London), Vol. 6, No. 1, 1981, pp. 28-60.

IMRAN, Muhammad. "Social justice in Islam", *Islamic Literature*, Vol. XIII, No. 7, 1967, pp. 5-16.

INSTITUT D'ETUDES POLITIQUES D'AIX. INSTITUTO DE CULTURA HISPANICA. *Las Casas et la politique des droits de l'homme*. Publié avec le concours du Centre national de la recherche scientifique. Aix-en-Provence, 1974, 373 p.

JAKOVLJEVIC, Bosko. *New International Status of Civil Defence: As An In-*

strument for Strengthening the Protection of Human Rights. The Hague, Martinus Nijhoff, 1981, 146 p.

JENKS, Clarence Wilfred. *The common law of mankind*. London, Stevens, 1956, 456 p. (The Library of World Affairs, No. 41).

JOBLIN, Joseph. "Solidarity, Human Rights and Basic Needs", *Labour and Society* (Geneva), Vol. 4, No. 4, 1979, pp. 355-71.

———. "Role of Human, Economic and Social Rights in the Advent of a New Society", *Labour and Society* (Geneva), Vol. 2, No. 4, 1977, pp. 349-76.

JOJIC, Branislava. *Covek v socijalismu. Ustavne koncepcije prava ooveka i njegove zastite v evropskim socijalisticskim zemljama* (Man in socialism. Basic concepts and protection of human rights in European socialist countries). Belgrade, Institut za medunarodni radnicki pokret, 1972, 149 p., bibliography.

JOYCE, James A. *The New Politics of Human Rights*. New York, St. Martin's Press, 1979, 305 p.

Jura hominis ac civis (Collection de l'Institut international des droits de l'homme), *René Cassin amicorum discipulorumque liber*. I: Problèmes de protection internationale des droits de l'homme (1969). II: Le difficile progrès du règne de la justice et de la paix internationales par le droit (1970). III: La protection internationale des droits de l'homme dans les rapports entre personnes privées (1971). IV: Méthodologie des droits de l'homme (1972).

JUVIGNY, Pierre. "La Déclaration universelle des droits de l'homme", *Revue de droit contemporain* (Paris), vol. 15, n° 1, 1968, pp. 7-167. Suite d'articles.

KADT, Emanuel de. "Some Basic Questions on Human Rights and Development", *World Development* (London), Vol. 8, 1980, pp. 97-105.

KALSHOVEN, Frits. "Reaffirmation and Development of International Humanitarian Law Applicable in Armed Conflicts: The Diplomatic Conference, Geneva, 1974-1977", *Netherlands Yearbook of International Law* (The Hague), Part I appears in Vol. 8, 1977, pp. 107-35 and Part II in Vol. 9, 1978, pp. 107-71.

KAMENKA, E., and TAY, A.E-S (Eds.). *Human Rights*. New York, St. Martin's Press, 1978, 148 p.

KARTASHKIN, V.A. *Mezhdunarodnaya zashchita prav cheloveka* (International protection of human rights). Mezhdunarodnye otnoshenija, Moscow, 1976. 222 p.

———. Uvazhenyije prav cheloveka i nevmeshatel'stvo vo vnutrenniye dela gosudastv (Respect for human rights and non-interference in domestic affairs of state). *Sovetskoye gosudarstvo i pravo* (Moscow), No. 6, 1974, pp. 35-41.

KEITH, K.J. (Ed.). *Essays on human rights*. N.Z., Sweet and Maxell, 1968. 199 p.

KHADDURI, Majid. "Human rights in Islam", *Annals of the American Academy of Political and Social Science* (Philadelphia), Vol. 243, 1946, pp. 77-81.

KHALAFFALA, Ahmad Mohammed. "The Islamic civilization's position toward human rights", (In Arabic.) *Egyptian review of international law* (Cairo), Vol. 12, 1956, pp. 1-27.

KHALIFA, Abdul-Hakim. *Fundamental Human Rights*. Lahore, Muhammad Ashrab, 1952.

KHOL, A. *Zwischen Staat und Welstaat. Die internationalen Sicherungsverfahren zum Schutze der Menschenrechte.* Vienna, Stuttgart, Braumüller, 1969, 628 p.

KHUSHALANI, Yougindra. *The Dignity and Honour of Woman as Basic and Fundamental Human Rights.* The Hague, Martinus Nijhoff, 1982, 280 p.

Kihonteki jinken (Fundamental Human Rights). Prepared by Shakaikagaku kenkyujo (Institute of Social Science). Tokyo University, Tokyo University Press, 1969/1970, 5 vol.

KIN, Tokun. *Jinkin: Jiketsuken to Gendai Kokusaiho* (Human Rights: The Right of Self-determination and Modern International Law). Tokyo, Sinyudo Press, 1979, 365 p.

KISS, Alexandre C. "La protection internationale du droit de l'enfant à l'éducation", *Revue des droits de l'homme/Human rights journal* (Paris), vol. VI, n° 3-4, 1973, pp. 467-487.

———, and DOMINICK, Mary. "The International Legal Significance of the Human Rights' Provisions of the Helsinki Final Act", *Vanderbilt Journal of Transnational Law*, Vol. 13, 1980, pp. 293-315.

KLAYMAN, J. "Definition of Torture in International Law", *Temple Law Quarterly*, Vol. 51, 1978, pp. 449-517.

KLENNER, H. "Human Rights under Materialistic Scrutiny", *GDR Committee for Human Rights, Bulletin No. 4/1978* (Berlin), pp. 3-25.

———. "Human Rights, Peaceful Coexistence and International Law in the Present Period", *GDR Committee for Human Rights, Bulletin No. 2/1979* (Berlin), pp. 16-37.

———. *Studien über die Grundrechte mit Dokumentanhang.* Berlin, Staatsverlag der D.D.R., 1964, 277 p., bibliography.

KOREY, T.W. "The key to human rights: implementation", *International Conciliation*, New York, November 1968, pp. 1-70.

KORSHUNOVA, E.N. *Diskriminatsija grazhdan v kapitalisticheskikh stranakh* (Discrimination against citizens in capitalist countries). Moscow, Jurid. Lit., 1973, 214 p., bibliography.

KOTB, Sayed. Al-'adâlah al-ijtimâ'yya fi-I-Islâm (Social justice in Islam). Maktabat Hisr., Cairo, 1945. Translated by John B. Hardie and published by the American Council of Learned Societies, Washington, D.C., 1953.

KOTHARI, Rajni, "Human Rights as a North-South Issue", *Bulletin of Peace Proposals* (Oslo), Vol. 11, No. 4, 1980, pp. 331-38.

KOZIEBRODSKI, Léopold Bolesta. *Le droit d'asile.* Leyden, Sijthoff, 1962, 374 p.

KRAMERS, J.H. "L'Islam et la démocratie", *Analecta Orientalia*, Leyden, 1956, pp. 168-83 (published for the first time in *Orientalia Neerlandica*, Leyden, 1948, pp. 223-39).

KUBOTA, Yo. "Kanshuhotekitenkai wo miru Kokusai Jinken Hosho" (The Development of International Protection of Human Rights under Customary Law). *The Review of Legal and Political Sciences* (Osaka), No. 17, 1981, pp. 102-15 with a summary in English, pp. 9-10.

KUTNER, L. (Ed.). *The human right to individual freedom: a symposium on world habeas corpus.* Coral Gables, Fla., University of Miami Press, 1970, 249 p.

LA CHAPELLE, Philippe de. *La déclaration universelle des droits de l'homme et le catholicisme.* Paris, Librairie générale de droit et de jurisprudence, 1967, 490 p.

LADOR-LEDERER, J. Josef. *International group protection: aims and methods in human rights.* Leyden, Sijthoff, 1968, 481 p., bibliography.

―――. "The role of treaty law in the protection of human rights", *Israel Yearbook on Human Rights* (Tel Aviv), Vol. 2, 1972, pp. 11-38.

LAUREN, P.G. "Human Rights in History", *Diplomatic History*, Vol. 2, 1978, pp. 257-78.

LAUTERPACHT, Eli, and COLLIER, J. (Eds.). *Individual Rights and the State in Foreign Affairs.* New York, Praeger, 1977, 762 p.

LAUTERPACHT, Hersch. *An international bill of the rights of man.* New York, 1945, 230 p.

―――. *International law and human rights.* New York, Praeger, 1950. 475 p.

―――. "The international protection of human rights", *Recueil des cours* (Hague Academy of International Law), Vol. 70, 1947, pp. 1-108.

LEE, Luke. "Law, Human Rights and Population: A Strategy for Action", *Virginia Journal of International Law*, Vol. 12, 1972, pp. 309-25.

LEVIE, Howard S. *Protection of War Victims: Protocol 1 to the 1949 Geneva Conventions*, 4 Vol., Dobbs Ferry, N.Y., Oceana, 1979-1981.

LILLICH, Richard. "Duties of States regarding the Civil Rights of Aliens", *Recueil des cours*, Hague Academy of International Law, 1978, Vol. 161, No. III, pp. 329-443.

―――, and NEWMAN, F.C. *International Human Rights: Problems of Law and Policy.* Boston and Toronto, Little, Brown and Company, 1979, 1030 p.

LIPPMAN, Matthew. "The Protection of Universal Human Rights: The Problem of Torture", *Universal Human Rights* (New York), Vol. 1, No. 4, 1979, pp. 25-56.

LITRENTO, Oliveiros Lessa. *O problema internacional dos direitos humanos.* Rio de Janeiro, Editôra Rio, 1973, 149 p., bibliography.

LUARD, David Evan Trent (Ed.). *The international protection of human rights.* New York, Praeger, 1967, 384 p.

LUINI DEL RUSSO, Alessandra. *International protection of human rights.* Washington, D.C., Lerner Law Books Co., 1971, 361 p., bibliography.

―――. "Prisoners' Right of Access to the Court: A Comparative Analysis of Human Rights Jurisprudence in Europe and the United States", *Journal of International Law and Economics*, Vol. 13, No. 1, 1978, pp. 1-39.

MACDONALD, R.; JOHNSTON, D.; and MORRIS, G. *The International Law and Policy of Human Welfare.* Alphen aan den Rijn, Sijthoff and Noordhoff, 1978, 690 p.

MADIOT, Yves. *Droits de l'homme et libertés publiques.* Paris, Masson, 1976, 298 p.

MAKI, Linda. "General Principles of Human Rights Law Recognized by All Nations; Freedom from Arbitrary Arrest and Detention", *California Western International Law Journal*, Vol. 10, 1980, pp. 272-313.

MANI, V.S. "Regional Approaches to the Implementation of Human Rights", *Indian Journal of International Law*, Vol. 21, 1981, pp. 96-118.

MARIE, Jean-Bernard. *Glossaire des droits de l'homme: termes fondamentaux dans les instruments universels et regionaux/Glossary of Human Rights: Basic Terms in Universal and Regional Instruments*. Paris, Editions de la maison des sciences de l'homme, 1981, 339 p.

———. "Les pactes internationaux relatifs aux droits de l'homme confirment-ils l'inspiration de la Déclaration universelle?", *Revue des droits de l'homme/Human rights journal* (Paris), vol. III, n° 3, 1970, pp. 397-423.

MARITAIN, Jacques. *Les droits de l'homme et la loi naturelle*. Paris, Hartmann, 1947.

———. *The rights of man and natural law*. New York, Scribner's, 1943, 119 p.

MARKS, Stephen P. "La Commission permanente arabe des droits de l'homme", *Revue des droits de l'homme/Human rights journal* (Paris), Vol. III, No. 1, 1970, pp. 101-8.

———. "Development and human rights: Some reflections on the study of development, human rights and peace", *Bulletin of Peace Proposals* (Oslo), Vol. 8, No. 3, 1977, pp. 236-46.

———. "Emerging Human Rights: A New Generation for the 1980's", *Rutgers Law Review*, Vol. 33, 1981, pp. 435-52.

———. "La notion de période l'exception en matière des droits de l'homme", *Revue des droits de l'homme/Human rights journal* (Paris), Vol. VIII, No. 4, 1975, pp. 821-58.

———. "The Peace/Human Rights/Development Dialectic", *Bulletin of Peace Proposals* (Oslo), Vol. 11, No. 4, 1980, pp. 339-48.

MARMORSTEIN, Victoria. "World Bank Power to Consider Human Rights Factors in Loan Decisions", *The Journal of International Law and Economics*, Vol. 13, 1978, pp. 113-36.

MASSIGNON, Louis. "Le respect de la personne humaine en Islam et la priorité du droit d'asile sur le devoir de juste guerre", *Revue internationale de la Croix-Rouge* (Geneva), No. 402, June 1952. Reproduced in *Opera Minora*, Vol. III, pp. 537-53.

MAUDOODI, Sayed Abdul Ala. "Islam and social justice", *Islamic Thought* (Rampur, India), Vol. X, No. 3-4, 1965, pp. 1-17.

M'BAYE, Keba. "Le droit au développement comme un droit de l'homme", *Revue des droits de l'homme/Human rights journal* (Paris), Vol. V, No. 2-3, 1972, pp. 503-34.

———. "Les réalités du monde noir et les droits de l'homme", *Revue des droits de l'homme/Human rights journal* (Paris), Vol. III, No. 3, 1969, pp. 382-94.

McCAMANT, John. "Social Science and Human Rights", *International Organization*, Vol. 35, No. 3, 1981, pp. 531-52.

McCARTHY, Thomas E. "The international protection of human rights—ritual and reality", *The International and Comparative Law Quarterly* (London), Vol. 25, April 1976, p. 261.

———. "Transnational Corporations and Human Rights", in Cassese (Ed.), *UN Law/Fundamental Rights: Two Topics in International Law*, Alphen aan den Rijn, Sijthoff and Noordhoff, 1979, pp. 175-96.

McCHESNEY, Alan. " 'Promoting the General Welfare in a Democratic Society': Balancing Human Rights and Development", *Netherlands International Law Review*, Vol. 27, 1980, pp. 283-334.

McDOUGAL, M.; LASSWELL, H.; and CHEN, L. "Human Rights and World Public Order: Human Rights in Comprehensive Context", *Northwestern University Law Review*, Vol. 72, 1977, pp. 227-307.

———. *Human Rights and World Public Order. The Basic Policies of an International Law of Human Dignity*. New Haven and London, Yale University Press, 1980, 1015 p.

———. "Human rights for women and world public order: the outlawing of sex-based discrimination", *American Journal of International Law* (Washington, D.C.), Vol. 69, 1975, p. 497.

———. "The protection of aliens from discrimination and world public order: responsibility of states conjoined with human rights", *American Journal of International Law* (Washington, D.C.), Vol. 10, July 1976, p. 432.

———. "The right to religious freedom and world public order; the emerging norm of nondiscrimination", *Michigan Law Review* (Ann Arbor, Mich.), Vol. 74, April 1976, p. 856.

MERON, THEODOR. "A Report on the N.Y.U. Conference on Teaching International Protection of Human Rights", *New York University Journal of International Law and Politics*, Vol. 13, 1981, pp. 881-957.

MERTENS, Pierre. *Le droit de recours effectif devant les instances nationales en cas de violation d'un droit de l'homme*. Brussels, Editions de l'Université de Bruxelles, 1973, 151 p.

———. "Les droits de *quel* homme?" *Synthèses* (Paris-Brussels), No. 273-274, March-April 1969, pp. 17-27.

———. *L'imprescriptibilité des crimes de guerre et centre l'humanité*. Brussels, Editions de l'Université de Bruxelles, 1974, 230 p. (Etudes de droit international et de droit pénal comparé, n° 6).

MESTDAGH, Karel de Vey. "The Right to Development", *Netherlands International Law Review*, Vol. 28, No. 1, 1981, pp. 30-53; and in *Development, Human Rights and the Rule of Law, op. cit.*, pp. 143-74.

MICHALSKA, Anna. "Uniwersalizm i regionalizm w miedzynarodowej ochronie praw czlowieka" (Universalism and regionalism in the international protection of human rights). *Ruch Prawniczy Ekonomiczny i Sociologiczny* (Poznan, Poland), Vol. 36, No. 2, 1974, p. 27.

MIRKINE-GUETZEVITCH, Boris. "Quelques problèmes de la mise en oeuvre de la Déclaration universelle des droits de l'homme", *Recueil des cours* (Hague Academy of International Law), 1954, pp. 255-375.

MODINOS, Polys. "Les droits de l'homme dans les écrits de Polys Modinos. Vingt-cinquième anniversaire de la Convention européenne des droits de l'homme", *Revue des droits de l'homme/Human rights journal* (Paris), Vol. VIII, Special issue, 1975.

MONROY CABRA, Marco Gerardo. *Los derechos humanos*. Temis Librería, Bogotá, Colombia, 1980, 371 p.

MONTEALEGRE, Hernan. *La seguridad del estado y derechos humanos*. Santiago, Chile, Academia de Humanismo Cristiano, 1979, 800 p.

MOREILLON, Jacques. *Le Comité international de la Croix-Rouge et la protection des détenus politiques*. Lausanne, Institut Henry-Dunant, Editions l'Age d'homme, 1973, 295 p.

MORSE, Bradford. "Practice, Norms and Reform of International Humanitarian

Rescue Operations", *Recueil des cours*, Hague Academy of International Law, Vol. 157, No. IV, 1977, pp. 121-94.

MOSKOWITZ, Moses. *Human rights and world order; The struggle for human rights in the United Nations*. Dobbs Ferry, N.Y., Oceana, 1958, 239 p.

———. *International concern with human rights*. Leyden, Sijthoff, 1974, 239 p.

———. *The politics and dynamics of human rights*. Dobbs Ferry, N.Y., Oceana, 1968, 283 p.

MOVCHAN, Anatolij P. *Mezhdunarodnaya zashchita prav cheloveka* (International Protection of human rights). Moscow, Jur. Lit., 1958, 167 p.

MOZOKHINA, Aleksandra Gavrilovna. *Svoboda lichnosti i osovnye prava grazhdan v sotsialisticheskikh stranakh Evropy* (Personal freedom and fundamental rights of citizens in the socialist countries of Europe). Moscow, Nauka, 1965, 294 p., bibliography.

MURPHY, J. "Objections to Western Conceptions of Human Rights", *Hofstra Law Review*, Vol. 9, 1981, pp. 433-74.

MUSHKAT. "The Development of International Humanitarian Law and the Law of Human Rights", *German Yearbook of International Law* (Berlin), Vol. 21, 1978, pp. 150-68.

NANDA, V.; and BASSIOUNI, C. "Slavery and Slave Trade: Steps towards its Eradication", *Santa Clara Law Review*, Vol. 12, 1972, pp. 424-42.

NAWAS, M.K. "The concept of human rights in Islamic law", *Howard Law Journal* (Washington, D.C.), Vol. 11, 1965, pp. 325-32.

———. "The Ratification of or Accession to Human Rights Conventions", *Indian Journal of International Law*, Vol. 13, 1973, pp. 576-88.

NDIAYE, B. "De l'individu et de sa collaboration avec les organismes internationaux de protection des droits de l'homme", *1974 Annales africaines* (Dakar), 1975, p. 25.

NEWMAN, Frank C. "Natural justice, due process and the new international covenants on human rights", *Public Law* (London), Winter 1967.

NICKEL, James W., "Is There a Human Right to Employment?", *The Philosophical Forum*, Vol. X, No. 2-4, 1979, pp. 149-70.

NOTRE DAME, Ind. University. Law School. Center for Civil Rights. *International human rights: a bibliography 1965-1969*. William Miller (Ed.). Notre Dame, The Law School, 1976, 125 p.

———. Center for Civil Rights. *International human rights: a bibliography 1970-1976*. William Miller (Dir. Publ.). Notre Dame, The Law School, 1976, 118 p.

NWABUEZE, B.O. *Constitutionalism in the emergent states*. C. Hurst and Co. (publishers) Ltd. in association with Nwamife Publishers Ltd., 1973, 316 p.

O'DONNELL, Daniel. "States of Exception", *Review of the International Commission of Jurists* (Geneva), No. 21, 1978, pp. 52-60.

O'GRADY, Ron. *Bread and Freedom: Understanding and Acting on Human Rights*. Geneva, World Council of Churches, 1979, 81 p.

OKOLIE, C.C. *International Law Perspectives of the Developing Countries. The Relationship of Law and Economic Development to Basic Human Rights*. New York, London, Lagos, NOK Publishers, 1978, 369 p.

O'MAHONY, Patrick J. *Multinationals and Human Rights*. Essex, Mayhew-McCrimmon, 1980, 318 p.

OPSAHL, Torkel. "Human Rights Today: International Obligations and National Implementation", *Scandinavian Studies in Law* (Copenhagen), 1979, pp. 151-76.

OSTROROG, Comte Léon. "Les droits de l'homme et l'Islam" (communication à l'Académie diplomatique internationale). *Revue de droit international* (Paris), 1930, p. 100 *et seq.*

OWEN, David. *Human Rights*. London, Cape, 1978.

PAUL, James. "Law, Socialism and the Human Right to Development in Third World Countries", *Review of Socialist Law*, Vol. 7, No. 3, 1981, pp. 235-42.

PÁSARA, Luis. "Human Rights and Development: A Difficult Relationship", in *Development, Human Rights and the Rule of Law, op. cit.,* pp. 181-86.

PECES-BARBA, G. *Derechos fundamentales. I. Teoría general.* Madrid, Biblioteca universitaria guardiana, 1973, 349 p.

PETERFI, W. "The Missing Human Rights: The Right to Peace", *Peace Research*, Vol. 11, 1979, pp. 19-25.

POLLIS, A., and SCHWAB, P. (Eds.).*Human Rights: Cultural and Ideological Perspectives*. New York, Praeger, 1979, 165 p.

POPESCU, Tudor R. "The significance of the Universal Declaration of Human Rights, Two decades after its adoption", *Revue roumaine d'études internationales* (Bucarest), No. 3-4, 1968, pp. 111-24.

POPPE, E. "The Right to Education—Reality for All in a Socialist Society", *GDR Committee for Human Rights, Bulletin No. 1/1979* (Berlin), pp. 9-21.

PRONK, Jan. "Human Rights and Development Aid", International Commission of Jurists, *The Review* (Geneva), No. 18, 1977, pp. 33-39.

PRZETACZNIK, Franciszek. "L'attitude des Etats socialistes à l'égard de la protection internationale des droits de l'homme", *Revue des droits de l'homme/Human rights journal* (Paris), vol. VIII, n° 1, 1974, pp. 175-206.

RAAFAT, W. "International Law and Human Rights", *Revue Egyptienne de Droit International* (Cairo), Vol. 33, 1977, pp. 13-66 (Text in Arabic).

RABBATH, E. "Le théorie des droits de l'homme dans le droit musulman", *Revue internationale de droit comparé* (Paris), Vol. 4, 1959, pp. 1-22.

RAMCHARAN, B.G. *Human Rights: Thirty Years after the Universal Declaration*. The Hague, Nijhoff, 1979, 274 p.

——. "Standard Setting: Future Perspectives", in Ramcharan (Ed.), *Human Rights, op. cit.*

——. "The Role of Regional, National and Local Institutions: Future Perspectives", in Ramcharan (Ed.), *Human Rights, op. cit.*

——. "Implementing the International Covenants on Human Rights", in Ramcharan (Ed.). *Human Rights, op. cit.*

——. "Equity in the International Law of Human Rights", *Dalhousie Law Journal*, Vol. 5, 1979, pp. 45-72.

RAMELLA, Pablo A. *Los derechos humanos*. Buenos Aires, Ediciones Depalma, 1980, 340 p.

RAMPHAL, Shridath. "Development and the Rule of Law", in *Development, Human Rights and the Rule of Law, op. cit.*, pp. 9-24.

REARDON, Betty A. "Human rights and educational reform", *Bulletin of Peace Proposals* (Oslo), Vol. 8, No. 9, 1977, pp. 247-50.

RECHETOV, Youri. "Responsibility for Violations of Human Rights", *Revue des droits de l'homme/Human rights journal* (Paris), Vol. 12, 1969, pp. 83-94.

The Recommendations from the Arusha Conference on the African Refugee Problem. Uppsala, Scandinavian Institute of African Studies, 1981 45 p.

REYNOLDS, Paul Davidson. "On the protection of human subjects and social sciences", *International Social Science Journal* (Paris, Unesco), Vol. XXIV, No. 4, 1972, pp. 739-69.

RIVERO, Jean. "Les droits de l'homme, catégorie juridique?", *Perspectivas del Derecho Público* (Madrid), Vol. 3, 1969, p. 21 *et seq.*

ROBERTSON, A.H. *Human rights in Europe.* 2nd edition. Manchester University Press, 1977, 392 p.

———. *Human rights in the world.* Manchester University Press, 1972, 280 p.

———. *Human Rights in National and International Law,* Dobbs Ferry, N.Y., Oceana, 1968, 412 p.

RODLEY, N.S. "Monitoring Human Rights by the UN System and Non-Governmental Organizations", in D. Dommers and G. Loescher (Eds.), *Human Rights and American Foreign Policy,* Notre Dame, London, University of Notre Dame Press, 1979, pp. 157-78.

RÖLING, B.V.A. "Human rights and the war problem", *Netherlands international law review* (Leyden), Vol. 15, 1968, p. 346.

RONEN, Dov. *The Quest for Self-Determination.* New Haven, Yale University Press, 1979, 144 p.

ROSENBAUM, A. (Ed.). *The Philosophy of Human Rights: International Perspectives.* Westport, Ct., Greenwood Press, 1980, 288 p.

ROSENBLAD, Esbjörn, *International Humanitarian Law of Armed Conflict: Some Aspects of the Principle of Distinction and Related Problems.* Geneva, Henry-Dunant Institute, 1979, 200 p.

ROZO ACÚNA, Eduardo. *Travectoría de los derechos humanos.* Bogotá, Universidad externado de Colombia, 1973, 2 vol.

RUIZ-GIMÉNEZ, J. "Vatican II et les droits de l'homme", *Revue des droits de l'homme/Human rights journal* (Paris), vol. II, n° 1, 1969, pp. 41-94.

SAID, Abdul Aziz (Ed.). *Human Rights and World Order.* New Brunswick, N.J., Transaction Books, 1978, 170 p.

———. "Precept and Practice of Human Rights in Islam", *Universal Human Rights* (New York), Vol. 1, No. 1, 1979, pp. 63-79.

SALZBERG, John, and YOUNG, Donald D. "The parliamentary role in implementing international human rights: a U.S. example", *Texas International Law Journal* (Austin, Tex.), Vol. 12, No. 2-3, 1977, pp. 251-78.

SANCHEZ DE LA TORRE. *Teoríay experienciade los derechos humanos.* Madrid, 1968, 183 p.

SANDOZ, Yves. "La place des Protocoles Additionnels aux Conventions de Genève du 12 août 1949 dans le droit humanitaire", *Revue des droits de l'homme/Human rights journal* (Paris), Vol. XII, No. 1-2, 1979, pp. 135-62.

SCHERMERS, H.G. "Judicial Protection of International Rights", *German Yearbook of International Law,* Vol. 23, 1980, pp. 181-95.

SCHINDLER, Dietrich, and TOMAN, Jiri. *The Laws of Armed Conflicts,* 2nd ed., Alphen aan den Rijn, Sijthoff and Noordhoff, 1981, 900 p.

SCHREUER, Christoph. "The impact of international institutions on the protection of human rights in domestic courts," *Israel Yearbook on Human Rights* (Tel Aviv), Vol. 4, 1974, pp. 60-88.

SCHWEISFURTH, Theodor. "Operations to Rescue Nationals in Third States Involving the Use of Force in relation to Protection of Human Rights", *German Yearbook of International Law*, Vol. 23, 1980, pp. 159-80.

SCHWELB, Egon. "Civil and political rights: The international measures of implementation", *American Journal of International Law* (Washington, D.C.), Vol. 62, pp. 827-68.

———. *Human rights and the international community. The roots and growth of the Universal Declaration of Human Rights, 1948-1963.* Chicago, 1964, 96 p.

———. "Human Rights and the Teaching of International Law", *American Journal of International Law*, Vol. 64, 1970, pp. 355-64.

———. *The influence of the Universal Declaration of Human Rights on international and national law.* New York, 1959.

———. "International conventions on human rights", *International Comparative Law Quarterly* (London), Vol. 9, October 1960, pp. 654-75.

———. "The law of treaties and human rights", in *Toward World Order and Human Dignity*, pp. 262-90. New York, The Free Press, 1976.

Seminario internacional sobre los derechos del hombre, Universidad Nacional Autonoma de México, 1968. *Veinte años de evolución de los derechos humanos: seminario internacional patrocinado por la Secretaría de Relaciones Exteriores de México y la Comisión Interamericana de Derechos Humanos.* 1 ed. México, UNAM, Instituto de Investigaciones Jurídicas, 1974, 603 p.

SHACHOR-LANDAU, C. "Protection of fundamental rights and sources of law in European Community jurisprudence", *Journal of World Trade Law* (Twickenham, Middlesex, U.K.), Vol. 10, May/June 1976, pp. 289-300.

SHELTON, Dinah. "Human rights within churches: a survey concerning discrimination within religious organizations", *Revue des droits de l'homme/Human rights journal* (Paris), Vol. VI, No. 3-4, 1973, pp. 487-563.

SHIMANE, Robert. *International Human Rights: A Selected Bibliography*, Los Angeles, University of Southern California Law Center, 1979, 81 p.

SINHA, S.P. *Asylum and international law.* The Hague, 1971, 366 p.

SKJELSBACK, Kjell. "Human rights and peace research", *Bulletin of Peace Proposals* (Oslo), Vol. 8, No. 3, 1977, pp. 195-97.

SOHN, Louis, and BUERGENTHAL, Thomas. *International protection of human rights.* Indianápolis, Ind., Bobbs-Merrill, 1973, 1,402 p. (republished in two bound volumes: 1. *The United Nations as protector of human rights*; 2. *Regional conventions on protection of human rights*).

SPERDUTI, G. "L'individu et le droit international", *Recueil des cours* (Hague Academy of International Law), Vol. II, 1956, pp. 729-839.

Spezialbibliographie über die in der Deutschen Demokratischen Republik zu Problemen der Menschenrechte und der verfassungsmässigen Grundrechte erschienene Literatur (Auswahl), Zeitraum 1945-1975. GDR Academy of Science for State and Law, Potsdam, 1975, 196 p.

SRNSKÁ, M. Socialistické mezinárodneprávni principy a normy a ochrana lidskych práv (Socialist principles and norms of international law and protection of human rights). *Pravnik* (Ljubljana, Yugoslavia), Vol. 115, 1976, pp. 94-106.

————. "Comparisons Between Universal and Regional Human Rights Conventions", *GDR Committee for Human Rights Bulletin No. 1/1980* (Berlin), pp. 40-49.

STONE, Julius. *Human Law and Human Justice.* Stanford, Calif., Stanford University Press, 1965, 415 p., bibliography.

STREETEN, Paul. "Basic Needs and Human Rights", *World Development*, Vol. 8, 1980, pp. 107-11.

SUZUKI, Eisuke, "A State's Provisional Competence to Protect Human Rights in a Foreign State", *Texas International Law Journal*, Vol. 15, 1980, pp. 231-60.

SWARUP, Jagadish. *Human rights and fundamental freedoms.* Bombay, Tripathi, 1975, 408 p., bibliography.

Symposium on human rights in health, London, 1973. Human rights in health, Amsterdam, Associated Scientific Publishers, 1974, 304 p. (CIBA Foundation Symposium 23, New Series).

Symposium on the Future of Human Rights in the World Legal Order, *Hofstra Law Review*, Vol. 9, 1981, pp. 337-592.

Symposium on the international law of human rights. Howard University, Washington, D.C., 1965. *Howard Law Journal* (Washington, D.C.), Vol. 2, No. 2, 1965.

SZABO, Imre. La portée juridique de la Déclaration universelle. *Revue de droit contemporain* (Brussels), nᵒ 1, 1968, p. 39, *et seq.*

————. "Remarques sur le développement du catalogue international des droits de l'homme", *René Cassin amicorum discipulorumque liber I*, Paris, 1969, pp. 347-61.

————. *Cultural rights.* Budapest, Akademiai Kiado, 1974, 116 p.

————. *Socialist concept of human rights, in fundamental questions concerning the theory and history of citizens.* Budapest, 1966.

TAKANO, Yuichi. *Kokusaishakai ni okeru Jinken* (Human Rights in International Society). Tokyo, Iwanami Press, 1977, 405 p.

TARDU, Maxime. "Coexistence des procédures universelles et régionales de plaintes individuelles dans le domaine des droits de l'homme", *Revue des droits de l'homme/Human rights journal* (Paris), vol. IV, nᵒ 2-3, 1971, pp. 614-20.

————. *Human Rights: The International Petition System, A Repertoire of Practice.* Dobbs Ferry, N.Y., Oceana, 1980-82, 3 vol.

THAMBYAHPILLAI, G. "The Right to Individual Property and the Problems of Agrarian Reform", *International Social Science Journal* (Paris, Unesco), Vol. XVIII, 1966, No. 1, p. 77.

THAPAR, Romila. "The Hindu and Buddhist traditions", *International Social Science Journal* (Paris, Unesco), Vol. XVIII, No. 1, pp. 34-44.

THOMPSON, Kenneth W., *The Moral Imperatives of Human Rights: A World Survey.* Washington, D.C., University Press of America, 1980, 254 p.

TIRUCHELVAM, Neelan. "The Legal Needs of the Poor: Towards an Alternative Model of Group Advocacy", in *Development, Human Rights and the Rule of Law, op. cit.*, pp. 199-206.

TRIKAMDAS, P. "Asian court of human rights", in SINGHIVI, L.M. (Ed.), *Horizons of freedom*. Delhi, Institute of Constitutional and Parliamentary Studies, 1969, pp. 106-10.

TRIVEDI, R.N. "Human Rights, Right to Development and the New International Economic Order—Perspectives and Proposals", in *Development, Human Rights and the Rule of Law, op. cit.*, pp. 131-42.

TYAGI, Yogesh. "Third World Response to Human Rights", *Indian Journal of International Law*, Vol. 21, 1981, pp. 119-40.

VALLAT, F. (Ed.). *An introduction to the study of human rights*, based on a series of lectures delivered at King's College, London, in the Autumn of 1970, London, 1972, 127 p.

VALTICOS, Nicolas. "Universalité des droits de l'homme et diversité des conditions nationales", *René Cassin amicorum discipulorumque liber I*, Paris, 1969, pp. 383-403.

VAN DER VYVER, Johan David. *Die Beskerming van menseregte in Suid-Afrika*. Juta en kie. Beperk, 1975, 211 p.

———. *Seven lectures on human rights*. Wynberg, South Africa, Juta, 1976, 182 p.

VAN DYKE, Vernon, "The Cultural Rights of Peoples", *Universal Human Rights*. Vol. 2, No. 2, 1980, pp. 1-21.

———. *Human rights, the United States and world community*. New York, Oxford University Press, 1970, 292 p.

VASAK, Karel. "L'application des droits de l'homme et des libertés fondamentales par les juridictions nationales", in *Droit communautaire et droit national*, Bruges, 1965, pp. 335-50.

———. "Les conseils de presse", *Revue des droits de l'homme/Human rights journal* (Paris), vol. VII, n° 2-4, 1974, pp. 617-23.

———. "Les droits de l'homme et l'Afrique", *Revue belge de droit international* (Brussels), Vol. 3, 1967, pp. 459-78.

———. "Le droit international des droits de l'homme", *Recueil des cours* (Hague Academy of International Law), Vol. IV, 1974, pp. 335-415.

———. "Egoïsme et droits de l'homme: esquisse pour un procès", in *Mélanges Modinos*, Paris, 1968, pp. 356-68.

———. "The European Convention on human rights beyond the frontiers of Europe", *The International and Comparative Law Quarterly* (London), October 1963, pp. 1206-31.

———. "Les institutions nationales, régionales et universelles pour la promotion et la protection des droits de l'homme", *Revue des droits de l'homme/Human rights journal* (Paris), vol. I, n° 2, 1968, pp. 164-79.

———. "Les problèmes spécifiques de la mise en oeuvre des droits économiques et sociaux de l'homme", Université de Louvain, 1974, in *Vers une protection efficace des droits économiques et sociaux*, pp. 11-34.

———. "Was bedeutet die Aussago, ein Staatsvertrag sei "self-executing"?, Juritische Blätter (Vienna), No. 24, December 1961, pp. 621-23.

VELU, J. "Les effets directs des instruments internationaux en matière de droits de l'homme", *Revue belge de droit international* (Brussels) Vol. 15, 1980, pp. 293-316.

VERDOODT, Albert. *Naissance et signification de la Déclaration universelle des droits de l'homme*. Louvain-Paris, 1964.

————. *La protection des droits de l'homme dans les Etats plurilingues*. Brussels, Editions Labor, Paris, Fernand Nathan, 1973, 210 p.

VERWEY, Wil D., "The Establishment of a New International Economic Order and the Realisation of the Right to Development and Welfare: A Legal Survey", *Indian Journal of International Law*, Vol. 21, 1981, pp. 1-78.

VEUTHEY, Michel. *Guérilla et droit humanitaire*. Geneva, Institut Henry-Dunant, 1976, 432 p.

VIERDAG, E.W. *The concept of discrimination in international law. With special reference to human rights*. The Hague, Nijhoff, 1973, 176 p.

WALKER, Dorothy Jean. "Statelessness: Violation or Conduit for Violation of Human Rights", *Human Rights Quarterly*, Vol. 3, No. 1, 1981.

WALTER SANCHEZ G. (Ed.). *Derechos Humanos y Relaciones Internacionales*, Santiago de Chile, 1979, Instituto de Estudios Internacionales de la Universidad de Chile and Instituto Chileno de Estudios Humanisticos, 240 p.

WEIS, Paul. "Legal Aspects of the Convention of 25 July 1951 relating to the Status of Refugees", *British Yearbook of International Law*, Vol. 30, 1953, pp. 478-89.

————. "The International Protection of Refugees", *American Journal of International Law*, Vol. 48, 1954, pp. 193-201.

————. "The 1967 Protocol relating to the Status of Refugees and Some Questions of the Law of Treaties", *British Yearbook of International Law*, Vol. 44, 1967, pp. 39-70.

————. *Nationality and Statelessness in International Law*, 2nd ed., Alphen aan den Rijn, Sijthoff and Noordhoff, 1979, 337 p.

————. "Recent developments in the law of territorial asylum", *Revue des droits de l'homme/Human rights journal* (Paris), Vol. I, No. 3, 1968, pp. 378-96.

WIJNGAERT, Christine van Den. *The Political Offence Exception to Extradition*. Deventer, Kluwer, 1980, 263 p.

WIRSING, Robert (Ed.). *Protection of Ethnic Minorities*. New York, Pergamon, 1981, 375 p.

WISEBERG, Laurie, and SCOBLE, Harry. "Bibliography of Women's Human Rights Publications", *Human Rights Quarterly*, Vol. 3, No. 2, 1981.

World Population Control: Rights and Restrictions. Edited by the Staff of Columbia Human Rights Law Review. New York, Family Service Association of America, 1975.

YOUNG-ANAWATY, Amy. "Human Rights and the ACP-EEC Lomé II Convention: Business as Usual at the EEC", *New York University Journal of International Law and Politics*, Vol. 13, No. 1, 1980, pp. 63-100.

ZIRS, S. *Human Rights: Continuing the Discussion*. Moscow, Progress Publishers, 1980, 187 p.

ZORIN, V. "International Cooperation in the Sphere of Human Rights", *International Affairs* (Moscow), Vol. 9, 1979, pp. 57-63.

B. References Relating to International and Regional Organizations

1. United Nations

ABRAM, J. "The United Nations and Human Rights", *Foreign Affairs*, Vol. 47, 1969, pp. 361-74.

ALSTON, Philip. "The United Nations' Specialized Agencies and Implementation of the International Covenant on Economic, Social and Cultural Rights", *Columbia Journal of Transnational Law* (New York), Vol. 18, No. 1, 1979, pp. 79-118.

Asociacion Costarricense Pro-Naciones Unidas. *La Declaracion Universal de Derechos Humanos.* San José, Editorial Juricentro, 216 p.

BOSSUYT, Marc. "Le règlement intérieur du Comité des droits de l'hômme", *Révue belge de droit international* (Brussels), Vol. XIV, 1978-1979, pp. 104-56.

BOVEN, T.C. Van. "The United Nations and Human Rights: A Critical Appraisal", *Bulletin of Peace Proposals* (Oslo), Vol. 8, No. 3, 1977, pp. 198-208.

———. "The United Nations Commission on human rights and violations of human rights and fundamental freedoms", *Nederlands tijdschrift voor internationaal recht* (Leyden), Vol. 15, No. 4, 1968, pp. 374-93.

———. "United Nations Policies and Strategies: Global Perspectives?", in Ramcharan (Ed.), *Human Rights, op. cit.*

BRUCE, Margaret K. "Work of the UN relating to the status of women", *Revue des droits de l'homme/Human rights journal* (Paris), Vol. IV, No. 2-3, 1971, pp. 365-412.

BUERGENTHAL, Thomas. "Implementing the racial convention", *Texas International Law Journal* (Austin, Tex.), Vol. 12, No. 2-3, 1977, pp. 187-221.

———. "To Respect and to Ensure: State Obligations and Permissible Obligations", in Henkin (Ed.), *The International Bill of Rights, op. cit.*, pp. 72-91.

———. "United Nations and the development of rules relating to human rights", *American Society for International Law Proceedings* (Washington, D.C.), Vol. 59, 1965, p. 132.

CAPOTORTI, Francesco. "The international measures of implementation included in the Covenants on Human Rights", in EIDE and SHOU, *Proceedings of the Seventh Nobel Symposium (Oslo, September 25-27, 1967)*, Stockholm, 1968, pp. 132-48.

———. "I diritti dei membri di minoranze: verso una dichiarazione delle Nazioni Unite", *Rivista di diritto internazionale* (Rome), Vol. 64, 1981, pp. 30-42.

CAREY, John. "United Nations Response to Government Oppression", *International Lawyer*, Vol. 3, 1968, pp. 102-8.

———. "United Nations scrutiny of South African prisons", *Revue des droits de l'homme/Human rights journal* (Paris), Vol. I, No. 4, 1968, pp. 531-43.

———. *UN protection of civil and political rights.* New York, 1970, 205 p.

CASSESE, Antonio. "The admissibility of communications to the UN on human rights violations", *Revue des droits de l'homme/Human rights journal* (Paris), Vol. V, No. 2-3, 1972, pp. 375-97.

———. "Il sistema di garanzia della Convenzione dell'ONU sull'eliminazione di ogni forma di discriminazione razziale", *Rivista di diritto internazionale* (Milan), 1967, pp. 270-336.

———. "The Self-Determination of Peoples", in Henkin (Ed., *The International Bill of Rights, op. cit.*, pp. 92-113.

———. (Ed.). *UN Law/Fundamental Rights: Two Topics in International Law*, Alphen aan den Rijn, Sijthoff and Noordhoff, 1979, 258 p.

CASSIN, René. "La Commission des droits de l'homme d l'ONU, 1947-1971",
    Miscellanea W.J. Ganshof van der Meersch, Vol. I, 1972, pp. 397-433.
CHAKRAVARTI, Raghubir. *Human Rights and the United Nations*. Calcutta,
    Progressive Publishers, 1958, 218 p.
CLARK, Roger S. *A United Nations High Commissioner for Human Rights*.
    The Hague, Nijhoff, 1972, 186 p.
———. "The United Nations and Religious Freedom", *New York University
    Journal of International Law and Politics*, Vol. 11, 1978, pp. 197-225.
COHEN, R. "International Covenant on Civil and Political Rights", *Interna-
    tional problems* (Tel Aviv), October 1968, pp. 38-49.
COLEMAN, Howard David. "The problem of anti-Semitism under the Interna-
    tional Convention on the Elimination of All Forms of Racial Discrimina-
    tion", *Revue des droits de l'homme/Human rights journal* (Paris), Vol. II,
    No. 4, 1969, pp. 609-31.
COMMISSION TO STUDY THE ORGANIZATION OF PEACE. *The United
    Nations and Human Rights*. Dobbs Ferry, N.Y., Oceana, 1968, 239 p.
DAS, Kamleshwar. "Measures of implementation of the International Convention
    on the Elimination of All Forms of Racial Discrimination with special ref-
    erence to the provisions concerning reports from States parties to the
    Convention", *Revue des droits de l'homme/Human rights journal* (Paris),
    Vol. IV, No. 2-3, 1971, pp. 213-62.
DECAUX, Emmanuel. "La mise en vigueur du Pacte international relatif aux
    droits civils et politiques", *Revue générale de droit international public*
    (Paris), Vol. 84, No. 2, 1980, pp. 487-534.
DECLEVA, M. "L'elezione del Comitato dei diritti dell'uomo" *Rivista di Diritto
    Internazionale* (Rome), Vol. 64, 1981, pp. 249-69.
DINSTEIN, Y. "The Right to Life, Physical Integrity and Liberty", in Henkin
    (Ed.), *The International Bill of Rights, op. cit.*, pp. 114-37.
DONNELLY, Jack. "Recent Trends in UN Human Rights Activity: Description
    and Polemic", *International Organization*, Vol. 35, 1981, pp. 633-55.
ELLES, D.L. "Aliens and activities of the UN in the field of human rights",
    Revue des droits de l'homme/Human rights journal (Paris), Vol. VII, No.
    2-4, 1974, pp. 291-320.
ERMACORA, F. "Human Rights and Domestic Jurisdiction: Art. 2, Sec. 7 of the
    United Nations Charter", *Recueil des cours* (Hague Academy of Interna-
    tional Law), Vol. 124, 1968, pp. 371-451.
GALEY, Margaret. "Promoting Nondiscrimination against Women: The UN Com-
    mission on the Status of Women", *International Studies Quarterly* (Bev-
    erly Hills Calif.), Vol. 23, 1979, pp. 273-302.
GONZALES, Theresa. "The Political Sources of Procedural Debates in the United
    Nations; Structural Impediments to Implementation of Human Rights",
    New York University Journal of International Law and Politics, Vol. 13,
    1981, pp. 427-72.
GRAEFRATH, Bernhard. *Die Vereinten Nationen und die Menschenrechte*.
    Berlin, Deutscher Zentralverlag, 1956, 171 p.
———. "Trends Emerging in the Practice of the Human Rights Committee",
    GDR Committee for Human Rights Bulletin No. 1/1980 (Berlin), pp.
    3-23.

GRAVEN, Jean. "Les crimes contre l'humanité sont imprescriptibles. Le signification et la portée de la décision de l'Assemblée générale des Nations Unies du 26 novembre 1968", *Revue des droits de l'homme/Human rights journal* (Paris), vol. II, n° 1, 1969, pp. 20-40.

GREEN, James Frederick. "Changing approaches to human rights; the United Nations, 1954 and 1974", *Texas International Law Journal* (Austin, Tex.), Vol. 12, No. 2-3, 1977, pp. 223-38.

GUGGENHEIM, Malvina H. "The implementation of human rights by the UN Commissioner on the status of women: a brief comment", *Texas International Law Journal* (Austin, Tex.), Vol. 12, No. 2-3, 1977, pp. 239-49.

———. "Key provisions of the new United Nations rules dealing with human rights petitions", *New York University Journal of International Law and Politics* (New York), Vol. 6, 1973, pp. 427-54.

GURADZE, Heinz. "Are human rights resolutions of the UN General Assembly law-making?", *Revue des droits de l'homme/Human rights journal* (Paris), Vol. IV, No. 2-3, 1971, pp. 453-62.

———. "Die Menschenrechtskonventionen der Vereinten Nationen vom 16 Dezember 1966", *German Yearbook of International Law*, Vol. 15, 1971, pp. 242-73.

HALDERMAN, J. "Advancing Human Rights through the United Nations", *Law and Contemporary Problems*, Vol. 43, 1979, pp. 275-88.

HANNUM, Hurst. "Thirty-third Session of the UN Sub-Commission on Prevention of Discrimination and Protection of Minorities", *Human Rights Quarterly*, Vol. 3, No. 1, 1981.

HENKIN, Louis (Ed.). *The International Bill of Rights: The Covenant of Civil and Political Rights*. New York, Columbia University Press, 1981, 523 p.

———. "The United Nations and Human Rights", *International Organization*, Vol. 19, 1965, pp. 504-17.

HEVENER, N.K., and MOSHER, S.A. "General Principles of Law and the UN Covenant on Civil and Political Rights", *International and Comparative Law Quarterly* (London), Vol. 27, No. 3, 1978, pp. 596-614.

HOLBORN, L.W. *Refugees, a problem of our time: the work of the United Nations High Commissioner for Refugees, 1951-1972*. Metuchen, N.J., Scarecrow Press, 1975, 2 vol.

HUMPHREY, John. "The right of petition in the United Nations", *Revue des droits de l'homme/Human rights journal* (Paris), Vol. IV, No. 2-3, 1971, pp. 463-75.

———. "The United Nations Commission on Human Rights and its parent body", *René Cassin amicorum discipulorumque liber I*, Paris, 1969, pp. 108-13.

———. "The United Nations Sub-Commission on the Prevention of Discrimination and the Protection of Minorities", *American Journal of International Law* (Washington, D.C.), Vol. 62, pp. 869-88.

———. "The Universal Declaration of Human Rights: Its History, Impact and Judicial Character", in Ramcharan (Ed.), *Human Rights, op. cit.*

International Committee of the Red Cross. *Annual Report*. Geneva, issued annually, *1980 Report* (Geneva), 1981, 110 p.

JAGERSKIOLD, Stig. "The Freedom of Movement", in Henkin (Ed.), *The International Bill of Rights, op. cit.*, pp. 166-84.

JENKS, C. Wilfred. "The United Nations Covenants on Human Rights come to life", in *Recueil d'études de droit international en hommage à Paul Guggenheim*, Geneva, 1968, pp. 765-73.

KISS, A.C. "Permissible Limitations on Rights", in Henkin (Ed.), *The International Bill of Rights, op. cit.*, pp. 290-310.

KRAMER, David, and WEISSBRODT, David. "The 1980 UN Commission on Human Rights and the Disappeared", *Human Rights Quarterly*, Vol. 3, No. 1, 1981.

KULIKOW, I.P., "Sub-Commission on Prevention of Discrimination and Protection of Minorities—Tasks and Results", *GDR Committee for Human Rights Bulletin No.1/1980* (Berlin), pp. 33-39.

LALIGNANT, M. "Le projet de convention des Nations Unies sur l'élimination de toutes les formes d'intolérance religieuse", *Revue belge de droit international* (Brussels), vol. 5, n° 1, 1969, pp. 175-206.

LANDERER, Lily E. "Capital punishment as a human rights issue before the UN", *Revue des droits de l'homme/Human rights journal* (Paris), Vol. IV, No. 2-3, 1971, pp. 511-34.

LERNER, Natan. "Anti-semitism as racial and religious discrimination under United Nations conventions", *Israel Yearbook on Human Rights* (Tel Aviv), Vol. I, 1971, pp. 103-15.

———. *The UN Convention on the Elimination of All Forms of Racial Discrimination*. The Hague, Martinus Nijhoff, 1980, 278 p.

LILLICH, R.B. (Ed.). *Humanitarian intervention and the United Nations*. Charlottesville, Va., University Press of Virginia, 1973, 240 p.

———. "The United Nations and human rights complaints," *American Journal of International Law* (Washington, D.C.), Vol. 64, July 1970, pp. 610-14.

———, and NEFF, S.C. "The Treatment of Aliens and International Human Rights Norms: Overlooked Developments at the U.N.", *German Yearbook of International Law* (Berlin, FRG), Vol. 21, 1978, pp. 97-118.

LIPPMAN, M. "Human Rights Revisited: The Protection of Human Rights under the International Covenant on Civil and Political Rights", *Netherlands International Law Review*, Vol. XXVI, 1979, No. 3, pp. 221-76.

MACCHESNEY, B. "International Protection of Human Rights in the United Nations", *Northwestern University Law Review*, Vol. 47, 1952, pp. 198-222.

MANSUY, Gérard. "Un médiateur des Nations Unies pour les droits de l'homme?", *Revue des droits de l'homme/Human rights journal* (Paris), vol. VI, n° 2, 1973, pp. 235-59.

MARIE, Jean-Bernard. *La Commission des droits de l'homme de l'ONU*. Paris, Pédone, 1975, 352 p.

———. "La Commission des droits de l'homme des Nations Unies à sa vingt-neuvième session", *Revue des droits de l'homme/Human rights journal* (Paris), vol. VI, n° 2, 1973, pp. 369-433.

———. "La pratique de la Commission des droits de l'homme de l'O.N.U. en matière de violation des droits de l'homme", *Revue belge de droit international* (Brussels), Vol. 15, 1980, pp. 355-80.

McDOUGAL, Myers S., and BEBR, Gerhard. "Human rights in the United Nations", *American Journal of International Law* (Washington, D.C.), Vol. 58, 1964, pp. 603-41.

MICHALSKA, Anna. "Podstawowe prawa czlowieka w systemie Organizacji Narodo Zjednoczonych", (The situation of human rights in the United Nations system). *Prawa i obowiazki obywatelskie w Polsce i swiecie* (Warsaw), 1974, pp. 394-435.

MILLER, Robert. "United Nations Fact-Finding Missions in the Field of Human Rights", *Australian Yearbook of International Law 1970-1973* (Melbourne), 1976, p. 40.

MIYAZAKI, Shigeki et al. *Kokusai Jinken Kiyaku* (The International Covenants on Human Rights). Hogaku Seminar (Tokyo), 1979, 287 p.

MÖLLER, Jakob. "Petitioning the United Nations", *Universal Human Rights* (New York), Vol. 1, No. 4, 1979, pp. 57-72.

MØSE, Erik, and OPSAHL, Torkel. "The Optional Protocol to the International Covenant on Civil and Political Rights", *Santa Clara Law Review* (Santa Clara), Vol. 21, 1981.

NEAL, M. The United Nations and human rights. *International conciliation* (New York), No. 489, 1953.

NEWMAN, Frank C. "Interpreting the human rights clauses of the UN Charter", *Revue des droits de l'homme/Human rights journal* (Paris), Vol. V, No. 2-3, 1972, pp. 283-91.

NJENGA, N. "The Role of the United Nations in the Matter of Racial Discrimination, *East African Law Review*, Vol. 1, 1968, pp. 136-57.

NOOR MUHAMMAD, Haji N. "Due Process of Law for Persons Accused of Crime", in Henkin (Ed.), *The International Bill of Rights, op. cit.*, pp. 138-65.

NOWAK, Manfred. "The Effectiveness of the International Covenant on Civil and Political Rights—Stocktaking after the First Eleven Sessions of the UN Human Rights Committee", *Human Rights Law Journal* (Kehl am Rhein), Vol. 1, 1980, pp. 136-70.

OSTROVSKIY, Y.A. *OON i prava cheloveka* (The United Nations and human rights). Moscow, Isdatelstvo mezhdunarodniye otnosheniya, 1968, 190 p.

PARTSCH, Karl Josef. "Elimination of Racial Discrimination in the Enjoyment of Civil and Political Rights. A Study of Article 5, subparagraphs (a)-(d) of the International Convention on the Elimination of All Forms of Racial Discrimination", *Texas International Law Journal*, Vol. 14, 1979, pp. 191-250.

———. "Freedom of Conscience and Expression, and Political Freedoms", in Henkin (Ed.), *The International Bill of Rights, op. cit.*, pp. 209-45.

PECHOTA, Vratislav. "The Development of the Covenant on Civil and Political Rights", in Henkin (Ed.), *The International Bill of Rights, op. cit.*, pp. 32-71.

PETRENKO, V. "The Human Rights Provisions of the United Nations Charter", *Manitoba Law Journal*, Vol. 9, 1978, pp. 53-92.

PREMONT, Daniel. United Nations Procedures for the Protection of All Persons Subjected to Any Form of Detention or Imprisonment", *Santa Clara Law Review* (Santa Clara), Vol. 20, 1980, pp. 603-32.

RAMCHARAN, B.G. "The Emerging Jurisprudence of the Human Rights Committee", *Dalhousie Law Journal*, Vol. 6, No. 1, 1980, pp. 7-40.

———. "Equality and Nondiscrimination", in Henkin (Ed.), *The International Bill of Rights, op. cit.*, pp. 246-69.

REANDA, Laura. "Human Rights and Women's Rights: The United Nations Approach", *Human Rights Quarterly*, Vol. 3, No. 2, 1981, pp. 11-31.

RESICH, Zbigniew. "La Commission des droits de l'homme des Nations Unies", *Revue de droit contemporain* (Brussels), n° 1, 1968, pp. 25-37.

———. Effectiveness of human rights defense in the UN Organization. (In Polish). *Nowe Prawo* (Warsaw), Vol. 30, March 1974, pp. 247-62.

RIGO, Sureda A. *The evolution of the right of self-determination. A study of UN practice.* Leyden, Sijthoff, 1973, 397 p.

ROBERTSON, A.H. "The Implementation System: International Measures", in Henkin (Ed.), *The International Bill of Rights, op. cit.*, pp. 332-70.

ROBINSON, N. *The Genocide Convention: A Commentary.* New York, Institute of Jewish Affairs, 1960, 158 p.

———. *The Universal Declaration of Human Rights: Its Origin, Significance, Application and Interpretation.* New York, Institute of Jewish Affairs, 1958, 173 p.

SAITO, Yasuhiko. "Kokuren no 1503 Tsuho Tetsuzuki ni tsuite" (The United Nations 1503 Communications Procedure). *Horitsujiho* (Tokyo), Vol. 53. No. 12, 1981, pp. 85-91.

SCHACHTER, Oscar. "The Obligation of the Parties to Give Effect to the Covenant on Civil and Political Rights", *American Journal of International Law* (Washington, D.C.), Vol. 73, 1979, pp. 462-65.

———. "The Obligation to Implement the Covenant in Domestic Law", in Henkin (Ed.), *The International Bill of Rights, op. cit.*, pp. 311-31.

SCHREIBER, Marc. "La pratique récente des Nations Unies dans le domaine de la protection des droits de l'homme", *Recueil des cours* (Hague Academy of International Law), Vol. II, 1976, p. 297 *et seq.*

———. "Les Nations Unies et les droits de l'homme", *Revue des droits de l'homme/Human rights journal* (Paris), vol. II, n° 1, 1969, pp. 95-112.

———. "Les organisations non-gouvernementales et l'oeuvre des Nations Unies dans le domaine de la protection des droits de l'homme", *Synthèses* (Dordrecht, Netherlands), 25 June 1970, pp. 58-63.

SCHWELB, Egon. "Complaints by individuals to the Commission of Human Rights: twenty-five years of uphill struggle (1947-1971)", in C. Boasson and N. Nurock (Eds.), *The changing international community*, The Hague, Mouton, 1973.

———. "The International Convention on the Elimination of All Forms of Racial Discrimination", *The International and Comparative Law Quarterly* (London). October 1966, p. 996 *et seq.*

———. "The International Court of Justice and the human rights clauses of the Charter", *American Journal of International Law* (Washington, D.C.), Vol. 66, 1972, p. 337.

———. "The international measures of implementation of the International Covenant on Civil and Political Rights and of the Optional Protocol", *Texas International Law Journal* (Austin, Tex.), Vol. 12, No. 2-3, 1977, pp. 141-86.

———. "The nature of the obligations of the States parties to the International Covenant on Civil and Political Rights", in *René Cassin amicorum discipulorumque liber I*, Paris, 1969, pp. 301-24.

——. "Notes on the early legislative history of the measures of implementation of the human rights covenants", *Mélanges Modinos*, Paris, 1968, pp. 270-89.

——. "Some aspects of the international covenants on human rights of December 1966", *Proceedings of the Seventh Nobel Symposium (Oslo, September 25-27, 1967)*, Stockholm, 1968, pp. 103-29.

——. "Some aspects of the measures of implementation of the International Covenant on Economic, Social and Cultural Rights", *Revue des droits de l'homme/Human rights journal* (Paris), Vol. I, No. 3, 1968, pp. 363-77.

SHIBAHARA, Kuniji. "Kokusairengo to Hikokinsha no Jinkenhosho" (The United Nations and the Human Rights Protection of Detained Persons), *Jurist* (Tokyo), Vol. 681, 1979, pp. 27-33.

SKOLER, D.L. *World implementation of the United Nations Standard Minimum Rules for Treatment of Prisoners.* Washington, D.C., American Bar Association Commission on Correctional Facilities and Services, 1975, 44 p.

SMOGER, Gerson. "Whither the Commission on Human Rights: A Report after the Thirty-Fifth Session", *Vanderbilt Journal of Transnational Law*, Vol. 12, 1979, pp. 943-68.

SOHN, Louis B. "A Short History of United Nations Documents on Human Rights", in Commission to Study the Organization of Peace, *The United Nations and Human Rights: 18th Report of the Commission*, Dobbs Ferry, N.Y., Oceana, 1968.

——. "The human rights law of the Charter", *Texas International Law Journal* (Austin, Tex.), Vol. 12, No. 2-3, 1977, pp. 129-40.

——. "The Improvement of the UN Machinery on Human Rights", *International Studies Quarterly* (Beverly Hills, Calif.), Vol. 23, 1979, pp. 273-302.

——. "The Rights of Minorities", in Henkin (Ed.), *The International Bill of Rights, op. cit.*, pp. 270-89.

——. "The United Nations, The next twenty-five years". *Twentieth report of the Commission to study the organization of peace.* New York, 1969.

SZABO, Imre. "The United Nations Human Rights Covenants, Problem of ratification and implementation", *American Society of International Law Proceedings* (Washington, D.C.), Vol. 62, 1968, pp. 83-123.

TABANDAHI, Sultan Husayn. *A Muslim commentary on the Universal Declaration of Human Rights.* (Translated from the Persian.) Guildford, Godding, 1970, 96 p.

TARDU, M., "UN Response to Gross Violations of Human Rights: The 1503 Procedure", *Santa Clara Law Review* (Santa Clara), Vol. 20, 1980, pp. 559-602.

TINKER, Catherine. "Human Rights for Women: The UN Convention on the Elimination of All Forms of Discrimination against Women", *Human Rights Quarterly*, Vol. 3, No. 2, 1981.

TRINDADE, A. "Exhaustion of Local Remedies Under the UN Covenant on Civil and Political Rights and its Optional Protocol", *International and Comparative Law Quarterly*, Vol. 28, 1979, pp. 734-65.

VIERDAG, E.W. "The Legal Nature of the Rights Granted by the International Covenant on Economic, Social and Cultural Rights", *Netherlands Yearbook of International Law* (The Hague), Vol. 9, 1978, pp. 69-105.

VINCENT-DAVISS, Diana, "Human Rights Law: A Research Guide to the Literature—Part I: International Law and the United Nations", *New York University Journal of International Law and Politics*, Vol. 14, No. 1, 1981, pp. 209-320.

VOLIO, Fernando. "Legal Personality, Privacy and the Family", in Henkin (Ed.), *The International Bill of Rights*, *op. cit.*, pp. 185-208.

2. International Labour Organisation

BARTOLOMEI DE LA CRUZ, H.G. *Protection against anti-union discrimination*, 1976, 123 p.

CAIRE, G. *Freedom of association and economic development*, 1977, 159 p.

ERSTLING, J.E. *The right to organise: a survey of laws and regulations relating to the rights of workers to establish unions of their own choosing*, 1977, 82 p.

HAAS, Ernest B. *Human rights and international action: The case of freedom of association*. Stanford, Calif., Stanford University Press, 1970, 184 p.

JENKS, Clarence Wilfred. *Human rights and the international labour standards*. New York, Praeger, 1960, 159 p.

———. "The international protection of freedom of association for trade union purposes", *Recueil des cours* (Hague Academy of International Law), Vol. I, 1955.

———. *The International protection of trade union freedom*. London, Stevens, 1957, 592 p.

———. *La Organización internacional del trabajo y la protección de los derechos humanos de América*. Buenos Aires, Universidad Nacional de Buenos Aires, 1962, 93 p.

———. *Social justice in the law of nations: the ILO impact after fifty years*. London, New York, issued under the auspices of the Royal Institute of International Affairs by Oxford University Press, 1970, 94 p., bibliography.

JOYCE, James Avery. *World Labour Rights and their Protection*. Croom Helm, London, 1980, 190 p.

LANDY, E.A. *The effectiveness of international supervision: three decades of ILO experience*. Dobbs Ferry, N.Y., Oceana, 1966, 268 p.

———. "The influence of international labour standards: Possibilities and performance", *International Labour Review*, June 1970, pp. 555-604.

LEARY, Virginia. *International Labour Conventions and National Law*. The Hague, Martinus Nijhoff, 1981, 214 p.

POTOBSKY, G. von. "Protection of trade union rights: Twenty years' work by the Committee on Freedom of Association", *International Labour Review*, January 1972, pp. 69-83.

POULANTZAS, N.M. "International protection of human rights: implementation procedures within the framework of the ILO", *Revue hellénique de droit international* (Athens), Vol. 25, 1972, pp. 110-41.

ROSSILION, C. "ILO examination of human rights situations", *The review of the International Commission of Jurists* (Geneva), No. 12, June 1974, pp. 40-49.

SAMSON, K.T. "The changing pattern of ILO supervision", *International Labour Review*, September-October 1979, pp. 569-87.

————. "The International Labour Organisation and human rights in 1970", *Revue des droits de l'homme/Human rights journal* (Paris), Vol. IV, No. 1, 1971, pp. 103-17.

VALTICOS, Nicolas. *Le droit international du travail*. Paris, Dalloz, 1970. 638 p. et supplément 1973.

————. "Fifty years of standard-setting activities by the International Labour Organisation", *International Labour Review*, September 1969, pp. 201-37.

————. "The future prospects for international labour standards", *International Labour Review*, November-December 1979, pp. 679-97.

————. Les normes de l'Organisation internationale du travail en matière de protection des droits de l'homme. *Revue des droits de l'homme/Human rights journal* (Paris), vol. IV, n° 4, 1971, pp. 691-771.

————. "The Role of the ILO: Future Perspectives", in Ramcharan (Ed.), *Human Rights, op. cit.*

WOLF, Francis. Aspects judiciaires de la protection internationale des droits de l'homme par l'OIT. *Revue des droits de l'homme/Human rights journal* (Paris), vol. IV, n° 4, 1971, pp. 773-838.

————. ILO experience in the implementation of human rights. *Journal of International Law and Economics* (Washington, D.C.), Vol. 10, August-September 1975, pp. 599-625.

3. United Nations Educational, Scientific and Cultural Organization

ALSTON, Philip. "Unesco's Procedure for Dealing with Human Rights Violations", *Santa Clara Law Review* (Santa Clara), Vol. 20, 1980, pp. 665-96.

BASTID, S. "Une nouvelle commission de conciliation?", in *Mélanges offerts à Henri Rollin*, Paris, Pédone, 1964, p. 1.

HEINTZE, H.J. "On the Unesco Declaration on Race and Racial Prejudice", *GDR Committee for Human Rights Bulletin No. 1/1981*, (Berlin), pp. 26-41.

LERNER, Natan. "New Concepts in the Unesco Declaration on Race and Racial Prejudice", *Human Rights Quarterly*, Vol. 3, No. 1, 1981.

LEWIS, Sulwyn. *The principles of cultural co-operation*. Paris, Unesco, 1971. 29 p. (Reports and papers on mass communication, No. 61).

MARKS, Stephen. "Unesco and Human Rights: The Implementation of Rights Relating to Education, Science, Culture and Communication", *Texas International Law Journal*, Vol. 13, No. 1, 1977, p. 35.

MERTENS, P. "L'application de la Convention et de la Recommandation de l'Unesco concernant la lutte contre la discrimination dans le domaine de l'enseignement: un bilan provisoire", *Revue des droits de l'homme/Human rights journal* (Paris), vol. I, n° 1, 1968, pp. 91-108.

NARTOWSKI, Andrzej S. "The Unesco system of protection of the right to education", *Polish Yearbook of International Law* (Wroclaw), Vol. 6, 1974, pp. 289-309.

SABA, Hanna. "La Convention et la Recommandation concernant la lutte contre la discrimination dans le domaine de l'enseignement", *Annuaire français de droit international* (Paris), vol. 6, pp. 646-59.

————. "Human rights", in *In the minds of men. Unesco, 1946-1971*, Paris, Unesco, 1972, pp. 251-69.

4. Food and Agriculture Organization of the United Nations

CHRISTENSEN, Cheryl. *The Right to Food: How to Guarantee.* World Order
    Models Project, Working Paper No. 6, 1978, New York, 40 p.
COLLINS, Joseph. "The Right to Food and The New International Economic
    Order". Paper presented to Unesco Expert Meeting on Human Rights,
    Human Needs, and the Establishment of a New International Economic
    Order, Paris, 1978, Unesco doc. SS-78/CONF.630/6, 33 p.
DOBBERT, J.P. "Right to Food", in *The Right to Health as a Human Right*,
    R.J. Dupuy (Ed.), Hague Academy of International Law/United Nations
    University, Alphen aan den Rijn, Sijthoff and Noordhoff, 1979, pp. 184-213.
The Right to be Free from Hunger: A Struggle for Self-reliance. International
    Youth and Student Movement for the United Nations, Geneva, 1978, 30 p.

5. Council of Europe

ANTONOPOULOS, Nicholas. *La jurisprudence des organes de la Convention
    européenne des droits de l'homme.* Leyden, Sijthoff, 1967, 262 p.
Arbeitskreis für Unwoltrecht (Bonn). *Le droit à un environnement humain:
    proposition pour un protocole additionnel à la Convention européenne des
    droits de l'homme.* (The right to a human environment/Das recht auf eine
    menschenwürdige Umwelt). By the working group for the right to envi-
    ronment (Bonn). Berlin, Schmidt, 1973, 58 p.
BUERGENTHAL, Thomas. "Domestic status of the European Convention on
    Human Rights: a second look", *Journal of the International Commission
    of Jurists* (Geneva), Vol. 7, Summer 1966, pp. 55-96.
———. "Effect of the European Convention on Human Rights on the internal law
    of Member States", *The International and Comparative Law Quarterly*
    (London), Supp. publ., No. 11, 1965, pp. 79-106.
CANÇADO TRINDADE, A.A. "Exhaustion of Local Remedies in the 'Travaux
    préparatoires' of the European Convention on Human Rights", *Revue de
    droit international*, 1980, No. 2, pp. 73-88.
CAPOTORTI, Francesco. "Sull'eventuale adesione della Comunità alla Convenzione
    europea dei diritti dell'uomo", *Rivista di Diritto Internazionale* (Rome),
    Vol. 63, 1980, pp. 5-28.
CASTBERG, Frede. *The European Convention on Human Rights.* Dobbs Ferry,
    N.Y., Oceana, 1974, 198 p.
Les clauses facultatives de la Convention européenne des droits de l'homme.
    Bari, Levante, 1974, 324 p.
COUNCIL OF EUROPE. *Bibliography Relating to the European Convention of
    Human Rights.* Strasbourg, 1978, 4th. ed., 173 p.
DANELIUS, Hans. "Conditions of admissibility in the jurisprudence of the Eu-
    ropean Commission of Human Rights", *Revue des droits de l'homme/Human
    rights journal* (Paris), Vol. II, No. 2, 1969, pp. 284-336.
DAUBIE, Christian. "La Convention européenne des droits de l'homme et la
    raison d'etat", *Revue des droits de l'homme/Human rights journal* (Paris),
    vol. III, n° 2, pp. 247-75.
DIJK, P. van, and HOOF G.J.H. van. *De Europese Conventie in theorie en
    praktijk*, Ars Aequi Libri, Utrecht, 1979, 452 p.

DRZEMCZEWSKI, Andrew. "The Sui Generis Nature of the European Convention on Human Rights", *The International and Comparative Law Quarterly* (London), Vol. 29, Pt. 1, 1980, pp. 54-63.

EISSEN, M.A. "La Cour européenne des droits de l'homme", *Annuaire français de droit international* (Paris), Vol. 5, 1959, pp. 618-58.

ERCMAN, S. *European Convention on Human Rights: Guide to Case Law.* Vienna, Wilhelm Braumüller, 1981, 528 p.

The European Convention on Human Rights. London, British Institute of International and Comparative Law, 1965, 106 p.

FAWCETT, J.E.S. *The application of the European Convention on Human Rights.* Oxford, Clarendon Press, 1969, 368 p.

FROWEIN, Jochen A. "The European and the American Conventions on Human Rights: A Comparison", *Human Rights Law Journal* (Kehl am Rhein), Vol. 1, 1980, pp. 44-65.

GANSHOF VAN DER MEERSCH, Walter. "Reliance, in the Case-law of the European Court of Human Rights, on the Domestic Law of States", *Human Rights Law Journal* (Kehl am Rhein), Vol. 1, 1980, pp. 13-35.

———. "La référence au droit interne des Etats contractants dans la jurisprudence de la Cour européenne des droits de l'homme", *Révue internationale de droit comparé* (Paris) 1980/2, pp. 317-37.

GAUTER, Hans Gerhard. *Die Spruchpraxis der europäischen Kommission für Menschenrechte auf dem Gebiet des Strafvollzuges.* Bonn, Ludwig Rohrscheid Verlag, 1974, 190 p.

GOLSONG, Heribert. "Control machinery of the European Convention on Human Rights", *The International and Comparative Law Quarterly* (London), Supp. publ., No. 11, 1965, pp. 38-69.

———. *Das Rechtsschutzsystem der Europäischen Menschenrechtskonvention.* Karlsruhe, C.F. Mueller, 1958, 115 p.

GURADZE, Heinz. *Die Europäische Menschenrechtskonvention.* Berlin, Vahlen, 1968, 276 p.

HELGESEN, Jan E. Access to Courts: Studies of Article 6(1) of the European Convention from the Perspective of the Sources of Public International Law. (In Norwegian.) Institutt for Statsrett og Folkerett Universiteti Oslo, 1975, 200 p.

HIGGINS, Rosalyn. "The Execution of the Decisions of Organs under the European Convention on Human Rights", *Revue Hellenique de Droit International* (Athens), Vol. 31, No. 1-4, 1978, pp. 1-39.

JACOBS, Francis G. *The European Convention on Human Rights.* Oxford, Clarendon Press, 1975, 286 p.

———. "The Extension of the European Convention on Human Rights to Include Economic, Social and Cultural Rights", *Human Rights Review* (London), Vol. 3, 1978, pp. 166-78.

KRÜGER, Hans Christian. "The European Commission of Human Rights", *Human Rights Law Journal* (Kehl am Rhein), Vol. 1, 1980, pp. 66-85.

MIKAELSEN, Laurids. *European Protection of Human Rights: The Practice and Procedure of the European Commission on Human Rights on the Admissibility of Applications from Individuals and States.* The Hague, Martinus Nijhoff, 1980, 280 p.

Modinos, Polys. "Coexistence de la Convention européenne des droits de l'homme et du Pacte des droits civils et politiques des Nations Unies", *Revue des droits de l'homme/Human rights journal* (Paris), vol. I, n° 1, 1968, pp. 41-69.

MONCONDUIT, François. *La Commission européenne des droits de l'homme.* Leyden, Sijthoff, 1965, 559 p.

MORRISSON, Clovis. *The Dynamics of Development in the European Human Rights Convention System.* The Hague, Martinus Nijhoff, 1981, 192 p.

MOWER, A. Glenn. "The Implementation of Human Rights through European Community Institutions", *Universal Human Rights*, Vol. 2, No. 2, 1980, pp. 43-59.

NEDJATI, Zaim. *Human Rights under the European Convention.* Amsterdam, North Holland Publishing Co., 1978, 298 p.

O'BOYLE, Michael. "Practice and Procedure under the European Convention on Human Rights", *Santa Clara Law Review*, Vol. 20, 1980, pp. 697-732.

O'HIGGINS, Paul, "The Closed Shop and the European Convention on Human Rights", *The Human Rights Review* (London), Vol. 6, No. 1, 1981, pp. 22-27.

OPSAHL, Torkel. "The Protection of Human Rights in the Council of Europe and in the United Nations", *European Yearbook* (The Hague), Vol. 26, 1980, pp. 92-118.

PARTSCH, Karl Josef. *Die Rechte und Freiheiten der Europäischen Menschenrechtskonvention.* Berlin, Duncker Humbolt, 1966, 263 p.

PEUKERT, Wolfgang, "Protection of Ownership under Article 1 of the First Protocol to the European Convention on Human Rights" *Human Rights Law Journal* (Kehl am Rhein), Vol. 2, 1981, pp. 37-78.

Privacy and human rights. *Reports and communications presented at the Third International Colloquy on the European Convention on Human Rights, Brussels, 30 September-3 October 1970.* Edited by A.H. Robertson. Manchester, Manchester University Press, 1973.

ROBERTSON, A.H. (Ed.). *Human Rights in National and International Law.* New York, 1968, proceedings of the Second International Conference on the European Convention on Human Rights, Vienna, 1965. Proceedings also published in French and German.

SARUP, R. "Torture under the European Convention on Human Rights", *American Journal of International Law* (Washington, D.C.), Vol. 73, 1979, pp. 267-76.

SCHERMERS, H. "The Communities under the European Convention on Human Rights", *Legal Issues of European Integration*, 1978/1, p. 1.

SCHWELB, Egon. "The abuse of the right to petition", *Revue des droits de l'homme/Human rights journal* (Paris), Vol. III, No. 2, 1970, pp. 313-32.

SWART, A.H.J. "The Legal Status of Aliens: Clauses in Council of Europe Instruments relating to the Rights of Aliens", *Netherlands Yearbook of International Law* (The Hague), Vol. XI, 1980, pp. 3-65.

TEUGEN, Piere-Henri. "The Temporal Effect of the Judgments of the European Court of Human Rights and the Court of Justice of the European Communities", *Human Rights Law Journal* (Kehl am Rhein) Vol. 1, 1980, pp. 36-45.

TRECHSEL, S. *Die Europäische Menschenrechtskonvention, ihr Schutz der persönlichen Freiheit und die schweizerischen Strafprozessrechte*. Berne, 1974.

———. "The Right to Liberty and Security of the Person: Article 5 of the European Convention on Human Rights in the Strasbourg Case-law", *Human Rights Law Journal* (Kehl am Rhein), Vol. 1, 1980, pp. 88-135.

VASAK, Karel. "Commission et Cour européennes des droits de l'homme", in *Jurisclasseur de droit international*, fascicule 155. Paris, Editions techniques, 1961; nouvelle édition, 1969.

———. *La Convention européenne des droits de l'homme* (prix Henri Texier; couronné par l'Académie des sciences morales et politiques, 1966). Paris, Librairie générale de droit et de jurisprudence, 1964, 327 p.

———. "La Convention européenne des droits de l'homme, complément utile des Conventions de Genève", *Revue internationale de la Croix-Rouge* (Geneva), August 1965 (English and French).

———. "De la Convention européenne à la Convention africaine des droits de l'homme", *Revue juridique et politique d'outre-mer* (Paris), n° 1, 1962, p. 59.

———. "The European Convention on human rights beyond the frontiers of Europe", *The International and Comparative Quarterly* (London), Vol. 12, 1963, pp. 1206-31.

WALDOCK, Humphrey. "The Effectiveness of the System set up by the European Convention on Human Rights", *Human Rights Law Journal* (Kehl am Rhein), Vol. 1, 1980, pp. 1-12.

WEIL, Gordon L. *The European Convention on Human Rights: background, development and prospects*. Leyden, Sijthoff, 1963, 260 p.

WILLIAMS, Anne M. "The European Convention on Human Rights: a new use?", *Texas International Law Journal* (Austin, Tex.), Vol. 12, No. 2-3, 1977, pp. 279-92.

ZANGHI, C. "La liberté d'expression dans la Convention européenne des droits de l'homme et dans le Pacte des Nations Unies relatif aux droits civils et politiques", *Revue générale de droit international public*, Vol. 74, 1970, pp. 573-89.

ZELLICH, Graham (Ed.). *European Human Rights Reports*. London European Law Centre Limited, issued annually.

6. Organization of American States

ABRANCHES, C.A. Dunshee. "La competencia actual de la Comisión Interamericana de derechos humanos y el requisito del agotamiento de los recursos internos", *Revista de derechos humanos* (San Juan, Puerto Rico), Vol. IV, No. 2-3, 1974.

BUERGENTHAL, Thomas. "The American Convention of Human Rights: an illusion of progress", *Miscellanea W.J. Ganshof van der Meersch*, Vol. 1, Brussels, Bruylant, 1972, pp. 385-96, 3 vol.

———. "The revised OAS charter and the protection of human rights", *American Journal of International Law* (Washington, D.C.), Vol. 69, 1975, pp. 828-36.

CABRANES, José A. "Human rights and non-intervention in the inter-American system", *Michigan Law Review* (Ann Arbor, Mich.), Vol. 65, April 1967, pp. 1146-82.

———. "The protection of human rights by the Organization of American States", *American Journal of International Law* (Washington, D.C.), Vol. 62, No. 4, 1965, pp. 889-908.

CAMARCO, Pedro Pablo. "The American Convention on Human Rights", *Revue des droits de l'homme/Human rights journal* (Paris), Vol. III, No. 2, 1970, pp. 333-56.

CHUECA SANCHO, Angel G. "Los derechos humanos protegidos en la Convención americana de San José de 1969", *Revista española de derecho internacional*, Vol. 32, 1980, pp. 33-79.

FOX, Donald T. "The American Convention on Human Rights and prospects for United States ratification", *Human Rights* (Chicago), Vol. 3, No. 2, 1973, pp. 243-81.

GROS ESPIELL, Hector. "Le système interaméricaine comme régime régional de protection internationale des droits de l'homme", *Recueil des cours* (Hague Academy of International Law), Vol. II, 1976.

JIMÉNEZ DE ARACHAGA, Justino. "La convención americana de derechos humanos y las posibilidades de su ratificación por los Estados americanos", *Revista de derechos humanos* (San Juan, Puerto Rico), Vol. IV, No. 2-3, 1974.

LEBLANC, L.J. *The OAS and the Promotion and Protection of Human Rights.* The Hague, Martinus Nijhoff, 1977, 180 p.

NORRIS, Robert. "Bringing Individual Petitions Before the Inter-American Commission", *Santa Clara Law Review*, Vol. 20, 1980, pp. 733-72.

———, and RETTON, Paula Desio. "The Suspension of Guarantees: A Comparative Analysis of the American Convention of Human Rights and the Constitutions of the States Parties", *The American University Law Review*, Vol. 30, 1980, pp. 189-223.

SANDEFER, Durward V. "Human rights in the inter-American system", *Howard Law Journal* (Washington, D.C.), Vol. 11, No. 2, 1965, pp. 508-28.

SCHEMAN, L. Ronald. "The Inter-American Commission on Human Rights", *American Journal of International Law* (Washington, D.C.), Vol. 59, No. 2, pp. 335-44.

SCHLEIFER, Nancy. "Territorial Asylum in the Americas: Practical Considerations for Relocation", *Lawyer of the Americas*, Vol. 12, 1980, pp. 359-80.

SCHREIBER, Anna P. *The Inter-American Commission on Human Rights.* Leyden, Sijthoff, 1970, 187 p.

THOMAS, A.V.W., and THOMAS, A.J. "Human rights and the Organization of American States", *Santa Clara Lawyer* (Santa Clara, Calif.), Vol. 12, 1972, p. 319.

URIBE VARGAS, Diego. *Los derechos humanos y el sistema interamericano.* Madrid, Ediciones Cultura Hispánica, 1972, 359 p.

VASAK, Karel. *La Commission interaméricaine des droits de l'homme.* Paris, Librairie générale de droit et de jurisprudence, 1968, 287 p.

―――. "La protection internationale des droits de l'homme sur le continent américain", *Österreichische Zeitschrift für öffentliches Recht* (Vienna), Vol. XVII, 1967, pp. 113-22.

7. Non-Governmental Organizations

ARCHER, A. "Action by Unofficial Organizations on Human Rights", in *The International Protection of Human Rights*, E. Luard (Ed.), New York, Praeger, 1967, pp. 160-82.

BAMBA, Nobuya. "Kokusai Jinken Mondai to NGO" (International Human Rights Problems and NGO", *Gendai Kokusai Kankeiron* (Modern International Relations), Tokyo, Tokyo University Press, 1980, pp. 251-74.

BISSELL, Thomas St. G. "The International Committee of the Red Cross and the protection of human rights", *Revue des droits de l'homme/Human rights journal* (Paris), Vol. I, No. 2, 1968, pp. 255-74.

CASSESE, Antonio. "How Could Nongovernmental Organizations Use U.N. Bodies More Effectively?", *Universal Human Rights* (New York), Vol. 1, No. 4, 1979, pp. 73-80.

―――. "Progressive Transnational Promotion of Human Rights by Non-Governmental Organizations", in Ramcharan (Ed.), *Human Rights, op. cit.*

CHIANG, P.L. *Non-Governmental Organizations at the U.N.* New York, Praeger, 1981, 260 p.

Conference of non-governmental organizations on human rights. *International labour review* (Geneva), Vol. 9, June 1968, pp. 585-87.

GREEN, J. "NGO's", in *Human Rights and World Order*, A. Said (Ed.), New Brunswick, N.J., Transaction, 1978, pp. 90-99.

LARSEN, E. *A Flame in Barbed Wire: The Story of Amnesty International.* New York, Norton, 1979, 152 p.

LEARY, Virginia. "The Right of the Individual to Know and Act upon His Rights and Duties: Monitoring Groups and the Helsinki Final Act", *Vanderbilt Journal of Transnational Law*, Vol. 13, 1980, pp. 375-95.

NANDA, V; SCARRITT, J.; and SHEPHERD, G. *Global Human Rights: Public Policies, Comparative Measures, and NGO Strategies.* Boulder, Colo., Westview Press, 1981, 318 p.

PECHOTA, Vratislav. "East European Perceptions of the Helsinki Final Act and the Role of Citizen Initiatives", *Vanderbilt Journal of Transnational Law*, Vol. 13, 1980, pp. 467-500.

POWER, Jonathan. *Against Oblivion: Amnesty International's Fight for Human Rights.* London, Fontana, 1981, 254 p.

PRASAD, N. "The Role of Non-Governmental Organizations in the New United Nations Procedures for Human Rights Complaints", *Denver Journal of International Law and Politics*, Vol. 5, 1975, pp. 441-62.

SCOBLE, Harry, and WISEBERG, Laurie. "Amnesty International: evaluating effectiveness in the human rights arena. There is a compelling need for protective associations to monitor governmental repression", *Intellect* (New York), September/October 1976, p. 79.

―――. "Human rights NGOs: Notes towards comparative analysis", *Revue des droits de l'homme/Human rights journal* (Paris), Vol. IX, No. 4, 1976, pp. 611-44.

————. "Human Rights and Amnesty International", *Annals of the American Academy of Political and Social Science*, No. 413, 1974, pp. 11-26.

SHESTACK, J. "Sisyphus Endures: The International Human Rights NGO", *New York University Law School Law Review*, Vol. 74, 1978, pp. 89-123.

WEISSBRODT, David. "The role of international non-governmental organizations in the implementation of human rights", *Texas International Law Journal* (Austin, Tex.), Vol. 12, No. 2-3, 1977, pp. 292-320.

WISEBERG, L., and SCOBLE, H. "The International League for Human Rights: The Strategy of a Human Rights NGO", *Georgia Journal of International and Comparative Law*, Vol. 7, 1977, pp. 289-313.

————. "Monitoring Human Rights Violations: The Role of Non-governmental Organizations", in D. Kommers and G. Loescher (Eds.), *Human Rights and American Foreign Policy*, Notre Dame, London, University of Notre Dame Press, 1979, pp. 179-210.

————. "Recent Trends in the Expanding Universe of Nongovernmental Organizations Dedicated to the Protection of Human Rights", *Denver Journal of International Law and Policy*, Vol. 8, special issue, 1979, pp. 627-58.

Index of International Instruments

CONVENTIONS

DECLARATIONS

General Index